The tax debt handbook

Written by advisers at

TaxAid

Sponsored by The Chartered Institute of Taxation

Published by

TaxAid Charitable Trust (Charity Registration 1017667)
Linburn House, 342 Kilburn High Road, London NW6 2QJ
Telephone: 0171 624 5216

© TaxAid Charitable Trust 1996

ISBN 1 900577 05 4

Printed in Great Britain by Communications in Print Plc, Basildon, Essex.

Contents

Preface		v
Foreword by Andrew Park QC		vii
The Chartered Institute of Taxation		ix
TaxAid		x
Abbreviations		xi
Terminology		xii

Chapter 1	The problem	1
Chapter 2	How tax is raised	7
Chapter 3	Legal and administrative safeguards	31
Chapter 4	Challenging excessive demands	64
Chapter 5	Status issues and other problem areas	96
Chapter 6	Negotiating with the Collector	140
Chapter 7	Introduction to recovery proceedings	172
Chapter 8	Distraint	181
Chapter 9	Summary proceedings	195
Chapter 10	County Court proceedings	204
Chapter 11	Bankruptcy proceedings	229
Chapter 12	Self-assessment	275
Chapter 13	Advice and advisers	296

Appendices

1	Distraint Notice and Inventory	309
2	Walking Possession Agreement	311
3	County Court Summons	312
4	Admission	314
5	Determination of Means Calculator	316
6	Defence and Counterclaim	317
7	Statutory Demand	319
8	Creditor's Bankruptcy Petition	322

Index		325

Preface

Over the last fifteen years tax debt has become a major problem in the UK and yet until now there has not been any specialist text on the subject. We hope that this handbook - which draws upon TaxAid's extensive experience in assisting individuals with tax arrears - will provide advisers and taxpayers with a much-needed source of help.

The scope of the handbook is explained in Chapter 1, but broadly it considers three areas: reviewing the sum demanded to see if it can be reduced in any way, negotiating with Collectors and responding to enforcement methods used by the Inland Revenue.

On the subject of reviewing tax liabilities, the handbook concentrates on the provisions applying for the years up to 1995/96, before the introduction of self-assessment. This is because advising on tax debt is usually a retrospective exercise. The Inland Revenue is still pursuing many liabilities from the 1970s and 1980s and it will be several years before it closes its books on the old regime.

While there are not yet any tax debts under self-assessment - the first payments do not fall due before January 1997 - this subject will eventually gain ascendancy. A separate chapter is therefore devoted to explaining how debts will arise under the new system, so that readers may be fully prepared (Chapter 12). The negotiation and enforcement methods discussed at chapters 6 - 11 will remain virtually unchanged.

The production of this guide has truly been a team effort and there is a long list of individuals and organisations to whom thanks are due.

The initial writing was done by David Brodie and Michael Old, but their work was then subject to considerable scrutiny and improvement by Stephen Lamb, Sharron West, Chris Chadburn, David Daws, Hywel Jones, Helle Sampson, Rachel Karp, Chris Lee and Deborah Russell.

We are also grateful to John Newth for his work on the chapter on self-assessment and to Mark Lee of Clark Whitehill for his comments on that chapter, to John Kruse for reviewing the chapters on enforcement and Zanita Thompson of Casson Beckman & Partners for her comments on bankruptcy and individual voluntary arrangements.

Anita Monteith bravely took on the task of editing the handbook and seeing it through the final stages of production, with assistance from Yolanda Moore and Matthew Hough. Kato Communications Limited kindly produced the design for the cover.

We also wish to thank the Inland Revenue for providing its views on a number of important subjects for publication within the handbook, the Insolvency Service for explaining many of its procedures, and Coopers & Lybrand for giving us access to their tax library.

And finally a special word of gratitude is due to Andrew Park QC for agreeing to write the foreword and to John Andrews, Deputy President of the Chartered Institute of Taxation, for his enthusiastic support which led to the Institute's very generous sponsorship of of this handbook.

TaxAid Charitable Trust
September 1996

Foreword by Andrew Park QC

I was very pleased to be invited to write a foreword to this handbook, for several reasons.

One is that it enables me to say how much I admire TaxAid and its dedicated team, who provide their time and expertise (at considerable financial sacrifice to themselves) so as to make available skilled and much needed guidance in a vast field where it is otherwise lacking. Another is the related point that the handbook covers an area of the tax system which is of immense importance to a great many taxpayers but of which most tax professionals know little or nothing. That is certainly true of me. The first time that I saw anything of what happens in practice when small or medium-sized tax debts have not been paid was not in the course of my practice but sitting as a part-time judge in a County Court.

The salient issues seem neatly encapsulated in the simple Inland Revenue statistic on page 182 of this handbook - that Collectors made 241,326 distraint visits in the year to October 1995, of which 395 led to the sale of taxpayers' goods at auction.

The large number of visits dramatically reveals the extent of tax debt, and TaxAid has estimated that over a million citizens are directly or indirectly affected by difficulties over tax liabilities each year. Apart from the individual trauma that this may entail, there is the consequential write-off of some £1 billion per annum in public revenues; money which could be used on vital social services.

I was very surprised to learn that only 395 visits led to sales at auction. No explanation is offered by the Revenue, but the low number must be attributable to many factors. In many cases the Collector's visit is the taxpayer's first personal contact with a tax official, which may provide the opportunity to explain verbally that an estimated tax assessment was excessive and perhaps that no tax was due. The formal written procedures for appealing are beyond most taxpayers, and many simply pay whatever the Revenue demands. But one of the things that I observed in the County Courts was that, even if there has been no appeal and the assessment is legally final, the staff of the Collector's office will always listen and refer a case back to the Inspector if, when they meet the taxpayer, it looks as though the tax ought not to have been fixed at the amount assessed. Self-assessment will change the procedures, but many of the same problems and consequences will remain.

The truth is that no change of procedures, or indeed anything else that any Government can realistically do, will remove the problem of tax debt. It is a problem which is here to stay. This makes a professional text on the subject essential reading for all tax practitioners.

It is particularly apt that the first handbook on tax debt has been written and published by TaxAid. As a unique charity specialising in providing free advice on tax matters to those unable to pay for professional help, much of TaxAid's work is in the field of tax debt and it can fairly lay claim to considerable expertise in this area.

And as the profits from the sale of the handbook will help to fund the continuation of TaxAid's admirable work, I encourage all practitioners to order a copy while stocks last!

Andrew Park QC

Grays Inn Chambers
Grays Inn
London WC1R 5JA

September 1996

The Chartered Institute of Taxation

The Chartered Institute of Taxation, the leading professional body in the United Kingdom concerned solely with taxation, was established in 1930 and received its Royal Charter in 1994. The Institute's primary purpose is to promote education in and the study of the administration and practice of taxation.

Membership of the Institute is open to individuals from all disciplines who are competent and qualified to advise on taxation matters. Entrance is through its associateship examination, from which members may advance to fellowship by thesis. An increasing number of members hold the Institute's qualification as their main professional qualification.

The Institute deals with all aspects of direct and indirect taxation. It is the United Kingdom member of the Confédération Fiscale Européenne, the umbrella body for taxation practitioners in Europe.

In 1989 the Institute sponsored the formation of The Association of Taxation Technicians. The two bodies maintain a close relationship.

The Chartered Institute of Taxation
12 Upper Belgrave Street
London SW1X 8BB
Telephone: 0171 235 9381

TaxAid

TaxAid is the operating name of TaxAid Charitable Trust, which was established in 1992 to provide free advice on tax and tax debt to people in financial need.

Advice is given by members of the Chartered Institute of Taxation, chartered accountants, solicitors and former Inspectors of Taxes, most of whom give their time as volunteers.

During the last four years, TaxAid has assisted hundreds of clients facing enforcement proceedings by the Inland Revenue for failure to pay taxes assessed on them. Frequently the charity succeeds in persuading the authorities that the amount demanded is excessive, which may lead to proceedings being withdrawn. Sometimes a client even receives a tax refund!

Even where the amount demanded is not in dispute, TaxAid's experience assists in negotiating manageable arrangements for 'time to pay' or in defending against distraint or Court proceedings.

In carrying out this work, TaxAid draws on its knowledge of tax law as well as many published and unpublished practices of the Inland Revenue.

This handbook has been written by advisers at TaxAid. It is a unique reference on all aspects of tax debt - from checking and challenging the amount demanded, through negotiating with the Collector, to the legal enforcement of tax debts. It also considers the changes to be introduced under self-assessment.

TaxAid Charitable Trust (Charity Registration 1017667)
Linburn House
342 Kilburn High Road
London NW6 2QJ
Telephone: 0171 624 5216

Abbreviations

All ER	All England Reports
AT	Inland Revenue Assessed Taxes Manual
CA	Court of Appeal
CAA	Capital Allowances Act
CAB	Citizens Advice Bureau
CCA	County Court Act
CCR	County Court Rules
Ch D	Chancery Division
CYB	Current year basis
E	Inland Revenue Enforcement Manual
FA	Finance Act
HL	House of Lords
IA	Insolvency Act
ICAEW	Institute of Chartered Accountants in England and Wales
ICTA	Income and Corporation Taxes Act
IPO	Insolvent Partnerships Order
IR	Insolvency Rules
IRRA	Inland Revenue Regulation Act
IVA	Individual Voluntary Arrangement
KB	King's Bench Division
Ord	Order
PAYE	Pay As You Earn
PCM	Inland Revenue Personal Contact Manual
PYB	Preceding year basis
QB	Queen's Bench Division
r	rule
Reg	Regulation
ROM	Inland Revenue Regional Executive Office Manual
RSC	Rules of the Supreme Court
s	section
Sch	Schedule
SI	Statutory Instrument
SSCBA	Social Security Contributions and Benefits Act
STC	Simon's Tax Cases
STI	Simon's Tax Intelligence
TC	Tax Cases
TCGA	Taxation of Chargeable Gains Act
TMA	Taxes Management Act
TR	Technical Release
VAT	Value Added Tax
WLR	Weekly Law Reports

Terminology

Collector and *Inspector* - These terms are used for Collector of Taxes and Inspector of Taxes respectively. For a discussion of how these roles are affected by the *New Office Structure* programme, see paragraph 2.9 *et seq*.

Gender - Except where the context requires otherwise, all individuals are referred to in the male gender, i.e. as *he* or *him*.

Inland Revenue - Some functions are described as carried out by the Inland Revenue where, by statute, they are required to be performed by the Board of Inland Revenue, or a specified officer. This approach has been adopted for ease of exposition, and reflects the fact that such functions are commonly delegated within the organisation. The strict statutory designation is used wherever it is significant.

Profits - This term covers both income and capital gains. Where a distinction is required, the terms *income* and *capital gains* are used.

Tax debt - This term is used to describe any sum payable by an individual to the Inland Revenue, in respect of income tax, capital gains tax or class 4 national insurance contributions, which has not been settled, or will not be settled, by the due date for payment. For further discussion, see paragraph 1.23 *et seq*.

Chapter 1

The problem

Every year tax debt shatters the lives of thousands of people across the UK and there may be over a million individuals whose lives are affected, directly or indirectly, by Inland Revenue demands that cannot be met. Yet the subject is not covered fully either by conventional texts on taxation or by general handbooks on debt. This chapter considers:

		From paragraph
■	The extent of tax debt	*1.1*
■	Difficulties faced by advisers	*1.4*
■	The need for specialist knowledge	*1.7*
■	A structured approach to tax debt	*1.12*
■	The scope of this handbook	*1.22*

The extent of tax debt

1.1   The latest annual Report of the Board of Inland Revenue reveals that it wrote off £1.16bn of unpaid tax, of which £860m 'related to money due from insolvent taxpayers'.[1] At the individual level, last year the Inland Revenue made 233,593 distraint visits and obtained 2,217 bankruptcy orders.[2]

1.2   These figures are just the tip of the iceberg. For every individual whose tax debt leads to enforcement proceedings, there may be a dozen struggling to find money to meet tax demands. While they may be successful in staving off legal action by the Collector, this may be at the cost of agreeing burdensome instalment arrangements or private borrowings, which can in turn have a heavy impact on members of their family or on their business.

1.3   A particular feature of tax debt is that the amounts demanded by Collectors are often based upon estimated or incorrect assessments, which are frequently unchallenged because the taxpayer does not understand complex tax procedures.

---

[1] Figures for the year ended 31 October 1994
[2] Figures for the year ended 31 March 1996

Difficulties faced by advisers

1.4   Even where an experienced tax adviser is involved, he may fail to obtain a reduction in his client's tax debt - or manageable instalment arrangements - through unfamiliarity with the Inland Revenue's collection practices and policies.

1.5   This stems, at least in part, from a tradition of official secrecy. Despite a long history of producing free leaflets on most aspects of taxation, the Inland Revenue offered no general guidance on collection matters until two *Codes of Practice* were published in November 1994. Even these omitted to mention the practice of *equitable liability* which remained unpublished until August 1995 (see paragraph 4.61 *et seq*). It also appears that several aspects of tax debt enforcement were omitted deliberately from the recently-published versions of the Inland Revenue's internal guidance manuals. Nevertheless, they still contain much useful information, which is mentioned in this handbook.

1.6   Furthermore, a tax adviser may feel out of his depth when advising on tax debts, through lack of experience. If most of his clients are financially solvent, he may rarely encounter some of the problems discussed in this book. However, the doubling of self-employed numbers during the last 15 years, combined with a growth in debt generally, makes it likely that in future every tax adviser will have to assist clients with tax debts more frequently. Responsible professionals will need to ensure that they can offer such advice with the same confidence that they have in other areas of their work.

The need for specialist knowledge

1.7   It is not uncommon for a person who employs a tax adviser, and who would not dream of conducting a complex business transaction without specialist advice, to enter negotiations over tax debts without any help. While this may be through fear of clocking up additional professional fees, it can also be based upon the premise that such negotiations require merely 'common sense'.

1.8   However, as in many other areas of taxation, the best way of dealing with a tax debt is not always the most obvious. A taxpayer threatened with County Court proceedings may offer to settle a tax debt by monthly instalments that he cannot actually afford. He may not realise that the threatened proceedings actually offer a rare opportunity to freeze interest on overdue tax, or that the Court itself has powers to grant time to pay which can be exercised very sympathetically. Similarly, a taxpayer fearing bankruptcy might negotiate a large loan to settle his tax debt, without stopping to consider whether bankruptcy may actually be a *solution* to his indebtedness.[3]

---

[3]   Clearly there are also significant *disadvantages* to such legal proceedings (see Chapters 10 and 11).

1.9 Sometimes 'common sense' might suggest that the best tactic is to do nothing at all. Inland Revenue Accounts Offices routinely issue computerised threats of legal action for tax 'not paid within seven days', while actually intending to do no more than pass the file to a local Collector, who in turn may take no action for months or even years. Anyone who has previously experienced such 'cries of wolf' might conclude that Inland Revenue demands should be ignored until the necessary funds are available for payment. However, Collection offices tend to be much more sympathetic towards those who have remained in touch and explained their difficulties, than towards those who appear to have ignored their obligations (see Chapter 6).

1.10 A further reason why tax debt negotiations can benefit from expert involvement is that Collectors generally are not trained to understand the *computation* of tax liabilities. Unless the taxpayer himself has an unusually good understanding of taxation, he may overlook opportunities for reducing his liability. For example, if the debt is based upon an estimated assessment, it may be possible to make a late appeal or to ask for relief under the practice of equitable liability. Even where the debt is based upon agreed profit figures, there may be scope for further relief for losses, allowances or other claims (see Chapter 4).

1.11 Some tax advisers fear that their involvement in tax debt negotiations could actually harm the client's position, as the Collector may simplistically assume that anyone who can employ an adviser must have the resources to settle his tax. Accordingly, if the adviser is currently acting without payment or on special terms, it may assist negotiations if he makes this clear to the Collector (see paragraph 13.25 *et seq*).

A structured approach to tax debt

1.12 This handbook has been written by advisers at TaxAid Charitable Trust, an agency that offers free advice on tax to individuals in financial need. Every year TaxAid is consulted by hundreds of individuals facing tax debts, many of whom bring no more than a single letter from a Collection office, threatening enforcement proceedings. Such clients cannot be advised properly until the background to the demand has been investigated fully and their personal and financial circumstances have been examined.

The three areas of consideration

1.13 Each of the following questions needs to be considered carefully:

- Can the size of the demand be reduced?

- Is there scope for negotiation with the Collector?

- What is the appropriate response to enforcement proceedings?

Can the size of the demand be reduced?

1.14 This involves examining the exact basis of the Inland Revenue's demand to ascertain whether it is stated correctly, and taking action as appropriate. At a simple level, an initial enquiry may reveal that a tax debt is based upon an estimated assessment, which may be remedied by a late appeal and the submission of accounts which demonstrate that the original estimate was excessive.

1.15 Where the taxpayer received competent professional advice over the period to which the tax debt relates, the amount demanded will often have been agreed with the Inland Revenue before the arrears arise. However, if he was unrepresented in the past, or had a less able adviser, there is frequently scope for significant reductions in the sum demanded. In practice, though, it is far less common for tax debts to be *under*stated.[4]

Is there scope for negotiation with the Collector?

1.16 To the extent that any tax remains properly due, consideration should be given to the prospect of reaching a mutually acceptable arrangement with the Collector for the debt to be remitted or settled over time. Care should be taken to ensure that any such arrangement will fall clearly within the taxpayer's means, and that it offers him a better overall 'result' than enforcement proceedings which might otherwise be instituted by the Inland Revenue. The factors that might assist in such negotiations are explored in Chapter 6.

What is the appropriate response to enforcement proceedings?

1.17 Where there is any possibility of enforcement proceedings, or where they have already commenced, consideration should be given to the steps that the Inland Revenue is likely to take in the particular case, the implications for the taxpayer, and the action he might take to mitigate their impact. The enforcement measures used by the Inland Revenue are discussed in Chapters 7 to 11.

Juggling the issues

1.18 To some extent the above division reflects the order in which matters should be considered: clearly there is no point in embarking on negotiations for time to settle a tax debt without first checking the scope for getting the demand withdrawn or reduced significantly. However, there remains a considerable degree of overlap. For example:

- The process of checking the amount due will usually necessitate contact with an Inspector, but at the same time it is vital to liaise

---

[4] The issues which need to be considered are covered in Chapters 2 to 5.

with the appropriate Collector. This is to ensure that enforcement action does not proceed regardless, through lack of liaison between different branches of the Inland Revenue (see paragraph 2.4 *et seq*).

- Strictly, an Inspector should establish an individual's tax liability without any reference to his actual ability to pay, since recovery of tax is solely the Collector's province. However, a responsible Inspector will appreciate the wider benefits of concentrating on cases with a good prospective yield and so, if he is told that the taxpayer has very limited resources, he may prove more amenable to a quick agreement of liabilities than would otherwise be the case.

- Even where enforcement proceedings have commenced, it is rarely too late to reach a negotiated payment arrangement. So frequently it is necessary to be negotiating and responding to enforcement measures at the same time.

- Even where legal proceedings have already been concluded, this need not be the end of the matter. For example, it may still be possible to have a judgment removed from the Register of County Court Debts, or a bankruptcy annulled, by reviewing the basis of the original debt and taking appropriate remedial action (see paragraphs 10.130 and 11.164 *et seq*).

1.19 Most of the strategies described in subsequent chapters of this handbook are of application in just one (or two) of the three areas of consideration mentioned in paragraph 1.13 above. For example:

- Reference to the existence of unclaimed allowances may help to reduce a sum assessed, but will not form the basis of a valid defence in legal proceedings for the recovery of tax.

- Pointing to a taxpayer's poor health may assist in negotiating remission of a tax debt, or time to pay, but will not affect the amount strictly due.

It is therefore vital to be aware of the limitations of any possible form of relief.

1.20 There is, however, a range of remedies that may apply across the whole area of tax debt, which are discussed in Chapter 3. In particular, the Taxpayer's Charter now offers increased protection against Inland Revenue maladministration.

1.21 Finally, tax debt should never be seen in isolation. The taxpayer may owe money to third parties, by way of mortgage or rent arrears, credit cards, overdrafts or business debts. The existence of such liabilities may assist in negotiations with a Collector if it is drawn to his attention that any assets or income ultimately may have to be shared with other creditors. This is particularly important where another creditor would take priority, for example because their debt is secured. Where other debts are significant, advice might be sought from an insolvency practitioner or money adviser with greater experience of multiple debts, as this could influence the way in which the tax debt is approached. There is little point in haggling over a £500 tax debt if there are other larger liabilities which will inevitably lead to bankruptcy. The roles of insolvency practitioners and money advisers are discussed in Chapter 13.

The scope of this handbook

1.22   This handbook is written as a practical guide for professional advisers assisting individuals who have problems in meeting their tax liabilities, but it may also be used by such individuals themselves.

1.23   Except where the context requires otherwise, the term *tax debt* is used to describe:

- any sum payable to the Inland Revenue,

- by an individual,

- in respect of income tax, capital gains tax or class 4 national insurance contributions, and

- which has not been settled, or will not be settled, by the due date for payment.

1.24   By far the largest category of individuals with tax debts are sole traders who have fallen into arrears with their Schedule D Case I or II liabilities, and class 4 national insurance contributions (which are collected on Schedule D assessments). However, the text also provides guidance for those who have been members of partnerships, company directors or employees, or those who have investment income or gains. Some of these special cases are considered in Chapter 5.

1.25   The law and practice described is that applicable in England and Wales at 31 May 1996. Important changes in tax assessment and payment procedures are currently being introduced under self-assessment, which is considered in Chapter 12, but familiarity with the old provisions will remain necessary for a considerable period as they will continue to apply indefinitely to any tax unpaid for the years up to 1995/96.

Chapter 2

How tax is raised

This chapter introduces the legislation, organisation and processes which underly the creation and enforcement of tax debts. It provides the context for the chapters that follow and covers:

		From paragraph
■	The duty to collect tax	*2.1*
■	The organisation of the Inland Revenue	*2.4*
■	The creation of a tax debt	*2.12*
■	Interest and penalties	*2.61*
■	Payment of tax	*2.88*
■	Proceedings to recover tax debts	*2.95*

The duty to collect tax

2.1   The Inland Revenue's statutory duty to collect tax is set out in the Inland Revenue Regulation Act 1890, s13(1):

> 'The Commissioners (of Inland Revenue) shall collect and cause to be collected every part of inland revenue, and all money under their care and management, and shall keep distinct accounts thereof at their chief office.'

'Inland revenue' is defined to cover stamp duties and taxes placed under the care and management of the Commissioners (IRRA 1890, s39).

2.2   This general duty is developed by the Taxes Management Act 1970, s1:

> 'Income tax, corporation tax and capital gains tax shall be under the care and management of the Commissioners of Inland Revenue (in this Act referred to as 'the Board'), and the definition of 'inland revenue' in section 39 of the Inland Revenue Regulation Act 1890 shall have effect accordingly.'

This section goes on to give the Board power to appoint Inspectors and Collectors, and to delegate its functions to them.

2.3 Statutory provision is also made for the Inland Revenue to collect certain national insurance contributions. In particular, class 4 national insurance contributions are charged on income tax assessments under Schedule D Cases I and II, while employers are required to account for primary and secondary class 1 national insurance contributions through the PAYE scheme which is administered by the Inland Revenue (SSCBA 1992, s15 and 1 Sch 3 and 6).

The organisation of the Inland Revenue

2.4 The Inland Revenue traditionally has split its core work into two functions:

- *Assessment*, which includes the making of assessments, the management of appeals, the issue and receipt of tax returns, the issue of notices of coding for PAYE, the conduct of tax investigations, and indeed most other functions apart from the actual collection of tax liabilities.

- *Collection*, which encompasses the receipt of tax payments, and the processes of negotiation and legal enforcement in cases of default.

2.5 Most *assessment* work has traditionally been carried out by *tax districts*, typically headed by a *District Inspector*, assisted by *Inspectors* of varying grades, under whom there are *officers* at different levels doing much of the day-to-day work.[1]

2.6 Assessment work for each taxpayer is normally managed within one tax district - commonly close to his place of work or residence, although taxpayers employed by organisations with London head offices are usually handled by one of the *London Provincial* tax districts outside the capital. Taxpayers with more than one source of income may be dealt with by two or more tax districts, but in such cases one district should be designated the General Claims District (frequently abbreviated to 'GCD'), which has overall responsibility for liaison between the offices concerned.

2.7 The general procedure for *collection* is that the taxpayer is initially instructed to send his payment to one of the Inland Revenue's two *Accounts Offices*, based in Shipley (West Yorkshire) and Cumbernauld (near Glasgow). Where payment is not received within an acceptable period, the matter is usually passed to a *local collection office* close to the taxpayer's residence or business premises, and larger debts may ultimately be referred on to the *Enforcement Office* in Worthing.

---

[1] There are also several specialist offices, such as the Special Compliance Office, The Pension Schemes Office, the MIRAS Central Unit and the Financial Intermediaries and Claims Office (FICO), which work closely with the tax districts.

2.8   All collection offices have powers to negotiate deferred payment arrangements, or to suspend or remit liabilities, which are examined in Chapter 6. Local collection offices and the Enforcement Office may also institute proceedings for recovery which are discussed in Chapters 7 to 11.

2.9   The tax districts and local collection offices are being reorganised under the *New Office Structure* programme. New-style *Taxpayer Service Offices* (TSOs) are being formed to take over most of the day-to-day work previously carried out within tax districts together with local collection office work. New-style *Tax District Offices* (TDOs) are handling more technical assessment work that was previously handled within tax districts. In addition, there is a chain of Tax Enquiry Centres (TECs) which offer face-to-face and telephone advice to any caller, as well as providing forms and leaflets, and can assist a taxpayer in making contact with other Inland Revenue offices.

2.10   Approximately 40% of taxpayers now fall within the reorganised areas. In the long run, this programme will end the strict division of responsibility - whereby Inspectors are concerned exclusively with assessment, and Collectors with collection - which is often confusing for taxpayers and can cause great problems where liaison breaks down. Ultimately the same officer will handle both aspects of an individual's tax, although at present the two functions are generally carried out within different sections of each TSO.

2.11   Under this reorganisation, all inspection and collection staff have been redesignated 'Officers of the Board of Inland Revenue'. However, for ease of exposition, this handbook uses the following terms according to their traditional meanings:

- *Inspector* refers to those officers concerned with assessment work, whether in old-style tax districts, TSOs or TDOs.

- *Collector* refers to those officers concerned with collection work, in the old-style collection offices or in TSOs.

- *Tax district* refers to the old-style tax districts, as well as TDOs and those sections of TSOs concerned with assessment work.

- *Local collection office* refers to old-style local collection offices, as well as those sections of TSOs carrying out local collection work.

The creation of a tax debt

2.12   A Collector has power to commence recovery proceedings in any circumstances where tax has become 'due and payable', but has not been paid (TMA 1970, s60).

2.13   Most commonly, tax becomes due and payable either:

- following the making of an *assessment* by an Inspector,

- under the terms of a *contractual settlement* between the taxpayer and the Inland Revenue following a tax investigation, or

- where the taxpayer has made a payment to a third party of a kind which is subject to a legal *requirement to deduct tax at source*, for example a salary payment to an employee.

Each of these is considered below.

Assessments

2.14   The power of an Inspector to make an assessment is set out in TMA 1970, s29:

- Where a tax return has been made and the Inspector is satisfied that it is correct and complete, he should make an assessment in accordance with the information reported on the return.

- Where no return has been made, or the Inspector is dissatisfied with a return, he may make an assessment 'to the best of his judgment'.

- Where tax is chargeable on the basis of income arising in the year, an assessment initially may be made to the best of the Inspector's judgment, but such assessments must be adjusted after the end of the tax year to reflect the actual income arising.

2.15   The power of an Inspector to make assessments *'to the best of his judgment'* is most commonly used where the taxpayer has failed to submit a tax return or business accounts on time. Such estimates are normally made in round numbers preceded by the letter 'E', for example 'E 15,000'. This power dates back to a time when the Inspector might have been personally familiar with the taxpayer's circumstances and in a position to make a reasonably accurate estimate. Nowadays the majority of estimates are at best a rough guess, perhaps by reference to previous accounts or the profits of other individuals engaged in similar activities, but the Courts have given Inspectors wide latitude. In the words of Fox L.J.:

> 'It is inevitable, in exercising the power which is plainly given to him by statute to assess to the best of his judgment, that the Inspector must, to some extent, be speculating because he is dealing with a situation in which the taxpayer has made no return, and so he has to attempt, himself, to guess what the true position may be.'[2]

---

[2] *Blackpool Marton Rotary Club v Martin* CA [1990] STC 1 p4

Making, issuing and serving assessments

2.16 An assessment is *made* when the Inspector completes a document or computer process, certifying details of the assessment. Although this activity is internal to the Inland Revenue, it can have significant practical implications. In particular, an assessment ordinarily is required to be made within six years of the end of the year of assessment to which it relates, and may be valid notwithstanding its issue to the taxpayer after that time limit (*Honig and another v Sarsfield* CA [1986] STC 246).

2.17 Details of the assessment are communicated to the taxpayer by the *issue* of a *notice of assessment*. This stage is critical because tax charged by an assessment cannot generally become 'payable' until at least 30 days after a notice of assessment has been issued for example ICTA 1988, s5(1)) (see also paragraph 2.29 below). Neither can interest on overdue tax begin to run before that time, unless the taxpayer has been guilty of failure to furnish information required by law, or of negligence or fraud (TMA 1988, s88; see paragraph 2.75 *et seq*).

2.18 The notice of assessment must also be *served* validly. It should be delivered or sent by post to the taxpayer's usual or last known place of residence, or his current place of business or employment, even if abroad (TMA 1970, s115 and *CIR v Huni* KB [1923] 8 TC 466). Service to the last known place of business is ineffective and a tax debt cannot be enforced if the requirements of service are not met (see *Re a Debtor (No 1240/SD/ 91) ex p. The Debtor v CIR* Ch D [1992] STC 771 and *Berry v Farrow* KB [1914] 1 KB 632).

2.19 Provided an assessment has been properly made, issued and served, the tax charged is recoverable by law even if the notice of assessment did not actually reach the taxpayer, for example because he had moved home. However, where a taxpayer alleges that he did not receive the underlying notice of assessment, *official policy* is to discontinue any enforcement proceedings to allow for a fresh notice to be served (unless there is evidence that the original was in fact received).[3] In fact, the *normal practice* is to supply photocopies of the original documents and to suspend enforcement proceedings to allow time for the taxpayer to respond, for example by making a late appeal (see paragraph 4.8 *et seq*).

The contents of a notice of assessment

2.20 Despite the importance of the notice of assessment, the legislation is poorly drafted and does not specify all the information that it should contain, this matter being left to TMA 1970, s113 which gives the Inland Revenue power to prescribe the form of documents that it uses. In particular, there is no requirement to state the *date* on which payment is

---

[3] *Inland Revenue Regional Executive Office Manual* paragraph 6.92

due, nor is there even a requirement to specify the *amount* of tax charged on the income assessed, although the Courts have held that this is implicit because:

> '(the contrary view) involves the proposition that the legislature envisaged the possibility of a taxpayer being liable to pay tax in an amount of which he has never been notified ... the words of the statute would have to be very clear to force the Court to this conclusion' (*Hallamshire Industrial Finance Ltd v CIR* Ch D [1979] STC 237 p241).

2.21   In practice, the Inland Revenue's computerised notices of assessment normally include:

- the date of issue of the notice,

- a description of the source(s) of profits assessed and the sum assessed for each,

- details of any deductions and allowances given,

- a calculation of the tax payable and credit for tax already paid,

- details of class 4 national insurance contributions due (if applicable),

- notes regarding the payment of tax and the right of appeal, and

- a detachable payslip to accompany the payment.

The notice is normally accompanied by detailed notes, which include a form on which to appeal against the assessment and a reply-paid envelope addressed to the relevant Collector.

2.22   An *error on a notice of assessment* will not necessarily render it invalid if the document 'in substance and effect' conforms with the tax legislation. In particular, it shall not be impeached or affected by reason of a mistake as to the person liable, the description of any profits or property, or the amount of tax charged (TMA 1970, s114; see paragraph 3.10 *et seq*).

Further and amended assessments

2.23   If an Inspector discovers profits which have not been assessed, or which exceed the amount assessed, or that excessive reliefs have been given, he may make what is called a *further assessment*, commonly called a *discovery assessment*, even if the original assessment is still under appeal (TMA 1970, s29(3) and *Duchy Maternity Ltd v Hodgson* Ch D [1985] STC 764).

2.24   A discovery may be one of law or fact. However, such an assessment may not be made on the basis of facts available to the Inspector, or a point of law considered, on the determination of an appeal against a previous assessment in respect of the same source (*Cenlon Finance Co Ltd v Ellwood* HL [1962] 40 TC 176 and *Olin Energy Systems Ltd v Scorer* HL [1985] STC 218).

2.25 A broad view is that the Inspector should, within reason, be deemed to have considered the information contained in any return and supporting documents submitted by the taxpayer at the time of the previous appeal. However, in 1991 the Inland Revenue issued *Statement of Practice SP8/91*, which stated that in general an Inspector would not be considered to be aware of information that was not expressly drawn to his attention, unless it was fundamental to the agreement of a computation. Leading counsel has expressed the view that:

> 'the Inland Revenue's interpretation of the *Olin Energy* decision ... is too narrow, i.e. the decision could apply (to protect the taxpayer) even where the point at issue is not fundamental to the agreement of the relevant figures, provided certain other conditions are satisfied ... it is counsel's view that the Inland Revenue could not raise a new assessment in any case where all such facts as it is reasonable to regard as relevant to considering the point at issue were disclosed and either:

> - the particular point had previously been raised expressly by the Inspector, the taxpayer or the taxpayer's agent; or

> - the point was so clearly presented that an 'ordinarily competent Inspector' would have or ought to have taken it into account.'[4]

2.26 *SP8/91* also sets out the Inland Revenue's practice where there was no appeal against the earlier assessment:

> 'a discovery assessment will not be made if the particular point on which the Inspector takes a revised view was, or ... could be said to have been, the subject of the specific agreement of the final figures for assessment purposes.'

2.27 While the same income may not be taxed twice without express statutory authority, the Inspector may make *alternative assessments* where, for example, it is unclear whether a particular receipt is liable to income tax or capital gains tax.[5] However, such double assessments are only provisional, as the taxpayer may ultimately claim relief from double taxation under TMA 1970, s32.

---

[4] *Ethical Rules and Practice Guidelines on Professional Conduct in Relation to Taxation*, published jointly by the Chartered Institute of Taxation and the ICAEW November 1995 p47

[5] Dictum by Lord Sumner in *Bradbury v English Sewing Cotton Co Ltd* HL (1923) 8 TC 481 p513, and *Bye v Coren* CA [1986] STC 393

2.28   Once an assessment has been served, it cannot be *amended* except in strict accordance with the Taxes Acts (TMA 1970, s29(6)). Effectively this requires that a written appeal must be made by the taxpayer and be determined subsequently by the Commissioners or settled by agreement between the Inspector and the taxpayer. The Inland Revenue may not unilaterally vacate (i.e. withdraw), reduce or otherwise amend an assessment (*Bayliss v Gregory* CA [1987] STC 297 pp321-322).

The normal due date for payment [6]

2.29   Where tax is charged by an assessment, payment falls due on the *later* of:

- 30 days after the issue of the notice of assessment, and

- the *statutory due date* which depends upon the source

Tax	*Due date*
Schedule D Cases I and II (income from a trade, profession or vocation)	Two equal instalments falling on 1 January in the tax year for which the tax is payable and 1 July immediately after the tax year.
Higher rate tax (income received net of tax deduction or credit)	1 December following the end of the tax year.
Schedule E (income from an office or employment)	14 days after the date on which the Collector makes application for payment. (There is a special regime allowing four direct payments by the employee on an assessment, where collection from the employer under PAYE is impractical, e.g. for non-resident employers.)
Capital gains tax	1 December following the end of the tax year.
Other assessed taxes	1 January in the tax year to which the tax relates.

(ICTA 1988, ss5 and 205, SI 1993/744 Regs 99 to 105, and TCGA 1992, s7).

---

[6]   As explained in the preface to this handbook, the new payment dates for self-assessment effective for 1996/97 onwards are not yet relevant in the context of historic tax debt. The new provisions are explained in Chapter 12.

In this handbook, the due date determined in accordance with the above rules is called the *normal due date*. It should be noted that payment may fall due later where tax is 'postponed' (see paragraph 3.42 *et seq*).

Contractual settlements

2.30   Certain taxpayers are selected by the Inland Revenue for in-depth *investigation* of their affairs.

> 'A set of accounts will be investigated only if the Inspector has reason to believe that the figures in them may not be correct. The sort of things that might lead to a closer look are:
>
> - A level of profits lower than in similar businesses in the area.
>
> - An amount taken out from the business which is clearly not enough for you to live on.
>
> - Unusually high business expenses, for instance a large claim for motor expenses when you do not appear to use a car much.
>
> - New funds being put into the business when it is not clear where they can have come from.
>
> - Savings which have grown faster than the Inspector would have expected given the profits of your business, or amounts drawn from your company.
>
> - Information from elsewhere (for example from a bank about interest credited to your account) which does not agree with your tax return.
>
> - Sending in your tax return or accounts late.
>
> - Failing to tell the Inland Revenue when you start in business and become liable to tax.
>
> Sometimes an investigation is necessary simply because your business records are muddled.'[7]

2.31   Most investigations involve the self-employed and are conducted by Inspectors within tax districts. A smaller number of more serious cases, which may involve fraud, evasion or significant tax avoidance, are handled by the Special Compliance Office.

2.32   Although a handful of investigations end in criminal prosecutions, the Inspector's usual objective is to reach a financial settlement, set out in an exchange of letters, under the terms of which the taxpayer agrees to settle any tax he has failed to pay for the period under review, together with interest and penalties.

---

[7]   *IR 72 Investigations: The examination of business accounts* p2

2.33   The exchange of letters at the conclusion of an investigation amounts to a binding contract between the taxpayer and the Inland Revenue.[8] Although there is no express statutory authority for the Inland Revenue to enter such contractual agreements, the Courts have confirmed the implied power of the Inland Revenue to adopt this method of revenue collection under its general duty of care and management. The sum payable by the taxpayer under such an agreement is enforceable as a debt under contract law and not as a tax liability *per se*. This may have implications, for example, as to the Inland Revenue's preferential rights on bankruptcy or the time limits for collection (*CIR v Woollen* CA [1992] STC 944; see paragraph 2.99 and 11.95).[9]

Elements of a typical investigation

2.34   Although each investigation is different and Inspectors have a considerable amount of discretion, investigations into the accounts of self-employed earners tend to have common elements described in the following paragraphs.

2.35   An investigation will usually commence with a letter from the Inspector raising queries about the taxpayer's accounting records or the basis upon which his accounts or return have been prepared. If the Inspector is not satisfied with the taxpayer's response to his first letter, he will inform the taxpayer that his accounts have become subject to an investigation, and send him copies of *IR 72 Investigations: The Examination of Business Accounts* and *Code of Practice 2 Investigations*.

2.36   An investigation may take several months and will generally include at least one meeting with the Inspector, at which the taxpayer will usually be given *IR 73 Investigations: How settlements are negotiated*.

2.37   The taxpayer will usually be asked to provide books and documents relating to his business affairs. The Inspector may also ask to see personal financial records if these may be relevant to the investigation.

2.38   The Inspector will be seeking to ascertain the true profits for the period under investigation. Typically, the initial review will concentrate on the latest year and, where the Inspector believes that a substantial adjustment should be made for that year, the enquiry may be extended to earlier years. In practice, the exercise may involve going back up to six years, although:

- In more serious cases, there are powers to go back further.

---

[8]   *IR 73 Investigations: How settlements are negotiated*
[9]   Also, for an interesting analysis of the Inland Revenue's powers, see *CIR v Nuttall* CA [1990] STC 194.

- In cases where the taxpayer has limited resources, the period covered may be much shorter (see paragraphs 2.60 and 5.83 *et seq*).

2.39 An investigation will usually include a 'business economics' exercise which considers, for example, mark-up levels within the business and profit levels enjoyed by similar businesses. The Inspector will have access to the Inland Revenue's *Business Economic Notes* which provide detailed financial statistics and information covering over 200 different types of business, 22 of which are now available to the public for a nominal charge. Published notes cover, *inter alia,* hairdressers, florists, licensed victuallers and the catering trade. In addition, or alternatively, the Inspector will seek to ascertain undisclosed profits by comparing the taxpayer's standard of living and financial resources with figures that have actually been declared. This may involve reviewing the financial affairs of other members of the household.

2.40 The Inspector will then produce calculations of the undisclosed profits and usually there will be some negotiation before an agreement of the final figures.

2.41 The Inspector will then calculate the tax considered to have been 'lost' through the taxpayer's fraudulent or negligent conduct, the interest thereon, and the maximum penalties that might be determined under the law, typically up to 100% of the tax 'lost'.

2.42 The taxpayer will be invited to propose an offer in full settlement and the Inspector will usually give an indication of the minimum figure that might be acceptable to the Inland Revenue. If he does not, the taxpayer may request such an indication.

2.43 The Inspector will explain that any offer must cover the full amount of tax lost and interest due, which the Inland Revenue considers merely to be financial restitution, together with a penalty, which is the only figure open for negotiation at this point. He will refer to leaflet *IR 73* which explains how penalties are mitigated to reflect:

- *disclosure* by the taxpayer, which may attract a reduction of up to 20% in the penalties demanded (or 30% for voluntary disclosure),

- *co-operation* in the investigation, which may earn a separate discount of up to 40%, and

- the *gravity* of the case, with less serious offences attracting a further reduction of up to 40%.

He will indicate the level of mitigation considered appropriate under each head for the case under consideration and indicate an expected penalty figure, which will usually fall between 10% and 40% of the maximum chargeable by law. Although mitigation of penalties is a matter for the

Board of Inland Revenue, tax districts are given considerable authority to agree settlements.

2.44   If the taxpayer indicates that he is prepared to make an acceptable offer covering tax, interest and mitigated penalties, the Inspector will draft a letter addressed to the Inland Revenue to be signed by the taxpayer. This sets out the taxpayer's offer of payment in consideration of the Inland Revenue taking no further proceedings against him in respect of the tax liabilities, interest and penalties concerned, which will be listed in the letter.

2.45   If the taxpayer has sufficient resources to settle the full amount stipulated, the letter will usually promise payment within 30 days of the date on which the offer is accepted. If there might be some delay in obtaining the necessary funds, the letter may provide for settlement within a longer period, or for payment by instalments over a timescale of months or even years. This is a rare situation where an Inspector - as opposed to a Collector - will be involved in discussions over payment arrangements.

2.46   If the taxpayer is content with the terms set out in the offer letter, he should sign it and return it to the Inspector, who will then issue a letter of acceptance together with a payslip giving details of the Accounts Office to which payment should be made. If the taxpayer complies with the agreement, the matter is settled.

2.47   At the end of an investigation, the taxpayer will also be asked to sign a formal Certificate of Disclosure confirming that he has not withheld any relevant information, and a statement of his assets and liabilities. If either of these documents proves false, criminal proceedings may be instituted.

2.48   Sometimes the Inspector will have issued assessments during the course of the investigation for the purpose of protecting the Inland Revenue's position. When a settlement is reached, normally the amount unpaid on these assessments is informally discharged.

Complaints about the conduct of investigations

2.49   The Adjudicator's Report for 1993/94 revealed that 19.5% of complaints about the Inland Revenue involved allegations of oppressive or unfair conduct by Inspectors during the course of investigations. This is not entirely surprising since:

- the essence of an investigation is that the Inspector is challenging information provided by the taxpayer and this can easily develop into a confrontational situation,

- although the Government has stated that Inspectors do not receive financial or non-financial rewards based upon the results they achieve[10], an Inspector's career prospects will be affected by the outcome of his investigation work, including the tax yield, and

- the Inland Revenue clearly relies upon the deterrent effect of its investigation work to encourage taxpayer compliance generally, a fact highlighted by its efforts to publicise the results of this work.

2.50 It is therefore to be expected that Inspectors will sometimes overstep the thin line between firmness and unreasonable conduct or duress. In such cases it should be remembered that an investigation is a non-statutory and essentially voluntary process, the purpose of which is to reach an agreement. The taxpayer is not obliged to enter into the negotiations and has the right to withdraw unilaterally at any time.

2.51 Nonetheless, co-operation is invariably beneficial for the taxpayer:

- In the event that an agreement cannot be reached, the Inspector is likely to resort to making estimated assessments and any appearance by the taxpayer before the Commissioners on appeal is likely to result in a full interrogation by the Inspector.

- The Inspector may use statutory powers to determine penalties and interest, and the taxpayer's 'non-co-operation' would influence the level of penalties sought (see paragraphs 2.43 and 2.87).

- The Inspector may use formal procedures to obtain information withheld by the taxpayer.

In consequence the tax assessed, and related interest and penalties, may be considerably higher than the figures that could have been reached by agreement.

Requirements to deduct tax at source

2.52 There is a wide range of circumstances where individuals are required to deduct tax at source from payments that they make, some important examples that arise in the context of tax debt being in respect of payments to:

- Employees, under Income Tax (Employments) Regulations 1993, SI 1993/744, commonly known as the *PAYE Regulations*.

- Self-employed sub-contractors in the construction industry, under Income Tax (Sub-contractors in the Construction Industry) Regulations 1993, SI 1993/743 (see further discussion in paragraph 5.101 *et seq*).

- Persons whose usual place of abode is outside the United Kingdom, in respect of income from UK property, under ICTA 1988, s43 (see further discussion in paragraph 5.166 *et seq*).

---

[10] Statement by the Financial Secretary to the Treasury, *Hansard* 28 January 1992

2.53 Where the law imposes an obligation to deduct tax, there is accompanying legislation requiring this to be paid to the Inland Revenue on a specified date falling shortly after the end of the period in which the payment was made. This obligation arises without any need for the Inland Revenue to issue a demand or assessment; i.e. the debt is created by the act of making the payment. In cases of non-payment, interest - and sometimes penalties - may be charged automatically, without prior warning from a Collector or Inspector.

2.54 The legislation also contains provisions for enforcement proceedings to be instituted where payment is not made timeously. Usually, this involves an Inspector or Collector having powers to issue a specified notice, with express powers for recovery of the tax as if it were an assessment.

2.55 For example, where an employer has not remitted sums due under the PAYE Regulations for a tax month or quarter, or the amount paid appears insufficient, the Collector may issue a *notice* of the amount considered payable. If this is not settled within seven days, he may issue a *certificate* of tax payable, on the basis of which recovery proceedings may be taken against the employer as if it were an assessment.[11] Quite separately, where the Inspector considers that tax due under the same Regulations is unpaid, but which is not covered by a Collector's certificate, he may issue a notice of *determination* and take recovery proceedings as if it were an assessment, and he has further powers to take action against the employees involved (SI 1993/744 *supra*, Regs 42 and 49; for further discussion, see paragraph 5.20 *et seq*).

Time limits for the creation of a tax debt

2.56 Normally, an *assessment* must be made within six years of the end of the tax year to which it relates (TMA 1970, s34(1)). In a small number of situations, this period is extended or reduced by specific provisions. For example, time limits are reduced after the death of a taxpayer (TMA 1970, s40; see paragraph 5.14).

2.57 Where an assessment is raised for the purpose of making good to the Crown any loss of tax attributable to 'fraudulent or negligent conduct' the time limit is extended to 20 years. For the years up to 1982/83, where such an assessment is attributable to 'fraud or wilful default', it may be made at any time although the Inspector must obtain leave of a Commissioner (TMA 1970, ss36 and 41).

2.58 Generally the same time limits also apply to the making of *determinations*, since the legislation usually 'imports' provisions governing

---

[11] SI 1993/744 *supra*, Regs 48 and 54. Note that this is a rare situation where there is no Inspector involved in ascertaining the quantum due.

assessments from the Taxes Management Act 1970. For example, a determination made on an employer under the PAYE Regulations is subject to the provisions in Parts IV, V and VI of TMA 1970 as if it was an assessment (SI 1993/744 *supra*, Reg 49(7)). It should be noted that this can be an imperfect method of drafting tax law, and Inspectors sometimes accept that Statutory Instruments do not always achieve the results intended by the draftsman.

2.59 In practice, assessments and determinations going back beyond the normal six-year limit are relatively rare, because cases involving fraud or negligence are normally handled through investigations aimed at contractual settlements.

2.60 In view of the non-statutory nature of *contractual settlements*, these may cover any number of years. However, in practice they rarely extend beyond the six years that would normally be open for assessment, unless the Inspector considers that he has very good evidence of serious neglect or fraud.

Interest and penalties

2.61 The taxes legislation contains numerous provisions for interest and penalties to be charged where a taxpayer fails to comply with its requirements. Perhaps the most common failures are delays in declaring income to the Inland Revenue and errors in tax returns and business accounts, and the relevant provisions are summarised in the following three paragraphs.

2.62 Anyone who has profits chargeable to tax, and who has not received a tax return form, must provide written details of his profits to the Inland Revenue within six months of the end of the tax year (TMA 1970, s7).[12] This requirement does not normally apply to income where the full tax liability is satisfied by deductions made at source.

2.63 The Inland Revenue has power to issue a tax return to any person for the purposes of assessing him to income tax or capital gains tax. Such a return must be completed and submitted to the Inspector within the time specified on the form, which is normally 30 days (TMA 1970, ss8 and 12, but see paragraph 2.77 *et seq*). There is considerable case law on the precise scope of this provision and, in particular, a return including the entry 'details to follow', 'as returned by my employer' or 'per accounts to follow' is incomplete (*Cox v Poole Commissioners & CIR* Ch D [1988] STC 66 and *Cox v Poole Commissioners & CIR (No 2)* Ch D [1990] STC 122).

---

[12] Note that, for tax years prior to 1995/96, notification had only to be made within 12 months of the end of the tax year in which the profits arose.

2.64 A tax return form ends with a declaration by the taxpayer that the information given is correct and complete to the best of his knowledge and belief. Accordingly, great care should be taken in completing the form. Where precise information is unavailable, estimates may be used and these should be accompanied by appropriate explanations (*Dunk v Havant Commissioners* Ch D [1976] STC 460).

Interest on unpaid tax

2.65 As a general rule, interest is chargeable on tax paid late. The charge is to *simple interest* (i.e. it is not compounded) and the rate is determined by a formula based upon the current average of the base lending rates of the six main clearing banks. Rate changes are publicised by way of Inland Revenue press releases (FA 1989, s178 and SI 1989/1297).[13]

2.66 Interest may also be levied on late payment of class 4 national insurance contributions, but only where charged on Schedule D Case I or II assessments issued on or after 19 April 1993 (SSCBA 1992, 2 Sch 6 and Social Security (Consequential Provisions) Act 1992, 4 Sch 8 and 9).

2.67 Where interest has been levied on tax charged by an assessment which is subsequently reduced, the interest charge should be reduced correspondingly and a refund made if appropriate (TMA 1970, s91). There are a few express exceptions, for example where the reduction follows a claim for relief under the Business Expansion Scheme or Enterprise Investment Scheme.

2.68 The Inland Revenue has powers to waive interest charges, although these are not exercised commonly.[14] The usual grounds for denying relief are that interest is not a penalty but represents merely commercial restitution to the Treasury for the late receipt of the money.

2.69 No tax relief is available for interest charged on unpaid tax (TMA 1970, s90).

2.70 Collection of interest may be enforced as if it were tax charged by the underlying assessment (TMA 1970, s69).

The period for which interest is charged

2.71 The date from which interest begins to accrue depends upon the particular provision under which it is charged. This may be either:

- *TMA 1970, s86*, which is the general charging provision, or

---

[13] At 31 May 1996, base lending rates were 6% and the interest charge generally applicable for unpaid tax was 6.25%.

[14] These powers are available generally under the care and management provisions in TMA 1970, s1 and specifically under TMA 1970, ss86(4B) and 88(4) and SSCBA 1992, 2 Sch 6(2).

- *TMA 1970, s88*, which may apply where the taxpayer has also been guilty of an error or default. This allows interest to run from an earlier date, and the charge may therefore be correspondingly higher.

The detailed provisions are discussed in the next two sections.

2.72   Interest stops running on the 'effective date of payment', which is normally the date that the payment is actually received by the Inland Revenue, although there are special rules for remittances by electronic means or bank giro described in paragraph 2.88 *et seq.*

Interest charges under TMA 1970, s86

2.73   Under section 86, interest runs from a 'reckonable date' which is typically the *normal due date for payment*, which can never be earlier than 30 days after the issue of the underlying assessment. The reckonable date may, however, be later where part or all of the tax charged by an assessment is postponed. For normal due dates, see paragraph 2.29, and for the rules following postponement see paragraph 3.42 *et seq.*

2.74   Interest charges are simply added to the tax due, as shown on the face of the tax assessment. For assessments made before 19 April 1993, the Inland Revenue will waive interest charges of up to £30.[15]

Interest charges under TMA 1970, s88

2.75   Interest may be charged under section 88 where an assessment is made for the purposes of 'making good to the Crown a loss of tax'. Interest then runs from the date on which tax 'ought to have been paid', i.e. the *statutory due date for payment*, regardless of whether any assessment was in issue at the time. For the table of statutory due dates, see paragraph 2.29.

2.76   Interest levied under section 88 is often referred to as *culpable interest* and this term reflects the origin of the provision. Before 27 July 1989, the taxpayer had to be guilty of 'fraud, wilful default or neglect' and could dispute the charge if he had a reasonable excuse. With effect from that date, the section may also apply in cases of wholly innocent error and there is no provision for reasonable excuse. The charge is most commonly invoked for failure to declare profits, or for errors or delays in submitting tax returns. The Inland Revenue's policy for determining whether s86 or s88 should apply is explained in *Tax Bulletin* May 1993 on page 61.

2.77   As regards late tax returns, the Inland Revenue recognises that the strict 30 day time limit for submission is frequently impractical, and so an

---

[15] Former TMA 1970, s86(6), repealed by FA 1989

extension is given by *Statement of Practice SP6/89*. This states that section 88 interest will be claimed only where the delay is 'substantial', and so will not be charged where a tax return, issued at any time on or before 1 October after the tax year end, is submitted by 31 October following the tax year end.

2.78   *SP6/89* explains that the Inland Revenue is particularly concerned to receive prompt details of new sources of income, continuing sources where inadequate estimated assessments have not been appealed against, or capital gains. It states:

> 'Where it is not possible to lodge the return, a section 88 charge will not be raised if the Inspector is provided, within these time limits, with sufficient information to enable an adequate estimated assessment to be made - e.g. in the case of the disposal of a chargeable asset, at least the sale price of that asset.'

2.79   Inspectors sometimes assume that section 88 interest is always chargeable where a taxpayer fails to meet the 31 October deadline. However, this view was rejected by the Court of Appeal in *Billingham v Myers* (CA [1996] STC 593) where a tax return reporting significant capital gains realised in 1987/88 was submitted on 3 November 1988. An estimated assessment was made on 7 November 1988, with the tax ultimately being settled by 1 June 1989. The taxpayer succeeded in arguing that the assessment could not have been raised for the purposes of making good a loss of tax, since it was issued prior to the earliest date on which the tax could have become payable (1 December 1988). Therefore, at the date of issue, there was only a potential loss of tax and section 88 did not apply.

2.80   A section 88 interest charge may be made by the issue of a formal *determination* showing the interest due, which has some of the features of a tax assessment, such as the right of appeal (TMA 1970, s88A). However, in practice such sums as would be due under this provision are usually collected within the framework of a contractual settlement and determinations tend to be restricted to those cases where an agreement cannot be reached.

Penalties

2.81   There is a wide range of provisions under which penalties may be charged. This section considers only those applicable where the taxpayer:

- has failed to declare profits,

- has been guilty of submitting an incorrect tax return, or

- has been late in submitting a tax return (for statutory requirements, see paragraph 2.62 *et seq*).

2.82   A penalty of up to 100% of any tax paid late as a result of the failure may be charged for failure to notify the Inland Revenue of income or gains. For this purpose, tax is paid late if it is not settled by 31 January following the tax year end (TMA 1970, s7(8)).[16]

2.83   Where a return is incorrect through fraud or negligence on the part of the taxpayer, a penalty of up to 100% of any tax undercharged in consequence of the error may be charged. Furthermore, where a taxpayer discovers an inadvertent error in a return, he will be deemed to have been negligent if he then fails to report the error to the Inspector without unreasonable delay (TMA 1970, ss95 and 97).

2.84   Where a tax return is not submitted within the 30 day time limit:

- The Inspector may apply to the Commissioners to impose a penalty of up to £300 and a further penalty of up to £60 per day if failure continues. In practice, this penalty is not sought where the return is submitted by the deadline laid down in *Statement of Practice 6/89* (see paragraph 2.77).

- There is a further penalty if the taxpayer's failure continues beyond the end of the tax year following that in which the return was issued. Any tax assessed after that date, in respect of profits which should have been included in the return, may attract a penalty of up to 100% of the tax (TMA 1970, s93(2)).

2.85   Under the taxes legislation, a penalty is normally imposed by the Inspector issuing a *determination*, and the amount charged is then recoverable as if it were tax charged by an assessment (TMA 1970, ss100 and 100A(3)). However, in practice such sums as might be charged by way of penalties are usually collected within the framework of a contractual settlement and determinations tend to be restricted to those cases where an agreement cannot be reached.

2.86   The taxpayer may appeal to the Commissioners against a penalty determination as if it were an assessment and the Commissioners may set aside, confirm, increase or reduce the determination. The Inland Revenue also has a general power to mitigate or remit penalties (TMA 1970, ss100B and 102).

2.87   The leading cases on the mitigation of penalties involve earlier legislation, where the quantum was normally determined by the Commissioners and not by the Inland Revenue. However, similar principles should still apply and the guiding factor is the extent to which the taxpayer was at fault. In a case where the Commissioners imposed a penalty of 40% of the statutory maximum, Mr Justice Vinelott refused to intervene on the grounds that:

---

[16] For the years up to 1994/95, the penalty was up to 100% of any tax not covered by assessments made within 12 months of the end of the tax year.

'the Court would only interfere with an award of penalties ... where plainly something had gone wrong ... where the penalty was plainly disproportionate to any possible fault.'

In contrast, penalties close to the statutory maximum were reduced by 20% in the case of an elderly taxpayer who had experienced problems with his professional advisers, as the judge considered the decision out of line with rulings by other panels of Commissioners (*Lear v Leek General Commissioners and CIR* Ch D [1986] STC 542 p543 and *Brodt v Wells General Commissioners* Ch D [1987] STC 207; see also *Stableford v Liverpool General Commissioners and others* Ch D [1983] STC 162).

Payment of tax

2.88   Tax may be paid by cash, postal order, cheque, bank giro, Girobank, or electronic funds transfer. The date on which the payment is treated as having been made is set out below:

Method of payment	*Effective date of payment*
Cheques, cash and postal orders handed in at an Inland Revenue office or received by post	Normally, the date of receipt by the Inland Revenue. However, for a postal receipt following a day on which the office was closed for any reason, the effective date of payment is the day the office was first closed. For example, a payment received by cheque on a Monday is treated as paid on the previous Saturday.
Electronic Funds Transfer by BACS or CHAPS	One working day immediately prior to the date that value is received.
Payments by Bank Giro or Girobank	Three working days prior to the date of processing by the Inland Revenue.[17]

2.89   A tax liability may also be met from a repayment due to the same taxpayer in respect of another assessment or different tax year, or by encashment of a Certificate of Tax Deposit (the detailed provisions are explained in paragraph 4.71 *et seq*).

2.90   Whenever a payment is made, it is advisable to attach a letter or Inland Revenue payslip indicating clearly the liability to which the payment relates. In the case of payment by cheque or postal order, the risk of error or fraud is reduced if the Inland Revenue's reference is included as part of the payee's name, for example 'Pay: INLAND REVENUE 111/D55555/9502'.

---

[17] Inland Revenue press release 1 April 1996

2.91   If the taxpayer does not know the full reference of an assessment, the covering letter should clearly indicate his name and tax district reference, the year of assessment and type of duty involved.

2.92   Where a single payment is made in respect of a number of assessments or liabilities, the allocation should be explained clearly in a covering letter. However, there is less risk of confusion if each liability is met by a completely separate payment.

2.93   The Inland Revenue does not routinely provide a receipt, but must provide one upon request (TMA 1970, s60(2)).

2.94   Cheques received by the Accounts Offices are processed through the normal clearing cycle. Following the abolition of the Town Clearing system in February 1995, the Inland Revenue has no special clearing arrangements for large cheques received by these offices.

Proceedings to recover tax debts

2.95   Where tax has become due and payable, but has not been settled, the Collector will first attempt to persuade the taxpayer to settle the arrears within an acceptable timescale (see Chapter 6).

2.96   If persuasion fails, the Collector may resort to one or more of the following *civil enforcement procedures*:

- Distraint upon goods and chattels - see Chapter 8.

- Proceedings through the Magistrates Courts - see Chapter 9.

- County Court proceedings - see Chapter 10.

- Bankruptcy - see Chapter 11.

2.97   Such proceedings must always be preceded by a demand being made on the taxpayer in person, or at his last place of abode (TMA 1970, s60(1)). In practice, a number of demands are issued before recovery proceedings commence.

Time limits for recovery action

2.98   In general, once a tax debt has become due and payable, action for recovery is never time-barred. Although the Limitation Act 1980 imposes an ordinary six-year time limit on proceedings by the Crown, section 37(2)(a) provides that:

> '... this Act shall not apply to ... any proceeding by the Crown for the recovery of any tax or duty or interest on any tax or duty'.

2.99   While the above provision clearly allows the Collector an indefinite period to recover income tax, capital gains tax and interest on those taxes, it is arguable that certain other tax debts are excluded:

- *National insurance contributions.* Published letters from the Contributions Agency state that proceedings cannot be taken for national insurance contributions after six years have elapsed and it is understood that this is based upon the view that such contributions are not 'a tax or duty'. It should be noted that in cases of concealment, the Contributions Agency considers that the six-year period runs from the date on which the liability is discovered, or could with reasonable diligence have been discovered.[18] These rules apply where contributions are recovered by the Inland Revenue and its manual confirms that the time limit is six years from the date that contributions became due and payable. However, it also states that the period for action starts afresh if the person liable, or their agent, acknowledges the debt in writing or makes a part-payment.[19]

- *Penalties.* On similar principles it may be argued that penalties are not a 'tax or duty' and that a six-year time limit applies to the enforcement of penalty determinations.

- *Payments due under contractual settlements.* In *CIR v Woollen* (CA [1992] STC 944), the taxpayer had entered a contractual settlement with the Inland Revenue jointly with three companies of which he had been a director. The companies had subsequently entered administrative receivership and the Inland Revenue had obtained a judgment against the taxpayer in respect of sums still outstanding under the settlement. The taxpayer appealed, contending *inter alia* that the Inland Revenue's decision not to lodge preferential claims in the receiverships was a breach of its equitable duty. The Court of Appeal held that sums due under the terms of a contractual settlement had lost their identity as 'tax', that the Inland Revenue could not rank as a preferential creditor and the only remedy open to it was an action in debt. This case provides authority for the general proposition that sums due under a contractual settlement lose their identity as 'tax' for other purposes too, and so the ordinary six-year limit should apply to the recovery of a payment promised under a contractual settlement.

Custodial sentences and criminal proceedings

2.100 Civil proceedings are normally aimed at securing funds or assets towards settlement of tax debts. Although the civil Courts do have reserve powers to impose custodial sentences on defendants in the event of non-cooperation, or non-payment, during or following proceedings to enforce tax debts (see paragraphs 9.34 and 10.122) these are very rarely used.

---

[18] Booths NIC Brief February 1993 p34 and May 1993 p61
[19] *Inland Revenue Enforcement Manual* paragraph E1.305

2.101 Although *criminal proceedings* are not instituted solely for non-payment of tax, such action may be considered by the Inland Revenue where other offences have also been committed. Prosecution is possible for a number of common law and statutory offences, including fraud on the Public Revenue, forgery, false accounting and conspiracy to defraud. In practice, such action is rare: in 1994/95 criminal proceedings were taken by the Inland Revenue against a total of 382 individuals, of whom 357 were convicted and only 19 cases related to false accounts or tax returns. The Report of the Board of Inland Revenue lists the offences for which charges were brought as follows:

Theft of payable orders or Giro cheques	240
Sub-contractors exemption certificates fraud	42
False PAYE returns by employers and pay clerks	25
False accounts or returns of income	19
Internal fraud	11
Other	45

2.102 This is probably a small fraction of the number of cases in which criminal offences are uncovered by the Inland Revenue, but the general policy is to seek a financial settlement, including interest and penalties. Factors influencing a decision to take criminal proceedings appear to include:

- The chances of securing successfully a conviction by a jury. This would involve consideration of the admissible evidence available, as well as the taxpayer's age and other personal circumstances.

- The seriousness of the offence. The following are considered particularly heinous:

    - false certificates of disclosure or statements of assets during an investigation,

    - second or subsequent offences by the same person,

    - conspiracies to defraud the Inland Revenue,

    - the creation of false documents, and

    - the involvement of accountants or other professional advisers.

This policy of selective prosecution has been approved by the Courts.[20]

2.103 Most cases of serious fraud are dealt with by the Special Compliance Office and these are usually opened by giving the taxpayer a leaflet, called the *Hansard leaflet*, which contains an extract from a

---

[20] See *R v CIR* (ex p. Mead and Cook) QBD [1992] STC 482, which provides an interesting analysis of the legal issues.

statement to the House of Commons. This explains that in cases of alleged fraud the Inland Revenue may accept a monetary settlement instead of instituting criminal proceedings. However, it reserves the right to take criminal proceedings even where the taxpayer makes a full disclosure and co-operates, although in practice prosecutions are unknown where full disclosure and compliance are given following a Hansard opening. If criminal proceedings are under serious consideration, then the taxpayer will be cautioned formally at the outset, while if the situation is unclear then neither a formal caution nor the Hansard leaflet will be given until the Inland Revenue has sufficient evidence to decide how to proceed.

2.104 Even where civil action is taken for penalties, this does not preclude criminal action in respect of the same matter (TMA 1970, s104). However, the Inland Revenue's practice is that a taxpayer should not suffer penalties and criminal sanctions for the same offence. The official policy applying from 10 May 1988 is:

'i.   to refrain (as previously) from taking steps to recover civil money penalties on the basis of fraud in respect of an offence which has been before the criminal Courts;

ii.   to seek appropriate civil money penalties in respect of any offence which has not been brought before the Courts;

iii.   to reserve the right to seek, where there are grounds to do so, a civil penalty in respect of negligence by a taxpayer who has been acquitted of criminal intent in respect of a prosecution for fraud.'[21]

---

[21] *Statement of Practice SP2/88*

Chapter 3

Legal and administrative safeguards

In view of the Inland Revenue's considerable powers to create and enforce tax debts, it is vital to appreciate the different safeguards available. This chapter examines:

		From paragraph
■	Tax appeals	*3.1*
■	Postponement of tax	*3.37*
■	How appeals and postponement affect payment dates and interest	*3.42*
■	Remedying unfairness through the Courts	*3.54*
■	Inland Revenue discretion and practice	*3.77*
■	The Taxpayer's Charter and complaints of maladministration	*3.96*
■	Selecting the appropriate course of action	*3.144*

The specific safeguards available to defendants in tax recovery proceedings are discussed, together with the respective methods of enforcement, at Chapters 8 to 11.

Tax appeals

3.1   If any assessment appears excessive or otherwise incorrect, the statutory mechanism for objection is for the taxpayer to make an *appeal* (TMA 1970, s31). There is a similar right of appeal against most types of Inland Revenue determination, see paragraphs 2.55 and 2.58, and most of the provisions discussed in this section apply also to appeals against determinations.

3.2   For practical purposes, an appeal is necessary for two reasons:

● It opens the way for amendment of any of the figures shown on the assessment, by agreement with the Inspector or by recourse to a Commissioners' hearing. In the absence of a valid appeal, the assessment is final and conclusive (TMA 1970, s29(6)).

● On making an appeal, the taxpayer may apply for *postponement* of part or all of the tax charged, to the extent that he considers it to be excessive. This procedure enables payment to be deferred beyond the date that it would otherwise be due and payable, pending the outcome of the appeal (see paragraph 3.42 *et seq)*.[1]

3.3   The legislation provides that appeals and postponement applications are made to the Commissioners, which are independent tribunals (see paragraph 3.21 *et seq)*. However, as the initial notice must be given to the Inspector who issued the assessment and as there are provisions for all subsequent matters to be agreed between the taxpayer and the Inspector, recourse to the Commissioners by either party is frequently unnecessary.

3.4   When a notice of an appeal is received, the Inspector should ascertain whether the matters in dispute can be resolved by agreement, which may result in the assessment being amended in some way, discharged or upheld without variation (see paragraph 3.14 *et seq)*.

3.5   If the parties cannot reach an agreement, the appeal is listed to be heard by the Commissioners. Upon considering the evidence, they may reduce or increase the amount assessed or tax charged, and the assessment shall be adjusted accordingly; otherwise it stands good. Their decision is commonly called a *Commissioners' determination* (TMA 1970, ss50(6) to 50(8)).

3.6   If either party is dissatisfied with a Commissioners' determination on a matter of law, he may take the matter to the Courts (see paragraph 3.30 *et seq)*.

Making appeals - specific provisions

3.7   A notice of appeal must:

●   be in writing,

●   state the grounds of appeal,

●   be given to the Inspector who made the assessment, in person or by post, and

●   be made within 30 days of the date on which the assessment was issued, which must be shown on the notice of assessment (TMA 1970, ss29(5), 31 and 115(2), but see paragraph 4.8 *et seq* for *late appeals)*.

3.8   The appeal may be made by letter, or on the standard Inland Revenue form to be found within the explanatory leaflet accompanying the assessment. In either case, the assessment reference number should be indicated clearly.

3.9   Although *grounds of appeal* must be given, additional grounds may be added later if the original omission was not wilful or unreasonable

---

[1]   For when tax is normally due and payable, see paragraph 2.29

(TMA 1970, s31(5)). Grounds of appeal are not limited to objections as to the profits assessed; any item affecting the amount of tax charged by an assessment may give rise to a valid appeal, for example the allowances given or the rates of tax charged (*Hallamshire Industrial Finance Trust Ltd v CIR* Ch D [1979] STC 237). In practice, it is common for appeals to be lodged on the grounds that 'the assessment is estimated and may be excessive', leaving scope for other specific grounds to be added at a later date if necessary.

3.10   Appeals on pure technicalities may be disallowed. An assessment may not be impugned for want of form by reason of a defect or omission if it:

> 'is in substance and effect in conformity with or according to the intent and meaning of the Taxes Acts, and if the person or property charged ... is designated therein according to common intent and understanding'

and, in particular, it may not be challenged by reason of a mistake as to the name of the person liable, the description of any profits or property, or the amount of tax charged (TMA 1970, s114).

3.11   Some examples of grounds of appeal which might be considered valid are:

- The assessment was made outside the statutory time limit (TMA 1970, s34(2); see paragraph 2.56 *et seq*).

- The source of income did not exist in the year of assessment, for example because it ceased in an earlier year (*Bray v Best* HL [1989] STC 159).

- The income assessed belongs to someone else (*Alongi v CIR* CS [1991] STC 517, although the argument failed on the evidence in that case).

- The assessment was made under the wrong Schedule or Case (*Pickles v Foulsham* HL [1925] 9 TC 261).

- The notice of assessment refers to the wrong tax year (*Bayliss v Gregory* CA [1987] STC 297).

- No proper *source* of income is shown. General Commissioners have held that an assessment on 'casual profits' was invalid. Another questionable description which is used is 'general income'. These are *descriptions* of profits, not sources.[2]

3.12   In contrast, appeals on the following grounds have been disallowed:

- The assessment was estimated, or was not made to the best of the Inspector's judgment (see paragraph 2.15).

---

[2] *Taxation* 27 January 1994 p344

- The assessment was made in the name of the wrong body of trustees where the error was clear from correspondence (*Hart v Briscoe and others* Ch D [1978] STC 89).

- The appellant is owed a refund under another head of tax (*Collis v Cadle* Ch D [1955] 36 TC 204).

- Claims for loss relief are to be, but have not yet been, made (*Khan v First East Brixton General Commissioners and CIR* Ch D [1986] STC 331).

- The appellant is not bound by the tax law, for example because he had been denied the opportunity to stand for Parliament (*Hebden v Pepper* Ch D [1988] STC 821).

- The tax will be used for nuclear weapons (*Cheney v Conn* Ch D [1967] 44 TC 217).

Settlement of an appeal by agreement

3.13   Once a valid appeal has been made, it cannot be withdrawn unilaterally by the taxpayer (nor can the Inspector unilaterally amend or discharge an assessment once it has been *served*).   The appeal must be settled by agreement or determined by the Commissioners (*R v Special Commissioners (ex p. Elmhirst)* CA [1935] 20 TC 381; see also paragraph 2.28).

3.14   In practice, more than 90% of appeals are concluded by the Inspector and taxpayer agreeing the adjustments to be made, if any. Generally the Inspector will require outstanding tax returns or business accounts, or other evidence or argument, in order to be satisfied of any adjustments required by the taxpayer.   These may be provided after the appeal itself is made.   In practice, the negotiations and the settlement are usually concluded by correspondence, although telephone calls and meetings may be used to clear up any areas of difference or confusion.

3.15   If an agreement is not reached within a timescale acceptable to the Inspector, he will arrange for the matter to be listed for a hearing by the Commissioners.   This occurs most commonly where the parties cannot agree on a contentious issue or if the taxpayer has failed over a period to provide business accounts or other information requested by the Inspector.

3.16   The listing of an appeal for a hearing does not imply that the Inspector is committed to a determination by the Commissioners.   Often it is simply a tactic to induce the taxpayer to compromise on a contentious issue, or to submit outstanding accounts or information.   There is still scope for an agreement to be reached before the date set for the hearing, which will then never take place.

3.17   A well-advised taxpayer will generally respond positively by taking such action as is necessary to secure an agreement. Indeed, in cases of tax debt, unless there is a clear dispute that requires independent intervention, generally a Commissioners' hearing should be avoided. Preparation and attendance are time-consuming and the outcome is unpredictable and in most cases is final (see further discussion in paragraph 3.33 *et seq*).

3.18   If a taxpayer wishes to reach an agreement but needs more time to consider his position or provide outstanding information, a telephone call to the Inspector will usually secure confirmation that the hearing will be postponed until the following meeting of the Commissioners, usually a month or two hence. However, prompt action is then required as many bodies of Commissioners are averse to hearings being postponed more than once (see further discussion in paragraph 4.34 *et seq*).

3.19   An agreement between the Inspector and the taxpayer, in settlement of an appeal, has the same legal effect as if the Commissioners had determined the matter. It may be a written agreement, or a verbal one confirmed in writing (TMA 1970, s54).

3.20   Following such an agreement the Inspector should issue an amended notice of assessment reflecting the agreed figures. If the taxpayer objects to any aspect of the amended assessment, or wishes to resile from the agreement for any reason, he should notify the Inspector in writing within 30 days (TMA 1970, s54(2)). If the agreement is to the effect that the original assessment should stand good, no amended assessment is issued although the taxpayer has the same right to resile.

Determinations by the Commissioners

3.21   The Commissioners are independent tribunals which determine appeals and other matters under the taxes legislation. There are two distinct types of tribunal - *General Commissioners* and *Special Commissioners*, more correctly known as Commissioners for the General Purposes of the Income Tax and Commissioners for the Special Purposes of the Income Tax respectively.[3]

3.22   *General Commissioners* consider the vast majority of tax appeals that reach a hearing. They are appointed by the Lord Chancellor in a similar way to Justices of the Peace. They are unpaid and require no special qualifications, and are most commonly local businessmen. They are advised on matters of law by their Clerk, who is usually a local solicitor who is also responsible for administration of the appeals that they hear. Their proceedings are held in private and their decisions are not published. They usually sit as a tribunal of three and their procedures are fairly informal, although they have recently been codified by Statutory

---

[3]   In this handbook, the term *Commissioners* refers to those tribunals constituted as General Commissioners or Special Commissioners.

Instrument, the General Commissioners (Jurisdiction and Procedure) Regulations 1994 SI 1994/1812. Further useful guidance is given in *Notes for Guidance of General Commissioners of Income Tax*, published by the Lord Chancellor's Department and reproduced by the Faculty of Taxation of the ICAEW on 24 July 1995.

3.23   *Special Commissioners* are barristers or solicitors of at least 10 years standing and are also appointed by the Lord Chancellor. They usually sit individually in public and their proceedings are rather more formal. Special Commissioners generally are considered more skilled at considering appeals involving technical points of tax law and, following changes in 1994, their decisions are normally published. Their procedures are codified in the Special Commissioners (Jurisdiction and Procedure) Regulations 1994, SI 1994/1811.   Further useful guidance is given in *Appeals and other proceedings before the Special Commissioners* obtainable from the Office of the Special Commissioners, 15-19 Bedford Avenue, London WC1B 3AS. Telephone: 0171 631 4242.

3.24   Most appeals lie automatically to the General Commissioners, although the taxpayer may elect to appeal to the Special Commissioners. Such an election must be made on the notice of appeal, or separately within the 30 day time limit for the appeal.   However, the election may be disregarded upon an application by the Inspector to the General Commissioners, if he considers that there is no merit in the election, for example where the hearing has become necessary because of delay by the taxpayer in providing information (TMA 1970, ss31 and 46(1)). There are certain exceptions: on certain more complex issues, appeals lie only to the Special Commissioners, while some appeals may be heard only by the General Commissioners (TMA 1970, 2 Sch). There are also provisions to transfer cases between General and Special Commissioners (TMA 1970, ss44(3)and 44(3A)). The specific body of General Commissioners which will hear any particular appeal will depend on a number of factors, such as the type of tax and the place of business (TMA 1970, 3 Sch).

3.25   At a Commissioners' hearing, the taxpayer has the right to present his case in person or to be represented by a person who is legally qualified or a member of an incorporated society of accountants. The Commissioners also have discretion to allow representation by any other person, which tends to be exercised flexibly (SI 1994/1811 Reg 14, SI 1994/1812 Reg 12).[4]

3.26   The detailed provisions for the conduct of an appeal - including the notification of hearings, summoning of witnesses, calling for the production of documents (known as the issue of *precepts*), the joinder of

---

[4]   See also *Cassell v Crutchfield* Ch D [1995] STC 663, where an individual suspended from membership of an accountancy body following convictions for fraud was denied the right of audience. For a list of incorporated societies of accountants, see the *Inland Revenue Inspector's Manual* paragraph 4908.

other parties, postponement or adjournment of hearings, and review of determinations - are now codified by statutory instrument (SI 1994/1811 and SI 1994/1812 *supra)*.

3.27   The *onus is on the taxpayer* to disprove any assessment appealed against and, in the absence of evidence that it is excessive, it cannot be reduced (*Haythornthwaite (T) & Sons Ltd v Kelly* CA [1927] 11 TC 657). Although costs normally are not awarded, the Special Commissioners may now do so if they consider that either party has acted 'wholly unreasonably' (SI 1994/1811 Reg 21).

3.28   A determination by the Commissioners is final and conclusive (TMA 1970, s46(2)). In particular, the Courts will not disturb a decision of the Commissioners on a question of fact if it could have been made reasonably on the evidence presented to them, even if a different body of Commissioners might have reached a different conclusion (*Edwards v Bairstow & Harrison* HL [1955] 36 TC 207).

3.29   Lord Brightman has stated:

> '... an appellate Court, whose jurisdiction is limited to questions of law, can and should interfere with an inference of fact drawn by the fact-finding tribunal which cannot be justified by primary facts. I do not agree ... that, if the primary facts justify alternative inferences of fact, an appellate Court can substitute its own preferred inference for the inference drawn by the fact-finding tribunal' (*Furniss v Dawson* HL [1984] STC 153 page 167).

Appeals to the High Court

3.30   The matter may be referred to the High Court by:

*   Asking the General Commissioners to state a case for the opinion of the High Court. This is sometimes called the *case stated procedure* (SI 1994/1812 Reg 20).

*   An appeal against a decision of the Special Commissioners (TMA 1970, s56A).

3.31   Under the case stated procedure:

*   The dissatisfied party must write to the Clerk to the Commissioners within 30 days of the determination, requiring the Commissioners to state and sign a case, and a fee of £25 must be paid (SI 1994/1812 Reg 20(1) and TMA 1970, s56(3)).

*   The case stated should set out the facts of the case and the Commissioners' determination. There is no requirement to explain any legal reasoning behind the determination (SI 1994/1812 Reg 20(2)).

- If the party has not paid the £25 fee or has, upon request, failed to identify the question of law involved, the Commissioners may refuse to state a case (SI 1994/1812 Reg 20(4)).

- There are provisions for both parties to make representations on the contents of the draft case, before it is finalised (SI 1994/1812 Reg 21).

- The case stated is sent to the party who required it, who has 30 days to transmit it to the High Court. A copy must also be sent to the other party, at or before the time of transmission (SI 1994/ 1812 Regs 22(3) and 22(4)).

For ease of exposition, this procedure is referred to as an *appeal* against a General Commissioners' determination.

3.32   The High Court may reverse, affirm or amend the determination, or make whatever other order seems fit. Appeals from the High Court lie to the Court of Appeal and, with leave, to the House of Lords. Further, any English Court could refer a question on a matter of EC law to the European Court, although this is *extremely* rare in direct tax appeals (TMA 1970, ss56(6), 56(7) and 56(8)). Exceptionally, certain appeals against Special Commissioners' determinations may be referred directly to the Court of Appeal (TMA 1970, s56A(2)).

The advantages of settling an appeal by agreement

3.33   Although the appeals procedures outlined above have their uses in contentious cases, generally it is advisable in cases of tax debt to settle any disputed assessments by agreement with the Inspector. There are a number of advantages to this approach.

3.34   Few Inspectors wish to devote time to cases where the taxpayer's ability to pay is in doubt. If the taxpayer's situation is made clear to the Inspector, it is generally possible to negotiate a settlement which is as good as any outcome that might be achieved at a hearing before the Commissioners.

3.35   The tax debtor faces significant barriers and risks in taking the matter to a hearing. In particular:

- Proper preparation is very time-consuming.

- Unlike the Inspector, the Commissioners will not generally be concerned with the appellant's ability to pay (although some do show sympathy).

- The outcome is unpredictable and generally an adverse finding on a question of fact cannot be reversed.

- Even if the taxpayer is successful, this is not the end of the matter. The Inland Revenue may appeal to the High Court.

- If the case proceeds to the High Court, legal representation is virtually essential and both parties' costs may be awarded against the losing side. (For further discussion on representation, see paragraph 13.48 *et seq.*)

- If the taxpayer cannot afford to risk a High Court hearing, the only recourse might be to seek the Inland Revenue's agreement for him to withdraw from the appeal. This may have to be on less favourable terms than might have been agreed originally and the Inland Revenue might also require payment of its costs (see *Toms v Sombreat Ltd* [1979] STI 313).

For an unrepresented taxpayer, or one who cannot afford the costs of representation on an appeal, the right to have the case heard by the Commissioners and the Courts is therefore of limited value.[5]

3.36 Sometimes, however, a taxpayer may by prior negotiation reduce some of the risks and costs he would face upon the matter proceeding to the High Court. If the case involves no significant point of law, both parties may be able to agree in advance to abide by the Commissioners' determination. In other cases, where the Inland Revenue wishes to test an important point of law in the High Court, which is out of proportion to the tax at stake in a particular case, it may agree not to ask for its costs, or even to indemnify the taxpayer for his own legal costs.[6]

Postponement of tax

3.37 The making of an appeal opens the way for the taxpayer to apply to postpone tax. Postponement is the statutory method of deferring payment of any tax considered overcharged, pending the outcome of the appeal, and the application must normally be made within 30 days after the issue of the assessment, i.e. the time limit for the appeal (TMA 1970, s55).

3.38 In the absence of postponement, tax is due and payable as if there were no appeal (TMA 1970, s55(2)). Exceptionally, tax charged under Schedule E does not require postponement because the Collector will defer issuing an application for payment until the appeal is settled by agreement or determined at a hearing.

3.39 Applications for postponement are considered promptly by the Inland Revenue, not least because no tax is payable pending the determination of the postponement application (see paragraph 3.44). The Inspector should consider whether there are reasonable grounds for admitting the application and he does not have unfettered discretion (*Savacentre Ltd v CIR* CA [1995] STC 867 page 875). In practice, tax

---

[5] For further discussion, see *Taxation* 18 April 1996 p55.
[6] This occurred in *Gray v Matheson* Ch D [1993] STC 178, see *Taxation* 9 November 1995 p142.

districts agree most applications fairly readily (see paragraph 4.19). The amount to be postponed is normally resolved by agreement between the taxpayer and the Inspector, who will confirm details in writing on a form 64-4.

3.40 If agreement as to the amount to be postponed cannot be reached, the matter is determined by the Commissioners in much the same way as an appeal, including the right of appeal to the High Court on a point of law (TMA 1970, s55(5) and *Parikh v Currie* CA [1978] STC 473).

3.41 Postponement applications may be admitted after the 30 day time limit in the event of a change in the circumstances of the case (TMA 1970, ss55(3A) and 55(4); see also paragraph 4.21). This includes cases where:

- An application has previously been made for a different sum to be postponed.

- An appeal was made earlier without any application to postpone tax.

- An appeal is admitted after the 30 day limit has elapsed.

How appeals and postponement affect payment dates and interest

Initial payment dates

3.42 The submission of an appeal alone - without a postponement application - ordinarily does not affect the date on which the tax becomes due and payable (TMA 1970, s55(2)).[7]

3.43 Exceptionally, payment of tax due under a Schedule E assessment is deferred automatically following the submission of an appeal, without the need for any postponement application. Once the appeal is determined, by agreement or by the Commissioners, a notice to pay is issued and tax becomes due and payable within 14 days.

3.44 Where a postponement application is made, any *tax not postponed* becomes due and payable on the *later* of:

- 30 days after the amount to be postponed is agreed or determined (usually the date the form 64-4 is issued), and

- the normal due date (TMA 1970, s55(6)(a)).

3.45 Where a revised postponement application is made, any tax that ceases to be postponed is due and payable on the *later* of:

---

[7] For the *normal due date*, see paragraph 2.29

- 30 days after the agreement or determination of the revised postponement application, and

- the normal due date.

In the event that the amount postponed is increased, any tax overpaid should be repaid (TMA 1970, s55(6)(b)).

Further payment dates

3.46 Further tax may become due and payable following the determination of an appeal by agreement or by the Commissioners. Where the amount of tax determined to be due exceeds any amounts previously due and payable under the above provisions, this additional tax becomes due and payable on the *later* of:

- 30 days after the Inspector issues a notice of the total amount payable in accordance with the determination, and

- the normal due date,

and any tax overpaid should be repaid (TMA 1970, s55(9)).

3.47 The Inland Revenue may enforce payment of tax under the above provision even where the taxpayer is taking the matter on appeal to the High Court, although it has discretion to defer collection pending the decision of the Court (TMA 1970, ss56(9) and 56A(8)). In contrast, the Inland Revenue appears to have the right to withhold repayment of tax where it is appealing against an unfavourable Commissioners' determination (*Collco Dealings Ltd v CIR* QB [1959] 39 TC 533).

3.48 If the High Court varies a Commissioners' determination, any further tax is due and payable 30 days after the Inspector issues a notice of the total amount payable in accordance with the order or judgment of the Court, while any tax overpaid should be refunded (TMA 1970, ss56(9) and 56A(9)). The Inland Revenue may not withhold repayment pending further appeal (*T & E Homes Ltd v Robinson* CA [1979] STC 351).

Interest charges under TMA 1970, s86

3.49 While the postponement of tax can suspend the Inland Revenue's right to recover a tax debt, it does not necessarily prevent interest accruing on payments which are deferred. The precise position depends upon the application of TMA 1970, s86, which provides that a postponement application *may* delay the date from which interest begins to run by a maximum of six months.[8]

---

[8] A postponement application would not affect interest chargeable under TMA 1970, s88 (see paragraph 2.75 *et seq*).

3.50 Where tax has been postponed, section 86 interest runs from the *reckonable date*, which is determined by reference to three different dates:

- The *enforceable date*, i.e. the date on which the tax actually becomes due and payable (see paragraph 3.42 *et seq*).

- The *normal due date* had there been no appeal (see paragraph 2.29).

- The *table date*, which is normally 1 July immediately following the tax year end (i.e. The normal due date for the second instalment of tax under Schedule D Cases I and II). However, for capital gains tax and higher rate tax chargeable on income received net of tax, the table date is 1 June falling 14 months after the end of the tax year.

3.51 The reckonable date is the *later* of:

- the normal due date, and

- the *earlier* of

  - the enforceable date, and
  - the table date.

3.52 In practice, this means:

- To the extent that tax becomes enforceable before the table date, interest runs from the enforceable date.

- To the extent that tax becomes enforceable after the table date, interest runs from the later of the table date and 30 days after the issue of the assessment.

3.53 A special regime applies for tax charged by an assessment under Schedule E. The submission of an appeal prevents section 86 interest from running until the tax itself becomes due and payable, which is 14 days after the issue of the demand note following the settlement or determination of the appeal (TMA 1970, s86(3)).

Remedying unfairness through the Courts

3.54 According to a traditional view, there is no room for equity in the interpretation of tax statutes - the overriding need for certainty justifies any unfairness that may result incidentally. There are powerful dicta in support of this position:

- 'In taxation you have to look merely at what is clearly said. There is no room for any intendment; there is no equity about a tax...' (Rowlatt J in *Cape Brandy Syndicate v CIR* CA [1921] 12 TC 358).

- 'If a person sought to be taxed comes within the letter of the law he must be taxed, however great the hardship may appear to the judicial mind to be...' (Lord Cairns in *Partington v Attorney General* HL [1869] LR 4E & I app HL100).

3.55 This conjures up a system where the only bulwark between the taxpayer and the Inland Revenue is a tribunal of Commissioners and, beyond that, a series of judges who will apply the strict letter of the law regardless of the outcome. While this may sometimes be true, recent decades have seen some developments.

The Courts' evolving approach to statutory interpretation

3.56 In recent years, the Courts have shown a greater flexibility in the interpretation of tax statutes in order to achieve a fairer or more reasonable outcome, or to give effect to Parliament's presumed intention. This development may sometimes assist the taxpayer - or the Inland Revenue - depending upon the circumstances of the dispute.

3.57 Early departures from the traditional approach involved cases where the legislation permitted alternative interpretations and the House of Lords opted for the interpretation that gave the 'fairer' or 'more reasonable' result in the particular circumstances.[9] More recently, the Court of Appeal permitted an individual partner to appeal against a joint partnership assessment, where a more literal approach might have denied that right. In its judgment:

> '... it would be easy to retreat into adopting a literal approach to the construction of statutory provisions ... We do not think that is the right approach. Legislation is to be interpreted so as to give effect to Parliament's presumed intention, so long as this is clear, provided always the language of the statute fairly admits of the interpretation in question' (*Re Sutherland & Partners' Appeal* CA [1994] STC 387 p391).

3.58 The 1980s saw the development of a 'new approach' to statutory interpretation in tax avoidance cases, which placed limits on the efficacy of circular transactions or pre-ordained series of arrangements in tax planning (see *WT Ramsay Ltd v CIR* HL [1981] STC 174, *Furniss v Dawson* HL [1984] STC 153, *Craven v White* HL [1988] STC 476).

3.59 In 1992 the House of Lords relaxed the long-standing rule prohibiting the Courts from referring to the record of parliamentary debates as an aid to interpreting legislation. Their Lordships held that such references should be permitted where:

- legislation was ambiguous or obscure, or led to an absurdity,

---

[9] Contrast *Vestey v CIR (Nos 1 and 2)* HL [1980] STC 10 and *CIR v Luke* HL [1963] 40 TC 630.

- the material relied upon consisted of one or more statements by a Minister or other promoter of the Bill, together if necessary with such other parliamentary material as was necessary to understand such statements and their effects, and

- the statements relied upon were clear (*Pepper v Hart and related appeals* HL [1992] STC 898).

3.60   Apart from the assistance that such developments may offer litigants in future cases, they may also assist in deliberations between taxpayer and Inspector aimed at settling an appeal by agreement.

The development of judicial review

3.61   In broad terms, judicial review involves the exercise by the High Court of a supervisory jurisdiction over the conduct of a tribunal or decision-making body, for example where it has abused its powers or acted in breach of natural justice. In tax matters, the Court examines the *way* in which the Commissioners or the Inland Revenue have conducted themselves, as opposed to the merits of the case.

3.62   Judicial review has assumed increasing importance in the tax field in recent years. Although most reported cases have been won by the Inland Revenue, the law is developing rapidly.[10]

3.63   In judicial review proceedings, the Court may make any of the following prerogative orders:

- *Certiorari*   an order to quash an action or decision

- *Mandamus*   an order to carry out a duty or perform an action

- *Prohibition*   an order to prohibit a future action

Alternatively, it may or grant one of the following equitable remedies:

- *Injunction*   an order to direct a person to carry out, or not carry out, a specific act

- *Declaration*   a statement as to the rights of the parties

- *Damages*   an order for financial compensation

Grounds for judicial review

3.64   The grounds for judicial review have been classified as:

- Want or excess of jurisdiction, i.e. that the Inland Revenue or Commissioners have acted *ultra vires*.

- Error of law on the face of the record.

---

[10] See article by Lord Woolf in (1993) *British Tax Review* 219.

- Failure to comply with the rules of natural justice.

- That no authority properly directing itself on the relevant law and acting reasonably could have reached the decision complained of.

The last-mentioned ground is known as *the Wednesbury principle* - after the decision in *Associated Provincial Picture Houses Ltd v Wednesbury Corporation* [1947] 2 All ER 680 - and is the test applied where it is alleged that the Inland Revenue has acted 'unfairly'.

3.65 The following paragraphs discuss conduct which might justify an application for judicial review.

3.66 Where the Inland Revenue has failed to follow a specific *assurance* given, for example that a particular transaction will not attract a tax liability. However, in the leading cases relief has been denied on the grounds that:

- the assurance was not completely unequivocal, or

- the applicant had not disclosed all the relevant details to the Inspector at the time, and there is a heavy onus on the taxpayer in this respect.

(*Aspin v Estill* CA [1987] STC 723, *R v CIR (ex p. Preston)* HL [1985] STC 282, *R v CIR (ex p. MFK Underwriting Agencies Ltd and others)* QB [1989] STC 873 and *R v CIR (ex p. Matrix Securities Ltd)* HL [1994] STC 272)

3.67 Where the Inland Revenue has failed to apply the terms of a published *Statement of Practice* or *Extra-statutory Concession,* which should be applied fairly to all taxpayers. However, the Inland Revenue may be able to claim protection by reference to published *caveats,* for example the general provision in *IR 1 Extra-statutory Concessions* that a concession will not be given in any case where an attempt is made to use it for tax avoidance (*R v Inspector of Taxes (ex p. Fulford-Dobson)* QB [1987] STC 344 and *R v Inspector of Taxes (ex p. Brumfield)* QB [1989] STC 151 - the applications failed in both cases; Statements of Practice and Extra-statutory Concessions are discussed in paragraph 3.78 *et seq).*

3.68 Where the Inland Revenue has acted *ultra vires,* i.e. outside the powers given to it by law. In *R v CIR (ex p. Woolwich Equitable Building Society)* (HL [1990] STC 682) the House of Lords held that some parts of Regulations made by the Inland Revenue were *ultra vires* the enabling legislation. In *CIR v National Federation of Self-Employed and Small Businesses Ltd,* the Federation argued that a tax amnesty given to casual workers in the newspaper industry was unlawful, and sought an order of *mandamus* directing the Inland Revenue to assess and collect tax from the casuals according to the law. However, the House of Lords held that the Inland Revenue had acted within its care and management powers. In the words of Lord Scarman:

'... in the daily discharge of their duties Inspectors are constantly required to balance the duty to collect 'every part' of due tax against the duty of good management. This conflict of duties can be resolved only by good managerial decisions, some of which will inevitably mean that not all the tax known to be due will be collected.' (HL [1981] STC 260 p279 - the Court referred to the care and management powers described in paragraphs 2.1 *et seq*).

3.69   Where there has been *procedural impropriety by the Commissioners*. The Commissioners must act within the rules of natural justice, designed to guarantee both sides a fair hearing and the absence of bias on the part of the tribunal. Successful applications have been made, for example where Commissioners have refused to adjourn hearings where the taxpayer was sick or abroad (*R v Sevenoaks Commissioners and CIR (ex p. Thorne)* QB [1989] STC 560 and *R v Hastings and Bexhill General Commissioners and CIR (ex p. Goodacre)* QB [1994] STC 799).

3.70   Where the Inland Revenue has acted *unfairly*. Although the judges have often reproached the tax authorities for 'unfairness', no application for judicial review had succeeded solely on that ground until the recent decision in *R v CIR (ex p. Unilever plc and related application)* (CA [1996] STC 681). In that case a group of companies had for 20 years been permitted to make informal loss relief claims, which were not finalised until after the statutory time limits. Without prior notice, the Inland Revenue then refused three claims on the grounds that they were finalised outside the periods permitted by statute. An application for judicial review was granted on the basis that the Inland Revenue's conduct was so unfair as to amount to an abuse of power.

Limitations on the scope for judicial review

3.71   An application requires leave from the Court to bring an action for judicial review and this is not granted lightly. Most commonly, it may be denied in the following circumstances.

3.72   Where there has been *delay* in bringing the application. An application for judicial review must be made promptly and in any event within three months from the date when grounds for the application first arose. The Court may extend this deadline, but not without good reason (RSC Ord 53, r4(1) and *R v Tavistock Commissioners (ex p. Worth and Another)* QB [1985] STC 564).

3.73   Where *other remedies* are available. Judicial review is invariably denied where an alternative remedy exists, particularly where the matter might be pursued by way of an appeal (*R v Special Commissioners (ex p. Philippi)* QB [1966] 44 TC 31 and dictum of Lord Scarman in *R v CIR (ex p. Preston)* HL [1985] STC 282 p299). However, this rule has been breached in exceptional circumstances, for example where the applicant might be prejudiced in taking proceedings before the Special

Commissioners because he would not be able to recover his costs (*R v Inspector of Taxes (ex p. Kissane and Another*) QB [1986] STC 152; for the present rules on costs in Special Commissioners proceedings, see paragraph 3.27).

3.74   Where the applicant lacks *sufficient interest* in the matter. In *CIR v National Federation of Self-Employed and Small Businesses Ltd*, discussed in paragraph 3.68 above, a further reason for denying the application was that the Inland Revenue's decision to grant a tax amnesty did not affect the applicant's own members directly.

3.75   There are also practical limitations on the availability of judicial review:

- The complexity of the procedures would almost certainly defy any taxpayer without legal representation (see paragraph 13.48 *et seq*).

- Where a taxpayer considers that he has been treated more harshly than others in similar circumstances, it may be impossible to obtain sufficient evidence. Inland Revenue officers work under a strict duty of confidentiality and the Inland Revenue has been supported by the Courts in refusing to disclose information relating to other taxpayers in the course of judicial proceedings (see *In re Joseph Hargreaves Ltd* CA [1900] 4 TC 173 and dicta in *Lonrho plc v Fayed and others (No 4)* CA [1994] STC 153).

3.76   Where it is considered that the Inland Revenue has acted *unfairly*, the most serious obstacle is the Courts' application of *the Wednesbury principle* discussed in paragraph 3.64. This requires gross unfairness on the part of the tax authorities, before the Courts will be prepared to intervene. The *Unilever* case discussed in paragraph 3.70 is a rare example of such judicial intervention.

Inland Revenue discretion and practice

3.77   It is well established that the Inland Revenue's powers of care and management allow it a degree of flexibility in assessing and collecting taxes, and that the full rigour of the law need not always be imposed where this can be justified on the grounds of good management (see *CIR v National Federation of Self-Employed and Small Businesses Ltd* HL [1981] STC 260 and paragraph 3.68).

Extra-Statutory Concessions

3.78   These are published in the free booklet *IR 1 Extra-Statutory Concessions* (June 1994) supplemented by *IR 1 Supp (November 1995)*. The introduction explains that most concessions are made to deal with minor or temporary anomalies under the taxes legislation and to meet cases of hardship where a statutory remedy would be difficult to devise or would be disproportionately long. It goes on to say that 'a concession will not be given in any case where an attempt is made to use it for tax avoidance'.

3.79   Although the operation of such concessions has received judicial approval (*R v CIR (ex p. Fulford-Dobson*) QB [1987] STC 344), many have in fact effected significant amendments to the taxes legislation. Following some criticism as legislation through the back door, there is now a programme to bring concessions within the statutory framework where this is considered possible (FA 1996, s201 and 39 Sch).

3.80   Nevertheless scores of concessions remain extra-statutory, some of which may be of assistance in cases of tax debt. Of particular importance is Concession A19, which allows arrears of tax to be waived where the Inland Revenue has been guilty of delay (see paragraph 4.99 *et seq*).

Statements of Practice

3.81   These are published in the free booklet *IR 131   Statements of Practice* (July 1994) with a supplement, also coded IR 131 (October 1995). The booklet explains that such statements explain the Inland Revenue's interpretation of legislation and the way that it is applied in practice. They do not affect the taxpayer's right to argue for a different interpretation, for example on a tax appeal.

3.82   Such statements apply in many different areas of tax law and administration, for example: ·

- Official policy for charging interest on overdue tax where tax returns are submitted late (SP 6/89, see paragraph 2.77).

- Discovery assessments (SP 8/91, see paragraph 2.25).

Assessing tolerances

3.83   Under *Statement of Practice A12*, last updated in 1987, tax offices would not take action to assess liabilities of up to £75 due from pensioners and war widows, because the administrative costs would be 'disproportionate to the amount of tax that would be charged'. According to *IR 131*, this Statement is not up to date and is being reviewed, and current experience indicates that liabilities of £100 or less are normally not assessed.

3.84   The Inland Revenue has advised TaxAid:

'Although the level of assessing tolerances was publicised in the past, current policy is not to publish the amount because it may prejudice the assessment or collection of tax.

'Under self-assessment, there will be no assessing tolerance because the calculation will need to be made in every case and the purpose of a tolerance - to avoid work which is not cost efficient - will not be in point. In this context, the question of tolerances for cases outside the scope of self-assessment is subject to internal review.'

Codes of Practice

3.85   These are published to provide guidance as to the way in which the Inland Revenue should conduct itself, with particular reference to the promises made in the Taxpayer's Charter. Although these booklets carry the *caveat* that they are for guidance only, generally the Inland Revenue will be bound by their contents. A number of these Codes are particularly relevant to cases of tax debt.

3.86   *Code of Practice 1 Mistakes by the Inland Revenue* (updated in March 1996) includes the following:

- The undertaking to respond to enquiries and correspondence within 28 days.

- The terms of Extra-Statutory Concession A19, covering delays in notifying taxpayers of arrears (see paragraph 4.99 *et seq*).

- The broad terms of Extra-Statutory Concession B41, permitting some claims for repayment after the normal six-year time limit (see paragraph 4.73).

- Details of compensation available in cases of Inland Revenue maladministration (see paragraph 4.109 *et seq)*.

It also explains how to make complaints.

3.87   *Code of Practice 2 Investigations* explains the process of investigating tax returns and accounts. It also mentions important taxpayer rights, for example:

- 'You are not obliged to come to any meeting we ask you to attend ...'

- 'If we have to keep (your records), we will give you copies of any documents which you need. We will do this free of charge, within 7 days.'

- 'You have the right at any time during the course of an investigation to ask for your case to be settled by the Appeal Commissioners ... (and this) will not be regarded as a lack of co-operation on your part' (for the relevance of 'co-operation', see paragraph 2.43).

3.88   *Code of Practice 6 Collection of tax* explains tax collection policy and has accompanying leaflets on:

- *Collection 1 - Distraint*
- *Collection 2 - Magistrates' Court Proceedings*
- *Collection 3 - County Court Proceedings*
- *Collection 4 - Bankruptcy and winding up*

These are referred to throughout Chapters 6 to 11 of this handbook. The specific positions of those who are required to deduct tax under PAYE, or from sub-contractors in the construction industry, are set out in *Code of Practice 7 Collection of amounts due from employers, and contractors in the construction industry.*

3.89   *Code of Practice 10 Information and advice* offers assistance to taxpayers in getting their affairs right. It explains the sources of information listed in this chapter and explains how taxpayers with complex affairs may obtain written interpretations of tax law, statutory clearances and approvals.

Practices published in the Inland Revenue manuals

3.90   In May 1996 the Inland Revenue completed the publication of its internal guidance manuals in collaboration with Tolley Publishing Co Ltd. In many respects, these manuals may assist by explaining official interpretation of complex areas of tax law as well as procedures for collection of tax.

3.91   However, the exercise has been criticised for the following reasons:

- The manuals are expensive. The complete set costs over £3,000 (or £1,750 on CD-Rom) which places it beyond the means of most tax practitioners and taxpayers. Although copies are available for public access at Inland Revenue offices, many do not hold the full set.

- Inconsistent layout together with incomplete and poor quality indexing can make it difficult to find specific information, although this problem is eased by using the CD-Rom version.

- The text omits certain information which the Inland Revenue considered too sensitive to publish.

3.92   Nevertheless the manuals remain a very useful source of information, setting out the way in which the Inland Revenue approaches a very wide range of complicated tax issues.

The Tax Bulletin

3.93   This is published every two months to inform tax practitioners about matters of technical interest, including the Inland Revenue's interpretation of different aspects of tax law. For example, the *Tax Bulletin* of August 1995 gave details of the hitherto unpublished practice of equitable liability (see paragraph 4.61 *et seq*).

Other publications

3.94 Specialist offices of the Inland Revenue sometimes produce guidance notes aimed at a specific group. For example, the MIRAS Central Unit has published *Guidance Notes for Lenders (MIRAS 30)* which contains details of a number of concessions (see paragraphs 5.151-5.152). There are also guides on self-assessment, written for tax practitioners, which are mentioned in Chapter 12.

3.95 The Inland Revenue publishes a wide range of free leaflets for the benefit of the public, which are listed in its *Catalogue (IR List)*. These tend to be written in fairly general terms and usually contain a note to the effect that the booklet is for guidance and does not affect the taxpayer's right of appeal. Occasionally the contents of such a leaflet will provide information to support a taxpayer in dispute with an Inspector.

The Taxpayer's Charter and complaints of maladministration

3.96 The Inland Revenue was one of the first Government Departments to publish a Charter setting out the standards of service that it seeks to attain. The Taxpayer's Charter was first published, jointly with HM Customs & Excise, in July 1986. It was relaunched in a different style in 1991 and the present version of the Charter is reproduced overleaf.

3.97 The Taxpayer's Charter, together with Codes of Practice discussed above, provide several protections and remedies particularly relevant to those with tax debts. Some of the most common issues are discussed in the following paragraphs.

The promise of 'equal fairness'

3.98 Inspectors and Collectors should treat all taxpayers fairly, and those in similar circumstances should be treated similarly. Historically there has been a particular problem with collection of tax debts, since there has been little published guidance as to how Collectors should conduct themselves. Accordingly, where it has been felt that a Collector was being oppressive in demanding payment, it has been difficult to demonstrate that he was not following normal procedures fairly.

The Taxpayer's Charter

You are entitled to expect the Inland Revenue

To be fair

- By settling your tax affairs impartially
- By expecting you to pay only what is due under the law
- By treating everyone with equal fairness

To help you

- To get your tax affairs right
- To understand your rights and obligations
- By providing clear leaflets and forms
- By giving you information and assistance at our enquiry offices
- By being courteous at all times

To provide an efficient service

- By settling your tax affairs promptly and accurately
- By keeping your private affairs strictly confidential
- By using the information you give us only as allowed by the law
- By keeping to a minimum your costs of complying with the law
- By keeping our costs down

To be accountable for what we do

- By setting standards for ourselves and publishing how well we live up to them

---

If you are not satisfied

- We will tell you exactly how to complain
- You can ask for your tax affairs to be looked at again
- You can appeal to an independent tribunal
- Your MP can refer your complaint to the Ombudsman

In return, we need you

- To be honest
- To give us accurate information
- To pay your tax on time

3.99 With greater publicity on collection processes now available, it is somewhat easier to identify cases where Collectors are being unfair (see Chapter 6). The standard retort that each case must be considered on its facts should not be accepted where it is clear that a Collector has strayed from normal Inland Revenue practice.

3.100 Nevertheless, there remain inconsistencies. For example, there is considerable variation in the practice of local collection offices with regard to remission of tax debts in the case of those who are unemployed or in receipt of welfare benefits. (*Remission* is discussed in paragraph 6.105 *et seq.*)

The promise to help you to get your tax affairs right

3.101 If there is any doubt about the amount of tax demanded by a Collector, the Inland Revenue should always provide appropriate assistance to enable the taxpayer to check his liability and to make any changes required by law.

3.102 If there has been any maladministration in arriving at the sum demanded by a Collector, this could justify a complaint which may lead to a reduction in the sum demanded or even an award of compensation to the taxpayer. The remedies available are set out in *Code of Practice 1 Mistakes by the Inland Revenue* (see paragraph 4.109 *et seq*) and some case studies are described in paragraphs 3.128 *et seq.*

The promise to settle matters promptly and accurately

3.103 This has been elaborated in the *Code of Practice 1 Mistakes by the Inland Revenue,* which sets out a 28 day time limit for dealing with most correspondence. If that time limit is exceeded, the taxpayer may demand a reply as a matter of urgency. Also, there are provisions for compensation or waiver of tax, in cases of excessive delay or serious or persistent errors (see paragraph 4.108 *et seq).*

The promise to keep your private affairs strictly confidential

3.104 The Inland Revenue works under a strict obligation of confidentiality and there are criminal sanctions, including imprisonment for up to two years, for breaches of confidentiality (TMA 1970, s6 and Sch 1, now reinforced by FA 1989, s182). Strictly, Inspectors and Collectors should not discuss a taxpayer's affairs with any third party in the absence of a written authority from the taxpayer, although a verbal authority may be accepted in appropriate cases.

3.105 Nevertheless certain problems can arise. For example:

• Taxpayers visiting Inland Revenue offices are often asked to discuss their affairs in public enquiry areas, within earshot of other people. Although they have the right to require a private hearing, individuals with tax debts may not feel easy about asking for this.

• A Collector making an unannounced home visit, to request or discuss settlement of a tax debt, may be told that the taxpayer is out or has moved elsewhere. The Collector may then seek the assistance of other residents or neighbours in tracing the taxpayer and in doing so may reveal the existence of a tax debt. This is a clear breach of confidentiality, which may in certain cases justify compensation for worry or distress.

The promise to keep your costs to a minimum

3.106 Inland Revenue maladministration may result in a taxpayer incurring unnecessary professional fees and other costs. This is a common cause of complaint and some case studies are described in paragraph 3.128 *et seq.*

3.107 Where a taxpayer has failed to keep proper records, it is not uncommon for Inspectors or Collectors to require duplicates of bank or building society statements covering a number of years. If the cost of obtaining such duplicates would be out of proportion to any enlightenment they might offer - particularly where some of the information may be available from alternative sources - the taxpayer reasonably may object to the Inland Revenue's request.

What the taxpayer must do in return

3.108 The Charter requires the taxpayer to be honest. The current version omits an undertaking given in the 1986 edition of the Charter that 'you will be presumed to have dealt with your tax affairs honestly, unless there is reason to believe otherwise'. However, the Financial Secretary to the Treasury stated on 21 November 1991 that this does not indicate a change of policy and that the presumption of honesty continues to apply. This undertaking may be particularly important during tax investigations or when a Collector is assessing a taxpayer's means to settle a tax debt.

3.109 The taxpayer is also required to pay his tax on time. Junior collection staff sometimes erroneously assert that the Charter does not apply to those with tax debts, since they are themselves in breach of its provisions! However, official policy is to apply the Charter equally to those with tax arrears (see paragraph 6.120).

Making a complaint under the Charter

3.110 In contrast with many other official bodies, the Inland Revenue takes complaints under its Charter very seriously and in 1993 it set up an independent Adjudicator's Office to consider complaints that could not be resolved between the taxpayer and the Inland Revenue. Elizabeth Filkin, a former Chief Executive of the National Association of Citizens Advice Bureaux, was appointed as the first Adjudicator and she is still in office. She was known initially as the Revenue Adjudicator but, having since assumed additional responsibility for complaints about HM Customs & Excise and the Contributions Agency, she is now known as the Adjudicator.

3.111 The procedures for making a complaint under the Taxpayer's Charter are set out in *IR 120 You and the Inland Revenue* and *AO1 - How to complain about the Inland Revenue*. The latter booklet is published by the Adjudicator's Office but is available from Inland Revenue offices. Both booklets make it clear that, before making a complaint to the Adjudicator, the Inland Revenue should be given an opportunity to settle the matter itself.

3.112 Initially, complaints should be addressed to the person in charge of the Inland Revenue office dealing with the matter. If he is unable to resolve it, the taxpayer should refer the matter to the Controller responsible for that office or unit. The Controllers' names and addresses are listed in booklet *AO1 How to complain about the Inland Revenue*.[11]

3.113 If the Controller is still unable to satisfy the taxpayer, the taxpayer may refer his complaint to the Adjudicator, and this should be done within six months.

3.114 If for any reason the taxpayer has difficulty managing any of the preliminary steps explained above, he may ask the Adjudicator's office to help him through the process. These are described by the Adjudicator as 'assistance cases'.

3.115 The preliminary steps should not normally take longer than two months, allowing 28 days for each stage, although in more complex cases they may take somewhat longer. If any delay might cause additional damage or hardship - for example, where a Collector has wrongly distrained on an asset which is about to be sold at auction - the Adjudicator will sometimes agree to waive the initial procedures and intervene directly as a matter of urgency.

The work of the Adjudicator

3.116 The purpose and guiding principles of the Adjudicator are set out in her latest Report:

'Our purpose is:

- to resolve complaints about the way the Inland Revenue have handled someone's affairs; and

- to suggest ways of improving the quality of service they provide.

---

[11] Exceptionally, complaints unresolved by the heads of the Accounts Offices or the Enforcement Office - who have the status of Controller - may be addressed directly to the Adjudicator.

Our guiding principles are at all times to be:

- impartial - we aim to deal with all matters fairly, thoroughly and objectively;

- speedy - we aim to deal with all complaints as quickly as we can without compromising the thoroughness of our investigations; and

- accessible - we aim to offer a service which is easy to use and understand. And we try to be flexible in our working methods, so that we can best meet the particular needs of each case.'

3.117 Although her office is funded by the Inland Revenue and staffed partly by Inland Revenue secondees, the Adjudicator is not part of its management structure and she adopts a rigorously independent position. This may be evidenced by the fact that, in the first two years of operation, she upheld the taxpayer's complaint in over 50% of cases.[12] Although her recommendations have no legal force, the Inland Revenue has undertaken to follow them in all but exceptional circumstances and she reports that all recommendations to date have been accepted. The service is free.

3.118 The Adjudicator's functions in relation to the Inland Revenue are described in the booklet *AO1 How to complain about the Inland Revenue*, which explains:

- The limits of her remit.
- How a complaint should be made.
- How complaints are dealt with.

Copies are obtainable from Inland Revenue offices or from the Adjudicator's Office at Haymarket House, 28 Haymarket, London SW1Y 4SP. Telephone: 0171 930 2292.

The Adjudicator's remit

3.119 The Adjudicator will only consider complaints about problems arising after 5 April 1993. Earlier matters may be addressed directly to the Inland Revenue, or possibly to the Parliamentary Ombudsman if the time limit explained in paragraph 3.144 is met (the role of the Parliamentary Ombudsman is discussed in paragraph 3.136 *et seq)*.

3.120 The Adjudicator will consider complaints about the way in which the Inland Revenue has handled a person's tax affairs, i.e. matters of *tax administration* including the exercise of Inland Revenue discretion. This covers complaints about:

---

[12] In 1994/95 the Adjudicator completed 381 investigations, upholding the complaint in 51% of cases. The comparative figures for her first year were 105 completed investigations and 64% of complaints upheld.

- discourtesy,

- delay,

- unfairness,

- the application of any concession or practice, or

- any other breach of the promises given in the Taxpayer's Charter or the Codes of Practice.

She cannot deal with complaints on matters of *law* which might be pursued through the tax appeals procedure.

3.121 This distinction between matters of *administration* and *law* is not as clear cut as it appears. For example, an inspector may have refused to agree a taxpayer's accounts, because of a heated dispute over the deductibility of a particular expense item. The taxpayer may consider that his interpretation of the law is supported by the Inland Revenue's own guidance manuals and that the Inspector is simply being unfair. In such a case, the taxpayer may:

- make an appeal and require the matter to be heard by the Commissioners, or

- complain of maladministration under the Taxpayer's Charter, on the grounds that for 'personal' reasons the Inspector is not following the Inland Revenue's published guidance.

3.122 The Adjudicator will not consider matters relating to a criminal prosecution brought by the Inland Revenue, until the legal proceedings are concluded.

3.123 The Adjudicator will not consider complaints which have been investigated by the Parliamentary Ombudsman, or are currently being investigated by him; however, the Ombudsman may review complaints already considered by the Adjudicator (see paragraph 3.136 *et seq)*.

The process of complaining to the Adjudicator

3.124 Complaints to the Adjudicator should ideally be made in writing and should include:

- The name and address of the taxpayer.

- The cause of dissatisfaction. It is sometimes simplest to enclose copies of correspondence with the Controller.

- The name of the Inland Revenue office responsible, and the taxpayer's reference within that office.

- The action required from the Inland Revenue to settle the complaint.

- Details of costs incurred as a result of the matter complained of.
- A daytime telephone number for contact, if possible.

3.125 Upon receipt of the complaint, the Adjudicator will first consider whether it falls within her remit and whether all the preliminary stages have been completed. She will then obtain the relevant Inland Revenue files, together with any explanations required, and may also contact the taxpayer if more information is needed. If appropriate, she may arrange a meeting with either or both parties.

3.126 Having ascertained the facts, the Adjudicator will consider whether there is scope for agreement between the parties. 38% of the 381 cases completed by her office in 1994/95 were settled by *mediation*. If agreement cannot be reached, she will make a *recommendation* which the Inland Revenue invariably will accept.

3.127 The Adjudicator's report for 1994/95 summarised the recommendations made as follows:

Compensation paid	80
Inland Revenue apology	43
Improved Inland Revenue service	30
Interest charges waived	28
Decision on discretion changed	19
Revised collection arrangements	16
Revised PAYE coding	5
Inland Revenue error corrected	7

Case studies from the Adjudicator

3.128 The Adjudicator's first two reports contain several anonymised case studies describing some of the complaints reviewed and their outcomes. Seven cases illustrating problems that arise commonly in cases of tax debt are summarised below, with the outcome in italics. It should, however, be emphasised that the reports do not always provide a full 'technical' explanation of the substance of the complaint.

Failure by the Inland Revenue to act on information received from the taxpayer

3.129 Mrs A had told the Inland Revenue that she had ceased working. The Inspector listed an appeal to be heard by the Commissioners and, as she was elderly, Mrs A was distressed by this and had to engage accountants to sort matters out. The Adjudicator found that the Inland Revenue had made some persistent errors and had also failed to act on receipt of the final accounts of the business. *The Inland Revenue agreed to pay £169 of the accountancy fees attributable to its error and to waive the £111 tax due on the final accounts under Extra-statutory Concession A19* (see paragraph 4.99 et seq).

Unnecessary bankruptcy following Inland Revenue errors

3.130   The Inland Revenue received an anonymous tip-off that Mr D had undisclosed income from ice-cream sales and casual work. The Inspector tried several times to arrange a meeting with Mr D, but he had always failed to attend. He also ignored most letters and tax returns sent to him. The Inspector eventually issued estimated tax assessments on the alleged earnings, to which Mr D did not respond properly, except to point out that he had not had the income, that he had nervous problems and that he did not understand tax. He was later visited by a local Collector who reported that Mr D had not worked during the period covered by the assessments, due to psychiatric and drink problems, and that he 'seemed genuine'. The Collector suggested that the tax be remitted, but this was rejected by the Inspector. Mr D was subsequently made bankrupt and his trustee in bankruptcy then satisfied the Inland Revenue that he had not had any income from ice-cream sales or casual work, and that his other tax liabilities on income from property had been settled in full by his wife. The Inland Revenue agreed to set aside the tax, but Mr D was faced with £15,000 in bankruptcy costs (see paragraph 11.159 *et seq*). *The Adjudicator considered that both parties shared responsibility for the bankruptcy and recommended that the Inland Revenue pay £8,000 compensation.*

Duplicate assessment leading to enforcement proceedings

3.131   Mrs F was erroneously sent a duplicate of a previous tax assessment. Despite efforts by Mrs F, her husband and their accountant to sort matters out, the Inland Revenue refused to recognise its error and proceeded to distraint and a County Court summons before the error was rectified. *The Inland Revenue agreed to compensate the couple for their accountancy fees, Mr F's loss of earnings and some typing and photocopying expenses.* This case provides the following insights into the remedies available: compensation was paid for the *spouse's* loss of earnings and also for incidental expenses, even though no receipts were available; a consolatory payment for distress was denied, although this may now be available (see paragraph 4.113).

Failure by second employer to operate PAYE

3.132   Mr H took on a part-time job with a burger bar to supplement his income. The burger bar failed to operate PAYE correctly and Mr H was assessed to tax of £1,492, which was required to be settled over three years. Mr H complained that the Inland Revenue should be responsible for ensuring that PAYE was properly operated, but admitted to the Adjudicator that he had been aware that this was not happening but had chosen to do nothing about it. *Mr H accepted the Adjudicator's view that the Inland Revenue were correct to assess him* (see paragraph 5.20 *et seq* for the law and practice relating to PAYE failures).

Unduly lengthy tax investigation

3.133 Mr I incurred £4,000 of accountancy fees in a prolonged tax investigation which led to a tax yield of £1,400. *The Adjudicator considered that the investigation had been twice as long as necessary and the Inland Revenue agreed to reimburse £2,000 of the accountancy fees and to make an apology.*

Inland Revenue refusal to continue instalment arrangement

3.134 Mr L complained that the Inland Revenue was refusing to continue with an instalment arrangement to pay off a tax debt, and was taking bankruptcy proceedings. *The Adjudicator found that he had defaulted on previous instalment arrangements and that, as the debt was for sums deducted from Mr L's employees under PAYE, Mr L was gaining an unfair advantage over businesses that remitted their PAYE on time. The complaint was not upheld.*

Bankruptcy partly attributable to Inland Revenue delay

3.135 Mr T complained that the Inland Revenue intended to take bankruptcy proceedings against him unless he settled his liabilities in full. He had offered to settle the debt over ten years on condition that no more interest would accrue. At that stage the arrears totalled £174,000, having risen steadily from £7,000 in 1983! He had made some payments during that period but had also taken on other personal debts, and the Inland Revenue had rejected his offer because of his poor payment history and the length of time it would take to clear the debt. *The Adjudicator did not uphold the complaint, considering that taxpayers should make every effort to pay their tax on time, agreeing with the Inland Revenue that it would be unfair to other taxpayers if Mr T's proposal was accepted. The Adjudicator also observed that the Inland Revenue could have taken a stronger line at an earlier stage, and that its conduct had allowed a relatively small, manageable debt to grow into a very large one.* The proposition that a proposal for time to pay would be 'unfair to other taxpayers' is commonly advanced by Collectors (see paragraph 6.19) and Inland Revenue failure to take early action frequently results in the problem illustrated, albeit usually in smaller figures.

Complaints to the Parliamentary Ombudsman

3.136 The Parliamentary Ombudsman - officially titled the *Parliamentary Commissioner for Administration* - is an officer of the House of Commons who reports to a Select Committee of MPs. The post is currently held by William Reid and his role is to investigate complaints by members of the public about the way that they have been treated by Government Departments and public sector bodies, including the Inland Revenue. Further information about the function of the Parliamentary Ombudsman may be obtained from his office at Church House, Great Smith Street, London SW1P 3BW. Telephone: 0171 276 3000.

3.137 In 1995 the Parliamentary Ombudsman received 160 complaints about the Inland Revenue which comprised 14.2% of his workload.

3.138 The role of the Parliamentary Ombudsman in handling complaints about the Inland Revenue is very similar to that of the Adjudicator. In both cases, the service is free and confidential. The range of matters investigated, and recommendations made, is broadly the same. However, there are certain differences.

Complaints must be made through an MP

3.139 Whereas the Adjudicator considers complaints made directly by members of the public, the Parliamentary Ombudsman can only investigate matters put to him through the individual's Member of Parliament. An MP may refuse to advance a constituent's complaint about the Inland Revenue, having regard to the Parliamentary Commissioner's workload and the fact that his office investigates many other departments and agencies.

Independence

3.140 The Parliamentary Ombudsman clearly is separate from the Inland Revenue, and should therefore be completely impartial. Although generally it is accepted that the Adjudicator is equally neutral, some critics have expressed concern that her office is funded by the Inland Revenue.

Speed

3.141 On average it takes the Parliamentary Ombudsman more than a year to complete an investigation. A complaint to the Adjudicator will generally be handled more quickly and urgent matters can be addressed within days (see paragraph 3.115).

Jurisdiction

3.142 The Adjudicator will not look at any matter already the subject of investigation by the Parliamentary Ombudsman, but the latter may review complaints considered by the Adjudicator.

3.143 In general, the Parliamentary Ombudsman will not investigate events that took place more than 12 months before the constituent contacted their MP.

Selecting the appropriate course of action

3.144 This chapter has considered four possible channels for objecting to tax assessments and demands, or complaining about the conduct of officials:

- Appeals to the Commissioners
- Applications for judicial review
- Complaints to the Adjudicator
- Complaints to the Parliamentary Ombudsman

It has also mentioned that there are many specific procedures for opposing recovery proceedings, which are discussed in Chapters 7 to 11.

3.145 To a large extent, these remedies are *mutually exclusive*. In particular:

- Judicial review is not generally available where an alternative remedy exists.
- The Adjudicator will not deal with appeals on matters of law, which may be properly addressed to the Commissioners.
- The Adjudicator will not consider any matter already placed before the Parliamentary Ombudsman, although the latter may review complaints already investigated by the Adjudicator.

3.146 In many circumstances, only one channel of objection or complaint will be available. In general, any matter which may be the subject of an appeal to the Commissioners cannot be considered by way of judicial review or a complaint of maladministration, although in practice there is a slight overlap (see paragraphs 3.73 and 3.121), nor in resisting legal proceedings for enforcement of a tax debt (see paragraph 7.19 *et seq)*. Also, the only channel for complaint about the conduct of the Commissioners is an application for judicial review.

3.147 However, many complaints about the Inland Revenue's discharge of its administrative functions could be addressed by any one of three channels: judicial review, the Adjudicator or the Parliamentary Ombudsman.

3.148 In most such cases, a complaint to the Adjudicator will be the appropriate approach, for reasons summed up by the Adjudicator herself:

> 'Where someone is unhappy with the way an administrative decision has been made, they can ask for judicial review. However, like many legal procedures, this can take a long time and be expensive. While judicial review is an important legal channel, it is not appropriate for a pensioner who sent in a claim form three months ago and wants to know why nothing has happened.

'The Parliamentary Commissioner for Administration ... can look at complaints of maladministration by any government department. While the Ombudsman undoubtedly does a good job, it is necessary for a taxpayer to complain via his MP, and the nature of the Ombudsman's investigation means that there can be a considerable period before the complaint can be resolved. Also he is not able to investigate every complaint of poor service made to him.

'My role as ... Adjudicator is to give an impartial view of a complaint at an earlier stage in the complaints procedure. I do not look at a matter which has already been considered by the Ombudsman, but he can be asked to look at complaints which I have investigated.'[13]

It should be noted that many complaints to the Adjudicator's Office are now taking some months to resolve. However, more urgent cases, for example where a bankruptcy hearing is imminent, will still be dealt with very quickly.

---

[13] Extract from article by Elizabeth Filkin in *Taxation Practitioner* April 1994

Chapter 4

Challenging excessive demands

This chapter explores action that may be taken by a taxpayer to reduce a sum demanded by the Inland Revenue - even after normal time limits have passed. It examines:

From paragraph

■   Appeals and postponement applications in   *4.4*
         difficult situations
■   Making claims   *4.45*
■   Relief for error or mistake   *4.55*
■   The practice of equitable liability   *4.61*
■   Repayments due to the taxpayer   *4.71*
■   Relief for Inland Revenue errors   *4.98*

Introduction

4.1   It will be appreciated from previous chapters that Collectors have comprehensive powers to recover tax debts based upon vague estimates of profits, or where not all reliefs have been claimed. Most Collectors do not understand the detailed processes for agreeing tax liabilities, while the Courts which hear tax recovery proceedings generally do not have jurisdiction to consider arguments about the accuracy of the underlying assessment(s) (see paragraph 7.19 *et seq*).

4.2   Accordingly, if enforcement proceedings are in prospect or have already commenced, the taxpayer should review the accuracy of the amount demanded as a matter of urgency. If he believes that it is excessive in any respect, he should apply immediately to the relevant Inspector to have it reduced. In most cases, this will involve taking steps described in this chapter and a taxpayer who has previously neglected his tax affairs may frequently achieve significant reductions in the tax debt.

4.3   In practice, the taxpayer should always keep the Collector informed of the progress of such negotiations with the Inspector. It is unwise to rely on the Inspector notifying the Collector directly, as liaison can be slow with the result that occasionally enforcement proceedings are carried out by the Collector at the same time as the Inspector is agreeing that no tax is due.

Appeals and postponement applications in difficult situations

The basic process

4.4   As explained in Chapter 3, the normal method for challenging any assessment, which is excessive by reason of an estimate or error, is to make an *appeal*. This opens the way for the taxpayer and the Inspector to reach an agreement on the proper figures. If the Inspector is made aware that the taxpayer has limited resources, generally it is possible to negotiate a reasonable agreement and rarely is it necessary for the appeal to be heard by the Commissioners (see paragraph 3.33 *et seq).*[1]

4.5   When making an appeal, usually it is appropriate to apply to the Inspector for *postponement* of tax considered overcharged by the assessment, as any amount postponed will not be recoverable by the Collector before the appeal is determined (see paragraph 3.37 *et seq).*

4.6   The process of appeal and postponement may be started by a taxpayer even *after* enforcement proceedings have been threatened or commenced by a Collector. Where it could lead to a significant reduction in the tax debt, the taxpayer simultaneously should ask the Collector to suspend recovery action to allow time for negotiation with the Inspector.

4.7   However, the process may falter in a number of ways. The following common problems, together with appropriate remedies and strategies, are discussed below:

- The statutory deadline for an appeal has passed.

- Difficulties arise over a postponement application.

- There are problems in demonstrating the true level of profits.

- Incorrect figures have already been agreed with the Inspector.

- A Commissioners' hearing is imminent.

- The Commissioners have already determined the appeal.

The statutory deadline for an appeal has passed

4.8   Upon an application by the taxpayer, the Inspector has discretion to admit an appeal after the 30 day time limit has passed, provided that

- there was a reasonable excuse for not making the appeal on time, and

- an application is thereafter made without unreasonable delay.

---

[1] The rules and procedures described in this section may also be applicable to *determinations*, although reference should be made to the underlying legislation in each such case, as there can be differences.

If the Inspector is not satisfied that these conditions are met, he must refer the application to the Commissioners and their decision is final (TMA 1970, s49 and *Inland Revenue Assessment Procedures Manual* paragraph 3396). The matter will usually be heard by the General Commissioners (TMA 1970, s49(2)).

4.9 The application to admit the appeal is completely separate from the appeal itself, although the two are often made together. There is no standard form or wording and a letter might simply commence, for example: 'Application is hereby made for an appeal against this assessment to be admitted out of time under the provisions of TMA 1970, s49. Please accept this letter also as a formal appeal against the same assessment on the grounds that it is excessive, and an application to postpone all the tax charged on the grounds that the assessable profits may fall within allowances/exemptions due.' The need for a prompt postponement application should not be overlooked (see paragraph 4.17 below).

4.10 In practice, most tax districts admit appeals received a month or two after the statutory time limit automatically, without requiring an express application under TMA 1970, s49 or even an explanation for the delay. However, in cases of longer delay the application will need to provide good reasons for:

•   the failure to appeal within 30 days, and

•   any subsequent delay in making the application.

4.11 Inspectors tend to exercise their discretion sympathetically and explanations of the following kinds are generally accepted where they reasonably justify the applicant's failure to act earlier:

•   Sickness or hospitalisation

•   A bereavement or serious illness in the family

•   Absence from home

•   Business or employment difficulties

•   Matrimonial or domestic problems

•   Language or literacy problems which prevented initial comprehension of the assessment

•   Non-receipt of the assessment (see paragraph 2.19)

The Inspector will not usually require evidence in support of the explanation given, unless there is reason to doubt its authenticity.

4.12 As the application is separate from the appeal, there is no requirement to provide details in support of the appeal itself when making the application. However, it may nevertheless be helpful to include such information - such as business accounts - where available. Apart from speeding up the process towards agreeing an acceptable liability, evidence which demonstrates that the assessment is excessive may persuade the Inspector to admit the appeal out of time, particularly if the grounds for delay are not thought absolutely persuasive. If accounts are not yet available, it may assist to provide a timetable for producing the figures, together with a payment on account (if applicable) to show good faith - this is particularly important where there is a history of non-compliance.

Referral to the Commissioners

4.13   If he refuses to accept the application, the Inspector will advise the taxpayer that the application is being listed for a determination by the Commissioners. Even at this stage, it may be possible to change his mind before the date of the hearing. The taxpayer could write to apologise for any lack of completeness in the original application and provide further details or evidence in support of his case. It may assist to refer, sensitively, to any lack of resources to settle the liability charged by the assessment, or to the likelihood of an application for relief under the practice of *equitable liability* in the event that a late appeal is not admitted (see paragraph 4.61 *et seq*). Indeed, the Inspector's own manual reminds him when making his decision to 'bear in mind ... that eventual recourse to 'equitable liability' to settle a case leads to extra work for the (Inland Revenue)' (*Inland Revenue Assessment Procedures Manual*, paragraph 3396).

4.14   Should the matter reach a hearing, this is held solely to determine whether the appeal should be admitted out of time. The appeal itself will not be considered at this point (although the taxpayer's chances of success may nevertheless be enhanced by producing evidence which demonstrates that the assessment is excessive). It is not uncommon for the Commissioners to determine that a late appeal should be admitted and for the substantive issues then to be settled by agreement between the taxpayer and the Inspector. Indeed, settlement by agreement remains desirable for the reasons explained in paragraph 3.35.

4.15   If the taxpayer is unable to persuade the Commissioners that an appeal should be admitted out of time, the assessment is final and conclusive. The Commissioners may also refuse the application if the taxpayer fails to attend the hearing. There is no further right of appeal and the Collector may recover the full amount charged (*R v Special Commissioners (ex p. Magill)* QB (NI) [1981] STC 479).

4.16   In the event of an adverse determination by the Commissioners, two possible remedies remain open to the taxpayer:

●   If there was any defect in the Commissioners' proceedings, he may apply for judicial review. Normally he would wish to obtain an order of *certiorari* quashing the determination, so that the matter may be reheard (*R v Special Commissioners (ex p. Magill)* QB (NI) [1981] STC 479; see paragraph 3.61 *et seq*)).

- If he can demonstrate that the amount charged by the assessment is excessive in relation to the actual profits of the relevant year, he may apply for relief under the practice of equitable liability (see paragraph 4.61 *et seq*).

Difficulty over a postponement application

4.17 The basic provisions for postponement of tax have been outlined in paragraph 3.37 *et seq*. The vast majority of applications are determined by agreement between the taxpayer and the Inspector, although some fail on substantive or procedural grounds, for example:

- The taxpayer's view of the amount overcharged by the assessment is not accepted by the Inspector.

- The application is made out of time.

4.18 By law an Inspector may admit a postponement application only if there are some grounds for believing that tax has been overcharged. He does not have unfettered discretion and he should refuse an application, in whole or in part, if there is insufficient evidence that the amount charged is excessive. The onus of proof rests on the taxpayer (*Savacentre Ltd v CIR* CA [1995] STC 867 and *Parikh v Currie* CA [1978] STC 473).

4.19 However, in practice generally an Inspector will accept a taxpayer's estimate of the amount overcharged unless he has reason to suspect that it is excessive. This approach reflects the view that it can be time-consuming to dispute the matter, that any excessive postponement will be corrected upon the determination of the appeal, and that the Exchequer ultimately will be compensated for any excessive claim by way of interest charged under TMA 1970, s86 (see paragraph 2.73 *et seq*). In fact, in some circumstances the interest provisions favour the taxpayer because of the delayed date from which interest accrues when an application for postponement is made (see paragraph 3.49 *et seq*).

4.20 Accordingly, a well-drafted letter of application for postponement of tax generally will be accepted. If not, the Inspector must list the application for a determination by the Commissioners, but even at this stage he will remain open to persuasion if the taxpayer can present further evidence that the charge is excessive. In appropriate cases the taxpayer might point out, sensitively, that he has insufficient resources to settle the liability that would be due and payable upon the failure of the application, and that the Collector's ensuing demands would cause him great stress and distract him from providing the information necessary to settle the appeal itself.

4.21 Applications for postponement may be made after the normal 30 day time limit

> 'if there is a change in the circumstances of the case as a result of which the appellant has grounds for believing that he is overcharged to tax by the assessment.' (TMA 1970, s55(3A)).

In practice, this provision is interpreted generously and late applications for postponement will be admitted, for example:

- Where, at the time of making an appeal, the taxpayer did not appreciate the need to apply separately for postponement of tax.[2]

- Where an application to make an appeal out of time is successful, and the application for postponement is submitted together with the appeal (see paragraph 4.9).

4.22 Even where an application for postponement has already been admitted or determined by the Commissioners, a further application may be made if there is a subsequent change in the taxpayer's circumstances, for example where draft accounts show that income was lower than had been estimated previously (TMA 1970, s55(4)).

Problems in demonstrating the true level of profits

Absence of business records

4.23 An appeal can be settled by agreement if the Inspector can be persuaded that accounts or other information presented by the taxpayer appear reasonable. A common difficulty in cases of tax debt is that the taxpayer cannot produce sufficiently reliable figures to displace the Inland Revenue's estimate, because he does not hold the necessary primary records.

4.24 Very often a former tax adviser will assert a right of lien over accounts and business records in respect of work for which he has not been paid, and may refuse to return them until his bill has been settled. He may rely upon the judgment of Lord Justice Lawton in the case of *Woodworth v Conroy* (CA [1976] QB 884 p890), with whom the other judges agreed:

> 'I would adjudge that accountants in the course of doing their ordinary professional work of producing and auditing accounts ... and carrying on negotiations with the Inland Revenue in relation both to taxation and rating have at least a particular lien over any books of account, files and papers which their clients delivered to

---

[2] Unrepresented taxpayers commonly assume that an appeal alone is sufficient to delay collection of the tax charged by an assessment and only discover the need for a postponement application upon subsequent receipt of demands for payment.

them and also over any documents which have come into their possession in the course of acting as their client's agents in the course of their ordinary professional work.'[3]

4.25   Even where there is doubt about a purported right of lien, legal proceedings to recover possession of books and records may nevertheless be prohibitively complex or expensive. Accordingly, it may sometimes be more practical to seek possession in another way, for example by asking the former adviser's professional institute (if any) to arbitrate over outstanding fees or to consider a claim of misconduct.

4.26   If it proves impossible to recover the documents on the grounds of unpaid fees, this point should be made clear to the Inspector. It provides independent evidence of the taxpayer's financial difficulties and may persuade the Inspector to settle the appeal quickly by agreement (see paragraph 3.34).

4.27   Records may be unavailable for many other reasons and it might help to explain the situation fully to the Inspector. For example:

- Where records have been lost for reasons genuinely beyond the taxpayer's control - such as in a fire or flood - this may sometimes assist negotiations by gaining sympathy for the taxpayer.

- If records were never maintained, the Inspector may be deterred from launching an investigation by the lack of prospective yield, if it is made clear from the outset that the taxpayer's resources are very limited (see paragraph 5.83 *et seq*).

Producing alternative information

4.28   Whatever the position regarding business records, the Inspector will not settle an appeal by agreement unless the taxpayer can present at least some evidence or argument in support of any profit figure advanced. Careful thought should be given as to appropriate ways of obtaining suitable information quickly and inexpensively.

4.29   Sometimes an Inspector will suggest that the taxpayer obtains evidence from a third party, e.g. bank statements or details from companies for which he has worked. This may well be mutually acceptable. However, if a significant charge were to be made for such information and an agreement might be reached in another way, the taxpayer might refer to the promise in the Taxpayer's Charter: *'To provide an efficient service ... by keeping to a minimum your costs of complying with the law'* (see paragraph 3.107).

---

[3]   For a fuller examination of a tax adviser's right of ownership and lien, reference should be made to section 6.12 of the *Members Handbook* of the Chartered Institute of Taxation and section 1.3 of the *Members Handbook* of the ICAEW.

4.30 Frequently, the matter can be resolved by the production of business accounts which are wholly or partly comprised of estimated figures. These are more likely to be acceptable to the Inland Revenue where:

- The accounts are derived from, or consistent with, agreed accounts for a previous period appropriately adjusted to reflect any changes in circumstances.

- Estimated entries are as far as possible consistent with other verifiable figures. For example, if cost-of-sales records are available, turnover might be estimated by using an agreed mark-up percentage.

- Estimates can otherwise be verified by reference to independent statistics or the Inland Revenue's own Business Economic Notes (see paragraph 2.39).

- Estimates that cannot be verified are mostly in respect of smaller sums.

Incorrect figures have already been agreed with the Inspector

4.31 A taxpayer may repudiate or resile from an agreement in settlement of an appeal, by giving written notice to the Inspector within 30 days of the agreement (TMA 1970, s54(2)).

4.32 There is no provision for extension of this deadline, but it may be possible to reduce an agreed figure at a later date by making a claim for *error or mistake* under TMA 1970, s33 (see paragraph 4.55 *et seq*).

A Commissioners' hearing is imminent

4.33 Where the Inspector does not receive sufficient information for an appeal to be settled by agreement within a timescale acceptable to him, he will list the matter for a hearing before the Commissioners and a notice should be sent to the taxpayer at least 28 days in advance (see paragraph 3.21 *et seq*).[4] While this may spur a tardy taxpayer into action, it may by then be too late to settle the appeal with the Inspector before the date set for the hearing.

Postponement of the hearing

4.34 In such circumstances the taxpayer should seek a *postponement* of the hearing - sometimes referred to as an *adjournment* - to allow more time for an agreement. The appeal is then relisted normally for the next meeting of the Commissioners, usually six to eight weeks later. Most, but

---

[4] General Commissioners (Jurisdiction and Procedure) Regulations 1994 SI 1994/1812 Reg 3(3). In this section, it is assumed that the listing will be for a hearing before the General Commissioners, as is invariably the position with 'delay' cases.

not all, panels of Commissioners will permit at least one such postponement in respect of any particular appeal before insisting on hearing the matter (SI 1994/1812 Reg 8(1)).

4.35   Some panels of Commissioners insist that any application for postponement should be made in person, normally at the time and place fixed for the hearing, or at least by prior written application to their Clerk. If so, the taxpayer (or his representative) will need to attend on the day of the hearing unless, exceptionally, the Clerk actually has confirmed postponement of the hearing beforehand. Merely having sent a letter requesting a postponement cannot be relied upon, as the Commissioners are not obliged to agree to it.

4.36   To avoid such inconvenience, postponements are usually arranged by telephoning the Inspector, before the date fixed for the hearing, and asking him to ensure that a postponement is granted. If he agrees, normally this can be relied upon and personal attendance at the hearing becomes unnecessary. (It may be prudent to confirm details of the telephone conversation in writing and to send a copy to the Clerk to the Commissioners.)

4.37   However, it should be appreciated that this is an informal procedure and paragraphs 7.41-42 of the *Notes for Guidance of General Commissioners of Income Tax* warn:

> 'The Inland Revenue may agree with the taxpayer that they will not oppose a request for adjournment, but they should also make it clear that they do not have the authority to grant adjournments ... whatever discussions take place with the Inland Revenue, the onus is on the taxpayer to ensure that attendance is not required. This may be done by submitting a letter to the General Commissioners explaining that both parties are requesting an adjournment or communicating with the Clerk to the General Commissioners. The final authority, however, rests with the Commissioners alone.' (See paragraph 3.22.)

Fortunately, most panels recognise the administrative advantages of arranging postponements through the Inland Revenue and do not adopt a rigid position.

Determinations in the taxpayer's absence

4.38   If the taxpayer fails to attend a hearing and a postponement is not granted, the appeal will be determined in his absence. This will generally be in the amount estimated by the Inspector, although the Commissioners may reduce the assessment by reference to their own local knowledge (*Hamilton v CIR* CS [1930] 16 TC 28 and *Noble v Wilkinson; Ridley v Wilkinson* Ch D [1958] 38 TC 135). The Commissioners may take some account of any evidence the taxpayer has sent by letter and they should not increase an assessment at the Inland Revenue's request without adjourning the hearing to enable the taxpayer to respond. However, such an adjournment is unnecessary if the Inland Revenue can demonstrate that a letter was sent to the taxpayer at least 28 days before the hearing warning him that the Commissioners would be asked to increase the assessment in the absence of further information (see *Notes for Guidance of General Commissioners of Income Tax* paragraph 5.11).

4.39 The following decided cases provide further guidance on postponements:

- A Commissioners' determination was quashed where it was made in the taxpayer's absence, following an assurance by the Inspector to the taxpayer that a postponement would be granted (*R v O'Brien (ex p. Lissner)* QB [1984] STI 710).

- Where the Commissioners were informed that accounts had been delivered to the Inspector, which should justify the reduction of the assessment to nil, it was a miscarriage of justice to refuse a postponement simply on the grounds that it was a second hearing (*Packe v Johnson* Ch D [1991] STC 1). Note that such facts would now justify a review of the Commissioners' determination (see paragraph 4.40 *et seq*).

- A determination was quashed where the tribunal had refused a second postponement, despite having received evidence that the taxpayer was unable to attend on grounds of ill-health, in a case where the taxpayer's evidence was reasonably necessary for his case to be properly presented and the Inland Revenue would not have suffered an irremediable injustice in consequence of a further postponement (*R v Sevenoaks General Commissioners and CIR (ex p. Thorne)* QB [1989] STC 560).

The Commissioners have already determined the appeal

4.40 The Commissioners may be asked to *review* their determination, following which it may be set aside or varied. If they agree, the appeal is effectively reopened and should be listed for a further hearing. This allows time for the taxpayer to submit information in support of the appeal to the Inspector and for figures to be agreed between the parties, which may then be simply endorsed by the Commissioners without the need for a hearing.

4.41 The Commissioners may review a determination if they are satisfied that:

- it was made wrongly as a result of an administrative error on the part of the Commissioners, their Clerk or staff, or any party to the appeal,

- a party who was entitled to be heard failed to appear or be represented for good and sufficient reason, or

- accounts or other information relevant to a party's case had been sent to the Clerk or appropriate Inland Revenue officer prior to the hearing but was not received by the tribunal until after the hearing (General Commissioners (Jurisdiction and Procedure) Regulations SI 1994/1812 Reg 17(1)).

4.42   An application for review must be made in writing to the Commissioners within 14 days of the date of the notice sent to the taxpayer recording the Commissioners' determination, or such later time as the tribunal may allow. Normally, an application for review should not be refused solely on the grounds that it was made late, if the taxpayer and inspector are in agreement that the appeal should be re-opened (SI 1994/ 1812 Reg 17(2) and *Notes for Guidance of General Commissioners of Income Tax*, paragraph 5.21).

4.43   The above provisions for review codify best practice prevailing prior to the promulgation of the General Commissioners (Jurisdiction and Procedure) Regulations in 1994, but there is not yet any case law on their application. In particular, there is no guidance on what constitutes a 'good and sufficient reason for failure to attend a hearing', but the following may suffice:

- Sickness on the day of the hearing.

- Non-receipt of the notice of the hearing because of absence from home, or because it was sent to an old address, even though it may have met the statutory conditions for *service* described in paragraph 2.18.

4.44   In the event that the Commissioners decline to review an adverse determination, three possible remedies remain open to the taxpayer:

- If the Commissioners' refusal is considered completely unreasonable, or there has been a defect in the proceedings, an application may be made for judicial review. A successful applicant may be granted an order of *certiorari* quashing the Commissioners' determination and the case should then be re-heard by a different panel (see paragraph 3.61 *et seq*).

- If it is considered that the Commissioners have made an error of law, the matter may be referred to the High Court by way of case stated or an appeal. Action is required within 30 days (see paragraph 3.30 *et seq*).

- If it is considered that the amount charged by the assessment is excessive in relation to the actual profits of the relevant period, the taxpayer may apply for relief under the practice of equitable liability (see paragraph 4.61 *et seq*).

Making claims

4.45 A taxpayer may reduce his liability for a tax year by submitting a claim for relief, for example for the married couple's allowance or for trading losses. Relief is given by discharge or repayment of tax, which is frequently effected by an amendment to an assessment for the relevant tax year, even where this has already been agreed or determined upon appeal and would otherwise be final and conclusive (TMA 1970, ss42(7) and 46(2)).

4.46 A claim should be made in writing to the Inspector. The Inland Revenue has statutory powers to prescribe the form to be used for any particular type of claim and, where there is no prescribed form, a claim should be made by letter. If the Inspector refuses to accept a claim, the taxpayer may appeal within 30 days of the date on which notice of the refusal was received (TMA 1970, ss42(3) and 42(5)).[5] Appeals lie to the Commissioners and thereafter to the High Court on a point of law, in much the same way as appeals against assessments.[6]

Time limits for claims

4.47 Most claims must be made within six years following the end of the year of assessment to which they relate, although for certain claims the legislation specifies a shorter time limit, typically two years. A claim may be made after its normal statutory time limit where it could not have been allowed but for the making of an assessment after the tax year to which the claim relates. In such cases a late claim will be admitted at any time before the end of the tax year following that in which the assessment was made (TMA 1970, ss43(1) and 43(2)). Note also that an assessment required to make adjustments consequent upon the admission of a claim may be made within 12 months of the determination of the claim, even if this falls after the normal statutory deadline for making assessments.[7]

4.48 The Inland Revenue's policy for admitting claims after the above statutory time limits was set out in a Government Statement:

> 'In cases where no statutory discretion is given to the Board of Inland Revenue to extend a time limit for a claim or election, it must be assumed that Parliament's intention is that the limit should be applied strictly, and the number of cases in which it would be appropriate to exercise discretion under the Board's powers of

---

[5] Certain claims must be made to the Board of Inland Revenue, in which case an appeal may be made within three months.

[6] Most appeals lie to the General Commissioners, with the taxpayer having the right to elect for a hearing by the Special Commissioners, although certain appeals must be heard exclusively by one tribunal or the other (see TMA 1970, 2 Sch 2(1)).

[7] With effect from 1996/97, following the introduction of self-assessment, these time limits for claims no longer apply.

care and management ... is correspondingly limited. Every such case has to be considered individually on its own merits, and in the light of all the factors relevant to the circumstances in which the claim was made late. However, there would be a presumption in favour of admitting a late claim where there has been a relevant error on the part of the Inland Revenue and the claim is made shortly after the error has been drawn to the taxpayer's attention; where a taxpayer has given clear notice of his intention to claim, but before the time limit expires, he has not completed any statutory requirement or specified the claim in sufficient detail; or where the reason for the delay in making the claim was clearly beyond the taxpayer's control (for example because he ... was seriously ill and there was no one else who could reasonably be expected to stand in his shoes).'[8]

4.49   Where an error or mistake has been made in a claim, a supplementary claim may be made within the time limit for the original claim (TMA 1970, s42(8)).

Practical points on claims

4.50   A detailed discussion of all possible claims is beyond the scope of this handbook, but the following practical points may be relevant in situations of tax debt.

4.51   While *personal reliefs* may not make an enormous difference to the liability for one year, a claim covering six years can achieve a significant reduction in outstanding tax liabilities and the repayments that follow may be enhanced by repayment supplement. Claims for, and transfers of, the married couple's allowance are often overlooked, as well as the potential for claiming the additional personal allowance (ICTA 1988, ss257A, 257BA, 257BB and 259).[9]

4.52   As regards claims for *trading losses*:

● An Inspector may be reluctant to admit a claim for a *trading loss* which would give rise to a refund of tax if business records are incomplete. A compromise agreement might be for the claim to be admitted only to the extent that it results in 'no gain/no loss', or reduces profits to the level of personal reliefs due.

---

[8]   Written answer by Financial Secretary to the Treasury, 10 December 1985. For detailed policy on late claims for loss relief, see *Inland Revenue Inspector's Manual* paragraphs 3357 to 3359.

[9]   It is not always appreciated that a non-custodial parent may qualify for the full additional personal allowance where a child spends perhaps just one night a week at his home - see 'Doubling up the Additional Personal Allowance', *TAXline* published by the Tax Faculty of the ICAEW November 1994 p11.

- Where taxable income is reduced in consequence of a trading loss claim, this may impact on the rate(s) at which capital gains for the same year should be charged and the Inland Revenue has confirmed that appropriate adjustments may be made by way of an appeal or a claim.[10]

4.53   Where an *employed* person has paid *personal pension contributions* without deducting basic rate tax relief at source, the Inland Revenue's official policy is to deny all relief for the payment, although some tax offices disregard this strict requirement and will admit claims for relief to be given by way of deductions on assessments.[11]

4.54   A *capital allowance* in respect of a trade or profession should be claimed on an income tax return and the provisions of TMA 1970, s42 are expressly disapplied. Strictly, relief for capital allowances cannot be revised after the corresponding assessment has become final and conclusive, but Inspectors should accept amendments where circumstances have changed, for example where other allowances and reliefs have subsequently become available (CAA 1990, s140(3) and *Inland Revenue Statement of Practice A26;* see also relief for error or mistake, paragraph 4.57).

Relief for error or mistake

4.55   Where an assessment which has become final and conclusive is considered to be excessive by reason of some error or mistake in a return, or in a supporting statement such as business accounts, the taxpayer may apply to the Inland Revenue for relief within six years of the end of the tax year in which the assessment was made (TMA 1970, ss33 and 118(1)).

4.56   Claims are submitted to the Inspector and, if appropriate, he should give relief on a just and reasonable basis. Strictly this should be effected by a repayment of tax, but in practice adjustments are commonly made to assessments instead. An appeal against the Inspector's decision may be made to the Special Commissioners, and thereafter to the High Court on a point of law.

4.57   The Inspector should have regard to all the relevant circumstances. In particular he must consider whether the relief claimed will result in the exclusion of any profits from the charge to tax, as well as the impact on the taxpayer's liability for other tax years (TMA 1970, ss33(2) and 33(3)). Accordingly, a claim that one figure in a badly-prepared set of accounts has given rise to an excessive liability is unlikely to succeed if the Inspector considers that there may be compensating errors elsewhere. On the other hand, a claim may succeed where the taxpayer's business accounts omitted significant categories of deductible expenditure, or if claims for capital allowances were overlooked.

---

[10] *Tax Bulletin* August 1993 p87
[11] *Taxation* 15 June 1995 p275 and *TAXline* November 1995 p4

4.58   The fact that an assessment has already been the subject of an appeal, which has been determined, does not preclude a claim for error or mistake relief. The Inland Revenue has stated:

> 'Relief will not be available (under TMA 1970, s33) where the substantive point was squarely in issue in the process of reaching agreement and determining the appeal under TMA 1970, s54. In these circumstances the assessment for the year (even if it later proved to be excessive) is not excessive by reason of some error or mistake in the taxpayer's return, but by reason of the taxpayer's failure to pursue his argument through the normal appeal channels.'[12]

This statement implies that errors in respect of substantive points which were *not* 'squarely in issue' in reaching an agreement *may* be remedied subsequently by an error or mistake claim. The Inland Revenue has confirmed to TaxAid that such claims would indeed be admissible. The Inland Revenue has also confirmed that the same principles apply where the appeal has been determined by the Commissioners.

4.59   No relief will be granted to the extent that the return was made in accordance with practice generally prevailing at the time. This may be a pure question of fact (TMA 1970, s33(2); *Rose, Smith & Co Ltd v CIR* KB [1933] 17 TC 586 and *Carrimore Six Wheelers Ltd v CIR* CA [1944] 26 TC 301).

Practical problems with error or mistake relief

4.60   The legislation requires that the applicant must have *paid tax* under an *assessment* and this might cause difficulty in various situations, for example:

- In cases of tax debt, the taxpayer might not actually have made any *payment* through insufficiency of funds. However, the Inland Revenue has confirmed to TaxAid that 'as long as all the other conditions of section 33 are satisfied, relief under section 33 may be given by way of discharge' (see also *Inland Revenue Inspector's Manual* paragraph 3751j).

- Taxpayers who are taxed under PAYE may not receive an *assessment* to collect outstanding liabilities which are simply coded out through PAYE. If it is desired to make a claim for relief under this provision, an employee may demand the requisite assessment under ICTA 1970, s205(3).

---

[12] *Tax Bulletin* February 1994 p117. See also the footnote to paragraph 4.63.

The practice of equitable liability

4.61 A tax liability may become final and conclusive, and recoverable by the Collector, where the underlying assessment is excessive, but the taxpayer is unable to benefit from any of the procedures discussed above.

4.62 Typically this will occur in one of the following circumstances:

- An application for an appeal to be admitted out of time has failed (see paragraph 4.8 *et seq*).

- A valid appeal was made and was listed to be heard by the Commissioners, but the taxpayer failed to attend the hearing and did not submit evidence in any other way. The Inspector's estimate has been confirmed by the Commissioners who, in the absence of good and sufficient reason for the taxpayer's non-attendance, have refused to review their determination (see paragraphs 3.27 and 4.40 *et seq*).

Publication of the practice

4.63 Until very recently, the Inland Revenue's public position was that in such situations there was no further avenue for reducing the liability which was due legally. It did not publish a practice known as *equitable liability*, whereby it might agree to accept a lesser sum in full settlement. This led to an uneven application of the practice, which was criticised in the Parliamentary Ombudsman's Annual Report for 1994, and the Inland Revenue has now published a statement which is set out below:

'The practice known as *equitable liability*

Most people keep their tax affairs up to date and pay their tax at the right time. If people have genuine difficulties in meeting their payments they should let us know as soon as possible. The more we are kept informed, the more we are likely to be able to help.

If a taxpayer receives an assessment and does not think it is right, he or she can appeal against it and has thirty days from the date on which the notice of assessment was issued to do so. Inspectors will accept appeals once that time limit has passed if they are satisfied that there was a reasonable excuse for not making the appeal within the time limit and the application to admit the appeal late was made without unreasonable delay thereafter. If the Inspector does not think these requirements have been met, the application must be referred to the Appeal Commissioners for a decision. The Appeal Commissioners are completely independent of the Inland Revenue and their decision on this matter is final.

Otherwise, an assessment is final and conclusive and the Inland Revenue is able to take recovery proceedings - through to bankruptcy if necessary - for the full amount. There is no legal right to adjustment of the liability.

However, where the taxpayer has exhausted all other possible remedies, the Inland Revenue may, depending on the circumstances of the particular

---

case, be prepared not to pursue its legal right to recovery for the full amount where it would be unconscionable to insist on collecting the full amount of tax assessed and legally due.

This practice is known as 'equitable liability' and was originally introduced to protect other creditors in a bankruptcy at a time when, prior to the 1986 Insolvency Act in particular, the Inland Revenue's preferential rights were wider. Crown preference meant that, if the Inland Revenue maintained an 'excessive' claim for a sum above that which would be due if based on the true profits, other creditors would be at a disadvantage. The term 'equitable liability' therefore reflects the original principle of fairness to other creditors.

It has become increasingly apparent to us that, while many practitioners know of this practice, some do not. To remedy this apparent unfairness, the Chairman of the Board of Inland Revenue confirmed in evidence to Select Committee on the Parliamentary Commissioner for Administration that we would publish an explanation of the practice in an article in Tax Bulletin.

The Inland Revenue may be prepared to consider applying 'equitable liability' where, in the circumstances of the particular case and in the light of all the evidence, it is clearly demonstrated that:

- the liability assessed is greater than the amount which would have been charged had the returns, and necessary supporting documentation, been submitted at the proper time, and

- acceptable evidence is provided of what the correct liability should have been.

In such cases the Inland Revenue may be prepared to accept a reduced sum based on the evidence provided, and not to pursue its right of recovery for the full amount.

This treatment will depend on the circumstances of the particular case, and is conditional on the taxpayer's affairs being brought fully up to date. The Inland Revenue would expect full payment to be made of the reduced sum. Furthermore, it would be most unusual for such treatment to be applied more than once in favour of the same taxpayer.

In determining the revised liability, the Inland Revenue will have regard to all the relevant circumstances of the case. Acceptable evidence of the reduced liability must be produced. It will not be sufficient to seek to replace the assessment merely with the taxpayer's or the accountant's estimate of the liability.

Cases are dealt with in the Inland Revenue's Enforcement Offices in Worthing and Belfast and Enforcement Section in Edinburgh, but Inspectors in local offices will be involved in considering the quantum of any claims for reduction of liability and the acceptability of the supporting evidence.'[13]

---

[13] *Tax Bulletin* August 1995 p245. The statement went on to explain the position under self-assessment which is reproduced in paragraph 12.91. In granting permission for extracts from *Tax Bulletin* to be reproduced, the Inland Revenue has asked that we indicate that each issue of *Tax Bulletin* contains certain qualifications which should be referred to before reliance is placed on an interpretation.

Procedures for relief

4.64   The normal procedure for obtaining relief under the practice of equitable liability is as follows:

- The taxpayer should write to the Collector currently pursuing the tax debt, requesting the application of equitable liability. The grounds for the application should be stated, at least in broad terms, for example: 'The Inland Revenue's demand is based upon estimated assessments confirmed by the Commissioners. Accounts which are now being prepared by my accountant will show that the true profits were considerably lower than those assessed.' If draft accounts are already available, it will assist to enclose copies.

- If the Collector is amenable to the application proceeding further, he sends a standard reply that the liability is final and conclusive in law but that the Inland Revenue may agree to accept a lesser sum in full settlement provided certain conditions are met. Usually these conditions are that the taxpayer must submit any outstanding tax returns, including business accounts as appropriate, to the Inspector within a period of six weeks. In the meantime, the Collector should agree to suspend enforcement action in respect of the disputed liability.

- Upon receipt of the tax returns, or whatever other information has been required, the Inspector reviews the figures and sends an internal report to the Collector indicating the amount which would have been due had the information been provided on time.

- The Collector writes to the taxpayer to advise on the lesser sum, if any, that should be paid in full settlement.

Practical points on equitable liability

4.65   Many Inland Revenue staff are unclear about the nature or mechanics of equitable liability and may wrongly deny its availability in cases which fall clearly within the ambit of the statement reproduced in paragraph 4.63. In such cases they should be referred to *Tax Bulletin* of August 1995, or to the Enforcement Office, for guidance.

4.66   Equitable liability is applied only to reduce or expunge amounts demanded by the Inland Revenue and will not give rise to a refund of tax. It is of no assistance to a taxpayer who has already paid the sum charged by an assessment which is shown subsequently to have been excessive.

4.67   Equitable liability is not limited to cases where a liability based upon an estimate is replaced by one based upon actual figures. The practice may also apply in more complex cases, for example to give effect to losses where the requisite claim for relief was not made in time.

4.68   Where profits have been assessed or agreed following a tax investigation (see paragraph 2.30 *et seq)*, it would be extremely unusual for the Inland Revenue to accept that those profits should be reduced subsequently under the principle of equitable liability, since one of the Inspector's main purposes in conducting the investigation will have been to establish the taxpayer's 'proper' profits. However, if the Inland Revenue is persuaded (perhaps following a complaint under the Taxpayer's Charter) that the investigation was conducted very unfairly, or that the Inspector's conduct was oppressive, an adjustment under equitable liability may be agreed.

4.69   The statement reproduced in paragraph 4.63 makes it clear that the practice is discretionary and will not commonly 'be applied more than once in favour of the same taxpayer'. So it may be denied if the Inland Revenue has doubts about the claimant's honesty. On the other hand, any application should mention factors that may generate sympathy, such as ill-health or unemployment. In appropriate cases a taxpayer might benefit from pointing out that he has insufficient assets to settle the assessed liability, but could meet the sum that would be due under the practice of equitable liability, since an astute Collector should recognise the practical advantages of a quick 'voluntary' settlement over protracted and unproductive legal proceedings.

4.70   Objections to the application of equitable liability may be pursued by way of an application for judicial review, although there are no reported cases, or complaints under the Taxpayer's Charter or to the Parliamentary Ombudsman (see Chapter 3).

Repayments due to the taxpayer

4.71   The taxpayer should review his affairs for all tax years ending within the last six years to identify any *refunds* due in consequence of overpayments made. A tax repayment may qualify for *repayment supplement* (i.e. interest).

4.72   Repayments are normally made in consequence of a *claim*, and the Inland Revenue will normally require the completion of a tax return or claim form R40. Claims are discussed in paragraph 4.45 *et seq.*

4.73   Applications must be made within the time limit for the relevant claim, although an extension may be given in the event of error by officials:

> 'Under the Taxes Management Act, unless a longer or shorter period is prescribed, no statutory claim for relief is allowed unless it is made within six years from the end of the tax year to which it relates.

> 'However, repayments of tax will be made in respect of claims made outside the statutory time limit where an overpayment of

tax has arisen because of an error by the Inland Revenue or another Government Department, and where there is no dispute or doubt as to the facts.'[14]

4.74 Where a claim is for the refund of tax deducted at source or tax credits, the Inland Revenue will usually require original vouchers (provided by the organisation that paid the income) as follows:

- If a person is not liable to tax for the repayment year, *all* vouchers should be sent.

- Where a repayment computation includes interest from a bank, building society or licensed deposit taker, the Inland Revenue will require certificates provided by the institution (under ICTA 1988, s352) *to cover at least the amount of the interest for which tax is repayable.*

- In other cases, the Inland Revenue will require vouchers sufficient to cover the amount of the *income* which is being relieved from tax by repayment.[15]

4.75 Where interest has already been paid or charged on an assessment which is subsequently reduced, interest in respect of the overcharged tax should be repaid or waived as appropriate (TMA 1970, s91).

4.76 A refund of national insurance contributions, where payments exceeded the relevant annual limit because there were two or more sources of earnings, should be claimed directly from the Contributions Agency even if payment was originally made to the Inland Revenue. The taxpayer should contact Contributions Agency, Refunds Group, Newcastle upon Tyne NE98 1YX.

Repayment supplement

4.77 Repayment supplement accrues at the same rate as interest on tax paid late and is exempt from income tax (ICTA 1988, s824). For the rates at which interest is charged, see paragraph 2.65.

4.78 Repayment supplement runs for the period:

- from the *relevant date*, which is the end of the tax year following the year of assessment to which the repayment relates, or the end of the tax year in which the overpayment was actually made (if later),

- to the end of the tax month in which the repayment is effected. Tax months run from the 6th of each calendar month to the 5th of the following month.

---

[14] *Extra-statutory Concession B41*
[15] *Tax Bulletin* February 1996 p291

It should be noted that, under these rules, interest may not begin to accrue until many months after the overpayment was made (ICTA 1988, s824(3)).

4.79   By law, repayment supplement is not available unless the claimant was resident in the UK for the year of assessment to which the refund relates. However, by concession it will be paid to residents of EC member states other than the UK, provided the other conditions of ICTA 1988, s824 are met (*R v CIR (ex p.) Commerzbank AG* QB [1991] STC 271 and *Extra-statutory Concession A82*).

Set-off against other liabilities

4.80   Where a taxpayer simultaneously owes tax while being entitled to a repayment in respect of a separate tax year or assessment, three points arise:

- Can either party demand a set-off? In particular:

    - Can the Inland Revenue insist on a set-off where the taxpayer would prefer a repayment so as to settle another debt which he regards as more pressing?

    - Can a taxpayer appeal against an assessment, and apply for postponement of tax, on the grounds that a refund is due elsewhere?

- What are the administrative arrangements for set-offs?

- What are the implications for interest and repayment supplement?

The parties' rights

4.81   Regarding its right to deny a repayment where tax is due elsewhere, the Inland Revenue has written to TaxAid as follows:

> 'The strict legal position on set-offs distinguishes between those which can be made unilaterally and those that are made in other circumstances.

> 'Unilateral set-off can occur in any case where, *inter alia*, both the amount available to be set-off and the debt to which it is directed are both due and legal proceedings have been commenced (in respect of the tax debt).

> 'Whilst some cases fit this situation, the majority fall outside and can only be made by agreement. Often the potential for set-off will have been recognised by the claimant who will authorise it in advance. But in the remainder of cases the situation is that the Revenue has no right of set-off unless the agreement of the taxpayer is first obtained.

'As a practical rule however to reduce work, and to avoid the absurdity of the Revenue sending out repayments while at the same time asking for payment where there is an amount due ... the Revenue will retain the amount and propose the set-off. The potential recipient may accept this suggestion (as most do) or may request that the amount be actually repaid (which will then be done).'

4.82   The Inland Revenue has stated further that where a tax debt is subject to a County Court judgment, which is subject to an instalment order (see paragraph 10.25 *et seq)*, then if a refund arises in respect of another tax year or assessment:

'The Inland Revenue has a right (of set-off) ... and in accordance with Order 42 Rule 10 of the County Court Rules such an action does not rank as a payment under the judgment.'[16]

4.83   An appeal will not be admitted against a tax assessment on the grounds that a repayment is due elsewhere (see paragraph 3.12). Accordingly, a postponement application cannot be made to reflect the anticipated refund. However, if the Inspector is satisfied that there are good grounds for believing that a repayment is due, the Collector may be instructed to make an informal set-off pending settlement of the claim.

The administrative machinery

4.84   On 6 April 1994 the Inland Revenue changed its computer systems so that most repayments are made automatically under a system called HEP (handle excess payments). This processes refunds arising through overpayments, assessments being amended to reduce the tax charged, or further postponement applications.

4.85   Under HEP a refund will be made automatically unless:

- the taxpayer is deceased,

- his address is unknown,

- the refund exceeds £150,000, or

- the case has been specifically identified as requiring manual intervention. (See *Taxation Practitioner* October 1994 p27.)

---

[16] Rule 10 states: 'Where the Crown has obtained judgment for taxes but subsequently the tax liability is reduced, whether by reason of an appeal against an assessment or otherwise, and the Crown has given notice of the reduction to the Court and to the debtor, the sum remaining unsatisfied under the judgment shall be reduced accordingly, but the amount of the reduction shall not rank as a payment under the judgment', i.e. instalments must continue to be paid without any break until the judgment debt (as reduced) is satisfied.

Small overpayments - £1 or less on an assessment, or £10 or less through PAYE - may be disregarded unless the taxpayer specifically requests a refund (*Inland Revenue Statement of Practice SP6/95*).

4.86   Before effecting a repayment the HEP system sets the repayment due against outstanding liabilities of the same taxpayer, including any payments that will fall due within the next 30 days, and repays just the balance.   In the minority of cases where the taxpayer has exercised his right to decline a set-off, as explained in paragraph 4.81, then no set-off should be made.

4.87   Overpayments are set against the oldest liabilities first - which will usually minimise interest charges - although the Collector should agree to a different order of set-off upon request. Collectors are sometimes criticised in the professional press for failing to do so, and mistakes may be remedied by complaints under the Taxpayer's Charter.

4.88   There are specific Regulations governing the order of set-off of PAYE overpayments against PAYE underpaid in two or more years, designed to ensure that as far as possible any repayment is allocated, for repayment supplement purposes, to the earliest possible year (SI 1993/ 744, Reg 106).   However, these provisions are nevertheless frequently criticised for denying repayment supplement where it might, 'in common sense', appear to be due.

Interest provisions on set-offs

4.89   In cases of set-off, disputes frequently arise over the interaction of the provisions for interest on tax paid late under TMA 1970, s86 and repayment supplement (for the provisions of TMA 1970, s86 see paragraph 2.73 *et seq*).   The Inland Revenue's general rule for these purposes, is that:

> 'The set-off is done in a way which gives the same result as if the overpaid tax had been repaid and then paid back against the other liability.   In other words, repayment supplement will run from the relevant date of the original payment up to the set-off date, and late payment interest will run from the reckonable date of the underpaid charge up to the date of set-off.'[17]

4.90   The above rule is weighted in the Inland Revenue's favour, because a relevant date can never fall earlier than 12 months after the tax year end, while a reckonable date will invariably fall earlier (see paragraph 2.73 and 3.42 *et seq*).   Accordingly, a net charge to interest may arise under TMA 1970, s86 where an underpayment and overpayment of identical

---

[17] *ICAEW Technical Release 13/92*, reporting a meeting with Inland Revenue officials. It should be noted that, strictly, the repayment supplement should run up to the end of the tax month of set-off (see 4.78 above).

amounts, originally made on exactly the same day, are set-off against each other at a later date.

The date of set-off for interest purposes

4.91   Because of the above rules, the date on which a set-off is treated as being made can be significant. Is it:

- when the repayment is requested (the taxpayer's likely preference), or

- when the refund is agreed to be due (the Inland Revenue's preference)?

4.92   In the Inland Revenue's view it is 'the date the Inspector established that an overpayment of tax existed and could therefore have been repaid.'[18]

4.93   This conflicts with a statement, reportedly made by the Inland Revenue, reproduced in the ICAEW's Technical Release 798 (1990):

> 'Where a taxpayer simultaneously has tax due under one assessment and has overpaid on another and he draws this fact to the Department's attention and asks for a set-off, we do not charge interest on the tax due as of the date that the set-off request is made (to the extent that it can be met from the overpayment). This is in accordance with the undertaking given by the then Chief Secretary during the debate on the Finance (No 2) Act 1975 (*Hansard*, Standing Committee H, 2 July 1975, col 746).'

4.94   Unfortunately, the Chief Secretary's statement does not clarify matters greatly. He said:

> 'In practice, the procedure in conformity with the Bill, will ensure that a taxpayer will not be exposed to a net charge for interest on unpaid tax, to any extent that and for any period in respect of which he has a repayment of tax owing to him, and the Inspector sets off tax due against tax repayable.'

Ultimately it comes down to an interpretation of the meaning of 'he has a repayment of tax owing to him'. If this is when the refund is agreed, then the Inland Revenue policy is unassailable.

Payments on account of disputed liabilities

4.95   Particular problems can arise where a taxpayer wishes to make a payment on account, to avoid interest running under TMA 1970, s86, where a tax liability is wholly or partly in dispute. If such a payment is

---

[18] *Inland Revenue Assessed Taxes Manual* paragraph 14.712

allocated directly against the particular assessment, but subsequently proves to be excessive, the interest provisions on repayment or set-off described above could be disadvantageous.

4.96   This may be avoided by asking the Collector to hold the payment in a suspense account. The Inland Revenue has confirmed that:

> '(As regards) unallocated payments ... held in a suspense account ... when the appropriate charge has been identified, the money is allocated to that charge and treated just as if had been allocated on the original date of payment. If that date was before the reckonable date for the receiving charge, then no late payment interest will arise on that amount.'[19]

Since Collection offices prefer to allocate all payments received against specific outstanding liabilities, a letter should accompany the cheque clearly requesting that it be held in suspense. Should a Collector later try to repay a sum held in suspense, it may be appropriate to preserve the protection against possible interest charges by returning the cheque with a clear explanation as to why the payment should be retained in suspense. (See *Taxation Practitioner* August 1994 p25 and October 1994 pp27-28.)

4.97   An alternative approach in cases of dispute is to purchase a Certificate of Tax Deposit (CTD). If the dispute is ultimately determined in favour of the Inspector, the liability may be settled by presentation of the CTD and, for interest purposes, payment is treated as made on the date the CTD was acquired. Should the dispute be determined in favour of the taxpayer, the CTD may be·used to settle other liabilities or encashed. Upon encashment, interest is paid at a very modest rate, which is taxable. The minimum investment is £2,000. Details of CTDs currently available are set out in Prospectus (Series 7), available from Collectors of Taxes, or from Financial Services Office (CTD), Inland Revenue (A), Barrington Road, Worthing, West Sussex BN12 4XH.

Relief for Inland Revenue errors

4.98   Where the Inland Revenue has been guilty of serious maladministration, the taxpayer may seek a waiver of part or all of the tax or interest due, or compensation for costs unnecessarily incurred.

Tax waived on grounds of Inland Revenue delay

4.99   By law an Inspector may raise assessments at any time up to six years following a year of assessment, however it is recognised that this is an unduly long period for a person to be uncertain about his tax position. Accordingly, concessional relief may be given under Extra-statutory

---

[19] *ICAEW Technical Release 13/92*

Concession A19 (ESC A19) where arrears of tax have arisen through failure by the Inland Revenue to take action at an earlier date. The provisions of ESC A19 are as follows:

'ESC A19 Giving up tax where there are Revenue delays in using information

Arrears of income tax or capital gains tax may be given up if they result from the Inland Revenue's failure to make proper and timely use of information supplied by:

- a taxpayer about his or her own income, gains or personal circumstances

- an employer, where the information affects a taxpayer's coding; or

- the Department of Social Security, about a taxpayer's State retirement, disability or widow's pension.

Tax will normally be given up only where the taxpayer

- could reasonably have believed that his or her tax affairs were in order, **and**

- was notified of the arrears more than 12 months after the end of the tax year in which the Inland Revenue received the information indicating that more tax was due, **or**

- was notified of an over-repayment after the end of the tax year following the year in which the repayment was made.

In exceptional circumstances arrears of tax notified 12 months or less after the end of the relevant tax year may be given up if the Revenue

- failed more than once to make proper use of the facts they had been given about one source of income

- allowed arrears to build up over two whole tax years in succession by failing to make proper and timely use of information they had been given.'

The above wording applies to arrears first notified after 10 March 1996 (for details of the earlier version, see paragraph 4.104 *et seq*). Certain practical aspects are examined below.

Arrears of ... tax may be given up

4.100 Despite the use of the word 'may' in the first line of ESC A19, the Inland Revenue has confirmed to TaxAid that the arrears are *always* waived where the necessary conditions set out in the concession are met.

Information routinely provided by employers and by the Department of Social Security

4.101 Employers should provide the Inland Revenue routinely with details of all payments to employees and occupational pensioners, and any benefits-in-kind and expenses, shortly after each tax year end. In such cases ESC A19 may apply to any arrears notified to the taxpayer more than two years after the year of assessment to which they relate (because this will be after the end of the tax year following that in which the information was submitted by the employer). Some details, such as changes in the provision of company cars, have to be reported by employers *during* the year of assessment, in which case ESC A19 may apply to arrears notified more than one year after the relevant year of assessment.

4.102 As regards information routinely provided by the DSS, the Inland Revenue has advised TaxAid:

> 'When someone first becomes entitled to a State retirement, disability or widow's pension, the DSS notifies the Inland Revenue of the award in all cases where the taxpayer has a known tax reference, or where a widow's pension is payable, and in other cases where the pension exceeds a certain amount (which is reviewed from time to time). The Revenue are *not* told about every taxable pension paid by the DSS.

> 'The DSS then give the Revenue information, usually in December - about how these pensions will be uprated from the following April.'

Accordingly, ESC A19 may apply to any arrears which arise from the receipt of such payments, where notified to the taxpayer more than one year after the end of the tax year in which details were notified to the Inland Revenue.

The claimant could reasonably have believed that his or her tax affairs were in order

4.103 It is a necessary condition for the application of ESC A19 that the taxpayer could reasonably have believed that his affairs were in order. So relief may be denied, for example, where a taxpayer has reported profits from self-employment which are clearly sufficient to attract a tax liability and the Inland Revenue has merely been slow to issue assessments. The official view, including the implications where a professional adviser has been involved, has been explained as follows:

> 'The test ... is not whether the taxpayer believed that his or her affairs were in order, but whether it was reasonable for him or her to so believe. Every case ... is considered on its individual merits, and in deciding in any particular case whether or not a taxpayer could reasonably be satisfied that his or her tax affairs were in

order, we look at all the circumstances. This exercise includes a judgment on the information that was both in the taxpayer's possession (or available to him or her) and also the nature and size of the error. But we also take a view on the taxpayer's ability to assess the significance of any information and to understand his or her tax affairs.

'The employment of skilled professional help does not of itself preclude remission under the concession, but it must have a bearing on the question of reasonable belief. The matter to be addressed therefore is whether assistance has been limited to the preparation of accounts or the completion of tax returns, or is there a broader checking and advisory role? We are more likely to decide that a particular error could not reasonably have been overlooked when an agent has been employed to look after tax affairs generally; but this will not always be conclusive ...'[20]

Arrears first notified to a taxpayer before 11 March 1996

4.104 Under the previous version of ESC A19, arrears would only be waived in part where the taxpayer's income was over £15,500. The provisions were:

'The proportion of arrears waived varies according to the size of the taxpayer's gross income (before personal allowances, deductions etc.) in the year in which the actual, or likely, amount of an arrear of tax is first notified. The current scale, which applies to arrears of tax which are first notified to the taxpayer or his or her agent on or after 17 February 1993 (and before 11 March 1996), is:

Gross income (£)	Remission
15,500 or less	All
15,501 - 18,000	3/4
18,001 - 22,000	1/2
22,001 - 26,000	1/4
26,001 - 40,000	1/10
40,001 or more	None

'A measure of relief may be given if the taxpayer's gross income marginally exceeds the limit set out above and he or she has large or exceptional family responsibilities.'[21]

---

[20] Extract from an Inland Revenue letter, *Taxation Practitioner* March 1993 p23

[21] This 'means test' was based upon the assumption that taxpayers with substantial income should find it easier to meet unexpected tax bills, but was abolished following representations by the Parliamentary Ombudsman and the Adjudicator that all taxpayers should be treated the same way. See *Inland Revenue Press Release* 11 March 1996.

4.105 Where some liability remained - because the taxpayer's income was above the £15,500 threshold - Collectors were instructed to be sensitive in enforcing payment of the tax, and this instruction remains in force where such liabilities are still unsettled (see paragraph 6.100).

4.106 The provision describing the requisite tax office delay was also expressed differently:

> '(The taxpayer) was notified of the arrear after the end of the tax year following that in which it arose, unless exceptionally the Revenue had made the repeated errors within that period or the arrear had built up over two whole years in succession as a direct result of the department's failure to make proper and timely use of information.'

This wording caused confusion, particularly with regard to when an arrear 'arose'. The Inland Revenue took the view that this was the point at which it received the necessary information to assess the income, and the new wording of ESC A19 makes this clear.

Disputes about the application of ESC A19

4.107 Disputes about the application of ESC A19 may be resolved by a complaint by any of the methods discussed in Chapter 3. The Adjudicator's report for 1995 describes the following four cases that she was asked to consider, although it should be noted that the first two complaints relate to the 'means test' which has now been abolished:

- Where the Inland Revenue had made serious errors, but the taxpayer's income was over £40,000, the Adjudicator concluded that ESC A19 did not apply, but persuaded the Inland Revenue to collect the arrears over a three-year period.

- Where the Inland Revenue had agreed to waive 10% of arrears that had arisen through incorrect PAYE codes, the Adjudicator accepted the taxpayer's complaint that the Inspector had not taken sufficient account of the exceptional financial hardship that the extra liability would create and the Inland Revenue agreed to increase the waiver to 25%.

- Where the Inland Revenue had issued a further assessment to collect tax wrongly refunded 12 months earlier, and the taxpayer had obtained telephone confirmation that the refunds were correct at the time that they were made, the Adjudicator concluded that he could reasonably have believed that his affairs were in order. Although the tax district's delay was not sufficiently long to meet the strict wording of ESC A19 she felt that 'the case fell within the limited flexibility which the Inland Revenue operate over time limits under the concession' and the Inland Revenue agreed to waive the tax.

• Where the Inland Revenue had repeatedly failed to take an occupational pension into account when calculating the taxpayer's liability, the Adjudicator concluded that ESC A19 did not apply because the mistakes had been corrected within the time limits allowed. However, the Inland Revenue agreed to compensate the taxpayer for professional fees and other costs incurred by reason of its 'persistent errors' (see paragraph 4.112).

Waiver of interest because of Inland Revenue delay

4.108 The Inland Revenue rarely waives interest charges but exceptional treatment should be given where it has been guilty of excessive delay in replying to a letter or enquiry:

> 'We aim to reply to all enquiries or letters within 28 days. Sometimes we cannot do so because of the amount, or complexity, of the information we have to examine. Or we might need advice, or information from someone else. When we know we will take longer than 28 days to give a full answer, we will tell you.

> 'If there is no good reason for a delay, and if we have taken more than six months in total - over and above the 28-day target we have set ourselves - we will, for amounts unpaid, or not repaid, because of our delay

> - give up interest that arose on unpaid tax during the period of our delay, or

> - pay you interest (called 'repayment interest') on money we owed you during the period of our delay, and

> - pay any reasonable costs which you incurred as a direct result of our delay.'[22]

Compensation for other costs

4.109 Even if the taxpayer does not qualify for any reduction in the tax or interest charged, the impact of a tax debt may be reduced by a claim for compensation where the Inland Revenue has not complied with the Taxpayer's Charter or has otherwise been guilty of maladministration or unfair exercise of discretion.

4.110 Specific relief is promised by *Code of Practice 1 Mistakes by the Inland Revenue* where a tax office has made serious or persistent errors. In such cases the Inland Revenue:

> 'will pay any reasonable costs you incur as a direct result of our mistake. Examples might be professional fees, incidental personal expenses, or wages or fees which you would have earned and

---

[22] *Code of Practice 1 - Mistakes by the Inland Revenue*

which you lost through having to sort things out. They could also include such items as postage and telephone charges.'

4.111 Each case will depend upon its facts but in broad terms a mistake will be considered *serious* if the Inland Revenue:

- took a wholly unreasonable view of the law, as opposed to a genuine difference of opinion,

- started or pursued enquiries into matters which, on the basis of facts available at the time, were obviously trivial, or

- made what would normally be a trivial mistake but should have known that in the particular circumstances such a mistake might lead to far more serious consequences.

4.112 Mistakes which are not serious may nevertheless be *persistent* where the Inland Revenue:

- continued with a mistake even after it was pointed out, unless there was a genuine difference of opinion,

- kept making the same type of mistake, for example having to issue an assessment three times to get it right, without any change in the underlying facts, or

- made a lot of unconnected mistakes in any 12 month period in connection with the same period of assessment.

Consolatory payments

4.113 The latest edition of *Code of Practice 1 Mistakes by the Inland Revenue* (March 1996) acknowledges that maladministration can cause worry and distress and offers compensation:

'In exceptional cases, we may make a serious error that results directly in a significant and unwarranted intrusion into your personal life. In such exceptional cases we will consider making a payment as consolation for any worry and distress you suffered as a direct result of that error. Similarly, if there is no good reason for our delay, or a series of delays on the same point, and, exceptionally, the unreasonable delay is more than two years in total, we will also consider making a payment as consolation for the delay. We will consider each case on its own merits. Typically any payment is likely to be in the range £50 to £250, but payments of higher amounts, up to £1,000, may be made in appropriate circumstances. In extreme cases a higher payment will be considered, but it is unlikely to exceed £2,000.'

This new form of compensation is available for cases settled after 8 March 1995.[23]

---

[23] *Accountancy Age* 18 April 1996

Mishandling of complaints

4.114 The new version of *Code of Practice 1 Mistakes by the Inland Revenue* also offers consolatory payments where the Inland Revenue mishandles seriously a complaint, or there is a significant delay in dealing with a complaint without good reason.

Chapter 5

Status issues and other problem areas

The law and procedures relating to tax debts can be affected significantly
by a taxpayer's personal status or the nature of his business organisation.
This chapter examines the following common problem areas:

		From paragraph
■	Personal status issues - marriage, death and legal incapacity	*5.1*
■	Employed or self-employed?	*5.20*
■	Company directors and other officers	*5.57*
■	Partnerships	*5.66*

It also considers some of the particular issues that arise in connection
with:

■	Tax investigations of individuals with limited means	*5.83*
■	Business cessations	*5.93*
■	Sub-contractors in the construction industry	*5.101*
■	MIRAS	*5.131*
■	International issues	*5.156*
■	Statutory reliefs for 'hardship'	*5.179*

Personal status issues

Marriage

5.1   For the years up to 5 April 1990, the tax law deemed a married
woman's income to belong to her husband and assessments would normally
be made in his name. A husband was also chargeable to tax in respect of
his wife's capital gains.[1]

5.2   With effect from 6 April 1990, following the introduction of
independent taxation, married persons are now charged to tax separately.

---

[1]   ICTA 1988, s279 and CGTA 1979, s45(1). Both of these provisions were repealed
with effect from 6 April 1990.

Although there are several ways in which the *quantum* of a person's tax liability may be affected by their marital status[2], each spouse is liable separately for the tax on their own income and gains.

5.3   A taxpayer's marital status is therefore of reduced significance in the area of tax debt, although it may still be relevant for the following reasons:

- Consideration of a taxpayer's marital status may assist in reducing his liability, for example by way of a claim for the married couple's allowance (ICTA 1988, ss258A to 258D).

- The position of a spouse may warrant special treatment in tax recovery proceedings - in particular where a family home is to be sold to meet the claims of creditors on a bankruptcy (see paragraph 11.124 *et seq)*. It should be noted that members of the household may be affected significantly by tax recovery proceedings. Their incomes and living expenses may need to be explained, if the taxpayer is negotiating time to pay. Also, their possessions may be seized erroneously in the course of distraint action and they may suffer indirectly from the listing of a tax debt by credit reference agencies (see paragraphs 8.40 *et seq* and 7.38 *et seq* respectively).

A married woman's profits up to 5 April 1990

5.4   Where a tax debt relates back to 1989/90 or an earlier year, it will fall within the old rules of joint taxation. Many outstanding arrears date back to that period and will remain enforceable indefinitely, as they are never time-barred (see paragraph 2.98).

5.5   Under the rules of joint taxation, a married woman's income and gains were assessable on her husband for the period:

- *From* the beginning of the tax year *following* that in which the marriage took place.

- *To* the date the wife ceased to be 'a married woman living with her husband', i.e. the date of the first death or the time of permanent separation.[3]

5.6   Where a tax debt still remains outstanding in respect of such a period, normally action for recovery should be taken against the husband and not the wife, even if the marriage has since ended. However, there are certain important exceptions to this general rule.

---

[2] It is beyond the scope of this handbook to examine all the situations where marriage may have an impact on an individual's liability.

[3] ICTA 1988, s279 and CGTA 1979, s45(1) now repealed

5.7   If their incomes were over certain thresholds, the couple may have sought to reduce their overall tax liabilities by electing for *separate taxation of the wife's earnings*. By doing so, the wife became personally liable for tax on her earnings for the tax years covered by the election.[4]

5.8   Either spouse could opt for *separate assessment* of their income and/or gains, in which case the wife would be liable for her own tax in respect of the years covered by that election. In practice, such elections were rare because they did not reduce the couple's overall liabilities and the provisions for splitting the tax bill were extremely complex.[5]

5.9   Where an assessment to tax was made on the wife's income, and this remained unsettled by the husband more than 28 days after becoming due and payable, the Inland Revenue had special powers to transfer the liability to the wife. This was effected by serving a notice on the wife, giving particulars of:

- the original assessment,
- the unpaid tax, and
- the amount which would have been due from her if separate assessment had been in force.

The issue of such a notice had the same consequences as if an assessment had been issued to the wife on the date of the notice. In particular, the notice itself had to be given within six years of the end of the year of assessment to which it related (ICTA 1988, s285 and *Johnson v CIR* CA [1978] STC 196).

5.10   A widower had the right to disclaim any tax in respect of his wife's income outstanding at the date of her death (ICTA 1988, s286). A written notice of disclaimer had to be served on the wife's personal representatives and on the Inspector, within two months of grant of probate or letters of administration, although this period could be extended with the consent of the personal representatives. If assessments had already been made on the husband, the Inland Revenue would then exercise its powers to transfer the liability to the wife's estate under the provisions of ICTA 1988, s285 just described. Insofar as assessments had not yet been issued, these would then be made on the wife's estate as if separate assessment was in force for the years in question. This provision to disclaim tax remains available, upon the death of a wife or former wife, where the widower still has unpaid liabilities relating to her income for the years up to 5 April 1990. If so, a disclaimer would effectively cancel the debt, since it is now beyond the six-year time limit for raising an assessment on the wife.

---

[4] ICTA 1988, s287 now repealed. For 1989/90, this election was generally beneficial where a couple's combined income exceeded £30,510, of which the lower income was at least £7,026.

[5] ICTA 1988, s283 and CGTA 1979, s45(2). Both provisions were repealed with effect from 6 April 1990.

5.11 Where a married woman was a member of a partnership, tax on her share of the partnership's trading income would normally be charged as part of an assessment on the firm (ICTA 1988, s111 and see paragraph 5.66 *et seq)*.

Death

5.12 On the death of a taxpayer, his personal representatives are liable for any outstanding tax (subject to the sufficiency of the deceased's estate). Upon non-payment, the Inland Revenue may proceed against the personal representatives in the same way as against any other defaulter (TMA 1970, ss74 and 77). The Inland Revenue as a creditor has no claim against assets that have passed by survivorship and which do not fall into the estate, for example where the deceased had an interest in a family home as a joint tenant.

5.13 Rights of recovery against the personal representatives extend to include:

- Interest chargeable under TMA ss86 and 88 (TMA 1970, s69; see paragraph 2.65 *et seq)*.

- Penalties determined under TMA 1970, s100; such determinations may be made after the date of death (TMA 1970, s100A; *Dawes v Wallington Commissioners and CIR* Ch D [1964] 42 TC 200; see paragraph 2.81 *et seq)*.

- Sums outstanding under contractual settlements (*A-G v Midland Bank Executor & Trustee Co Ltd* KB [1934] 19 TC 136; see paragraph 2.30 *et seq)*.

5.14 Assessments in respect of profits arising or accruing prior to death, which are still outstanding at the time of death, must be made on the personal representatives no later than the end of the third tax year following the year of death. Where the deceased taxpayer had been guilty of fraudulent or negligent conduct, an 'extended time limit assessment' (under TMA 1970, s36) may not extend back to any year ending more than six years prior to the date of death (TMA 1970, s40). These provisions override the 'normal' time limits discussed in paragraph 2.57.

5.15 If a taxpayer dies before tax charged by an assessment falls due for payment, and his personal representatives do not have the funds to meet the liability immediately, concessional treatment is given for interest charged under TMA 1970, s86. The 'reckonable date' may be deferred until 30 days after the date on which probate or letters of administration are granted (*Extra-statutory Concession A17;* see paragraph 2.73 *et seq)*.

5.16 For special rules relating to a married woman's death, see paragraph 5.10 above.

Legal incapacity

5.17   The 'trustee' or 'guardian' of an incapacitated person is chargeable to tax on his behalf, in the same way as that person would be charged if he were not incapacitated. The trustee or guardian has the right to retain money coming into his hands on behalf of such a person, sufficient to meet tax liabilities and is indemnified for payments made from his own resources (TMA 1970, ss72(1), 72(3) and 77).

5.18   The trustee or guardian is also required to meet other obligations imposed by the taxes legislation for the purpose of assessment and payment of tax, for example the completion of tax return forms (TMA 1970, s72(2)).

5.19   The above provisions do not preclude the making of an assessment directly on a person who is legally incapacitated, such as a minor. They merely offer the Inland Revenue an alternative method of assessing and collecting tax. If a legally incapacitated person is assessed in his own name and fails to pay the tax charged, the Collector may take recovery action against his parent or guardian in the same way as any other defaulter (*R v Newmarket Commissioners ex p. Huxley* CA [1916] 7 TC 49 and TMA 1970, s73).

Employed or self-employed?

5.20   Disputes over tax debts frequently centre around a disagreement over whether a particular contract for the provision of services was one of employment or self-employment. In this section, the word *individual* designates the provider of services and the word *organisation* designates the person or body to which they are provided.

5.21   If the contract is designated an *employment*:

- Income tax is chargeable under Schedule E and the organisation is usually responsible for deduction of tax at source under PAYE.

- The individual's responsibility may be limited to providing the Inspector with details of his personal circumstances, so that the organisation may be issued with the appropriate PAYE code to ensure that the deductions are correct. There is little tax relief for work-related expenses.

- Employee's class 1 national insurance contributions should be deducted and the organisation will also be liable for employer's contributions.

- There may be statutory entitlement to employment protection.

5.22   If the contract is designated one of *self-employment*:

- The individual is responsible for his own tax affairs, including the making of tax returns and direct payment of tax under Schedule D.

- Tax is paid later, under complex rules of assessment, and work-related expenses are generally tax-deductible.

- Class 2 and class 4 national insurance contributions are payable. The total due will usually be less than the class 1 contributions payable by an employee on the same level of earnings, with a correspondingly lower entitlement to state welfare benefits.[6]

- There is no statutory entitlement to work protection.

- There may be an obligation to register for VAT.

The statutory fiction

5.23   The law is built upon the supposition that every contract to provide services will fall neatly into one category or the other - being either:

- an employment, under *a contract of service*, which is sometimes described as covering situations where he works as *part and parcel of the organisation*, or

- a self-employment, under *a contract for services*, where the individual may be characterised as being *in business on his own account*.

5.24   While there is some historical justification for this dichotomy, recent changes in work patterns have created a growing class of workers who do not fit neatly into either category, such as home-workers providing services to a single organisation, former employees retained as consultants, and freelance workers providing services traditionally performed by employees to a number of different organisations on a part-time basis.

5.25   Despite this expanding 'grey area', the law requires that all contracts for the provision of services must be categorised as employments or self-employments. In consequence two individuals performing similar functions may attract different classifications. Furthermore, because classification is carried out by a variety of offices and tribunals, and is not an exact science, identical arrangements may be classified differently in different cases. Indeed it is not unknown for the same contract to be classified differently for separate purposes (e.g. for income tax and national insurance contributions) because conflicting views were taken of the same facts by different officers (see paragraph 5.52 *et seq*).

5.26   Because of the significant tax and other consequences that may flow from it, generally it is preferable for the individual's classification to be clear from the outset.

---

[6] It should be noted that at very low income levels - between £65.96 and £109.30 per week, an employee's class 1 liability is *lower* than the fixed sum of £6.05 per week due from a self-employed person under class 2.

5.27   The Inland Revenue's advice to organisations is clear. In answer to the question 'Is everyone who works for me an employee?' it states:

> 'Normally, yes. But if you are in doubt about whether they are employed or self-employed, ask your Tax Office or Social Security (DSS) office for advice. Until a decision is made, you should operate PAYE/NICs on their earnings.'[7]

5.28   This advice suggests a predilection on the part of the Inland Revenue, borne out in practice, to rule that individuals in borderline cases should generally be classified as employees. This reflects the significant administrative advantages of collecting tax from employers under PAYE, as compared with assessment under Schedule D.

5.29   However, the Inland Revenue's approach tends to discourage organisations and individuals, who wish their arrangements to be treated as self-employments, from seeking official confirmation of this in advance. A 'tactical' decision is sometimes made to proceed on the assumption that the contract is one of self-employment, with a view to arguing the point with the Inland Revenue at a later date, should a dispute ever arise. However, this does expose the organisation to the significant risk that the Inland Revenue may seek back taxes, interest and penalties for failure to make deductions under PAYE.[8]

The proper approach

5.30   The proper basis for deciding whether a person is employed or self-employed has been developed by the Courts over many years. The same tests apply for the purposes of income tax, national insurance contributions and employment law, although there are special rules which may override them in particular cases. Some exceptions applicable to national insurance contributions are discussed in paragraph 5.54 *et seq.*

5.31   A summary of the points to be considered is provided by the Inland Revenue and Department of Social Security in their booklet *IR 56/NI 39 Employed or Self-employed? A guide for tax and national insurance*, which concedes that the matter is complex, but suggests the following pointers:

'*Employed*

If you can answer 'yes' to the following questions, you are probably **employed**.

- Do you yourself have to do the work rather than hire someone else to do it for you?

---

[7] *IR 53 Thinking of taking someone on?*
[8] In such circumstances, it would be prudent for the organisation to get the individual to confirm his understanding of the arrangements in writing and to supply details of his tax office and reference number.

- Can someone tell you at any time what to do or when and how to do it?

- Are you paid by the hour, week, or month? Can you get overtime pay?

- Do you work set hours, or a given number of hours a week or month?

- Do you work at the premises of the person you work for, or at a place or places he or she decides?

'Self-employed

If you can answer 'yes' to the following questions, it will usually mean you are **self-employed**.

- Do you have the final say in how the business is run?

- Do you risk your own money in the business?

- Are you responsible for meeting the losses as well as taking the profits?

- Do you provide the main items of equipment you need to do your job, not just the small tools many employees provide for themselves?

- Are you free to hire other people on your own terms to do the work you have taken on? Do you pay them out of your own pocket?

- Do you have to correct unsatisfactory work in your own time and at your own expense?'

These are not the sole considerations, but they give a flavour of the issues to be considered.

5.32 How classification should be approached was explained in the High Court decision of Mr Justice Mummery in *Hall v Lorimer* Ch D [1992] STC 599 p612:

'In order to decide whether a person carries on business on his own account it is necessary to consider many different aspects of that person's work activity. This is not a mechanical exercise of running through items on a check list to see whether they are present in, or absent from, a given situation. The object of the exercise is to paint a picture from the accumulation of detail. The overall effect can only be appreciated by standing back from the detailed picture which has been painted, by viewing it from a distance and by making an informed, considered, qualitative appreciation of the whole. It is a matter of evaluation of the overall effect of the detail, which is not necessarily the same as the sum total of the

103

individual details. Not all details are of equal weight or importance in any given situation. The details may also vary in importance from one situation to another.'

This passage was cited with approval in the Court of Appeal, which upheld the decision of the High Court.[9]

5.33 In *Hall v Lorimer* the Courts refused to overturn a decision of a Special Commissioner that a freelance vision mixer in the television industry was self-employed. Apart from the pointers listed in paragraph 5.31, the Court was influenced by the fact that the taxpayer performed his services for many different organisations on short-term contracts. This particular point has been acknowledged by the Inland Revenue in a more recent booklet, where it states that:

> 'a series of short-term engagements with many different contractors may be a pointer towards self-employment.'[10]

5.34 It should be noted that in certain situations the taxes legislation overrides the above tests, and an individual may be liable for income tax under Schedule E, with deductions due under PAYE, even though he would otherwise be categorised as self-employed. Examples are certain workers contracted through employment agencies, and divers and diving supervisors working in the North Sea and other designated areas (ICTA 1988, ss19, 134 and 314). For further examination of agency workers, see paragraph 5.55 below.

Status disputes and tax debts

5.35 Tax debts linked with status disputes may arise in various ways, for example:

* The organisation and the individual may agree to treat their contract as one of self-employment, with the individual undertaking to account for tax under Schedule D. This does not prevent the Inland Revenue from taking the view, at a later date, that the contract should have been treated as an employment and that the organisation is liable for deductions that should have been made under PAYE.

* Organisations frequently advise individuals that they will be 'treated as self-employed' and such individuals may not dispute the matter through ignorance or fear of losing the work. In such cases the individual may, or may not, proceed to account for tax under Schedule D and the Inland Revenue may later argue that tax should have been deducted under PAYE.

---

[9] [1994] STC 23

[10] *IR 148/CA 69 Are your workers employed or self-employed? A guide for tax and national insurance for contractors in the construction industry* p10

- The organisation may proceed unilaterally on the basis that an individual is self-employed, and pay him without deduction of tax. In such cases the individual may assume that 'tax is taken care of', or give no thought to his tax obligations, with the result that no tax is paid until the matter is uncovered by the Inland Revenue.

5.36   Discrepancies may come to light in different ways, for example:

- An audit of an organisation's PAYE records by the Inland Revenue or Contributions Agency may reveal payments being made without deduction of tax to individuals whose self-employed status cannot be substantiated easily.

- An individual may notify the Inland Revenue that he has received income from an employment, where there is no reference to him on the annual return of PAYE (P35) submitted to the Inland Revenue by the organisation for which he has worked.

- An individual may report income assessable under Schedule D, on the basis that he is self-employed, but the circumstances may suggest to the Inspector that he should be classified as employed. This may be because the occupation reported is one which ordinarily is carried out by employees (e.g. a receptionist or a waiter).

5.37   The Inland Revenue has a range of powers to recover tax debts arising in such circumstances - from employers and employees. Although generally it may go back up to six years, it may agree to limit the exercise of its retrospective powers, for example where tax has been fully accounted for under Schedule D or where it is very clear that there will not be the means to settle such a liability in full (see paragraph 5.83 *et seq*).

Regulation 49 determinations on employers

5.38   Where it considers that an organisation has failed to operate PAYE correctly in respect of one or more individuals, the Inland Revenue may make a *determination* of the tax which has not been paid. This is subject to the same provisions of the Taxes Management Act 1970 as if it were an assessment to income tax made on the employer (Income Tax (Employments) Regulations 1993 SI 1993/744, Reg 49; see also paragraph 2.55). Frequently this exercise involves 'grossing up', i.e. computing the outstanding tax on the basis that the amount received by the individual was a net 'after tax' sum, which increases the outstanding tax due.

5.39   An organisation in receipt of a determination under Regulation 49 might appeal on the grounds that the individual(s) concerned were not employees but were in fact self-employed. Other possible grounds of appeal might be that the amount charged is excessive, for example because the Inland Revenue's calculations make no provision for personal allowances that would have been given had PAYE been operated correctly. A set-off should always be claimed for any tax paid by the individual(s) under Schedule D and the Inspector should be asked to check their files if necessary. It should be noted that a Collector may opt not to collect unpaid liabilities from an employer for errors made in good faith where reasonable care has been taken to operate PAYE correctly (SI 1993/744, Reg 42(2)).

5.40   An employer has only a limited right to recover any tax paid under a Regulation 49 determination from the employee concerned. The only available remedy is to make deductions from subsequent remuneration (understood to be restricted to subsequent payments in the same tax year) and there may be no right of recovery if the employment has already ceased (*Bernard & Shaw Ltd v Shaw* KB [1951] 2 All ER 267). Nor would there appear to be any right of recovery from the employee if the Regulation 49 determination was calculated upon the basis that the employee was paid net, i.e. if the payments were grossed up (see paragraph 5.38), since the deduction will already have been 'made'. Exceptionally, an employer may recover the tax from a former (or current) employee if there is a separate agreement to this effect between them (*Philson & Partners Ltd v Moore* [1956] 167 Estates Gazette 92).

5.41   Regulation 49 determinations commonly follow PAYE audits and any default found may also give rise to penalties and interest charges. Reference to the way in which such audits should be conducted may be found in the following Inland Revenue booklets:

- *Code of Practice 3 Inspection of employers' and contractors' records*

- *IR 71 PAYE inspections - employers' and contractors' records*

- *IR 109 PAYE inspections and negotiations - employers' and contractors' records - How settlements are negotiated*

If it is felt that the procedures set out in these publications have not been followed, a complaint may be made by way of the procedures described in Chapter 3.

Recovery from the employee

Directions under the PAYE Regulations

5.42   Where tax determined under Regulation 49 is not paid within 30 days of the date on which it becomes final and conclusive, the Inland Revenue may *direct* that the tax underdeducted be recovered from the employee(s) to whom it relates (SI 1993/744, Reg 49(5)). Alternatively, the Inland Revenue may make a *direction* on an employee without any prior determination on the employer (SI 1993/744, Reg 42(3)).

5.43 However, in both cases the power to make such directions is dependent upon the Inland Revenue being satisfied that the individual received the emoluments *knowing* that his employer had *wilfully failed* to deduct the tax properly due under the PAYE Regulations. Because of this stringent requirement, the powers are rarely used against individuals who are not company directors or other company officers. The detailed provisions are considered in paragraphs 5.57 *et seq.*

5.44 Where a direction is made against an employee, credit should be given for any amounts paid previously under Schedule D in respect of the same income.

Schedule E assessments

5.45 The Inspector may make an *assessment* on the individual under *Schedule E* to recover any underpayment. In such cases, the appropriate response will depend upon whether the individual considers that he was actually an employee, as opposed to self-employed.

5.46 If the individual believes that he was employed, there may nevertheless be grounds for appealing against the assessment if it contains any computational errors. Alternatively, if it is considered that the liability has arisen through failure by the employer to take adequate care in applying the PAYE Regulations and the employee was an 'innocent' party, the Inland Revenue may be persuaded to exercise its powers against the employer under Regulation 49 instead.[11] This approach is more likely to bear fruit if it is made clear that the employee lacks funds to meet the tax due. In this connection, the Inland Revenue has advised TaxAid:

> 'The operation of PAYE is the employer's responsibility and it falls on the employer to make good any shortfall of tax deductible from emoluments. The employee is thereby usually protected from an employer's mistake in not deducting a sufficient amount of tax. Where however the employer can demonstrate to the satisfaction of the Collector that an error was made in good faith despite the employer taking reasonable care, the Collector can direct that the employee and not the employer will be responsible for payment of the under-deducted tax. The tax recoverable from an employee in this way will be collected either through a coding adjustment or a Schedule E assessment.'[12]

5.47 Where the individual considers that he was actually self-employed, he may appeal on the grounds that he had no income assessable under Schedule E. Although the matter may take some time to resolve, no interest

---

[11] Ideally, such a suggestion should be made before the Inspector actually makes the Schedule E assessment.

[12] The reference to the employer taking 'reasonable care' may be found in SI 1993/744, Reg 42(2).

accrues on the Schedule E assessment while it is under appeal (see paragraph 3.43). If the appeal succeeds, the Inland Revenue will almost certainly exercise its powers to assess the individual under Schedule D, although the liability may well be lower, primarily because of the different rules for deduction of expenses.

Schedule D assessments

5.48 Sometimes an Inspector will decide to collect an outstanding liability by way of an *assessment* on the individual under *Schedule D*. This may be as an administrative convenience or because the Inspector has concluded that the taxpayer has been self-employed.

5.49 Where an individual receives a Schedule D assessment, the appropriate response will again depend upon his view as to his proper status.

5.50 If he considers that he was indeed self-employed, then it may be a matter of considering merely whether the assessment is correctly made, and that all reliefs, etc. have been given.

5.51 If the individual considers that he was actually an employee, an appeal may be made on the grounds that there was no source of income assessable under Schedule D. If the appeal succeeds, the assessment should be withdrawn. The Revenue may then resort to one of its other powers against employers and employees discussed above.

National insurance contributions aspects

5.52 Historically, individuals have often been categorised differently by the Inland Revenue and Department of Social Security. Such discrepancies should now be less frequent following the adoption of the Common Approach:

> 'Under joint working arrangements (the 'Common Approach'), if one Department makes a written decision based on a **full investigation** of the facts of a particular case, and these facts remain the same, it will normally be accepted by the other Department.'[13]

5.53 Accordingly, in cases of dispute with either Department, it may assist to check whether the matter has been considered previously by the other Department. Such enquiries should be assisted by the fact that each office should now have a specialist officer who is designated to deal with status issues.

---

[13] *IR 148/CA 69 Are your workers employed or self-employed? A guide for tax and national insurance for contractors in the construction industry* p11. The 'Common Approach' applies to other industries as well.

5.54 It should, however, be noted that there are certain earners whose categorisation for national insurance purposes is defined by the nature of their activity, without regard to the normal tests of status.

5.55 The following are invariably regarded as *employees* for national insurance purposes:

- Workers supplied by agencies to render personal services to third parties, who are subject to supervision, direction or control in the way in that they do their work. This covers most temporary secretarial workers, supply drivers and nurses, but specifically excludes entertainers, models, people employed in their own homes, or where the payment to the agency is solely an introductory fee (Social Security (Categorisation of Earners) Regulations 1978, Sch 1). It should be noted that many such individuals may also be deemed employees for income tax purposes (see paragraph 5.34).

- Certain ministers of religion (Social Security (Categorisation of Earners) Regulations 1978, Sch 1, Part I(5)).

- Office cleaners (Social Security (Categorisation of Earners) Regulations 1978, Sch 1, Part I(1)).

- Lecturers, teachers or instructors paid by the institutions within which they work. This provision does not apply to correspondence or videotape teaching (except in the case of the Open University), nor to public lectures nor to work under agreements covering less than three days in three consecutive months (Social Security (Categorisation of Earners) Regulations 1978, Sch 1, Part I(4)).

- Au pairs (following a decision of the Secretary of State M67).

- Rent officers (Rent Act 1977, s63(3)).

- Live performers, such as actors.[14]

5.56 The following are invariably regarded as *self-employed* for national insurance purposes:

- Examiners, moderators, invigilators and people setting questions for examinations leading to degrees, certificates, diplomas and professional qualifications, where contracted by the organisation setting the examination and where the contract is for a period of less than 12 months (Social Security (Categorisation of Earners) Regulations 1978, Sch 1, Part II(6)).

---

[14] Following the successful appeal by Sam West and Alex McCowen to the Special Commissioners in 1993, such individuals are generally treated as self-employed for income tax purposes. At the time of going to print, the Contributions Agency was reviewing its traditional categorisation of such individuals as employed earners.

- Certain share fishermen (Social Security (Contributions) Regulations 1979, Reg 98).

- Certain homeworkers and outworkers (following decisions of the Secretary of State M17, M25 and M35).

- Sports umpires paid for each match and tennis coaches (following decisions of the Secretary of State M38 and M51).

Company directors and other officers

5.57 Special considerations apply to emoluments received by office-holders of companies, in particular directors and company secretaries. Tax debt problems arise commonly where such an individual has been drawing sums from the company with a view to 'sorting out the tax' later.[15]

Directions against the individual

5.58 The Inland Revenue may exercise its powers to make determinations, directions or assessments under all the provisions discussed in paragraphs 5.38-5.51 above where it considers that PAYE has not been properly applied. However, the fact that usually a company officer will have been closely involved in the company's financial affairs gives particular scope for the use of directions under Regulations 49(5) and 42(3).

5.59 The Inland Revenue has confirmed to TaxAid that it considers that there is no right of appeal against such directions. Accordingly, the decision to proceed is made at a senior level.

> 'The Department must be able to demonstrate having made reasonable enquiries in order to be absolutely sure that the necessary basis for a direction exists. At the same time, the employee must have been given every opportunity to provide an explanation for the apparent under-deduction of tax.'[16]

5.60 Usually the Inland Revenue will write to the individual first, setting out its view of the situation in full and asking for his comments, before issuing a direction. The burden of proof imposed on the Inland Revenue is considerable - the individual must have received the income *knowing* that the organisation was *wilfully failing* to deduct tax. In this context:

- *knowing* means 'knowing' and not 'ought to have known' or 'should have been suspicious', and

---

[15] Such arrangements frequently lead to a full-scale investigation of the company and the implications for the company itself are beyond the scope of this handbook.

[16] *Inland Revenue Regional Executive Office Manual* paragraph 8.218

- *wilfully* means 'intentionally' or 'deliberately', and it should not be presumed that a failure is 'wilful' without evidence (*R v CIR (ex p. Chisholm)* QB [1981] STC 253).

5.61   While it might be difficult to demonstrate that these conditions are fulfilled in the case of a mere employee, the Courts have experienced less difficulty in the case of company officers. In *R v CIR (ex p. Chisholm)* (QB [1981] STC 253 p259), the Court considered that 'there was an abundance of material' on which the Inland Revenue could conclude that these conditions were met.[17] In a more recent case, sums had been credited to a director's loan account net of the PAYE deductions calculated to be due. The deductions so calculated were never paid over to the Inland Revenue and the company went into liquidation. Directions were made against the director under Regulation 49(5) and an application for judicial review failed (*R v CIR (ex p. McVeigh)* QB [1996] STC 91). However, the decision has received critical comment in recent articles in *Taxation* 11 July 1996 p400 and 22 August 1996 p560.

5.62   It is not absolutely clear that the Inland Revenue is correct in its view that no appeals may be admitted against these particular forms of direction. However, in the absence of a right of appeal, objections to such directions should be made by way of the channels for complaint described in Chapter 3.

Other company office-holder issues

5.63   It is difficult for an office-holder to contend that earnings from his company have arisen from self-employment. As a general rule, the Inland Revenue will insist that such payments arise from 'an office or employment' and are therefore assessable under Schedule E. However, in some specific cases it is possible to structure arrangements so that payments fall outside Schedule E. For example, *Extra-statutory concession A37* permits certain directors' fees received by partnerships to fall within Schedule D.

5.64   Investigations into companies often reveal undeclared receipts, where it is unclear whether an assessment should be made on the company or on an office-holder. The Inland Revenue's normal policy is to adopt the approach likely to generate the greatest yield (typically by assessing the company for the receipt and treating it as a distribution or remuneration paid to the director(s) or shareholder(s) with all the consequential tax implications). Accordingly, where an individual lacks resources to settle any prospective liability, this fact should be made clear to the Inland Revenue at an early stage.

---

[17] See also *R v CIR (ex p. Sims)* QB [1987] STC 211.

5.65 The taxes legislation contains no provision for office-holders to be made liable personally for corporation tax due from a company. However, where non-payment of corporation tax is revealed in the course of an investigation, an Inspector may require that an office-holder should join the company in offering to settle outstanding liabilities by way of a contractual settlement (see paragraph 2.30 *et seq*). While it might be argued that such a contract is unenforceable against the individual through lack of 'consideration', the Inland Revenue may point either to:

- the benefit derived, *qua* shareholder or office-holder, from the Inland Revenue's agreement to enter the contractual settlement with the company, or

- a parallel agreement not to assess the individual personally.

Accordingly, the office-holder may be jointly liable (see *CIR v Woollen* CA [1992] STC 944 and see paragraph 2.99).[18]

Partnerships

5.66 Under English law, a partnership is constituted by two or more persons engaged in business together and has no separate legal identity. However, for the purposes of assessing its trading profits to income tax and class 4 national insurance contributions, a partnership is deemed to have a separate identity from the individual partners and a joint assessment is made in the partnership name (ICTA 1988, s111 and TMA 1970, s9).[19]

5.67 The partnership assessment should be made on the profits of the firm calculated under the normal rules of Schedule D Cases I and II, apportioned between the partners in accordance with their entitlement to profits in the year of assessment, with the tax liability on each partner's allocation computed by reference to his individual tax allowances and rate bands. The aggregate of the partners' liabilities, so computed, is then due on the partnership assessment. The complexity of this procedure invariably results in most partnership assessments initially being made in estimated sums, leading to appeals which are usually settled by agreement (see paragraph 3.13).

5.68 The same time limits apply for making assessments on partnerships as apply to individuals. Any assessment which purports to include a liability of a deceased partner must be made within the time limits set out in paragraph 5.14 above (*Harrison v Willis Bros* CA [1965] 43 TC 61).

---

[18] The general law in this area is developing and there is the possibility that the Inland Revenue may pursue a director for losses arising from breaches of director's duties, or attempt to lift the 'veil of incorporation' and pursue shareholders.

[19] Note that there are new rules for partnerships established after 5 April 1994 or deemed to have commenced trading after that date, see paragraphs 5.77 and 12.69 *et seq*.

5.69 Appeals against partnership assessments are made invariably by the partners acting together. However, in the absence of agreement between them, one or more of the partners may appeal against an assessment on the firm (*Re Sutherland & Partners' Appeal* CA [1994] STC 387).

Problems with joint liability

5.70 Tax assessed on a partnership is a debt for which all current partners are jointly liable (Partnership Act 1890, s9). Where the partners are still in business together at the time that tax is payable, usually they will be able to agree on the apportionment of the liability between them, commonly by reference to their shares of the total liability, as computed in paragraph 5.67.

5.71 Tax debt problems tend to arise where a partnership has ended prior to the settlement of a liability. In such situations the Inland Revenue may pursue every person believed to have been a partner in the business, for the full amount due and payable, subject to the overriding obligation to collect no more than the full amount due. Where one or more of the former partners is insolvent, has disappeared or has left the UK, this can impose a heavy burden on the others, and the following points might be considered.

5.72 It is sometimes possible to argue that an individual in receipt of demands for the firm's tax was not in fact a partner, but perhaps a mere employee or self-employed sub-contractor. It should assist to demonstrate as far as possible that the individual:

- took no part in managing the business,

- was not able to sign business cheques or contracts,

- was not shown as a partner on any business stationery, and

- was not regarded as a partner by customers and/or suppliers.[20]

While it will not help matters if the individual has signed a partnership agreement, this fact alone should not determine the matter either way.[21]

5.73 If an individual is successful in his contention that he was not a partner, he should be relieved of joint liability, although he may remain chargeable on his own income from the business, if he was an employee or sub-contractor. (For the position of an employee, see paragraph 5.42 *et seq*).

---

[20] See *Saywell and Others v Pope* Ch D [1979] STC 824 where wives of existing business partners were held not to have been admitted as new partners.

[21] *Dickenson v Gross* KB (1927) 11 TC 614. Ironically, in most leading cases concerning the *existence* of a partnership, the Inland Revenue has been successful in contending that an individual was *not* a partner, having taken this position to counter a specific tax planning advantage.

5.74 Disputes about an individual's status should be raised ordinarily by way of an appeal within 30 days against a partnership assessment. The fact that an individual is considered by the Inspector to be (or to have been) a partner, may be apparent from:

- the service of the partnership assessment on him personally, or

- the service on him of a *notice of partnership share*, being the document which is sent ordinarily to each member of a partnership, stating his share of profits included in the partnership assessment.

5.75 In practice, however, an individual may not have appreciated the need for such prompt action and disputes about partnership status arise frequently only when enforcement action commences, commonly upon receipt of a County Court summons. In such cases, it is helpful to note the Inland Revenue's internal procedures below.

5.76 Whenever a Collector receives a defence - in response to a County Court summons - to the effect that a defendant was not a partner for the year or years in question, or at all, he is instructed to send the relevant papers to his Regional Executive Office. That office should obtain the tax district file immediately to check details of the assessment:

- If the partnership assessment was issued to the defendant concerned, the Collector will be told that the defence can be answered readily by reference to the income tax legislation, and finality principles, and will be instructed to seek a judgment and enforce the debt as necessary. It may nevertheless be possible to seek a suspension of proceedings by submission of an application to make a late appeal (see paragraphs 4.8 *et seq* and 10.44 *et seq).*

- If the notice of assessment was not issued to the defendant or there is doubt whether it arrived, then proceedings should be discontinued. A fresh notice of assessment will be served on the individual, who may then make his appeal. The Collector should send notices of discontinuance of the proceedings to the defendant and to the Court (*Inland Revenue Regional Executive Office Manual* paragraphs 6.61-6.62 and 6.92-6.94).[22]

5.77 Joint liability will cease to apply following the introduction of self-assessment. Under the new provisions, partners are chargeable only on their own share of profits:

- For any partnership established after 5 April 1994, from commencement of the business.

---

[22] If an appeal was made by another partner, the case will be sent for review to the Inland Revenue's Business Services Office in Shipley.

- For partnerships already trading at 5 April 1994, from the earlier of:

  - the date of the first change in the composition of the partnership for which no 'continuation election' is made under ICTA 1988, s113(2) (this is known as a *deemed cessation*), and

  - 6 April 1997.

  (See paragraph 12.69 *et seq*).

5.78   Accordingly, where a partner is pursued for a liability of his firm for 1994/95, 1995/96 or 1996/97, this may be challenged if there was a change in the members of the partnership after 5 April 1994 but before the end of the year of assessment to which the demand relates. Where a continuation election has already been made in respect of such a change, this may be revoked to create a deemed cessation, provided a signed notice of revocation is given to the Inland Revenue within two years of the partnership change (*Inland Revenue Statement of Practice A4*). If this deadline has passed, it *may* be possible to secure the Inspector's agreement to a late revocation by reference to the criteria for late elections set out in paragraph 5.81. This strategy may assist, for example, in reducing the exposure of remaining members of a firm where a partner becomes insolvent. However, it should be noted that a revocation may also have the effect of increasing the aggregate amount of tax due from the partners. As a result, it may be blocked by anyone affected, since the notice of revocation must be signed by all those who were partners immediately before and after the date of the change.

5.79   An individual who meets the tax liability of a partner, or former partner, has a quasi-contractual right under the common law to be indemnified by him. In practice, this right can be difficult to enforce and so, in cases of tax debt, generally an individual partner should try to avoid responsibility for more than his own share of the firm's liability.

5.80   A Collector is not bound by any contractual rights of indemnity between the partners, but he should at least pursue the members of the firm on an even-handed basis. If it is considered that a Collector has pursued one partner far more vigorously than another, without good reason, a complaint might be made by one of the methods discussed in Chapter 3. However, such a complaint is unlikely to succeed if the Collector can demonstrate, for example, that there was little point in pursuing the other partner because he was clearly insolvent.

Late partnership continuation elections

5.81   In some circumstances the members of a partnership which was trading before 6 April 1994 may be more concerned with reducing the firm's overall taxable profits, by making a continuation election outside the two-year period permitted by ICTA 1988, s113(2).

5.82   In this situation they may seek to rely upon the following statement by the Financial Secretary to the Treasury, Mr Stephen Dorrell, in 1992:

> 'there would be a presumption in favour of admitting an election ... which is made as soon as is reasonably possible in all the circumstances, but after the statutory time limit has expired, if the reason for the late election being late was one of the following:
>
> -   some relevant and uncorrected error on the part of the Inland Revenue has had the effect of misleading the partners or their agent about whether the requirements of the legislation had been met; or
>
> -   at a crucial time, one of the required signatories was not available for unforeseeable reasons (e.g. because of serious illness); or the agent of a signatory was similarly not available and there was no one else who could be expected reasonably to stand in the agent's shoes; or
>
> -   there was some other difficulty about obtaining all the required signatures to the election within the time limit, and the Inland Revenue had, before the time limit expired, both been clearly notified that each of the signatories had individually decided to make an election, and been given the reasons why the election could not be made within the time limit ...'.[23]

Tax investigations of individuals with limited means

5.83   Where a taxpayer's affairs attract a formal investigation, normally the Inspector will be seeking a contractual settlement, whereby the taxpayer promises to settle unpaid tax, interest and penalties, by way of a lump sum or instalments (for a detailed discussion, see paragraph 2.30 *et seq).*

5.84   As such investigations are time-consuming, the Inland Revenue tries to concentrate its resources on cases offering a good prospective yield. The recently-published *Inland Revenue Investigation Handbook* explains how the conduct of an investigation, and the sum sought by an Inspector, should be altered where the taxpayer has limited means.

5.85   The *Investigation Handbook* states that there is no point in trying to negotiate a contractual settlement which clearly cannot be met. If a taxpayer indicates that he lacks the means to make what would be regarded in the circumstances of the case as a 'standard offer' - or it appears to the

---

[23] *Hansard* 23 November 1992

Inspector that this is so - then the taxpayer should be asked to provide a written statement. This will provide details of:

- his assets and liabilities,

- his income and expenditure,

- similar information in respect of his spouse or children, or anyone else to whom he may have transferred assets, and

- any likely changes in the next three to five years (*Inland Revenue Investigation Handbook*, paragraph 6015).

The Inspector will review such statements critically, on the premise that a person who has concealed or understated taxable profits might be expected equally to conceal the means to settle the tax.

5.86 The taxpayer will be told that he is expected to use every possible means to settle the liability, for example by realising his assets or raising loans. In this connection:

- Business assets and debtors should be realised, but only to the extent that this does not prevent the continuation of trading.

- In extreme cases it may be suggested that the taxpayer's home should be sold, although the *Investigation Handbook* warns that this is a sensitive subject which should be approached with tact!

- The Inspector should be alert to any assets having been transferred at undervalue, since such transfers may be voidable on a bankruptcy (*Inland Revenue Investigation Handbook*, paragraph 6016 and see paragraph 11.106).

Basic guidelines

5.87 If the taxpayer has resources, but *lacks the cash* to meet the terms of a settlement within the normal 30 days:

- The settlement may provide for full payment to be made within a specified period of no longer than six months, and interest should be calculated up to the anticipated date of payment.

- If payment is dependent upon an uncertain event, such as the sale of a house, an initial period of not longer than six months may be allowed. In the event of non-payment within that period, a further deferment may be allowed, although the rate of interest will be increased by 1%. However, if payment does not appear to be in prospect at the end of the initial period, the Inspector may resort to formal means of collection (i.e. assessments with or without interest and penalty determinations).

- A legal charge on a property may be agreed with the taxpayer as an alternative to a forced sale, but only as a last resort in the case of those 'at or near retirement age', and this should be accompanied by payment of a lump sum and/or instalments if feasible. The balance of the tax, plus interest, will then be recovered on the death of the survivor of the taxpayer and their spouse (*Inland Revenue Investigation Handbook*, paragraph 6032).

Inspectors can be very flexible in reaching arrangements for the realisation of assets - in one case it was agreed that the funds could be generated by property sales on which no capital gains tax would be charged.

5.88 If the taxpayer has only a *small amount of capital*, and insufficient income to justify an instalment arrangement, the Inspector should negotiate with the taxpayer to establish the level of payment that he could make. The number of years covered by the contractual settlement should then be 'tailored', so that the level of offer required by the Inspector matches the funds available (*Inland Revenue Investigation Handbook*, paragraph 6034).

5.89 Where the taxpayer has *no capital, limited earning capacity and no other substantial sources of income*, the Inspector should not seek a contractual settlement. He is instructed to raise an assessment covering just the current year's liability, and not to exercise his powers to go back to earlier years (*Inland Revenue Investigation Handbook*, paragraph 6033).

5.90 Where the taxpayer's *income is uncertain, or may fluctuate wildly*, an informal arrangement may be reached for the taxpayer to make payments to the Accounts Office over a two-year period, and any sums still unpaid are then normally written off (*Inland Revenue Investigation Handbook*, paragraph 6034).

Special cases

5.91 If a taxpayer explains that he is *bankrupt*, or facing bankruptcy proceedings, the Investigation Handbook warns that this does not necessarily imply insolvency. However, the Inspector should recognise that a genuinely insolvent taxpayer may see no benefit in co-operating with him and in such cases an investigation should not be prolonged unduly. A settlement may be negotiated with a trustee in bankruptcy, although penalties should not be claimed where they would be borne effectively by 'innocent creditors'. If the trustee objects to the inclusion of an amount to reflect interest chargeable under TMA 1970, s88, a formal determination should not be made unless justified by the collection prospects (*Inland Revenue Investigation Handbook*, paragraph 6017).

5.92 Where a *taxpayer has died*, a settlement with his personal representatives may be sought. If estate funds are inadequate, action may be considered against persons who have benefited from gifts, prior distributions from the estate, or assets that passed by survivorship (but see paragraph 5.12), although the *Investigation Handbook* points out that this raises difficult legal points on which the Inspector should obtain advice. Normally, an Inspector should not be swayed by suggestions that action against a deceased estate simply penalises innocent third parties but, where estate funds are limited, he should have regard to the financial position of any widow or widower and any immediate dependants, if they have no other adequate means of support (*Inland Revenue Investigation Handbook*, paragraphs 6020 and 6021; see also paragraph 6.86).

Business cessations

5.93   Particular tax problems arise where a taxpayer ceases trading in circumstances of financial difficulty. In such cases:

- He will need to submit final accounts for the business, together with any accounts for previous periods which have not already been presented.

- He may face complex adjustments to his tax liabilities for the last three tax years of trading.

- He may have limited means to pay for professional assistance to sort matters out.

Most such individuals will in the past have been charged to tax on the 'preceding year basis' of assessment and in these circumstances the following points may be of relevance.[24]

The closing year rules

5.94   For the tax year in which trading ceases, the assessment should be based upon profits arising in that year (ICTA 1988, s63(1)(a)). This provision overrides the normal preceding year basis, even if an assessment on that basis has already been finalised following an appeal. A revision of the final year's assessment may lead to a significant reduction in the tax charged where, for example:

- the business ceases part of the way through a tax year, and/or

- the profitability of the business has fallen.

Accordingly, if a Collector is pursuing a tax debt for the year of cessation, it is particularly important to check that all appropriate adjustments have been made.

5.95   The Inspector should also review the profits *arising* in the two tax years immediately preceding the tax year of cessation, and compare them

---

[24] With effect from 1997/98, all self-employed persons will be charged to tax on the current year basis. Transitional rules apply.

with the profits originally assessable for those years (normally on the preceding year basis).

- If the profits arising were greater than the profits originally assessable, the Inspector must revise the assessments for both years to reflect the profits arising (ICTA 1988, s63(1)(b)). Such revisions will occur where income has been increasing steadily, and may occur where profits have fluctuated.

- If the profits arising were not greater than the profits originally assessable, no adjustment is made. In general, this will occur where income has been steady or has been declining.

5.96 Adjustments to assessments for the two years preceding cessation will often give rise to additional liabilities for which the taxpayer may not have set aside sufficient funds. There is rarely any point in asking the Inspector to waive the statutory provisions, as the Courts have ruled that they are mandatory (*Bayliss v Roberts and another* Ch D [1989] STC 693). Nevertheless, if a proposed adjustment would be small, and the Inspector is made aware that the taxpayer would not have the funds to settle the additional liability, he may agree not to issue revised assessments.

5.97 A technical anomaly arises upon the making of revisions under ICTA 1988, s63(1)(b). If the assessments for the relevant years have already been finalised, then the adjustments are effected by 'further assessments' and the reckonable date for interest charges under TMA 1970, s86 cannot be earlier than 30 days after the issue of each further assessment. If, however, an original assessment for either of the relevant years is still under appeal, then the revision for that year is effected in settling or determining the appeal. In such cases the reckonable date for s86 interest will be the date set by reference to the original assessment, usually 1 July following the end of the year of assessment (see paragraph 3.50 *et seq*). Thus interest may run from a year or two prior to the amendment of the assessment and even prior to the cessation of the business.

Closing years' accounts

5.98 The preparation of closing accounts can cause particular difficulties where business records are incomplete, or where the taxpayer lacks the resources to pay a tax adviser and has no access to free assistance.[25]

5.99 If the Inspector is made aware that the taxpayer is no longer in business, he should be amenable to accepting reasonable estimates, and consideration should be given to the suggestions in paragraph 4.30.

5.100 A further short cut may be possible in cases where the Inspector requires accounts covering two years prior to cessation, merely in order

---

[25] See Chapter 13 for sources of free help.

to check whether the adjustments described in paragraph 5.95 should be made. If it is clearly demonstrated that the *turnover* of the business has been falling steadily, to an extent that profits must also have fallen, the Inspector may agree that detailed accounts are unnecessary.

Sub-contractors in the construction industry

5.101 A number of tax debt problems are specific to self-employed taxpayers in the construction industry, who are subject to a special tax deduction scheme which was introduced in 1972 to counter widespread evasion of liabilities by casual workers. The thrust of the regime is to divide *self-employed construction industry workers* into two groups:

- The majority of workers who should be paid net of tax at the basic rate.

- Those who hold *tax certificates* entitling them to be paid gross.

5.102 The main legislative provisions are contained in ICTA 1988, ss559 to 567 and Income Tax (Sub-contractors in the Construction Industry) Regulations 1993 SI 1993/743, as amended, with further explanations in Inland Revenue booklets:

- *Code of practice 7 Collection of amounts due from employers, and contractors in the construction industry*

- *IR 14/15 Construction industry tax deduction scheme*

- *IR 117 A sub-contractor's guide to the deduction scheme*

- *IR 116 Guide for sub-contractors with tax certificates*

5.103 The detailed operation of the regime is beyond the scope of this handbook, but the essential elements affecting the sub-contractor are summarised in the following paragraphs.

Taxation at source

5.104 The law places an onus on a *contractor*, when making a payment to a *sub-contractor* who does not hold a tax certificate, to deduct income tax at the basic rate and remit this to the Inland Revenue, where it is credited against the individual's tax liabilities.

5.105 For each such payment, the contractor should provide the sub-contractor with a certificate called an *SC60*. This shows, *inter alia*, the gross earnings and the tax deducted at source. The tax deduction should be made from the labour element of a payment only and not from payments for materials provided by the sub-contractor.

5.106 Like other self-employed taxpayers, the sub-contractor is required to submit tax returns to the Inland Revenue, reflecting details of his business profits. Income tax under Schedule D Case I or II, and class 4 national insurance contributions, are assessed in the normal way.

5.107 Relief for tax shown on SC60s should be given by way of deduction from the total amount of income tax and class 4 national insurance charged by the assessment for the tax year in which the deduction was made. In practice, the sums deducted at source will usually exceed the liability for the year concerned and the Inspector must then refund the difference. Any disputes may be resolved by appeals to the Commissioners under the same provisions as apply for claims under TMA 1970, s42 (SI 1993/743, Reg 20 and see paragraph 4.46).

5.108 A sub-contractor should receive credit for, or a refund of, the tax shown on an SC60, even if the sum deducted was not remitted to the Inland Revenue. This may happen, for example, where the contractor has become insolvent.

Missing SC60s

5.109 The deduction scheme depends upon the sub-contractor being able to present SC60s to the Inspector, to claim his tax credits. Usually this should be done upon submission of the tax return. However, things can go wrong in several ways.

5.110 Many working arrangements in the construction industry are very informal, with the sub-contractor being unsure whether a weekly amount is paid net or gross. If the sub-contractor is not given an SC60, the Inspector will invariably contend that the payment was gross.

5.111 By law an SC60 should be given 'on the making of any payment', although the contractor and sub-contractor may agree for composite certificates to be provided at longer intervals (SI 1993/743, Reg 7). In the absence of any such agreement, the sub-contractor should be given an SC60 every time he is paid, but in practice many contractors unilaterally assume the right to provide certificates at longer intervals. This can sometimes mean that an SC60 is not issued at all, where for example:

- the contractor's business fails, or

- the parties fall out.

5.112 Some sub-contractors make a practice of delivering or posting SC60s to their tax district as soon as they are received. These should be placed on file for credit in due course, but they do occasionally go astray. If the SC60s cannot be found, and it is considered that this is due to inefficiency on the part of the Inland Revenue, a complaint might be made under the Taxpayer's Charter.

Asking the Inspector to help

5.113 Where an SC60 is unavailable for any reason, the Inspector may be asked to check the deduction claimed, by reference to the annual return of payments to sub-contractors (SC35), which should have been submitted by the contractor. For this purpose the sub-contractor should provide the name and address of the contractor, (approximate) details of dates worked and amounts earned, and any other evidence of tax deduction that he holds. If confirmation of the deduction is found on the contractor's SC35 return, due credit for the missing SC60 should be given (*Inland Revenue Sub-contractors in the Construction Industry Manual*, paragraph 1748).

5.114 If the Inspector cannot confirm the deduction at source because the contractor has made no SC35 return, or if the return makes no mention of the sub-contractor, strictly speaking credit should be refused. However, an Inspector may agree to a refund, or at least be persuaded to settle the matter on the basis that no further tax is due, if there is some alternative evidence in support of the sub-contractor's contention. Ideally, this might be regular payslips which correspond with gross amounts due under a written contract and net sums shown by cheques banked, although less compelling evidence may be acceptable according to the circumstances of the case.

Other problems with SC60s

5.115 A sub-contractor holding SC60s may also have received some earnings gross, from work falling outside the deduction scheme (e.g. from 'domestic' jobs), and this income should still be included in his annual accounts. If his turnover appears to be low, the Inspector may contend that the income received gross has been understated and, if the sub-contractor has not maintained good records, this will be difficult to refute. Sometimes it will be possible to explain reduced income by reference to periods spent out of work, in which case the Inspector may require evidence of having 'signed on' for welfare benefits. If the sub-contractor did not sign on, perhaps because he expected further work very soon, other evidence of 'unemployment' may need to be provided.

5.116 Occasionally an innocent or naive sub-contractor may get caught up in a fraud (see paragraph 2.101 concerning the Inland Revenue's prosecution policy). One case involved sub-contractors who had been told to give their SC60s to their foreman, who then disappeared and created false identities to claim back the tax deducted at source. Refunds were eventually made to the innocent sub-contractors, but only after the Inland Revenue had completed its investigations into the fraud.

5.117 Credit for the deduction shown on an SC60 is given against the liability for the tax year in which the deduction was made. However, the related earnings might be taxed in a different year, depending upon the basis of assessment. This can cause difficulty where income fluctuates.

For example, where a sub-contractor assessable on the preceding year basis had high earnings in 1994/95, he may have a high tax liability for 1995/96. But if he had less work in 1995/96, his tax credits for that year may be insufficient to cover the liability for that year, and he may not have set aside any funds to make up the difference.

5.118 Where a sub-contractor ceases working, he may experience the problems described under *Business Cessations*. In particular, there may be tax due under revised assessments for the two years prior to cessation, see paragraph 5.96. If the sub-contractor has received tax refunds each year historically, he is unlikely to have set aside any funds to meet such unexpected tax liabilities (which will usually arise after he has received tax refunds for the same years, which will have given the impression that his liabilities had been finalised).[26]

Holders of tax certificates

5.119 Where a contractor is satisfied that a sub-contractor holds a valid tax certificate, no deduction should be made at source. The sub-contractor is then taxed in much the same way as any other self-employed worker.

Obtaining a tax certificate

5.120 Normally, a sub-contractor may qualify for a tax certificate if he can demonstrate that:

- He works in a businesslike manner; in particular that he maintains proper business records and operates a business bank account.

- He has been employed or self-employed for a continuous period of three years within the six years preceding his application, although short breaks may be disregarded.

- He has previously complied with his tax obligations under the Taxes Management Act 1970.

5.121 The certificate is issued by the Inspector and is often referred to as a *714*, being the Inland Revenue reference on the certificate. There are four different categories:

- 714I Issued to sole traders

- 714P Issued to members of partnerships or directors of companies

- 714C Issued to companies

---

[26] Similar problems will remain on cessation in the future despite the introduction of the current year basis of assessment. In particular, individuals who prepare accounts to a date early in the tax year may be affected.

- 714S Issued, subject to certain conditions, to individuals who cannot meet all the normal requirements. In particular, there is a specified limit on the amount that may be paid gross in any week.

A certificate must be renewed every three years and the Inland Revenue has powers to cancel it before expiry where it has been issued on the basis of false information or where it has been misused.

5.122 For many workers in the construction industry, a tax certificate is a 'passport to work' since many contractors are not willing to operate the statutory scheme for deduction of tax at source described above. Holders of tax certificates also enjoy significant cash flow advantages, as their tax is payable later.

Tax arrears and tax certificates

5.123 An individual may be denied a new certificate, or the renewal of an existing certificate, if he has failed to comply with his obligations under Taxes Management Act 1970, which includes failure to settle tax liabilities on time. However, minor or technical failures should be disregarded unless they suggest that the applicant will not meet his obligations in future (ICTA 1988, s562 and *IR 40 Construction industry - Conditions for getting a sub-contractor's tax certificate* p2).

5.124 Accordingly, modest arrears in paying tax charged by Schedule D assessments should not prevent the issue or renewal of a tax certificate, provided the sub-contractor has reached some arrangement with the Collector to settle the debt. However, other arrears may cause more difficulty, for example:

- If a sub-contractor has been the subject of a tax investigation which revealed any irregularities, a certificate should not be granted or renewed until the outstanding liability has been settled, or the initial payment has been made in the case of an instalment agreement (*Inland Revenue Sub-contractors in the Construction Industry Manual*, paragraph 1078).

- Inspectors are instructed to pay particular attention to cases where a sub-contractor holds, or has previously held, a 714P on behalf of a company which he controlled. In such cases, a certificate may be denied if the company has had any tax arrears (*Inland Revenue Sub-contractors in the Construction Industry Manual*, paragraph 348).

Status issues in the construction industry

5.125 Many workers in the construction industry are *employees*, and their earnings should be taxed at source under the normal provisions of PAYE.

The construction industry rules discussed above do not apply, since they relate only to payments to *self-employed* sub-contractors.

5.126 However, in practice many contractors assume improperly that their entire workforce is self-employed and apply the construction industry rules throughout. Despite its declared position that construction industry employees should be taxed under PAYE (*IR 148/CA 69 Are your workers employed or self-employed? - A guide for tax and national insurance for contractors in the construction industry*), the Inland Revenue does not appear unduly concerned to enforce this policy where the construction industry rules appear to be working smoothly.

5.127 While such misclassification is not always a matter of particular concern, problems can arise where a worker cannot prove that tax was deducted at source because he does not hold the requisite SC60s. In such cases, normally the Inspector will seek to recover the outstanding tax by way of a Schedule D assessment, against which the worker may appeal on the grounds that there was no Schedule D source, since he was an employee assessable under Schedule E. The matter should then be resolved by consideration of the normal tests of employment/self-employment and, if the worker succeeds, it may be possible to persuade the Inland Revenue to seek collection from the employer for failure to operate PAYE (see paragraph 5.38 *et seq*).

5.128 Given the Inland Revenue's relatively relaxed attitude towards the proper classification of employees, inconsistencies can arise regarding income tax and national insurance. The DSS has stated that holders of tax certificates will *prima facie* be regarded as self-employed, although it does not feel bound by individual Inland Revenue decisions when it discovers 'that forms 714 are being used in cases where they should not be'. This conflicts with the normal 'Common Approach' (ICAEW TAX 18/95 20 June 1995 paragraph 31 and paragraph 5.52), and there are increasing reports of the DSS insisting upon 'employed earner' status where the Inland Revenue has been collecting tax under Schedule D.

Future changes

5.129 It has long been agreed that the construction industry rules are unsatisfactory, and the Inland Revenue has been particularly concerned about fraudulent use of tax certificates and related documentation. Accordingly, major reforms are to be introduced, most of which will take effect from 1 August 1998.

5.130 The most important changes are:

- The introduction of a 'turnover test' - sub-contractors will not qualify for tax certificates unless their turnover exceeds a specified level, still to be announced. The intention is to exclude most 'labour only' sub-contractors.

- Gross payments to holders of tax certificates will be made by electronic transfer to their bank accounts.

- The obligation to have complied with all the provisions of the Taxes Management Act 1970 will be applied more strictly. A sub-contractor with any tax arrears since 1995 may be denied a certificate.

- Deduction of tax at source from payments to sub-contractors without certificates will be at a rate slightly lower than the basic rate of income tax. This will be set to reflect the effective rate of income tax and class 4 national insurance contributions payable by most sub-contractors.

MIRAS

5.131 Mortgage interest relief at source (MIRAS) was introduced in 1982. The scheme enables a borrower to receive tax relief in respect of interest payable on a home loan, by entitling him to make a reduction from each interest payment due under his mortgage. Lenders in turn make periodic claims to the Inland Revenue, to recover the amounts deducted at source by borrowers.

5.132 The main legislative provisions are contained at ICTA 1988, ss369 to 379 and Income tax (Interest relief) Regulations 1982 SI 1982/1236 as amended. A useful 'plain English' explanation of the rules and administrative procedures is given in the Inland Revenue's *MIRAS (30) - MIRAS - Guidance Notes for Lenders*.

5.133 Broadly, a loan may qualify for inclusion within MIRAS if it was taken out for the *sole* purpose of acquiring the borrower's main residence. The interest is then described as *relevant loan interest* and this may be paid net of a tax deduction which is currently 15%.

5.134 A new loan may be included within MIRAS if the borrower completes a form *Miras 70*, on which he certifies that the loan meets the conditions for deduction of tax relief at source.[27]

5.135 Interest on the loan may cease to qualify subsequently for relief and the Inland Revenue has summarised the position to TaxAid as follows:

> 'Lenders must remove loans from MIRAS where the borrower gives notice that interest on a loan has ceased to be relevant loan interest or (much more rarely) that he/she is no longer a qualifying borrower. It is however unusual for a borrower to make a clear statement that interest has ceased to be relevant loan interest.

---

[27] It should be noted that a loan made before 6 April 1988 may qualify for inclusion within MIRAS if it was for the purpose of *improving* a main residence, or for certain other purposes.

Normally he/she simply advises the lender of a change in circumstances.

'The lender is not required to take the loan out of MIRAS unless the interest has clearly ceased to be relevant loan interest, but must provide information to the Inland Revenue if there is reason to believe that interest is no longer relevant loan interest. If appropriate, the Inland Revenue then instruct the lender to remove the loan from MIRAS.

'Where lenders fail to act on information from borrowers giving details of changes in circumstances any excessive relief given is recovered from the lender. Otherwise excessive relief is recovered from borrowers.'

5.136 The operation of MIRAS is supervised by the Financial Intermediaries and Claims Office of the Inland Revenue. The scheme is policed primarily by Inland Revenue audits of samples of lenders' records, although some errors come to light upon review of individual taxpayers' returns. If the Inland Revenue finds that a lender reclaimed excessive relief, it may recover the overclaim:

● directly from the lender, or

● by assessments on borrowers who have been given incorrect relief.

In either case, there are also provisions for interest to be charged, as well as penalties for incorrect statements.

5.137 It should be noted that staff in tax districts are generally not familiar with the details of MIRAS and complex questions are usually forwarded to the Inland Revenue's *MIRAS Central Unit* for a ruling.

Home loans outside MIRAS

5.138 If part of the capital sum outstanding on a mortgage has been advanced for other purposes than those described at paragraph 5.133, the loan is described as a *mixed loan* and cannot be included within MIRAS.

5.139 Also, a home loan may not be within MIRAS because:

● The mortgagee is not approved by the Inland Revenue as a 'qualifying lender'.

● The borrower has not applied for MIRAS relief. A qualifying lender should provide each borrower with a form *Miras 70,* but some borrowers fail to complete these forms.

5.140 Where a home loan is not within MIRAS, this does not preclude the granting of tax relief. If the advance was *wholly or partly* for the purpose of acquiring the borrower's main residence, the Inspector may grant appropriate relief by way of a reduction in liability under PAYE or on an assessment. However, these alternative methods rely upon reducing the amount of tax that would otherwise be due from the claimant and therefore are of no assistance to non-taxpayers.

Tax debt problems

5.141 The mechanics of MIRAS described above give rise to a number of tax debt problems which are discussed below.

Failures by borrowers

5.142 A borrower may fail to notify a lender of a change in circumstances requiring the loan to be removed from MIRAS, for example because the property has ceased to be his main residence. The Inland Revenue may recover any tax relief given subsequently under MIRAS by an assessment on the borrower, often called a *clawback assessment* (ICTA 1988, ss374A(3), 375(1) and 375(3); see also paragraph 5.136). In practice, the Inland Revenue does not always exercise its powers to add interest and penalties.

5.143 As such errors are often discovered some years after the event, the tax assessed for several years may be substantial. Often there is little that can be done by the taxpayer, apart from negotiating time to settle the liability. However, consideration should be given to whether the interest might have qualified for relief in some other way. For example:

- If the loan should have been removed from MIRAS because it had become a mixed loan, relief may be due in respect of the qualifying element of the loan by way of a reduction in the taxpayer's income tax liabilities. This may be set against any liability charged by the clawback assessments.

- It is often the case that the loan should have been removed from MIRAS because the borrower had moved from the property in order to rent it out. Although disqualified from MIRAS, the interest may attract relief in computing the tax due on the rental income received. The provisions are complex, but consideration should be given to *Extra-statutory Concession A27* - which extends MIRAS to cover properties temporarily not in use as the borrower's main residence - and ICTA 1975, s375A, which grants an irrevocable option for the loan interest to be given as a deduction from the rental income instead.[28]

Failures by lenders

5.144 Many problems arise because of failure by lenders to operate MIRAS properly, or to grant practical assistance to borrowers.

---

[28] The latter provision applies with effect from 1995/96; different rules applied in earlier years.

5.145 A common problem relates to 'mixed loans'. In *R v Inspector of Taxes and another (ex p. Kelly)* CA [1991] STC 566 the taxpayer had remortgaged his home, taking out a larger loan and applying the excess to meet living expenses. The Court of Appeal conceded reluctantly that the Inland Revenue was correct in requiring the mortgage to be removed from MIRAS, because it was a mixed loan. However, the Court observed that the problem could have been avoided if the lender had made the additional advance by way of a separate loan. It is a common problem that lenders do not give consideration to splitting loans, merely to keep borrowers within MIRAS.

5.146 Other difficulties arise through bureaucratic failure on the part of lenders to respond to notifications received from borrowers of changes in their circumstances which might require that their loans be removed from MIRAS. Although ICTA 1988, s375(1) states that a borrower should stop making deductions at source as soon as he is aware that his loan has ceased to qualify, most borrowers will wait to be notified of the increased instalment due. If the lender continues to demand net payments, most borrowers will simply comply. The Adjudicator has reported on a complaint by a taxpayer who received a clawback assessment in such circumstances, even though he had notified both his tax district and his lender of his change in circumstances. The Adjudicator ruled that the Inland Revenue was not responsible for the failure and the lender agreed concessionally to meet one-half of the tax charged. It will be noted that this report by the Adjudicator suggests that the Inland Revenue did not follow its own practice as stated in paragraph 5.135.[29]

5.147 Where a lender has been subject to an Inland Revenue audit and has refunded excessive relief claimed in error in respect of net interest received from borrowers, the settlement may include a provision that the Inland Revenue will not make clawback assessments on any borrowers in respect of the same period. This is appropriate, since the settlement is usually based upon an extrapolation of errors found within a sample. However, the terms of such a settlement are not publicised and clawback assessments have sometimes been made inadvertently in breach of such a settlement. A borrower should therefore check the position with his lender, or MIRAS Central Unit, before agreeing to settle tax charged by a clawback assessment.

Retrospective relief

5.148 Where a loan has qualified for inclusion within MIRAS, but the necessary form *Miras 70* was not completed at the outset, the borrower

---

[29] *The Adjudicator's Office Annual Report 1995* p23. It is likely that the tax district did not appreciate that the changed circumstances would affect the taxpayer's entitlement to MIRAS relief, as complex issues are handled exclusively by MIRAS Central Unit (see paragraph 5.137).

may have been paying interest gross. In many cases this creates little difficulty, since he may claim relief for the interest by way of a reduction in his tax liabilities, which will normally lead to a tax refund (see paragraph 4.71 *et seq*).

5.149 However, problems occur if the borrower has not been liable for sufficient tax during the relevant period. In such cases he should claim the benefit of a little-known procedure - called *retrospective MIRAS* - whereby MIRAS Central Unit may repay relief that could have been given at source had the loan been included within MIRAS (ICTA 1988, s375(8) and SI 1982/1236 Reg 8A). Before making such refunds, MIRAS Central Unit will check carefully to ensure that the loan could properly have been within MIRAS. In particular, it will refuse a claim in respect of a 'mixed' loan, since it could never have qualified for inclusion within MIRAS. Such claims are normally made through the taxpayer's own tax district, which should be asked to refer the matter to MIRAS Central Unit.

Capitalisation of arrears

5.150 Sometimes a lender will add arrears of interest to the capital outstanding on a mortgage. While this may assist a borrower with cash-flow difficulties, it may also result in the loan becoming 'mixed' and lead to its exclusion from MIRAS. If the borrower is a non-taxpayer, this will add a serious additional burden, as no other form of relief is available.

5.151 By concession, the Inland Revenue allows such loans to remain in MIRAS, provided the arrears capitalised are less than the greater of:

- one year's interest on the loan, and

- £1,000 (*MIRAS (30) MIRAS - Guidance Notes for Lenders* paragraph 10.4).

5.152 Even if this limit is exceeded, the Inland Revenue states:

'the loan may remain in MIRAS provided:

- some arrangement has been made between the lender and the borrower for the borrower to reduce the arrears; or

- the arrears are accruing because, due to hardship, a borrower has reached an agreement with the lender to reduce temporarily his monthly payments.

Lenders will wish to explain this to borrowers who fall into arrears'.[30]

5.153 Despite the Inland Revenue's generous attitude, most lenders operate a far more restrictive policy in such cases. Typically, loans are

---

[30] *MIRAS (30) MIRAS - Guidance Notes for Lenders* paragraph 10.5

removed from MIRAS automatically, if arrears exceed £1,000 on the annual review date.

5.154 TaxAid asked the Inland Revenue for its observations on this subject and the following reply has been received which may be of practical assistance:

> 'Where interest is 'capitalised' and loans become of mixed purpose the interest ceases to be relevant loan interest. In these circumstances the lender may not remove a loan from MIRAS (because the borrower has not given notice that interest has ceased to be relevant loan interest) but must inform the Inland Revenue that there is reason to believe that interest is no longer relevant loan interest. If appropriate the Inland Revenue then instruct the lender to remove the loan from MIRAS.

> 'Where the loan falls within the scope of paragraphs 10.4 and 10.5 of the *Guidance Notes for Lenders* the lender need not inform the Inland Revenue and the Inland Revenue would not instruct the lender to remove the loan from MIRAS.'

5.155 The above statement makes it clear that the concessions set out in paragraphs 5.151 and 5.152 are mandatory for lenders, who *must* apply them. However in practice many loans are in fact removed from MIRAS against the wishes of borrowers, even though the capitalised arrears are within the limits allowed, in direct contravention of Inland Revenue policy.

International issues

5.156 There are numerous provisions in UK tax legislation and practice aimed specifically at transactions with an international aspect, or at individuals who have links with more than one country. It is beyond the scope of this handbook to address the issues beyond raising a few points relating to the collection of liabilities.

Territorial limitations

5.157 As a general rule, the courts of one country will not assist in the enforcement of revenue debts due to another country (*re Delhi Electric Supply & Traction Co Ltd, Government of India v Taylor* HL [1955] 1 All ER 292).

5.158 There do appear to be certain exceptions to this general principle:

- English and foreign courts may grant assistance to trustees in bankruptcy seeking recovery of assets abroad, which might be used to settle tax claims.

- English courts may permit trustees to transfer assets abroad to meet a tax claim, if the trustees would otherwise be liable personally for the debt.[31]

5.159 In light of the general rule, usually the Inland Revenue does not seek to enforce tax debts against individuals currently resident outside the UK (except where there are valuable assets in the UK which might be made the subject of a charging order or a Mareva injunction). Instead it tends to rely upon provisions in the taxes legislation giving it power to assess a non-resident in the name of a branch or agent in the UK, whether or not that person was in receipt of the profits concerned. Assessment and enforcement is in like manner and in the same amount as the non-resident might be charged if he were resident in the UK (TMA 1970, s78).

5.160 An assessment may nevertheless be made on a non-resident, upon the basis that he may wish to comply voluntarily so as to prevent any difficulties upon returning to the UK. Such an assessment is not invalidated by the fact that the Inland Revenue also has the power to assess a branch or agent (*Tischler v Apthorpe* QB [1885] 2 TC 89).

5.161 Where a taxpayer who is subject to a tax investigation has left the UK permanently, and has taken all his assets with him, the Inland Revenue's policy is that an Inspector should not accept a 'substandard' offer in full settlement - thereby giving the taxpayer the opportunity to return to the UK with impunity - simply because of the difficulties of enforcing payment of the debt.[32] In practice, however, some Inspectors take a more pragmatic view.

Non-resident employers

5.162 A separate enforcement difficulty arises in respect of employees working in the UK, where there is no 'employer' whom the Inland Revenue may require to operate PAYE. Broadly, this applies in the case of:

- A person employed by a foreign embassy or consulate, or international body, whose employer declines to operate PAYE on the grounds of 'immunity'.

- A person working for a foreign employer which does not have a place of business in the UK.[33]

---

[31] For an interesting discussion of this area of the law, see *The Transnational Enforcement of Tax Liabilities* by Philip Baker, *British Tax Review* October 1993 Volume 93 Issue 5 p314.

[32] *Inland Revenue Investigations Handbook* paragraph 6018

[33] A consideration of the *extent* to which such individuals are liable to UK income tax and national insurance contributions is beyond the scope of this handbook.

5.163 In such cases, the Inland Revenue may raise the income tax by 'direct collection' - a Schedule E assessment is issued and payment is required in four equal instalments, while national insurance contributions should be paid directly in accordance with instructions obtainable from the Contributions Agency (Income Tax (Employments) Regulations 1993, Paragraphs 99 to 105 and *CA 65 (NP 16) National insurance contributions for people working for embassies, consulates and overseas employers).*[34]

Unremittable income and gains

5.164 Payment of tax in respect of overseas income or gains may be deferred to the extent that the taxpayer is prevented from transferring those profits to the UK, by reasons of:

- exchange control restrictions,

- executive action of the foreign government, or

- the impossibility of obtaining foreign currency in the territory.

If the taxpayer claims that such profits are unremittable, despite reasonable endeavours on his part, the relevant amounts should be omitted from assessments and then assessed at such time as the funds become remittable. There are special provisions for non-domiciled taxpayers assessable on the remittance basis (ICTA 1970, ss584 and 585 and TCGA 1992, s279).

5.165 Interest under TMA 1970, s86 is waived from the date that the Inland Revenue is advised that funds cannot be remitted, and if notice is given within three months of the date the tax was due and payable, interest is waived in full. Interest starts accruing again if the tax is not settled within three months of a demand for payment made after the tax has become remittable (TMA 1970, s92).

Tenants of non-resident landlords

5.166 Income arising from property in this country is chargeable to income tax, regardless of the landlord's place of residence, with special provisions enabling tax to be recovered from a UK resident tenant or agent if the landlord's *usual place of abode is outside the UK.* The rules changed significantly with effect from 6 April 1996, and each regime is considered separately.

Payments due up to 5 April 1996

5.167 Two separate sets of rules applied, according to the way in which payments were made:

---

[34] From 1996/97, such individuals will pay tax at six-monthly intervals under the normal provisions of self-assessment, see paragraph 12.19 *et seq.*

- A tenant making payments directly to his landlord, including payments into a UK account in the landlord's name, was required to deduct income tax at the basic rate from each payment and remit this to the Inland Revenue (ICTA 1988, s43). Insofar as such deductions exceeded the landlord's true liability, the sums deducted could be reclaimed by the landlord.

- In any other case, assessments would be made on a UK agent under the provisions discussed in paragraph 5.159. Usually this would be the person to whom the payment was made initially, which could be a commercial agent or a friend or relative of the landlord.

5.168 Tax debts have often arisen in the former situation through tenants' ignorance of the obligation to deduct tax at source. Gross payments might have been made for some years before the failure was discovered, and the Inland Revenue would then exercise its power to assess the tenant for sums which were never withheld. Indeed, many individuals remain exposed to such assessments because payments erroneously made gross, during the period prior to 5 April 1996, have yet to be reported or discovered.

5.169 Such difficulties may be resolved easily with the landlord's co-operation. He may agree, for example:

- to return the sums which should have been deducted at source, or

- to submit tax returns which demonstrate that ultimately there would not have been any liability because of deductions available against the rental income, which should enable the Inspector to withdraw the assessment on the tenant.

5.170 In other cases, a tenant may avoid liability by demonstrating either:

- that the landlord's usual place of abode was not outside the United Kingdom, or

- that he had no reason to suspect that it was outside the United Kingdom. This approach is hindered by the Inland Revenue's view that the onus has always been on the tenant to check the position, and if in doubt to clarify it with an Inspector (*IR 27 Notes on the taxation of real property* paragraph 60).[35]

It should be noted that the legislation did not define 'usual place of abode'.

5.171 If none of the above options is available, the tenant will remain liable personally and he cannot recoup the liability by making deductions in excess of the basic rate from future payments (*Tenbry Investments Ltd*

---

[35] This publication was withdrawn in 1991.

v Peugeot Talbot Motor Co Ltd Ch D [1992] STC 791). However, Collectors tend to be sympathetic towards individuals in this situation and will often accept proposals to settle the debt over a number of years.

Payments due after 5 April 1996

5.172 The regime described above was unsatisfactory and was enforced inconsistently. It has now been replaced by a different code introduced to coincide with self-assessment (TMA 1970, s42A and Taxation of Income from Land (Non-residents) Regulations 1995 SI 1995/2902).[36]

5.173 Under the new rules - unless there is a UK 'agent' (see paragraph 5.177) - a tenant must normally deduct income tax at the basic rate from payments to a non-resident landlord (see paragraph 5.178 for definition of 'non-resident'). The sums deducted must be paid to the Inland Revenue within 30 days of the end of each calendar quarter and the landlord may set such deductions against his liability for the corresponding tax year under the normal rules of self-assessment.

5.174 While tax debts may arise in similar ways as before, there are certain provisions which should ameliorate the situation.

5.175 Firstly, a landlord may obtain approval from the Inland Revenue to be paid gross, thereby relieving his tenant of any obligation to account for tax. The landlord must satisfy the Inland Revenue that:

• he has complied with all his obligations under Taxes Management Act 1970 prior to the date of application; *or*

• he has not had any such obligations prior to the date of application; *or*

• he does not expect to be liable to UK tax for the year for which the application is made,

and he must undertake to comply with all his UK tax obligations in future. It will be noted that a landlord should not be denied approval solely because he has tax debts; he may still qualify for approval on the third ground given above, despite a published Inland Revenue statement that he would first need to bring his affairs up to date (SI 1995/2902 Reg 17 and *IR 140 Non-resident landlords, their agents and tenants* p15).

5.176 In addition, two new protections are given to tenants:

• A tenant paying less than £100 per week is not liable to make deductions unless and until he is instructed expressly to do so by the Inland Revenue (SI 1995/2902 Reg 3(5)).

---

[36] The rules are explained in *Tax Bulletin* December 1995 pp261-263.

- A tenant is entitled to be indemnified by his landlord, and may retain sums out of payments due to the landlord, in respect of *past* liabilities under the new provisions. This reverses the situation following the decision in *Tenbry Investments Ltd v Peugeot Talbot Motor Co Ltd* discussed in paragraph 5.171 (ICTA 1970, s42A(3)).

5.177 For the purposes of these new provisions, an *agent* is defined as a person 'who acts on behalf of the non-resident in connection with the management or administration' of the property, although the Inland Revenue has stated that it will not be taken to include:

- An accountant who does no more than prepare accounts and tax computations.

- A solicitor who provides only legal advice or legal services, such as taking proceedings to recover rent arrears.

- A bank or building society into which rental income is paid and withdrawals for expenses made (TMA 1970, s42A(2)(b)).[37]

5.178 Unfortunately the authorities did not take the opportunity of the new legislation to define a *non-resident*, beyond being 'any person who has his usual place of abode outside the United Kingdom' and the Inland Revenue says only that it will not apply to a person living abroad temporarily for 'say, six months' (SI 1995/2902 Reg 2 and *IR 140 Non-resident landlords, their agents and tenants* p3).

Statutory reliefs for 'hardship'

5.179 The taxes legislation contains a handful of provisions which grant a taxpayer extra time to settle a liability, where there is express reference to the alleviation of *hardship*.

Unpaid rental income

5.180 Under the rules for taxing income from property applicable up to 1994/95, a taxpayer was assessable on the rental income *due* in each year of assessment, regardless of whether it was actually received. In the event of non-payment, a claim may be made for the relevant assessment to be adjusted as if the taxpayer was not entitled to the rental income concerned. Such claims must be made within the normal six-year time limit.

5.181 This relief is conditional upon the taxpayer being able to demonstrate either:

- that the non-receipt was attributable to a default by the person liable to pay him the income and that he has taken any reasonable steps available to him to enforce payment, or

---

[37] See also *Tax Bulletin* December 1995 pp261-263. The article describes the detailed regime for agents, which is beyond the scope of this handbook.

- that he waived payment for no consideration in order to avoid hardship on the part of the person from whom payment was due (ICTA 1988, s41(1)).

5.182 Relief is subject to the condition that the taxpayer should notify the Inspector of any subsequent recovery, within six months, whereupon appropriate readjustments of the liability will be made (ICTA 1988, s41(2)).

5.183 The above provisions became obsolete for liabilities from 1995/96, following the introduction of a new basis for assessing rental income by FA 1995, s39. Property income is now computed as if it arose from a 'Schedule A business', permitting relief to be claimed for non-payment of rent in the same way as for a bad debt of a trade.

Premiums receivable under a lease

5.184 A premium, or other amount assessable on the grant of a lease, is taxable normally as if due in one sum at the time of the grant (ICTA 1988, s34).[38]

5.185 Where the amount so assessable is due to be received by instalments, there is provision for the Inland Revenue to allow the tax to be spread over a period of up to eight years, or the period to be covered by the instalments if shorter. The taxpayer needs to satisfy the Inland Revenue that he would otherwise suffer undue hardship, and a Government undertaking has been given to the following effect:

> 'In considering whether undue hardship would arise, the Revenue would look primarily to the question whether the (taxpayer) could reasonably be expected to pay the tax on the full amount immediately, in the light of the resources made available by the particular transaction involved. Regard would not normally be paid to the other resources of the taxpayer if it could be shown that the instalment arrangement was ... a normal commercial arrangement ...'[39]

5.186 Where an amount due by way of a premium is unpaid, similar relief is given as for unpaid rents as described in paragraph 5.180 above.

Capital gains tax

5.187 Where part or all of the consideration receivable on the disposal of an asset is payable over a period exceeding 18 months, and the taxpayer

---

[38] The charge is, however, subject to special rules for computing the *amount* of tax assessable.

[39] ICTA 1988, s34(8) and *Hansard* 22 June 1972. The full statement is reproduced in *Inland Revenue Assessment Procedures Manual* paragraph 1532.

demonstrates that he would otherwise suffer undue hardship, the Inland Revenue may allow for payment of tax to be deferred in the same way as described for premiums on leases above. The Inland Revenue should set the level of tax instalments so as to collect no more than 50% of each instalment of the disposal consideration, as it becomes payable. Interest is chargeable under TMA 1970, s86, in respect of the payment so delayed (TCGA 1992, s280 and *Inland Revenue Capital Gains Manual* paragraph 14912).

Chapter 6

Negotiating with the Collector

This chapter explores an area of tax debt that has traditionally been shrouded in mystery - how Collectors negotiate with taxpayers who are unable to meet their liabilities on time. Initially, it examines:

From paragraph

■   The purpose of negotiation   *6.8*
■   Inland Revenue policy and practice   *6.14*

It then goes on to discuss the key points to consider before entering negotiations:

■   The roles of the different collection offices   *6.47*
■   The taxpayer's circumstances   *6.81*
■   The size, history and type of tax debt   *6.97*
■   Waiver and remission   *6.104*
■   Time to pay   *6.109*
■   The enforceability of negotiated arrangements   *6.149*

Introduction

6.1   Despite its long history of producing free leaflets on most aspects of taxation, the Inland Revenue had not until very recently published any significant guidance on how it treats taxpayers who have difficulty in meeting their liabilities on time.

6.2   To some extent, such reticence has been understandable. If Collectors were to recover tax debts as effectively as possible, they could not enter negotiations with their cards face-up on the table. Also, a comprehensive set of published guidelines on the acceptance of late payments might minimise the scope for discretion to be exercised in particular cases, and might also persuade more compliant taxpayers that prompt payment was unnecessary.

6.3   Nevertheless, the absence of any publicity led to unfairness. Unrepresented taxpayers have had no idea of the factors taken into account in considering requests for time to pay, which meant that they might not receive the same latitude as individuals having tax advisers with some experience of negotiations with Collectors. Also, the knowledge of tax advisers has varied considerably, usually in proportion to the indebtedness of their client base.

6.4   The lack of information and the resulting unfairness was clearly not in keeping with the promises in the Taxpayer's Charter, and in November 1994 the Inland Revenue published two Codes of Practice:

- *Code of Practice 6 Collection of tax*

- *Code of Practice 7 Collection of amounts due from employers, and contractors in the construction industry*

and four leaflets:

- *Collection 1 Distraint*

- *Collection 2 Magistrates' Court Proceedings*

- *Collection 3 County Court Proceedings*

- *Collection 4 Bankruptcy and winding up*

6.5   The Codes of Practice are fairly informative and the first Code, in particular, is referred to throughout the remainder of this handbook. The leaflets explain some of the potential consequences of each enforcement measure, and the importance of contacting the Collector urgently with a view to arranging to settle the debt.

6.6   Further guidance has emerged with the publication of the Inland Revenue's internal guidance manuals (see paragraph 3.90 *et seq*). They contain useful source material for those engaging in negotiations with Collectors, although there is little guidance on more sensitive subjects, such as the remission of tax liabilities. This chapter refers to four of the manuals, by use of the prefixes below:

AT   -   *Assessed Taxes Manual*

E   -   *Enforcement Manual*

PCM   -   *Personal Contact Manual*

ROM   -   *Regional Executive Office Manual*

e.g. ROM 6.201 refers to paragraph 6.201 of the *Regional Executive Office Manual*.

6.7   This chapter considers the published guidance in the light of TaxAid's own experience of advising on tax debts and negotiating with Collectors in many hundreds of cases over the last four years.

The purpose of negotiation

6.8   The purpose of negotiating with a Collector is to avoid or delay formal action for recovery of a tax debt (by one or more of the enforcement procedures discussed in the next five chapters).

6.9   So before launching into negotiations, it is advisable to consider:

- whether the Collector is likely to take enforcement proceedings in the event of non-compliance, and

- in those cases where there is a real threat of enforcement proceedings, what the consequences of such proceedings would be.

6.10   In certain limited circumstances the risk of enforcement action is quite low, which assists the taxpayer in negotiations. For example:

- Where the debt is very small. If the taxpayer's indebtedness to the Inland Revenue is below £100 in total, proceedings will not be taken (E1.303).

- If the Collector is made aware that the taxpayer is frail, for example very elderly or suffering long-term ill-health, or that recovery proceedings may give rise to adverse publicity, the risk of recovery action is relatively low (see paragraph 6.81 *et seq*).

6.11   In the vast majority of cases a Collector will fully intend to pass the matter on for enforcement action, in the event that a suitable arrangement is not agreed. However, this is not always disadvantageous to the taxpayer. In particular:

- Threats of distraint may be discounted if the taxpayer has no assets of any significant value (see paragraph 8.21).[1]

- County Court proceedings offer many tax debtors the only realistic way of arranging manageable instalments and freezing interest on the debt. Indeed, Collectors are warned not to commence such proceedings solely to help the taxpayer by stopping interest (see paragraph 10.52).

- Bankruptcy may offer a welcome relief from the pressures of creditors, and may hardly impact on the life of an individual who has no significant assets (see paragraph 11.20).

In such circumstances there may be no advantage in trying to dissuade a Collector from taking enforcement action.

6.12   However in most cases a tax debtor will benefit from seeking an agreement with the Collector, whether this be a short-term deferral of payment, a longer-term arrangement for time to pay, or complete remission of the liability and the detailed considerations are discussed below.

---

[1]   Although, even if the taxpayer has explained that he has no valuable assets, a distraint *visit* may be made nevertheless to check the sitaution.

6.13 It should be noted that negotiations are possible even after enforcement proceedings have commenced - for example, the Inland Revenue may accept an 'improved' offer to clear a debt by instalments literally in the waiting room of the Bankruptcy Court.

Inland Revenue policy and practice

General principles

6.14 The *Code of Practice 6 Collection of tax* sets out the following general principles:

> 'We set high standards for the way in which we carry out our collection work. Our aim is to collect only the right amount of tax at the right time, along with any interest which may be due if you have paid your tax late.
>
> 'Most people pay their tax at the right time and it would be unfair to them if we did not pursue those who do not pay. If people have genuine difficulties in meeting their payments, and tell us about them, we will do what we can to help. If we are not told about your difficulties, all we can do is resort to the legal methods open to us to enforce payment of the debt...
>
> 'If you know that you will have difficulty paying your tax when it is due you should tell us as soon as possible. The more you keep us informed, the more we are likely to be able to help.'

The duty of fairness

6.15 The Code refers to two kinds of fairness:

- The Collector's duty to the tax debtor
- The Collector's duty to taxpayers as a whole

Fairness to the tax debtor

6.16 Collectors should treat taxpayers with equal fairness, as promised by the Taxpayer's Charter (which is reproduced in the Code of Practice), and this should theoretically guarantee a consistency of approach to tax debtors (see paragraph 3.96).

6.17 Where it is felt that a Collector has rejected unfairly proposals from a taxpayer, this may justify a complaint under the Taxpayer's Charter and 14% of complaints received by the Adjudicator in 1993/94 related to the actions of Collectors.[2]

---

[2] Comparable statistics were not given for 1994/95. Some case studies are provided in paragraphs 3.130, 3.134 and 3.135, although it will be noted that two of the three complaints failed.

6.18   However, a recurring difficulty in tax debt negotiations is that the Collector is required to consider a range of information, most of which is specific to the particular taxpayer. A decision which appears unfair will be justified usually by reference to the special circumstances of the case. Accordingly, it is difficult to succeed with a complaint except in cases of gross unfairness or maladministration.

Fairness to the body of taxpayers

6.19   The statement reproduced in paragraph 6.14 refers to the Collector's duty to other taxpayers, and it is absolutely proper that he should not allow any individual simply to avoid his liability. It is therefore quite common for a proposal to a Collector to be turned down on the basis that *'it would be unfair to the general body of taxpayers'*.

6.20   Unfortunately, the latter phrase is often trotted out in cases where the disadvantage to other taxpayers is far from apparent. Indeed, quite often it is used as 'grounds' for rejecting proposals which offer the Inland Revenue the greatest possible yield at the lowest possible cost, and where no public policy issues appear to be involved.

6.21   If it is considered that the Collector is refusing to provide a sensible reason for rejecting a reasonable proposal, the taxpayer is perfectly entitled to demand a proper explanation. This should at least ensure that the Collector gives due regard to the proposal, even if it is then rejected on the grounds that its acceptance would fall outside Inland Revenue policy.

The Inland Revenue as a creditor

6.22   In many respects negotiations with Collectors are quite similar to those with other creditors. The debtor is seeking to make an offer that is at least as attractive to the creditor as any alternative way forward, and the process is governed largely by common sense.

6.23   However, several aspects of Inland Revenue collection policy are unusual and differ from practices adopted by other creditors. Sometimes this will give rise to a decision that appears perverse on the facts of a particular case, even though it may be justifiable in a broader context.

Issues of public policy

6.24   Decisions by Collectors are not necessarily taken solely by reference to the maximum yield achievable at the lowest cost in the particular case. In enforcing tax debts, the Inland Revenue is also concerned with ensuring better compliance by the same taxpayer in future, and the wider deterrent effect of treating individual defaulters firmly.

6.25   This may explain the following statement on the subject of bankruptcy:

'In some cases we may decide, in the light of (the circumstances of the case), that we need to start bankruptcy ... proceedings even though there may appear to be little prospect of recovering the debt owed at the time.'[3]

6.26   On the other hand, Collectors are instructed to take account of the wider consequences of refusing a taxpayer's proposal, such as the risk of putting a taxpayer out of business or causing his employees to become redundant (PCM 4.8).

6.27   The Inland Revenue is sensitive about attracting adverse publicity. The managers of local collection offices are told to be alert to cases 'which may attract the attention of the media' and to seek guidance from the Controller's office (ROM 6.201). This is not to suggest that a threat of 'going to the papers' will necessarily cause the Controller to back down - he may welcome the opportunity to appear tough in the particular case.

Negotiations can be quite 'personal'

6.28   Whereas a commercial creditor will usually be seeking a quick financial settlement, often with little regard to the past conduct or present circumstances of the debtor, Collectors pay some attention to such issues.

6.29   This can be of great assistance to the individual. The Collector's manuals are scattered with requirements to be particularly sympathetic to taxpayers who are elderly, fragile or otherwise disadvantaged. Such circumstances should always be drawn to the Collector's attention, since he may not be aware of them, although this will not necessarily guarantee preferential treatment.

6.30   It should be emphasised that Collectors appreciate politeness and a taxpayer who conducts himself sensitively throughout negotiations is likely to receive a sympathetic hearing.

6.31   On the other hand, Collectors' discretion to consider 'personal' issues can also count against a taxpayer. Tax debtors sometimes feel that Collectors appear set against them on the grounds of previous heated disputes with colleagues, which may have occurred years earlier but are recorded on their files.

6.32   There is also an unfortunate tendency of a minority of Collection staff to make decisions that are based upon unchecked adverse inferences that they have drawn about a taxpayer. A typical example is the assumption that the inability of a self-employed taxpayer to meet his Schedule D liabilities must *necessarily* be due to his failure to set aside money for tax.

---

[3] *Code of Practice 6 Collection of tax* p8

6.33   The possibility of misunderstandings reinforces the need to obtain a clear explanation when proposals are rejected by a Collector.

Time to pay

6.34   The subject of allowing time to pay is discussed in detail at paragraph 6.109 *et seq*. This makes it clear that a primary consideration by any Collector is the time the taxpayer will take to clear the debt, which will rarely be allowed to extend beyond a year or two.

6.35   This has certain implications, in particular:

- It is sometimes advantageous to allow County Court proceedings to be taken, because the Court may allow much smaller instalments than would be acceptable to a Collector (see paragraphs 6.124 *et seq* and 10.122 *et seq)*.

- A Collector may be prepared to remit a tax debt (see paragraph 6.105 *et seq)* rather than accepting small instalments over a period of years, even if the instalments on offer might be acceptable to a commercial creditor.

Part payments in full settlement

6.36   As a general rule, a Collector will not accept part payment in full settlement of a tax debt (sometimes referred to as *compounding* the debt) even if the amount offered is substantial and far greater than the sum likely to be realised by formal recovery action.

6.37   However, it should be noted that an offer of a substantial lump sum may, in some cases, facilitate an agreement for the balance of a tax debt to be paid by instalments which would otherwise be unacceptable.

Freezing of interest

6.38   As a general rule, Collectors will not agree to freeze interest, despite the positive influence that this may have in motivating the taxpayer to clear the debt.

6.39   This policy can obstruct negotiations even where the interest involved would actually be quite small, given that the rate charged is relatively modest and it is not compounded (see paragraph 2.65 *et seq)*. Unrepresented taxpayers rarely pause during negotiations to quantify the amount of interest that will accrue under a proposed arrangement, while Collectors are unlikely to point out that it will not reach the levels charged by commercial creditors.

Writing off a tax debt

6.40   While Collectors may sometimes agree to *remit* tax liabilities (see paragraph 6.105 *et seq)* the amount is never formally written off and there is no limitation period for reinstating proceedings for recovery (see paragraph 2.98 *et seq)*. At present, relatively few remitted debts are 'revived' because there are no formal procedures for periodic review, but this may change with the introduction of *taxpayer statements* under self-assessment (see paragraph 12.82).

6.41 A taxpayer who has been granted remission may be inhibited from starting a new business, for fear that future profits will be demanded by the Inland Revenue to settle back taxes. The only way of clearing a tax debt completely is through the process of bankruptcy, but this route may be equally unattractive given the likely difficulties in obtaining credit for some eight years after bankruptcy (see paragraph 7.40).

Points to consider before entering negotiations

6.42 The remainder of this chapter is devoted to the detailed issues that may influence the progress of tax debt negotiations.

6.43 It is first necessary to understand the structure of the Inland Revenue's collection function and the role of Collectors at each stage, as well as differences between individual Collectors and collection offices. A taxpayer is more likely to achieve a satisfactory outcome if he understands the factors influencing the person with whom he is negotiating.

6.44 Consideration should then be given to the taxpayer's own circumstances which may have a significant bearing on the arrangement that might be achieved in any particular case. The taxpayer should give careful attention to ensuring that the Collector is aware of all factors which may attract sympathy, with explanations given (or prepared) for those factors which might count against him.

6.45 The Inland Revenue's policy on remission and time to pay should also be understood clearly, so that proposals may be designed as far as possible to fall within the scope of the Collector's authority. Different considerations apply at different stages of the collection process. Sensitive conduct during the course of negotiations is essential, and consideration should also be given as to how any proposed payments will be made or secured.

6.46 The chapter concludes with a brief examination of the enforceability of arrangements made between a taxpayer and a Collector.

The roles of the different collection offices

6.47 Tax debts normally pass through a hierarchy of collection offices.[4]

---

[4] It may be helpful to refer to the Inland Revenue structure explained at paragraph 2.4 *et seq.*

The Accounts Offices

6.48   The Accounts Offices in Shipley or Cumbernauld are responsible for issuing *routine reminders* where payment has not been made by the date a liability is due and payable. These are computerised forms - usually red - which state the sum(s) due and warn of enforcement action in the event of non-payment within seven days. Typically the first reminder will be issued within a week or two after the due date, with a second more sternly worded form a few weeks later.

6.49   The matter may be concluded by the taxpayer settling the liability, or a written application for time to pay which falls within the limited authority of the Accounts Offices (see paragraph 6.140 *et seq)*.

6.50   If no response is received and the taxpayer lives within the London region, the case may be referred to the *London Telephone Unit* (LTU) at Shipley. The LTU tries to establish contact with the taxpayer by telephone 'with a view to obtaining payment or identifying and resolving any areas of dispute or difficulty' (AT 7.105). The objective is to resolve the case without reference to the local collection office, and the LTU may consider granting time to pay within the limits discussed at paragraph 6.140 *et seq*. The LTU does not deal with Schedule E liabilities or 'permanent local action cases' (see paragraph 6.55).

6.51   If the matter is not satisfactorily concluded by the Accounts Office, and enforcement action or personal contact is considered necessary, the case will be referred to the taxpayer's local collection office (AT 7.105). This implies that in some cases no referral is made, for example where the debt is trivial and falls within (unpublished) limits. The Accounts Offices never institute enforcement proceedings.

6.52   It should be observed that the Collector responsible for a particular tax debt within an Accounts Office is normally contactable easily, using the telephone number and reference shown on the reminder received. If there is any dispute about the sum demanded, a telephone request for demands to be suspended pending further enquiry will normally be agreed to.

The local collection offices

6.53   The bulk of recovery work is handled by local collection offices across the UK, which handle tax debts due from taxpayers resident or carrying on business within their areas. Each office is headed by a Collector in Charge.[5]

---

[5]   The work of local collection offices is now being merged within the new-style Taxpayer Service Offices (TSOs) headed by Officers in Charge, although the role of the local Collector has not yet changed and the term *local collection office* is used to include those cases where work is done from a new-style TSO. See paragraph 2.9.

6.54   The role of each local collection office is to pursue quick recovery of tax debts by negotiation under the threat of enforcement by way of distraint, summary proceedings or action through the County Courts. They also take further action where judgment debts are unpaid (see Chapters 8, 9 and 10).

6.55   Debts are notified to the local collection offices by the Accounts Offices, where they have failed to secure payment, or when agreed instalment arrangements have broken down. Certain liabilities are referred automatically to local collection offices without any prior reminders by the Accounts Offices, in particular:

- where the debt is £100,000 or more (AT 1.303), and

- *permanent local action* cases, which are potentially sensitive or more complex cases including tax debts of insolvent taxpayers and deceased estates (AT 6.501).

Priorities

6.56   Tax debts are normally allocated to local collection office staff according to the sums involved. Where the amount is £4,500 or more it is given priority treatment and should be allocated as follows:

- £20,000 or more: it requires the attention of the Collection Manager.

- £10,000-£19,999: it should be allocated to a Revenue Executive.

- £4,500-£9,999, is should be allocated to a Revenue Officer (AT 6.201).

These bands should be borne in mind in the course of negotiations.

6.57   If the debt falls within or below the lowest band, the taxpayer is likely to be negotiating with a relatively junior Collector (perhaps at the grade of 'Revenue Officer') who may lack experience or knowledge of the relevant procedures, and have limited powers of discretion. If it is considered that the taxpayer's circumstances or proposals have not received appropriate consideration, the Collector may be asked to refer the matter to a more senior officer. Unfortunately, this will often yield the response that the matter has already been considered by his manager, in which case a reference to an even more senior officer may be requested.

6.58   On the other hand, if the debt is in the top band, it is likely to have been considered by a senior Collector, whose decision is less likely to be varied upon internal review. In cases of unfairness, a complaint under the Taxpayer's Charter may be considered appropriate, subject to the difficulty mentioned in paragraph 6.18.

6.59 It should also be noted that debts below £4,500 are not given priority treatment (AT 7.203). In practice this can mean that taxpayers with smaller debts are not contacted until some months after details have been received by the local collection office, which may even give the erroneous impression that the matter has been dropped. It also causes problems where the taxpayer wants to organise a payment arrangement promptly, but does not know whom to approach until initial contact is made by the local collection office.

Handling of cases

6.60 The Collector's task is to secure payment, or institute acceptable arrangements for time to pay, as quickly and efficiently as possible. Local collection offices also have powers to remit liabilities (see paragraph 6.105 *et seq)*.

6.61 Initial contact is normally made with the taxpayer by a letter from the Collector, which will set out the tax due, sometimes with details of accrued interest, requiring payment within a short period (typically seven days). The taxpayer is told that if he cannot do so, he should contact the Collector immediately. Further contact may be made by letter, telephone or personal visit to the taxpayer's home. Frequently the taxpayer will be asked to visit the local collection office to discuss action to clear the debt.

6.62 If the Collector considers that the taxpayer is not being cooperative, threats of enforcement proceedings will be made (AT 7.205).

- *Summary proceedings* will be considered early, because of the strict time limits involved, although these are subject to a £1,000 monetary limit (see paragraph 9.9 *et seq)*.

- *Distraint* is the next option and large numbers of distraint visits are made although very few lead to the sale of goods by auction (see paragraph 8.5).

- *County Court proceedings* are usually the final option and it is unusual for a summons to be issued until the case has been with the local collection office for some months, and other methods of negotiation and recovery have failed. County Court proceedings are unattractive to the Inland Revenue because of the length of time it may take to clear the debt.

6.63 Local collection office staff tend to rely upon taxpayers being frightened by generalised threats of recovery proceedings, and ignorant of the safeguards and the benefits they may sometimes confer. Indeed, recovery action is often taken by a different section and so a Collector who is negotiating with the taxpayer may not have detailed knowledge of what enforcement proceedings will actually entail.

6.64 Although the Inland Revenue's internal guidance manuals devote extensive coverage to collection matters, considerable scope is given for *discretion* to be exercised at local collection office level, because of the personal and subjective issues involved:

- Even at a very junior level, Collection staff are given responsibility for assessing taxpayers' circumstances and variations in approach will inevitably occur. For example, a tax debtor who appears quite ill to an inexperienced new recruit may be adjudged a malingerer by a case-hardened colleague.

- There are wide variations of practice between different local collection offices. Some appear quite ready to remit smaller tax debts owed by individuals dependent upon state welfare benefits, while others will 'work' the case for months.

This can often lead to the impression of unfairness.

The Enforcement Office

6.65 The larger more difficult cases are referred to the Enforcement Office, which will seek to secure a quick settlement of the tax debt, failing which bankruptcy proceedings will be considered. The factors which will influence such a decision are listed in paragraph 11.25 *et seq.*

6.66 Most referrals to the Enforcement Office follow failure by the local collection office to secure payment by agreement or recovery action, or where payments due under a judgment obtained by a local collection office have not been made.

6.67 There is no published threshold, although it would appear that debts below £5,000 are not referred. However, it should be noted that once the file has been passed to the Enforcement Office, bankruptcy proceedings may be taken for debts which have been reduced below that figure, subject to the legal minimum of £750 (see paragraph 11.54).

6.68 The Enforcement Office normally handles matters by correspondence. After a review of the file, a letter will be sent to the taxpayer threatening bankruptcy proceedings unless payment, or an acceptable offer of settlement, is made within a short period (typically 14 days). Contact is not usually initiated by other means, although the taxpayer may contact the Collector at the Enforcement Office by telephone.

6.69 The Enforcement Office will be seeking to clear the debt relatively quickly and usually within 12 months (see paragraph 6.146). If after that period it appears unlikely that an agreement will be reached, consideration will be given to the issue of a Statutory Demand followed by a petition for bankruptcy which is arranged by the Inland Revenue Solicitor's Office.

6.70   Collectors at the Enforcement Office also have discretion to consider the particular facts of each case. As with local collection offices, this can give rise to apparent discrepancies although variations appear less extreme, perhaps because:

● All the work is within one office.

● Negotiation is mostly by correspondence.

6.71   The Enforcement Office also has powers to remit larger tax debts, including consideration of applications for remission made to local collection offices, where the sum involved exceeds their (unpublished) authority (see paragraph 6.60).

Further points relating to collection offices

Liaison issues

6.72   Communication between Inland Revenue offices can be slow and imperfect.

6.73   A taxpayer negotiating with a Collector about settlement of a tax debt should make sure that the Collector is kept abreast of any concurrent arrangements with the Inspector to postpone or reduce any part of the same liability. Direct communication between Inspectors and Collectors can be slow, and enforcement action is occasionally taken in respect of a debt which the Inspector has actually agreed is not due.

6.74   A taxpayer should not assume that the Collector with whom he is negotiating is aware of personal circumstances justifying compassionate treatment, where details have been given to another Inland Revenue office. Such information is not always passed on.

Collectors are not experts in tax assessment

6.75   A Collector's duty is to recover tax liabilities determined by the Inspector, and few have any detailed understanding of how such sums have been assessed. Accordingly, there is rarely any point in entering discussions with a Collector about the accuracy of an assessment. In cases of dispute, the Collector should be advised of the issues that need to be raised with the Inspector, and asked to suspend action to allow the necessary time for them to be resolved.

6.76   Where just part of a tax debt is in dispute, the Collector may require that the balance be settled immediately (AT 7.205).

The Collector's powers

6.77   Negotiations should always be conducted in the context of the particular collection office involved.

6.78   If the taxpayer is dealing with an Accounts Office:

- Enforcement action will not be imminent, as the matter must first be transferred to a local collection office.

- It may be difficult to negotiate remission, as this will have to be considered by a local collection office.

6.79   Where the file is at a local collection office:

- If the taxpayer's primary fear is of bankruptcy (and the possible consequential loss of his home), this will not be imminent since the file must first be transferred to the Enforcement Office and such a transfer is unlikely while his indebtedness remains below £5,000.

- There is the possibility of a distraint visit or Court summons, which may occur with little advance notice.

- The taxpayer should not assume that he will be treated in the same way as a friend or relative who has been in a 'similar' situation. Each case is considered individually and there are variations of practice between different local collection offices.

6.80   If the matter has been transferred to Enforcement Office:

- The risk becomes one of bankruptcy proceedings but, for all except the very largest debts, some months will first be allowed for negotiation.

- Even after negotiations have failed, it usually takes at least a few months before the matter reaches a bankruptcy hearing, after allowing for the issue of a statutory demand followed by the service of a bankruptcy petition (see Chapter 11).   This allows further time for the taxpayer to improve on any offer of settlement.

The taxpayer's circumstances

6.81   Negotiations should always be influenced by the taxpayer's personal circumstances.

Age

6.82   Compassion may be shown towards elderly taxpayers, particularly where they are on low incomes.

6.83   For example, where a Schedule E direct collection assessment is raised on a *limited income pensioner* - one whose income is below £6,000 or where payment by the statutory four instalments would clearly cause hardship - Collectors are instructed to give 'especially sympathetic treatment' and not to cause worry by over-emphasising the fact that interest may be charged on late payment (PCM 4.10 and AT 6.303).

Health and domestic circumstances

6.84   Collectors will generally be sympathetic to taxpayers suffering from ill-health or disability, or where there are serious problems within their families or homes (see *Code of Practice 6 Collection of tax* p8).

6.85   Such factors might lead to a more generous arrangement for time to pay or affect decisions about enforcement. For example, where the only material asset is the family home and the taxpayer's spouse is disabled to the extent that a sale of the property would cause extreme hardship, this *may* help to dissuade the Enforcement Office from taking bankruptcy proceedings.[6]

Deceased estates: 'Widow's Clemency Cases'

6.86   Where the taxpayer has died and:

- the estate comprises only (or mainly) the matrimonial home,

- the widow is the sole beneficiary, and

- the widow cannot pay the tax without selling the property,

then the matter must be referred to the Enforcement Office for special consideration (ROM 6.186).

6.87   The Enforcement Office should consider the case in some detail, including the widow's age, dependants and financial means, before deciding how to proceed. The guidance manual does not refer to widowers, but presumably the same considerations should apply.[7]

Unemployment or dependence upon state welfare benefits

6.88   Generally, Collectors will agree to a brief suspension of recovery action where the taxpayer is in short-term financial difficulty through unemployment. Beyond that, practice varies between local collection offices. Some will remit smaller tax debts if the problem continues beyond a few months, while others will not readily do so.

Treatment of other creditors

6.89   Where the taxpayer has one or more creditors apart from the Inland Revenue, for example in respect of rent arrears or electricity bills, the Collector should recognise the need for payments to be made to them too. A typical approach adopted by money advisers (see paragraph 13.40 *et seq)* is for the debtor to offer to divide the payments that he is able to make between his 'priority creditors' (this term includes the Inland

---

[6]   For the treatment of the home after bankruptcy, see paragraph 11.115 *et seq.*
[7]   See also paragraph 5.92 regarding the conduct of tax investigations in such cases.

Revenue), in proportion to the amounts owed to them. This reflects how the Courts might deal with the situation, for example on making an administration order or bankruptcy order (see paragraphs 10.77 *et seq* and 11.94 *et seq)*. The existence of any other creditors should therefore be pointed out to the Collector, and it is sometimes helpful to provide a schedule of all debts and payments to be made by the debtor.

6.90   If any preference has been shown to other creditors, this may count against a tax debtor, for example:

- Where a person with unsettled tax liabilities has taken out a loan which is secured on his property, thereby giving it precedence over the unsecured tax debt.

- Where another creditor has been paid in priority to the Inland Revenue. If such preference was necessary, for example to prevent gas or electricity being cut off or a property repossessed, it may assist to explain the precise circumstances to the Collector.

Previous compliance history

6.91   Considerable attention is given to the taxpayer's compliance record (see *Code of Practice 6 Collection of tax* p8). If he has normally settled his liabilities on time, this will assist negotiations.

6.92   Negotiation will be more difficult where:

- There is a history of tax liabilities having been settled late.

- The present debt has been outstanding for a long time and there is little evidence that the taxpayer has attempted to clear it in the absence of pressure from the Collector.

- There is a file record of threatening or abusive conduct towards Inland Revenue staff in the past.

Current tax status

6.93   Where a taxpayer is self-employed, the Collector may need particular assurance that a proposal for settlement takes proper account of prospective future tax liabilities. In particular, if the taxpayer's proposal is dependent upon increasing his business profits, he should be setting aside a greater sum for current tax.

6.94   In other cases it may assist to emphasise that no future liabilities will accrue, for example because the taxpayer is:

- An employee or pensioner who is fully taxed under PAYE.

- Unemployed and receiving benefits which fall within his tax allowances.

- A sub-contractor in the construction industry who has tax deducted at source (see paragraph 5.101 *et seq)*. In such cases it may assist to offer that the annual tax refunds be set against the tax debt.

Residence abroad

6.95 Where a Collector learns that a tax debtor is about to leave the UK, immediate action may be taken to recover the debt by legal proceedings. If local action is not practicable, the file is referred to Enforcement Office for immediate consideration (AT 11.803).

6.96 If the taxpayer is living abroad, it is considerably more difficult for the Inland Revenue to enforce payment. Overseas courts are not likely to assist, and enforcement against UK assets can be impractical (see paragraphs 5.157 *et seq* and 11.54). Accordingly, the Collector may be more amenable to reaching a voluntary settlement.

The size, history and type of tax debt

The size of the liability

6.97 For reasons of efficiency and effectiveness, Collectors attach greater priority to the settlement of larger liabilities (see paragraph 6.56 for details of the bands used by local collection offices).

6.98 For larger debts:

- The file may be expected to be passed up the hierarchy of collection offices, and be 'actioned', more quickly.

- Less time will be allowed for negotiations over a taxpayer's proposal for settlement.

- Recovery action may be commenced more quickly.

Also, the Collector may (wrongly) assume greater 'culpability' on the part of the taxpayer for failing to set aside sufficient funds to pay the tax.

6.99 For smaller debts:

- Several months may pass between communications from collection offices.

- Negotiation should be easier.

- Remission is more likely to be considered.

Also, the Collector is more likely to be sympathetic to the taxpayer.

The history of the debt

6.100 Collectors should have regard to the way in which the debt arose, and should show greater understanding where it was unexpected or due to an administrative error. For example:

- 'An employee with a Schedule E net underpayment who genuinely believed PAYE deductions had settled all tax in full' will 'attract sympathy' (PCM 4.8).

- Where the liability arises 'from an error or delay within the Inland Revenue', Collectors should relax the normal standards by which they judge the taxpayer's ability to pay and accept any reasonable proposals which would clear the liability within three years (PCM 4.10). Taxpayers should also be handled more sensitively (AT 6.505).[8]

- Particular sensitivity should be applied to the recovery of tax which was over-repaid in error, or where a liability is reinstated following discovery of an incorrect allocation of payments on the Inland Revenue computer. Subject to the amount involved and the facts of the case, such errors may justify remission (ROM Chapter 10).[8]

- An assessment and routine reminders may have been sent to the wrong address. Quite often such errors are only discovered when the matter is passed to a local collector, who obtains the taxpayer's new address.[9]

6.101 A separate consideration is the *promptness* of a request for time to pay. Relatively favourable consideration should be given to requests made before, or very shortly after, the due date for payment. On the other hand, Collectors will be wary of requests made just before enforcement action, as they 'may be no more than deliberate stalling tactics' (PCM 4.8).

The nature of the debt

6.102 Collectors may be influenced by the type of tax liability involved. Certain liabilities are generally expected to be settled promptly, for example:

- Capital gains tax liabilities. A Collector may start from the presumption that it is always possible to set aside the necessary funds from the disposal proceeds of the asset sold. It is then necessary to distinguish those cases where no funds were actually received, perhaps because there was no equity in the property sold.

- Assessments raised during a tax investigation. Collectors are instructed that these are raised in cases of non-cooperation or failure to make an acceptable offer and that such 'taxpayers are unlikely to pay the liability willingly'. Prompt consideration will be given to recovery proceedings (AT 6.609).

---

[8] Consideration should also be given to waiver of the liability under Extra-statutory Concession A19. See paragraph 4.99 *et seq.*

[9] In such cases, the assessment may not have been served validly. See paragraph 2.18.

- Schedule D liabilities of self-employed taxpayers. Collectors often start from the presumption that funds should be set aside for tax at the time that income is earned. While unobjectionable in principle, this disregards the complexities of assessment under Schedule D, and the need to meet 'costs of sales' and overheads.

6.103 Collectors may be more sympathetic in other cases, where the matter is very complex or a third party was involved who might have been expected to account for the tax. For example:

- Unexpected Schedule E liabilities - see paragraph 6.100 above.

- Where an individual is required to settle more than 'his share' of a partnership liability (see paragraph 5.70 *et seq)*, perhaps because another partner is insolvent or has disappeared.

- Tenants of non-resident landlords who have failed to account for tax through ignorance of their obligations (see paragraph 5.171*)*.

- Where MIRAS relief has been given incorrectly through administrative failure of the lender or a misunderstanding on the part of the taxpayer (see paragraph 5.141 *et seq)*.

- Tax due on bank and building society interest erroneously paid gross. Where the Inland Revenue considers a depositor has been incorrectly registered to receive interest gross, and it is unable to locate a tax office reference, an assessment is raised under Schedule D Case III. In the event of non-payment, local collection offices are instructed to make three attempts at personal contact before considering any form of enforcement action (AT 6.612).

Waiver and remission

Waiver

6.104 It may be of assistance to list the significant situations described elsewhere in this handbook where the Inland Revenue does not recover the full amount of tax due, or the full amount which might be charged.

- Tax waived on the grounds of *Inland Revenue delay*, under Extra-statutory Concession A19 (see paragraph 4.99 *et seq)*.

- Sums not recovered under the practice of *equitable liability* (see paragraph 4.61 *et seq)*.

- Settlements and assessments following *tax investigations*, where the Inspector finds that the taxpayer has limited means (see paragraph 5.83 *et seq)*.

- Profits falling within *assessing tolerances* (see paragraph 3.83 *et seq)*.

- Where a tax debt becomes incorporated within a *composition order* (see paragraph 10.83*)*.

- Where a tax debt is comprised within an *individual voluntary arrangement* (see paragraph 11.182 *et seq)*.

Remission

6.105 Where it appears to a Collector that tax is irrecoverable, because the taxpayer cannot make an acceptable offer for time to pay and enforcement action is considered inappropriate, he will consider remitting the debt. Remission differs from a permanent 'write off' for the reasons explained at paragraph 6.40 *et seq*.

6.106 For obvious policy reasons the Inland Revenue does not publicise the details of its remission policy, although the occasional reference appears in the published Inland Revenue guidance manuals. On the subject of enforcement, Collectors are advised:

> 'Where an individual has been ill or unemployed for a period of six months or more and hardship may apply ... consider remission ... **Note**: Despite illness/unemployment, remission will not be appropriate in *every* case. For example, the taxpayer may have distrainable effects or sufficient equity in a property to make bankruptcy proceedings a possibility. You should consider each case on its merits' (E1.303).

6.107 Broadly it may be observed that remission tends to be limited to those individuals who have very low incomes and no significant savings, such as pensioners and people who are long-term sick or unemployed. It is unlikely to be offered to a self-employed person, unless his income is extremely low.

6.108 One feature of remission is that Collectors are not always willing to confirm it in writing. At best the taxpayer will receive a letter stating that the Inland Revenue does not propose to take action in respect of the debt at the present time.

Time to pay

6.109 The guiding principle was set out in a Parliamentary statement:

> 'The first duty of the Inland Revenue is to collect tax that is properly due and in carrying out this duty it aims to treat all taxpayers fairly and impartially.

> 'The Revenue recognises that businesses may face temporary financial difficulties and in such circumstances the Collector should be contacted at the earliest opportunity to discuss how the difficulty may be resolved.

'All reasonable offers of payments, including payment by instalments, are considered. This practice will continue to operate.'[10]

6.110 Not all time to pay arrangements are actually *agreed*:

• Some taxpayers respond to Inland Revenue demands solely by sending the Collector payments of varying or regular amounts - without entering into negotiations - in the hope that this will defer enforcement action long enough for the debt to be cleared. While this will often have the desired effect, such an approach is disliked by Collectors and may harm the taxpayer's compliance record. Also, if there is no agreement, there is nothing to prevent the Collector from commencing enforcement action before the debt is cleared.

• In the short term, it may assist a taxpayer to make payments on account during the course of negotiations with a Collector, as a demonstration of 'good faith'.

6.111 Most negotiations for time to pay are conducted with local collection offices, and this chapter concentrates on the factors that will be considered by them. Some arrangements are made with the Accounts Offices and the Enforcement Office and, while many of the same considerations will apply, they are subject to particular constraints which are discussed at the end of this section (paragraph 6.140 *et seq)*.

The different kinds of arrangement

Short-term difficulties

6.112 Where a taxpayer needs no more than a few months to clear a tax debt, perhaps because he is temporarily out of work, there should not be any difficulty in reaching an agreement with the Collector that no recovery action will be taken for a period of perhaps three months, although the taxpayer will be warned that interest will be charged to reflect the late payment.

6.113 Such arrangements reflect Collectors' instructions that 'there is little point in refusing time to pay if the normal course of Collection action to obtain full payment is likely to take longer than the duration of settlement under an arrangement' (PCM 4.8) and, except in the case of very large tax debts, enforcement action would rarely be taken within the first few months.

6.114 Nevertheless, such arrangements should not be sought too often, as they do not enhance the taxpayer's compliance record.

---

[10] Statement by the Financial Secretary to the Treasury, Stephen Dorrell, *Hansard* 8 February 1993

6.115 If at the end of the agreed period, the taxpayer is still unable to settle the debt, the Collector might agree to extend the arrangement for a further period of perhaps three months and, if the taxpayer remains unable to pay after that time, remission might possibly be considered.

Instalments

6.116 Normally the Collector will be seeking an arrangement to pay by instalments. If the taxpayer's income and outgoings are relatively constant, then these will be set at a fixed amount each week or month.

6.117 However the agreed payments may fluctuate. For example:

- If the taxpayer has some savings available, the collector may expect an initial lump sum from those savings, followed by periodic instalments out of income.

- If the taxpayer's circumstances are expected to improve, perhaps through seasonal fluctuations in trading or the clearing of a personal loan commitment, the agreement will provide for corresponding increases in the payments required (PCM 4.11).

Guiding principles

6.118 Collectors will generally *not* agree time to pay where the taxpayer has the ability to meet the liability in full, even if this means using funds which he has personally 'earmarked' for other purposes (PCM 4.1).

6.119 Collectors will make it clear that a time to pay arrangement is a *concession*. Taxpayers should not be given the impression that their application is a routine matter, or that the granting of their request implies that it will be granted on a future occasion (PCM 4.3).

6.120 Collectors are nevertheless instructed that a taxpayer's request for time to pay 'in no way reduces any right to efficient, prompt and courteous attention' under the Taxpayer's Charter (PCM 4.3). So if the taxpayer considers, for example, that the Collector is demanding too much information from him in relation to the proposal he has made, or has not considered a proposal properly, a complaint may be made (paragraph 3.109 *et seq*).

6.121 The fact that the Inland Revenue will claim *interest* to reflect any deferral in payment is not regarded as sufficient justification for granting time to pay. Collectors are instructed that they should 'not agree to any proposal to delay payment on those grounds alone' (AT 14.101).

6.122 A time to pay arrangement should include all debts owed by the taxpayer to the Inland Revenue and the Collector should be careful to ensure that sufficient provision is made to meet further liabilities that are expected to fall due during the period of settlement. It will normally be a condition that such liabilities are met on time.[11]

6.123 The fundamental principle is that any agreement should be fair to the taxpayer, reasonable in relation to his ability to pay, while taking the interests of the Exchequer properly into account (PCM 4.13).

The taxpayer's financial situation

6.124 The Collector will consider how long the proposed arrangement will take to clear the debt.

'If

- a taxpayer's time to pay proposals involve settlement over a period in excess of six months,

- there is a history of the taxpayer requesting a time to pay concession (for example, for last year's liability and now for this year's), or

- you believe that the taxpayer may be requesting time to pay with no valid basis for requiring this

you must obtain in-depth information about the taxpayer's financial situation before deciding whether time to pay is appropriate.

In simple terms (this) means obtaining details of the taxpayer's

- income,   ·

- expenditure, and

- assets' (PCM 4.11).

6.125 The Collector may be prepared to accept a proposal to settle the tax over a year or two, or even longer in certain cases. In doing so, he will be taking account of the issues discussed in this chapter, as well as the detailed financial situation of the taxpayer. If the taxpayer declines to co-operate in providing the information requested, time to pay will be refused.

6.126 The taxpayer will be asked to complete a statement and a specimen list that may be used by Collectors appears as follows (PCM 4.11):

---

[11] Some Collectors are less particular about this requirement and will be prepared to renegotiate instalment terms to incorporate future liabilities as they arise.

	Amount £ (weekly/monthly)
Income	
- Net average income, including any overtime, bonus, commission, tips	....
- Work-related benefits, such as expenses, meal vouchers, petrol allowances	....
- Contributions from a spouse, child earning and living at home, other dependant relative(s)	....

- Other income, such as from
  - property
  - second job
  - lodgers
  - pension
	....

- Interest from savings or investment accounts	....
- Dividends from shares	....
- Child benefit	....
- Other state benefits	....
Total income	_____
Outgoings	
- Mortgage repayments/rent/board and lodgings	....
- Council tax	....

- Rates
  - commercial
  - water
	....

- Housekeeping (food, cleaning materials, and so on)	....
- Electricity Gas Other fuel	....
- Telephone	....

- Insurance
  - life/endowment
  - structural/building
  - home contents
  - car
	....

- TV/video rental/licence	....
- Travel expenses to and from work	....
- School meals	....
- Credit commitments	....
- HP payments (ending .... (*date*))	....
- bank credit cards and store credit cards (Access, Barclaycard, Marks and Spencer, and so on) (amount outstanding ....) (*enter approx. weekly/monthly payment*))	....
- Maintenance or other Court orders	....
Total outgoings	_____

	Details	Amount
Assets		

- Property (house, business or other)
  - estimated current value
  - amount of mortgage outstanding		

- Bank/building society accounts - current balance(s)		
- Savings/investments		

- Deposit etc. account(s)
    - type of account
    - current balance(s)
    - period of notice required for withdrawals		

- Savings certificates and premium bonds		
- Stocks and shares - current value		

- Life or endowment policies
    - date of maturity
    - approximate current surrender value		

- Other assets Give brief details of any saleable items of value which belong wholly to the taxpayer, such as a motor vehicle, boat, caravan, paintings, antiques, jewellery		

- Debts owed to the taxpayer
  - amount owed
  - date(s) payment expected		

Completing the Collector's form

6.127 The forms used by local collection offices may vary from the above example, but they are generally designed to arrive at a 'surplus' of *income* over *essential outgoings*, which may then be applied towards settlement of the tax debt.

6.128 This is based upon the assumption that this 'surplus' would normally be applied towards non-essential expenditure or savings, which the taxpayer should be prepared to forego. While unobjectionable in principle, the Collector's view of 'non-essential expenditure' might be somewhat severe.

6.129 For example, Collectors are advised to be wary of forms 'containing no evident 'surplus' for everyday personal expenses (hairdressing, leisure activities, cigarettes and so on)' of which no details are even requested (PCM 4.12). This implies that such items are necessarily dispensible, which is not always the case, and so it is advisable to include a list of all reasonable personal expenditure to ensure that it is not overlooked. In practice, Collectors can be quite reasonable about such matters.

6.130 Any standard form should be considered very carefully to ensure that the taxpayer is providing a complete picture. The above list has a number of omissions, for example:

- While requesting details of assets, it does not ask for a statement of liabilities. The Collector will obtain only limited information about other liabilities from the questions about credit commitments under 'outgoings'.

- Oddly, the list of assets does not refer to cash-in-hand.

6.131 While the specimen list has the advantage of being relatively straightforward and general, it does not cope well with particular circumstances, for example:

- If the taxpayer has responsibility for children or other dependants, there will be many further costs beyond school meals.

- If the taxpayer is self-employed, it should be established clearly whether the Collector requires details of business income and outgoings, or merely net business earnings after expenses. The above list seems to adopt the latter approach, but anomalously asks for details of commercial rates.

6.132 Given the limitations involved in the use of any standard list, the taxpayer should not be blinkered by the categories set down. He should ensure that he provides a full picture of his situation, if necessary by attaching extra sheets to the Collector's form. Since irregular items of expenditure are frequently overlooked, it is best to ask for a week or two to complete the exercise, and to maintain a detailed record of all transactions during that period.

Review and decision by the Collector

Review

6.133 The Collector is instructed to review financial statements carefully, by the application of logic and intuition. For example, he will be wary if:

- Expenditure exceeds income.

- There is no evident surplus for personal items, unless these are included in the statement of outgoings (see paragraph 6.129).

- The taxpayer's lifestyle or possessions appear incompatible with the statement. Relevant information may have been gleaned from a home visit (PCM 4.12).

- The taxpayer is offering an amount which exceeds the surplus shown on the form (PCM 4.13), although in practice this may be explained away by offers of contributions from friends or relatives.

The Collector may ask for supporting information, such as sight of a telephone bill or rent book.

6.134 If the taxpayer has assets which might be used to meet part or all of the liability, he will usually be expected to realise them, and detailed guidelines are given (PCM 4.13):

- For *bank and building society accounts* offering instant access, or where any notice period may be overridden (even if this is on payment of a penalty), the whole of the deposit may be requested. However, if the taxpayer's wages or salary is paid into the account, the last such credit may be disregarded.

- For *bank and building society deposits* requiring notice of withdrawal which cannot be overridden, the taxpayer might be required to contribute the amount on deposit at the earliest possible date of withdrawal.

- *Savings certificates, Premium Bonds, shares, stocks and bonds* may be taken into account if the investment can be encashed within the period covered by time to pay proposals, and its value is a substantial proportion of the amount due.

- The proceeds of *life insurance and endowment policies* due to mature within a short period (perhaps, six months) may be expected to be paid upon maturity. In other cases, the taxpayer may be asked to surrender the policy early.

- The sale of *personal possessions* such as cars, boats, caravans and valuable jewellery, may be required, although the sale of a valuable item to pay a small debt would only be expected as a last resort.

- Where *debts are owed to the taxpayer*, any arrangement should be structured so that money coming in is applied towards settlement of the tax debt.

6.135 Having digested all the above information, the Collector must then decide whether the taxpayer's proposal is reasonable and should be accepted. If it is consistent with the taxpayer's declared financial circumstances and is not otherwise objectionable, then it may be accepted.

6.136 If the offer is too low, the Collector might suggest a rate of payment which he considers is fair and acceptable. In such cases he might make suggestions as to how the taxpayer might 'tailor' his financial circumstances to meet the proposed payments. Collectors are instructed that:

> 'what is fair and acceptable should be conditioned to the taxpayer's ability to pay; not internal Collection targets or statistics' (PCM 4.13)

although in practice Collectors' suggestions frequently are designed to clear the debt within an arbitrary period, typically six months, which would seem to breach the above instruction.

6.137 Sometimes a Collector might be more inclined to agree a proposal if it will be settled by a particular method of payment, for example post-dated cheques or a solicitor's undertaking that the debt will be cleared from the proceeds of an imminent property sale.

The Collector's decision

6.138 If the Collector agrees proposals for time to pay, he should indicate this clearly to the taxpayer and confirm it by letter (PCM 4.14). The following points should be covered:

• Where and when the payments should be sent.

• Any conditions attaching to the agreement.

• Any arrangements for interim review in the case of longer-term settlements.

• The obligation to inform the Collector of any changes in the taxpayer's circumstances.

• It will be explained that:

- Payments must be made on time, without any reminder.

- Interest will be accruing on overdue amounts.

- The Collector will be monitoring the arrangement, which will be cancelled if breached.

- The arrangement is a 'once only' concession and that future liabilities must be met on time.

• The taxpayer should be given sufficient payslips to accompany each payment.

6.139 If the Collector refuses an arrangement for time to pay, the taxpayer should be informed of the decision and the underlying reasons, told of the need to meet the liability in full, and warned of enforcement action in default.

Negotiating with an Accounts Office

6.140 The Accounts Offices have limited authority to grant time to pay where the following conditions are met (AT 8.401):

• The total tax collectible during the period will not exceed £4,500.

• The taxpayer has put forward good reasons for his request, demonstrating a genuine financial problem.

- A clear and definite proposal for clearing the debt is made.

- Full settlement will be achieved by the *earlier* of:

  - the date tax is expected to fall due on the next assessment

  or

  - within nine months of the date of the time to pay request (this latter category does not apply to Schedule D and class 4 national insurance contributions liabilities).

- All outstanding tax is included in the proposal, including any future instalment that will fall due during the period covered.

- No tax debts are currently being pursued by a local collection office.

- The Accounts Office has no knowledge of previous time to pay arrangements having broken down.

- There is nothing to suggest that the taxpayer should be interviewed, to check any of the information provided.

6.141 If a request is made which does not contain a clear proposal, or insufficient reasons are given as to why it is necessary, then the Accounts Office will make further enquiries and reconsider the proposal.

6.142 In other cases, the correspondence will be referred to the relevant local collection office for further consideration.

6.143 Taxpayers are often confused by a continuing flow of routine reminders from an Accounts Office, when they have written to apply for time to pay. This is because applications can take some weeks to consider, and there is no automatic procedure for stopping demands during this period. In such cases, a request by telephone call to the Accounts Office, pointing out that a request for time to pay is under consideration, will usually prevent the issue of further demands.

6.144 Where payments agreed with an Accounts Office are not made on time, the taxpayer will be warned that the arrangement will be cancelled unless it is brought up to date immediately. Where an arrangement is then cancelled, the case is referred to the local collection office.

Negotiating with the Enforcement Office

6.145 Negotiations with the Enforcement Office are conducted under the constant threat of bankruptcy proceedings, and the Collector will only be interested in proposals for relatively quick clearance of the debt.

6.146 While local collection offices are told:

'Where the taxpayer is able to bring his tax position up to date within three or four years, favourable consideration should be given to making an instalment arrangement in preference to bankruptcy proceedings' (E4.752).

the position changes once the file reaches the Enforcement Office. TaxAid has been advised by the Inland Revenue:

'If a taxpayer makes a request to pay tax arrears by instalments and responsibility for the case is in the hands of the Enforcement Office, it has to be remembered that the taxpayer will already have had an opportunity to put forward proposals for settlement to the local Collector. The Enforcement Office only becomes involved when it has proved impossible to negotiate a settlement locally.

'In certain circumstances the Enforcement Office may agree that payment can be made by instalments. The determining factor will be the taxpayer's financial position and the ability to pay in one sum. The Enforcement Office will expect settlement under an instalment arrangement to be made in the shortest time possible, and usually within 12 months of the arrangement being implemented. In cases of genuine hardship, consideration will be given to instalment arrangements over a longer period although it would be unusual for these to extend for longer than 24 months.'

6.147 The above statement suggests that the Enforcement Office may institute bankruptcy proceedings rapidly in the absence of an acceptable short-term agreement for time to pay and this may be true of very large debts. In practice, the pressures of work on the Enforcement Office are substantial, and relatively few cases seem to progress to bankruptcy within less than a year or two. For further discussion of the Enforcement Office's policy on taking bankruptcy proceedings, see paragraph 11.25 *et seq*.

6.148 A taxpayer will usually benefit from making whatever possible arrangements he can with a local collection office, so as to avoid the file being transferred to the Enforcement Office. One consideration is to ensure that the debt remains below the (apparent) £5,000 threshold for such transfers. It should be noted that once the debt has been passed to the Enforcement Office, bankruptcy proceedings may ensue even if the debt has since been reduced below that threshold (see paragraph 6.67).

The enforceability of negotiated arrangements

6.149 In practice, a Collector who has granted time to pay will invariably adhere to the arrangement, although the taxpayer should always ensure that the details are confirmed in writing (see paragraph 6.138). Where complaints are made, it usually transpires that the taxpayer has failed to meet one of the conditions laid down.

Re Selectmove Ltd

6.150 Nevertheless, it is instructive to consider the extent to which the Inland Revenue is legally bound by such an agreement and some of the salient issues were considered by the Court of Appeal in *Re Selectmove Ltd* ([1995] STC 406).

6.151 In that case a company had for some time failed to make remittances due under the PAYE Regulations, and in July 1991 the managing director made a verbal proposal to the Collector that the company would:

- from August 1991 pay its current liabilities as they fell due, and

- begin to clear the arrears at the rate of £1,000 per month with effect from 1 February 1992, by which time trading should have improved.

6.152 The Collector responded that the proposal went further than he would like and that he lacked the authority to agree to it. However, he would recommend the proposal to his superiors and would revert to the company if it was unacceptable.

6.153 The company heard no further from the Collector until October 1991, by which time it had missed paying a further month's liability. It then received a letter demanding immediate payment of all the arrears.

6.154 Thereafter the company made some (but not all) payments of £1,000 due under the purported agreement, and a number of the current liabilities were settled late. In January 1993 the company was compulsorily wound up by the Companies Court on the petition of the Inland Revenue, and it appealed to the Court of Appeal.

6.155 The Court had to consider three issues:

- Whether the taxpayer's offer was accepted validly by silence on the part of the Inland Revenue.

- Whether the agreement was supported by consideration moving to the Inland Revenue, under normal principles of contract law.

- Whether, if there was no agreement, the Inland Revenue was estopped from asserting that the money was due.

6.156 On the first point, the Court considered that there was no valid acceptance. Silence cannot amount to acceptance 'save in the most exceptional circumstances'. Furthermore, there was a more substantial objection in that the Collector had made it clear that any agreement was outside his powers. He therefore had no actual or ostensible authority to bind the Inland Revenue.

6.157 On the question of consideration, the Court considered that it was bound by the decision in *Foakes v Beer* (HL (1884) 9 App Cas 605), where a creditor agreed that if £500 of a judgment debt was paid immediately and the balance by instalments, he would not take any proceedings under the judgment. After the payments were made, the creditor sued for interest under the judgment, in breach of his undertaking. The House of Lords held that this undertaking was not enforceable under the law of contract, since there is no *consideration* given where a creditor simply agrees to allow a debt - which is already due - to be paid off over time. In *Re Selectmove* the amounts covered by the company's proposal were already due under the fiscal legislation and, if there was an agreement, it was unenforceable for want of consideration.

6.158 The company's final argument was that the Crown was estopped by the doctrine of promissory estoppel, and could not go back on an implied agreement not to enforce a debt. Without needing to examine whether such an argument might have force in other circumstances, the Court dismissed it on the grounds that:

- the Collector lacked authority to bind the Crown, and

- having not met its side of the purported agreement, the company could not argue that it was inequitable or unfair of the Crown to enforce the debt.

6.159 Although the taxpayer failed on all counts in that case, the judgment offers some ideas for tax debtors who wish to secure a legally binding agreement for time to pay, the minimum requirements being:

- The arrangement must be with a Collector having sufficient authority. If the particular Collector's actual authority is unclear, it may be that a *letter* from a collection office overcomes this difficulty on the basis that the writer then has ostensible authority.

- There needs to be *consideration,* to obtain a binding contract. The fact that interest will be charged is probably insufficient, since this would in any event be due under tax law. While a peppercorn is sufficient, few Collectors would accept such an offer without suspecting that the taxpayer was trying to achieve an undesirable advantage! Perhaps an offer to round the payments up to the nearest £ might have the desired effect.

As an alternative to relying upon a binding contract, the taxpayer might argue promissory estoppel. If so, he would need to show that he had kept his payments completely up to date, and even then it is thought unlikely that the Courts would wish to extend the doctrine of promissory estoppel to cover such a case.

Chapter 7

Introduction to recovery proceedings

This chapter discusses legal and procedural aspects of tax collection which are common to all enforcement methods. It also considers issues which may be relevant once the Collector has instigated proceedings. In particular, the following areas are covered:

From paragraph

- Background   *7.1*
- Inland Revenue procedures before comencing proceedings   *7.10*
- Evidence of the debt required by the Courts   *7.17*
- Stopping or suspending collection action   *7.29*
- Representation and legal aid   *7.36*
- Credit reference agencies   *7.38*

Background

7.1 If a taxpayer fails to pay his tax liability voluntarily and negotiations with a Collector prove unsuccessful, the Inland Revenue may resort to one or more of its legal powers to enforce payment of the debt.

Enforcement methods and the roles of collection offices

7.2 Chapters 8 to 11 describe the methods most commonly used by the Inland Revenue to recover such liabilities:

- Distraint   - Chapter 8
- Summary proceedings   - Chapter 9
- County Court proceedings   - Chapter 10
- Bankruptcy   - Chapter 11

In a few complex cases, the Revenue instigates High Court proceedings. However, these are increasingly rare - only 36 High Court judgments were obtained in 1995/96 - and so such proceedings are outside the scope of this handbook.

7.3   Enforcement action generally starts at a *local collection office*, which may institute local enforcement procedures - distraint, summary proceedings or County Court proceedings.

7.4   Certain larger debts are referred to the *Enforcement Office* at Durrington Bridge House, Barrington Road, Worthing, West Sussex BN12 4SE. Generally this occurs where the sum due is over £5,000 and local recovery action has not succeeded in securing payment. In such cases, the Enforcement Office will attempt to negotiate speedy settlement by full payment over a relatively short period, failing which *bankruptcy proceedings* will be considered. The Enforcement Office does not take any other kind of enforcement action.

7.5   The Enforcement Office has other important powers in relation to tax collection. For example:

- It acts for the Inland Revenue in relation to all individual voluntary arrangements (see paragraph 11.182 *et seq*).

- It has administrative control over the practice of equitable liability by collection offices (see paragraph 4.61 *et seq*).

- It considers remission of larger debts which exceed the (unpublished) authority of local collection offices (see paragraph 6.105 *et seq*).

Law and practice

7.6   When it enforces tax liabilities, the Inland Revenue is exercising powers granted by the Taxes Management Act 1970, subject to the provisions of general law pertaining to the enforcement method involved.

7.7   Beyond that, Collectors should also conduct themselves within the limits prescribed by their own instructions, now published in the *Inland Revenue Enforcement Manual*, which will often provide the taxpayer with greater protection. To assist readers, several references to provisions within its volumes are made in the following chapters and they are prefixed by the letter 'E'.

Content of chapters

7.8   This chapter introduces enforcement by examining issues that are common to the enforcement measures discussed in Chapters 8 to 11.

7.9   Because those enforcement procedures will be unfamiliar to some readers, each of the next four chapters ends with a list of *Key points to consider*, which summarises some of the more important practical points that have been raised in the chapter.

Inland Revenue procedures before commencing proceedings

Warning to the taxpayer

7.10 When tax becomes due and payable, the Collector is required to demand payment from the taxpayer. The demand may be made on the taxpayer in person, or by post to his last place of abode, or at the premises to which the tax charge relates (TMA 1970, s60).

7.11 The Collector's internal instructions expand on this:

'In **all** cases, **before** starting enforcement proceedings you should

- warn the defaulter in writing that you will start enforcement proceedings if payment is not made within the time specified

- ask for payment to be made to your office

- inform the defaulter that interest (where appropriate) chargeable on the unpaid amount will be included in the proceedings' (E1.208)

The period specified for payment is normally seven days.

7.12 In practice, a series of warning letters are normally issued before enforcement proceedings commence. Usually, the Accounts Office will issue a warning within days of a taxpayer defaulting on a payment, threatening enforcement action in the event of non-payment. Following one or two further reminders from the Accounts Office, it may then be several months before the taxpayer hears from the Inland Revenue again, while the file is transferred to the relevant local collection office. Even then, the local collection office may negotiate for several months before instigating recovery proceedings. These delays are often helpful to a taxpayer with short-term 'cash flow' difficulties.

7.13 However, they may also give rise to complaint, since taxpayers often gain a false sense of security from the Inland Revenue's initial failure to carry out its threat. Many infer that the Inland Revenue is not to be taken seriously and may subsequently be devastated to discover how tough a Collector can become. For example, unlike most commercial creditors, the Inland Revenue may take bankruptcy proceedings even where the taxpayer has no significant assets.

Internal checks

7.14 Before commencing enforcement, the Collector will also need to confirm with the relevant Inspector that the tax he is seeking to recover remains correctly due and payable, i.e. to ensure that the Inspector has not agreed to an adjustment of which the Collector is not yet aware.[1] This is done by the Collector issuing an internal Form C87, which must be sent in time to reach the relevant tax district at least 14 days before proceedings can be taken (E1.209). If the liability stated on the Form C87 is not due, the Inspector must advise the Collector within 14 days of receiving the form.

7.15   A serious weakness in this procedure, which is designed to provide an important safeguard for the taxpayer, is that it relies upon a timely response from the Inspector. It does not allow a significant margin for delays due to postal or tax district backlogs nor for a transfer of files between districts and so proceedings do sometimes commence in respect of incorrect sums. In such cases, the taxpayer should draw the error to the Collector's (or Court's) attention as soon as it becomes apparent and recovery proceedings should be suspended or adjourned until the matter is resolved.

7.16   Even where the Inspector does not object to the proposed recovery proceedings notified on Form C87, he is asked to provide the Collector with specified information which may assist the Collector in carrying out the recovery, or deciding whether or not to proceed. In particular, the Inspector is asked to advise on the source assessed (e.g. the type of trade), any change of address, private addresses of members of a partnership, whether the taxpayer is under 18 or over 70 years old and whether the taxpayer has died.

Evidence of the debt required by the Courts

7.17   The history behind a particular tax debt may be extremely complex. For example, there may have been an appeal against the original assessment, followed by a Commissioners' determination necessitating an amendment to the assessment, followed by a claim for allowances or loss relief which might have altered the liability still further.

7.18   The Courts in which recovery proceedings are taken are not suited to the detailed examination of such issues and, from an administrative viewpoint, the recovery of tax debts could be held up indefinitely by arguments over the minutiae of tax assessments.

7.19   Accordingly, the Taxes Management Act 1970, s70(1) adopts the following approach regarding evidence:

'Where tax is in arrear, a certificate of the Inspector or any other officer of the Board that tax has been charged and is due, together

---

[1]   One exception, where no such confirmation is necessary, is where the debt relates to a certificate issued by a Collector in cases where an employer's PAYE remittances fall into arrears, as this process does not involve an Inspector (Income Tax (Employments) Regulations 1993/744, Reg 47).

with a certificate of the Collector that payment of the tax has not been made to him, or, to the best of his knowledge and belief, to any other Collector ... shall be sufficient evidence that the sum mentioned in the certificate is unpaid and due to the Crown ...'

Put simply, a taxpayer may not dispute the correctness of an assessment in proceedings brought by the Inland Revenue to enforce payment of a tax debt.

CIR v Pearlberg

7.20   In *CIR v Pearlberg* (CA [1953] 34 TC 57) the taxpayer had been assessed to tax on income from property under Schedule A. He did not appeal and the Inland Revenue took recovery proceedings against him. The taxpayer sought to resist the proceedings on the grounds that he was at no time the owner-occupier or landlord of the premises in question and so he was not within the charge to tax. The Court of Appeal held that the points raised by the taxpayer should have been made on an appeal against the underlying assessment and were not admissible as a defence in collection proceedings.

7.21   In *CIR v Soul* (CA [1976] 51 TC 86) an appeal by the taxpayer had been determined by the Commissioners and he had asked for a case to be stated for determination by the High Court. The Collector sought to collect the liability corresponding with the Commissioners' determination, in accordance with his powers under TMA 1970, s56(9) (see paragraph 3.47). Opposing recovery proceedings, the taxpayer asserted that he had an arguable defence, but this was rejected in the Court of Appeal where Bridge L.J. (with whom the other judges agreed) said:

> '... the short answer to Mr Soul's point is that there is not now open to him in the present proceedings to raise any issue by way of challenge to the assessments ... That is the clear result of the decision of this Court in the case of *CIR v Pearlberg*.'

The Collector's instructions

7.22   Applying the above law, the Collector is instructed:

> 'In practice, TMA 1970, s70 means that *if the statutory requirements are met* then the only defences to a claim for tax are those that relate to the tax itself and not to the assessment, for example, disputes about payment or reliefs. Such defences are, of course, simply matters of evidence and are easily answered.' (E4.312)

7.23   Taking account of the proviso in italics, the only admissible defences in recovery proceedings are:

- The statutory requirements in relation to the assessment were *not* met, the most promising argument being that the assessment was not properly served (see paragraph 2.18 and *Berry v Farrow* KB [1914] 1 KB 632).

- The Collector has not given appropriate credit for payments made by the taxpayer, or set-offs due (see paragraphs 2.88 *et seq* and 4.71 *et seq).*

- Claims for relief have been made which would serve to reduce the liability (see paragraph 4.45 *et seq).*

The approach of the Collector

7.24 A Collector will attend any hearing in the course of enforcement proceedings armed with certificates as required by TMA 1970, s70.

7.25 Should the taxpayer raise questions about the liability, the Collector will cite *CIR v Pearlberg.* If the Court hesitates to enter judgment on this basis, the Collector may go on to quote what the Inland Revenue calls the 'finality principles':

'- the taxpayer must be served with a notice of assessment (TMA 1970, s29(5))

- the taxpayer has a right of appeal to the Commissioners (TMA 1970, s31(1))

- if the taxpayer does *not* appeal, the debt is held to be absolute ... and is recoverable (TMA 1970, ss65 and 66)

- if the taxpayer does appeal and the case is either

  - heard and determined by the Commissioners (TMA 1970, s50) or
  - determined by agreement (TMA 1970, s54)

  then the debt is final and conclusive (TMA 1970, s46(2)) and recoverable (TMA 1970, ss65 and 66)

- the taxpayer may appeal to the High Court but the tax remains payable anyway (TMA 1970, s56(9)).' (E4.312)

In consequence, Collectors tend to have little difficulty in persuading the Courts that orders for payment should be made. Indeed, if the Collector is over-zealous, he may obtain a judgment even where there is a valid defence, for example a dispute over a claim or the service of the assessment.

7.26 It should be appreciated that few Collectors understand precisely how tax liabilities are finalised and Courts to which enforcement proceedings are taken rarely have the necessary expertise to appreciate the subtle distinctions involved.

7.27 Accordingly, even where there is a valid defence, it will usually be better for the taxpayer to raise the matter with the Collector prior to the date of any hearing or other enforcement action. Should it be necessary for a disputed liability to be examined further, for example:

- by checks between collection offices regarding payments made, or

- by communication between Collector and Inspector regarding amendments to an underlying assessment,

the Collector will usually agree to suspend recovery proceedings to allow for this.

7.28 In the event that a dispute is not raised until the matter has already reached a hearing, the Court should be asked to adjourn proceedings to allow the parties to resolve it as a matter of urgency between themselves.

Stopping or suspending collection action

7.29 Sometimes a taxpayer does not become aware of action that might be taken to reduce a liability, or otherwise avoid legal proceedings, until after he has received a distraint visit or summons. In such circumstances, he should ask for enforcement to be suspended to allow for the following points to be considered.

Late appeals, postponements and claims

7.30 Despite the wide powers of enforcement described in the previous section, Collectors are instructed to suspend recovery action at any time if:

- A late appeal and accompanying postponement application is made (see paragraph 4.8 *et seq*).

- A late claim for relief is made (see paragraph 4.45 *et seq*).

7.31 The relevant instructions are at E2.501 *et seq*, E3.501 *et seq*, E4.901 *et seq*. Although these refer to *late* claims for relief, such a claim might not necessarily be late. Quite commonly assessments are finalised before the expiry of the time limit for making claims and the submission of a timely claim should reduce the liability as of right.

7.32 In all cases, the taxpayer should provide the Collector with copies of correspondence sent to the tax district, to ensure that the Collector is aware of the situation.

7.33 The Collector should suspend recovery proceedings until the tax district advises him of the outcome. If a hearing date has already been set, the Collector may agree to arrange for it to be adjourned. If there is any doubt over whether a hearing will be adjourned, it is generally advisable for the taxpayer to attend the Court on the hearing date so as to request an adjournment personally. A case can be adjourned either generally or to a specified date.

Instalment arrangements

7.34 At any time during enforcement proceedings, the Collector may agree to suspend his action in return for an undertaking by the taxpayer to settle the debt within a reasonable timescale. The repayment terms that are likely to be demanded will depend on the local rules adopted by the collection office, the stage reached in the proceedings and the taxpayer's personal circumstances (see Chapter 6).

Unemployed or genuine hardship

7.35 Where a taxpayer has been unemployed for a period of six months and further enforcement action may cause genuine hardship, the collection office should consider remitting the tax debt (E1.303). Any proceedings already commenced will be discontinued if the debt is remitted (see paragraph 6.105 *et seq* regarding remission generally).

Representation and legal aid

7.36 In all proceedings for recovery of tax debts in the Courts, the taxpayer is entitled to be legally represented. He may also qualify for legal aid, the conditions for which are discussed in paragraph 13.55 *et seq*.

7.37 Furthermore, most Courts will be prepared to hear a representative authorised by the taxpayer, even if he is not legally qualified. Indeed, where the issues to be raised relate mostly to the administrative processes of assessing and collecting tax, some Courts prefer to hear a tax adviser (who might be an accountant), who has expert knowledge of these areas.

Credit reference agencies

7.38 There are four main credit reference agencies in the UK which hold basic details on individuals and their credit records. These agencies provide information to lenders, which is used by them in determining whether an applicant for credit represents an acceptable risk.

7.39 An individual's credit record will normally include County Court judgments, bankruptcy orders made against him and individual voluntary arrangements made to avoid bankruptcy. It should be noted that there is no record of summary proceedings in the Magistrates' Courts nor of distraint levied by the Inland Revenue.

7.40 Details of debts are normally held on an individual's credit record for six years, although some agencies retain records of bankruptcy for longer (typically about eight years). An individual may ask an agency to record the fact that a bankruptcy has been annulled or discharged, or that a County Court judgment has been satisfied. (For the detailed process following a County Court judgment, see paragraphs 10.36 and 10.130.)

7.41 Inclusion of tax debts on an individual's credit record may make it difficult for him to obtain credit through the normal channels. For this reason, it is sometimes called *credit blacklisting*, although it does not necessarily mean that credit will be denied. This will always be a matter for an individual lender to decide, by reference to its own 'scoring system' for assessing applicants.

7.42 The procedures are explained in the leaflet *No Credit? Know Your Rights 2*, published by the Office of Fair Trading which describes the work of credit reference agencies and how mistakes on credit records can be corrected.

Chapter 8

Distraint

Distraint is a powerful weapon, which offers the Collector a quick and cost effective method of recovering a tax debt. This chapter considers the situations in which it may be used, what will happen during the distraint visit and possible remedies. This chapter covers the following:

From paragraph

■	Background	*8.1*
■	The basic conditions	*8.8*
■	Preliminary checks	*8.11*
■	The distraint visit	*8.12*
■	Prior distraint by another creditor	*8.32*
■	Exempt goods	*8.34*
■	Possession and sale	*8.42*
■	Costs and fees	*8.59*
■	Key points to consider	*8.62*

Background

8.1   Under its powers of distraint, the Inland Revenue may remove a taxpayer's possessions for sale at auction to satisfy an unpaid tax debt. In practice, this power cannot be exercised without certain preliminary procedures which are described in this chapter and which offer some protection for a tax debtor.

8.2   A Collector is given power to distrain for unpaid tax and interest by TMA 1970, ss61(1) and 69(a). Unlike most other creditors, he does *not* require a Court order to do so. Distraint is carried out by local collection offices. It is the most common method of recovery action undertaken by the Inland Revenue, which sees it as quick and effective.

8.3   The origins of distraint pre-date the earliest legal records and the current law remains rooted in the nineteenth century. It is therefore necessary to explain certain terms which are still in use:

- *Levy* or *levy distraint* - This refers to the whole process, from the initial visit by the Collector to the application of the proceeds of sale by auction towards satisfaction of the debt.
- *Seize* - This is the formal act of taking control of goods, usually by preparing a list (or inventory) of the goods which may be sold at public auction if the tax is not paid within a specified period.

It should be noted that the words *distraint* and *distress* are commonly used interchangeably.

8.4 In many ways distraint is an archaic process, governed by case law dating back to previous centuries. It gives the Inland Revenue power to effect a swift sale of a debtor's goods, without much time for intervention by the Courts. This leaves any taxpayer who lacks immediate access to competent legal advice extremely vulnerable.

8.5 Fortunately distraint is used more as a threat to encourage compliance, than as an actual method of recovery. In the year to October 1995, there were 241,326 distraint visits, of which just 395 led to goods being sold at auction.[1] This indicates that over 99% of visits do *not* lead to the sale of goods, often because:

- Entry to the premises leads the Collector to the conclusion that there are no valuable assets worth seizing.
- The taxpayer is able to negotiate an alternative method of settling the liability before assets are removed for auction.
- Personal contact with the Collector gives the taxpayer the opportunity to find out about appealing against an excessive assessment.

8.6 In many other cases the process is abandoned because the Collector cannot gain access to the premises, either because nobody is there or because entry is denied.

8.7 In all cases, the Inland Revenue should comply with the law governing distraint and Collectors should also follow normal Inland Revenue practice which offers taxpayers further protection (see paragraph 7.7). Most of the relevant guidelines are to be found in the *Inland Revenue Enforcement Manual* and, in this chapter, the relevant paragraph numbers are shown in brackets, prefixed by the letter 'E'.

The basic conditions

8.8 Distraint may be levied against an individual, partnership or limited company. There is no time limit within which action may be taken, nor any monetary ceiling on the size of the debt.

---

[1] Source: Inland Revenue

8.9   However, a Collector should **not** levy distraint if:

- The taxpayer owes the Inland Revenue less than £100 in total (E1.303).

- The taxpayer is a seafarer (E1.303).

- The taxpayer is an undischarged bankrupt (E1.303).

- Application has been made for an interim order in respect of an individual voluntary arrangement (E1.303).

- The tax is due under a *contractual settlement*, following a tax district investigation or PAYE Audit inspection (E1.105). For discussion of the legal status of tax debts under such settlements, see paragraph 2.33.

8.10   While the above rules place few limitations on a Collector, he should nevertheless be conscious of the effect that distraint action might have. If he considers that his actions could close down a large business or attract the attention of the press, radio or television, then application must be made to a higher office for authority to proceed (E2.105).

Preliminary checks

8.11   Inland Revenue instructions state that a distraint visit should be preceded by a *pre-distraint call* to check that the address is correct. The Collector should also obtain advance evidence, usually from such a pre-distraint call, that there will be 'enough effects' to justify distraint (E2.303). However, in practice such calls are often not made.

The distraint visit

8.12   The distraint process commences with a visit by the Collector, who has an implied right of peaceful entry into a taxpayer's home or business premises to distrain on his goods, subject to the conditions described below.

The time and place of the visit

8.13   A distraint visit may be made to the taxpayer's residential or business premises during normal working hours. The Inland Revenue follows the common law practice that calls must **not** be made:

- After sunset or before sunrise.

- On a Sunday, bank or public holiday.

Furthermore, a Collector should not levy distraint at an address outside his collection area (E2.402).

The officers involved

8.14 Until 1993 every distraint visit was carried out by a Collector accompanied by a local private bailiff. The bailiff might be of assistance in advising on the value of goods, helping with the removal of goods (in the unusual event that immediate removal was necessary), and might also act as an independent witness in cases of complaint.

8.15 In 1993 the Inland Revenue began a pilot exercise in which Collectors carried out distraint calls on their own, referred to as *non-bailiff calls*. The pilot was viewed as a success and nowadays distraint calls are a mixture of non-bailiff, or Collector and bailiff, depending on local management of collection offices.

8.16 It should be emphasised that distraint action cannot be delegated to a private bailiff. In response to reports that such delegation may be occurring in some areas, the Inland Revenue has advised TaxAid:

> 'The Inland Revenue is not aware of such practices and could not condone them. Distraint by the Inland Revenue is carried out under the provisions of TMA 1970, s61 and this requires that it is an officer of the Inland Revenue who conducts the process.

> 'Distraint may of course be used to enforce Magistrates' Court orders and County Court judgments for tax debts but in those circumstances the Collector is not directly involved in the distraint execution.'

Arrival and entry

8.17 The Collector will not necessarily identify himself or the bailiff prior to entering the taxpayer's premises, although an Inland Revenue leaflet states that the taxpayer 'should ask to see the callers' identification which they will carry to confirm who they are' *(Collection 1 Distraint)*. If identification has not been given before entry (because it was not requested), the Collector should always identify both himself and the bailiff after access has been gained to the taxpayer's premises (E2.404.)

8.18 By law a Collector should not force his way in, nor allow the bailiff to do so. If the Collector cannot gain peaceful access, he should defer distraint action and consider alternative forms of recovery (E2.403).

8.19 The taxpayer has the right to refuse entry, which can offer an important safeguard, particularly where he considers that there has been a mistake and that no tax is due, or that there is still scope for negotiating a manageable instalment arrangement. (Indeed, it is not unknown for a distraint call to be made while the taxpayer is in the middle of negotiations with another Inland Revenue officer.)

8.20 However, in practice it is not always possible to prevent entry, for example:

- Where a visit is to business premises, doors may be left open for public access which will allow unimpeded entry to the Collector during office hours.

- Even where the visit is to the taxpayer's home, access may be given by another member of the household who does not realise the purpose of the visit.

8.21 Furthermore, in many cases the taxpayer will actually benefit from granting the Collector access. If, apart from any exempt assets (see paragraph 8.34 *et seq*), there are no possessions of particular value, the Collector may conclude that distraint is inappropriate, which will remove a cause of worry for the taxpayer. It will have been noted in paragraph 8.5 that very few visits actually lead to sales at auction.

8.22 Collectors are instructed that they should not normally make more than two distraint calls to the same address for the same liability, where they have not been able to obtain entry (E2.303).

Forced entry

8.23 If the Collector cannot gain peaceful access, he may apply to a Justice of the Peace for a warrant to break open the premises so as to levy distraint (TMA 1970, s61(2)). However, this power is used extremely rarely.

Action within the premises

8.24 Upon gaining entry to the premises, the Collector should advise the taxpayer 'what is owed and how it is made up, including any interest which has been charged, and ask you to pay' *(Collection 1 Distraint)*.

8.25 If the taxpayer believes that the tax demanded is not due, he should point this out to the Collector and it may be possible to persuade him to return to his office to clarify the matter before carrying out further action.[2]

8.26 Otherwise, unless the taxpayer pays the sum demanded, the process of *seizure* will commence. The Collector will exercise his right to survey the taxpayer's premises and prepare a list of the goods which might be taken for sale at auction, i.e. those which are not exempt and which are of sufficient value to justify seizure.

8.27 Collectors should recognise that few items realise more than a fraction of their value at auction and that there is no point in seizing items

---

[2] See paragraph 7.15 which discusses how Collectors may not have up-to-date information concerning liabilities.

that will fetch less than the costs that will be incurred in the process. This rules out the seizure of most ordinary household possessions. Indeed, the Collector's instructions state:

> 'You should only seize sufficient goods to recover the amount of the debt and the costs incurred. Where more than one item of tax, etc. is due from the defaulter

- make a comprehensive distraint to recover the whole amount.

> 'In *all* cases

- take into account

  - the worth of the asset to the debtor
  - that any sale of goods will be by public auction
  - the possible costs of removal, appraisal and sale
  - VAT on the costs of removal, appraisal and sale, where appropriate
  - the cost of an electrical safety check where the item(s) is domestic electrical equipment.

> 'If only a single high-value item is available

- seize that item.' (E2.406)

8.28   The first sentence in the above extract is somewhat ambiguous, since it may be taken to imply that distraint should be discontinued if the total value of available goods is found to be less than the tax debt. However, the Inland Revenue has advised TaxAid that in such circumstances:

> 'The Collector is expected to apply his/her skill and experience in deciding how to proceed. In some cases (those where the estimated value of the assets available would cover a reasonable part of the debt) he/she will continue the action levying on what is available, in others he/she will withdraw.'

8.29   In practice, the Collector will rarely have much information concerning the likely efficacy of distraint action prior to the visit. In the absence of a pre-distraint call, he may have just the following information which is routinely provided by the Inspector (and even this may be incomplete):

- The amount of the debt.
- A history of demands issued.
- The taxpayer's type of trade.
- The taxpayer's age if over 70 or under 18.

- A note of any special circumstances, for example whether the debt arises because of an official error (see paragraph 7.16).

For the relevance of these factors, see paragraphs 8.9, 6.82 and 6.100 respectively.

8.30 The Collector may therefore be unaware of special circumstances which should deter him from levying distraint, for example where such action might close down a large business or attract adverse media publicity (see paragraph 8.10). If so, such special circumstances should be pointed out to him immediately, with the suggestion that he returns to his office for further guidance before proceeding.

8.31 Where distraint is carried out at a taxpayer's home, it should be done in his presence. In the case of a visit to business premises for business tax debts, it must be carried out in the presence of someone who can 'accept responsibility for the distraint action'. The Collector's instructions do not define that term but expressly exclude a waiter, shop assistant or receptionist (E2.415).

Prior distraint by another creditor

8.32 Sometimes a Collector will find that another bailiff has levied previously. In such circumstances the Inland Revenue has a limited right to claim the following liabilities, in priority, from the third party:

- Sums due from an employer and related interest, under Income Tax (Employments) Regulations 1993 SI 1993/744.

- Sums due from a contractor and related interest, under Income Tax (Sub-contractors in the construction industry) Regulations 1993 SI 1993/743 (TMA 1970, ss62(1) and 62(1A)).

If the other creditor settles the outstanding amount with the Inland Revenue, they will be free to proceed with their enforcement of the debt.

8.33 Such claims may be made in respect of liabilities for the 12 month period immediately before the date of the third party seizure. However, claims cannot be made against a landlord who has distrained for rent due nor does the Inland Revenue make claims against other Government departments (E2.408).

Exempt goods

8.34 For reasons of policy, the Inland Revenue voluntarily imposes certain restrictions on the assets that may be seized, beyond those imposed under the common law.

8.35 The Inland Revenue's leaflet *Collection 1 Distraint* makes the following general statement:

'Are there any assets that we cannot seize?

We have no right to seize property which you can prove belongs to someone else or which is jointly owned. We will not seize perishable food, beds and bedding, clothes, sufficient furniture for you to sit at a table and basic cooking equipment. Nor will we seize livestock or the necessary tools of your trade.'

8.36 The Collector's instructions also list the following exempt items (E2.405):

- Goods belonging to individual partners, where the debt is a partnership one.

- Goods subject to a hire purchase agreement.

- Goods in which the taxpayer has only a life interest.

- Goods hired out to, or by, the taxpayer.

- Goods subject to a retention of title clause.

- Goods subject to a fixed charge in favour of a third party.

- Goods included in a Bill of Sale (E2.411).

- Loose money (coins or notes), although a coin collection is not exempt.

- Meters, fittings, and other apparatus which belong to the gas, electricity or water authorities.

- Coin slot meter-operated television sets.

- Fixtures and fittings which, if removed, would cause damage to the fabric of the building.

Domestic items and equipment necessary for work

8.37 In addition, the Inland Revenue chooses to observe certain exemptions which would apply upon the issue of a warrant of execution following a County Court judgment (see paragraph 10.96 *et seq*). The Collector should not seize:

- Such tools, books, vehicles, and other items of equipment as are necessary for use personally in an employment, business or vocation.

- Such clothing, bedding, furniture, household equipment, and provisions as are necessary for satisfying basic domestic needs of the taxpayer and family. These are further defined by the Inland Revenue to include a cooker, refrigerator and microwave oven if this is the only means of cooking (E2.405). The taxpayer should always be left with at least one table and a sufficient number of chairs.

8.38   The Lord Chancellor's Department has produced guidelines on implementing these exemptions for County Court bailiffs which define 'necessary' items for a business as those which are so essential that there is no way that the individual could continue working without them. Consequently, the Collector should not close a business down by the seizure of equipment, although this may be done by seizure of trading stock which falls outside the exemption (subject to the restriction in paragraph 8.10).

8.39   It is only in exceptional circumstances that a taxpayer will be allowed to retain a motor vehicle as a necessary item, since the Collector will generally take the view that he may use alternative means of transport, if necessary hiring a replacement vehicle (E2.405). Nevertheless, a Collector may accept that a car used as a chauffeured limousine, taxi or minicab is a necessary tool of the taxpayer's trade, if he can demonstrate that it would be impossible (or prohibitively costly) to continue the business in a rented vehicle, for example because of insurance difficulties.

Assets which are jointly owned or belong to someone else

8.40   The Collector is expressly instructed to 'obtain specific verbal confirmation of ownership from the defaulter' (E2.407). If such confirmation is not given, then normally the item should not be seized.

8.41   Accordingly, the taxpayer should ensure that any items which are owned by another person, or jointly owned, are clearly identified and excluded from distraint. With household items, it is not always possible to provide documentary evidence of ownership, but any relevant facts should be drawn to the Collector's attention. For example, if a stereo was given to a married couple as an anniversary present, this indicates that it is jointly owned.

Possession and sale

The distraint notice and inventory

8.42   Having identified the taxpayer's goods available for seizure, the Collector will list them on a *Distraint Notice and Inventory* (Form C204A - see copy in Appendix 1). If payment is not made, all goods listed on the notice can be sold to satisfy the debt.

8.43   The Collector should prepare the notice carefully, since goods not listed cannot be added subsequently.

8.44   Also, where an item comprises more than one part, each should be listed separately. In the case of a computer, for example, the monitor, keyboard and disk drive should be recorded individually. Similarly, a car radio and other accessories should be listed separately from the car itself (E2.406).

8.45 The list may include goods near the premises, such as a vehicle parked on the road. However, it cannot include items which the Collector does not actually see, even if he has reason to believe that such items may be on or near the premises.

8.46 The notice also shows details of the liabilities due, including related interest if the interest charge is above £30 for each assessment. This *de minimis* limit does not apply to interest under TMA 1970, s88. Interest is calculated to the actual date of the levy; it is not recalculated thereafter (E1.207).

Walking possession (E2.415)

8.47 In the vast majority of cases, the next stage is a *walking possession agreement* between the taxpayer and the Collector, which is recorded on an Inland Revenue Form C204B (see Appendix 2). The Collector agrees not to take close possession (see paragraph 8.50) in return for which the taxpayer acknowledges and agrees that:

- The distress has not been abandoned.

- He will pay the fees for walking possession.

- The Inland Revenue may have continued access to inspect the goods seized.

- He will not allow the distrained goods to leave his possession.

- He will inform any third party seeking to levy on the same goods that they have already been seized by the Inland Revenue and will inform the Collector of any such visits made for this purpose.

8.48 While it is not obligatory to sign a walking possession agreement, it is generally advantageous to do so because it removes the threat of immediate removal or close possession, discussed below. This allows the taxpayer to retain his goods while having a short period (see paragraph 8.52) to:

- check with the Collector and Inspector whether or not the liability is actually due,

- arrange finance to settle the debt if it is payable,

- persuade the Collector to accept an instalment arrangement, although an extended arrangement will only be allowed in 'very exceptional circumstances' (E2.508), or

- demonstrate to the Collector that sale of the goods would give rise to 'genuine hardship', and ask him to consider remitting the debt (E2.504).

The terms in quotes above are not explicitly defined.

Alternatives to walking possession

Immediate removal (E2.416)

8.49   If a taxpayer refuses to enter into a walking possession agreement, or the nature of the case warrants instant removal, the seized goods may be removed immediately and held in storage. It is understood that such action is rare and occurs only where the Collector fears that the debtor might abscond with the assets.

Close possession (E2.417)

8.50   Alternatively, where immediate removal cannot be arranged, close possession may be taken. The Collector leaves the premises, but instructs the bailiff to remain in physical possession of the goods until such time as they are removed.

Sale

8.51   Whatever form of possession is taken, the taxpayer is then given a specified period to settle the underlying debt plus costs, or reach an alternative arrangement with the Collector, after which time the seized goods may be sold.

8.52   By statute the taxpayer is given five days, but in practice Collectors will normally allow a longer period, often 14 days, before taking further action (TMA 1970, s61(4)).

8.53   After this time, the goods can be appraised and sold. *Appraisal* is an independent valuation normally carried out by an auctioneer and the taxpayer will not be liable for appraisal costs if a sale does not take place (E2.509).

8.54   The distrained goods are normally removed from the taxpayer's premises to be sold elsewhere. In a small number of cases, where goods are difficult to remove, the sale may take place on the taxpayer's premises.

8.55   The sale is by public auction. The auction is advertised and the taxpayer informed of the date and place of the sale. There is no reserve price and goods are frequently sold for just a fraction of their true value. The manager of the collection office will attend the auction but must not bid for any items in the sale (E2.509).

8.56   If the taxpayer offers full settlement of the debt and costs, before the sale takes place, it will be accepted, but it is then his responsibility to transport the goods back to his premises (E2.511).

8.57   Where a sale of distrained goods results in a shortfall, the Collector should not carry out a further distraint action for the balance (E2.515). Alternative forms of recovery action should be considered instead.

8.58 In exceptional cases, the goods realise more than the debt and costs, and the balance should then be returned to the taxpayer.

Costs and fees

8.59 The Inland Revenue has powers to charge costs and fees, which are set by Statutory Instrument and vary from time to time. The current costs are set out in Distraint by Collectors (Fees, costs and charges) Regulations 1994 SI 1994/236, as amended by SI 1995/2151. The proceeds of sale are set first against costs and fees, with the balance being applied towards settlement of the tax debt (E2.604).

8.60 For *visiting premises* with a view to levying distraint, an amount may be charged not exceeding £12.50.

For *levying distress*, the costs are based upon the size of the tax debt involved. Where the total sum *excluding* costs is:

- Up to £100, the costs charged are £12.50.

- More than £100, the costs charged are:

    - 12.5% on the first £100 to be recovered.

    - 4% on the next £400.

    - 2.5% on the next £1,500.

    - 1% on the next £8,000.

    - 0.25% on any additional sum.

The costs charged for *possession* are:

- For walking possession, 45p per day up to a maximum of £6.75.

- For immediate removal or close possession, a flat sum of £4.50.

For *appraisal*, the taxpayer may be charged reasonable fees, charges and expenses of the person appraising.

For *removal and storage of goods*, the taxpayer may be charged reasonable costs and charges.

The costs charged for the *sale* of distrained goods depend upon the place of auction:

- If the sale is on the auctioneer's premises: 15% of the sum realised, plus the reasonable costs of advertising.

- If the sale is on the debtor's premises: 7.5% of the sum realised, plus advertising costs and the auctioneer's actual and reasonable out-of-pocket expenses.

A bailiff is paid an *attendance fee* of £4.00 (plus VAT if applicable) for each distraint call made. Although the Inland Revenue has powers to re-charge the taxpayer for this, it is normally waived.

8.61 Should the tax debt be remitted after distraint has commenced, the process should be discontinued and costs are not recovered from the taxpayer (E2.503). Costs may also be remitted in cases of hardship (E2.504).

Key points to consider

8.62 By law, distraint may be levied even where the implications for the taxpayer or his business could be disastrous. However, a Collector is required to consider such implications in advance and recovery may be halted if, for example:

- It may have the result of closing down a large business (see paragraph 8.10).

- The taxpayer's age, health or other circumstances are such that the action may attract adverse media coverage (see paragraph 8.10).

8.63 Since the Collector may have very little information concerning these issues before his arrival, any special factors should be drawn to his attention immediately.

8.64 The taxpayer has the right to refuse the Collector access to the premises. However, in practice it is not always possible to prevent entry, nor is it invariably beneficial (see paragraph 8.19 *et seq)*.

8.65 A Distraint Notice and Inventory should not include any exempt goods, in particular:

- items which are jointly owned, or owned by another member of the household, or
- equipment necessary for work.

All items listed must actually have been seen by the Collector (see paragraph 8.34 *et seq)*.

8.66 It is generally preferable to sign a walking possession agreement, as the alternatives may be considerably more disruptive (see paragraph 8.48).

8.67 Interest is calculated up to the actual date of the levy; it is not recalculated thereafter. There is a *de minimis* disregard of interest falling below £30, except where this falls under TMA 1970, s88 (see paragraph 8.46).

8.68 Distraint proceedings do not give rise to any credit blacklisting, as there is when judgment is entered in the County Court or when a taxpayer is made bankrupt (see paragraph 7.38 *et seq*).

8.69 Distraint is a rapid form of recovery. It frequently gives rise to complaints that the Collector has not obeyed the rules, with complaints ranging from:

- discourtesy or aggressiveness, to
- mistakes as regards the existence of a liability, to
- the sale at a 'knock-down' price of assets which should have been treated as exempt.

If it is considered that the Collector is not following his internal instructions, or is otherwise in breach of the Taxpayer's Charter, it may be possible to get the Adjudicator's Office to intervene as a matter of urgency (see paragraph 3.115).

Chapter 9

Summary proceedings

Summary proceedings before a Magistrates' Court may be used to recover relatively small amounts of tax. Nevertheless, the extensive powers which are available to Magistrates make this an effective means of collecting debts. This chapter covers the following:

	From paragraph
■ Background	*9.1*
■ Limitations on summary proceedings	*9.8*
■ Procedure	*9.25*
■ Enforcement	*9.28*
■ Fees and costs	*9.37*
■ Other implications	*9.39*
■ Key points to consider	*9.41*

Background

9.1   Summary proceedings are taken in Magistrates' Courts before Justices of the Peace or Magistrates. They are also commonly called *Magistrates' Court proceedings*. The Magistrates are assisted by a Clerk of the Court, normally an experienced solicitor or barrister.

9.2   Magistrates deal mainly with criminal offences, rather than civil disputes such as tax debts which are more commonly handled by the County Courts. Since Magistrates are accustomed to wielding extensive powers under the criminal law, they may not feel squeamish about using their considerable powers in civil cases too.

9.3   Indeed the Inland Revenue's leaflet on summary proceedings spells out that, where a taxpayer fails to pay an amount ordered by the Court, the Collector may obtain a judgment summons. If so:

> 'You will have to explain to the Magistrates why you have not paid. Failure to attend Court or pay what the Magistrates order may result in a prison sentence.' (*Collection 2 Magistrates' Court proceedings* and see also paragraph 9.33 *et seq)*

9.4 This tends to reinforce the public perception that summary proceedings commonly lead to custodial sentences in civil cases. Although this is untrue, it has the result that most tax debts are settled before the date set for the hearing. Since summary proceedings are also relatively quick and cheap to administer, they are viewed by the Inland Revenue as an effective method of recovery.[1]

9.5 However, summary proceedings are subject to significant limitations - in particular, they must be commenced within a very short timescale and cannot be used to recover sums of £1,000 or more.

9.6 The power to take summary proceedings to recover tax and interest is given to the Inland Revenue under TMA 1970, ss65 and 69. Such action is normally initiated by local collection offices.

9.7 In all cases, the Inland Revenue must comply with the law governing summary proceedings. Furthermore, Collectors should also follow normal Inland Revenue practice, which tends to offer the taxpayer further protection (see paragraph 7.7 *et seq*). Most of the relevant guidelines are to be found in the *Inland Revenue Enforcement Manual* and, in this chapter, the relevant paragraph numbers are shown in brackets, prefixed by the letter 'E'.

Limitations on summary proceedings

9.8 Summary proceedings are subject to certain significant restrictions in the form of:

- monetary limits
- time limits
- types of tax which qualify
- the taxpayer's personal circumstances
- procedural difficulties

Monetary limits (E1.305 and E3.203)

9.9 The debt to be recovered must be less than £1,000 (TMA 1970, s65(1)).[2] For this purpose, Schedule D tax and class 4 national insurance contributions are considered separately although any related interest is included with the specific duty to which it relates.

9.10 For example, a taxpayer may owe the Inland Revenue £1,255 comprising:

- income tax - £950,

---

[1] The Inland Revenue has advised TaxAid that 24,442 summary actions were started in 1995/96.

[2] For liabilities of 1996/97 and subsequent years, proceedings may be taken for sums not exceeding £2,000 (FA 1994, 19 Sch 19).

- interest on the income tax - £30, and

- class 4 national insurance - £275.

Summary proceedings may be taken for the full amount. However, if the interest due on the income tax is £55, then proceedings cannot be taken to include the interest charge (because the tax plus interest would exceed £1,000).

Time limits (E1.305)

9.11   Summary proceedings must be started within a relatively short period which is determined by the type of duty involved. The main provisions are as follows.

9.12   Action must commence within six calendar months from the date on which the sum involved became due and payable, in respect of an assessment to:

- income tax

- capital gains tax

- class 4 national insurance contributions

It must commence within the same period for any charge to interest under TMA 1970, s86 in respect of any of the above liabilities (Magistrates' Court Act 1980, s127).

9.13   Action must commence within 12 calendar months from the date on which tax became due and payable in respect of tax charged by an assessment under Schedule E (TMA 1970, s65(3)).

9.14   Action must commence within 12 calendar months from 19th May following the end of the year of assessment, in the case of non-payment by employers and contractors of sums due under the PAYE Regulations and the construction industry rules. Where the defendant's annual return was submitted late (i.e. after 19th May following the year of assessment), action may commence within 12 months of the date of submission.

9.15   The start of summary proceedings is defined as the day on which complaint is lodged before a Magistrate and application is made for a summons to be issued (E1.305).

Types of tax

9.16   Summary proceedings are commonly taken to recover outstanding liabilities on assessments under Schedules D and E and capital gains tax.

9.17   Certain duties charged on individuals *cannot* be recovered by way of summary proceedings. Important examples are debts due under:

- Determinations or directions under Income Tax (Employments) Regulations 1993 SI 1993/744, Regulation 49 (E1.306) (see paragraphs 5.38 *et seq* and 5.58 *et seq).*

- Contractual settlements (E1.105) (see paragraph 2.30 *et seq).*

Personal factors (E1.303)

9.18   A collection office should **not** take summary proceedings if:

- The taxpayer is 70 years old or more.

- The taxpayer is not in good health.

- The taxpayer owes the Inland Revenue less than £100 in total.

- The taxpayer is a seafarer.

- The taxpayer is an undischarged bankrupt.

- Application has been made for an interim order in respect of an individual voluntary arrangement.

Procedural difficulties

9.19   Each local collection office will have its own views as to the efficacy of summary proceedings. In practice, local problems with the workings of Magistrates' Courts may deter some collection offices from taking such proceedings at all. There are wide variations in the way Magistrates' Courts work and some procedural difficulties facing Collectors are examined below.

The need for a hearing

9.20   In contrast with County Court proceedings, where judgments can be entered without any need for a hearing, summary proceedings require a personal appearance before the Magistrates by the Collector.

Home Court

9.21   The area covered by a local collection office may include a number of Magistrates' Courts. In such cases the Inland Revenue may, for administrative convenience, seek agreement of the Magistrates that proceedings for unpaid tax against taxpayers working or living in the collection area will normally be heard at one particular Court. This is then referred to as the *home Court* and invariably this will be the Court nearest to that collection office.

9.22   However, in some areas Magistrates may insist that each action normally should be commenced in the taxpayer's local Court. Collectors will then have to cover a number of Courts in their area, increasing the time that has to be spent on recovery.

9.23   In any event, proceedings should not be taken against a taxpayer who does not live or work within the collection area, or within a reasonable travelling distance of the Court. In such cases, proceedings may be commenced in the home Court of another Collector, provided that at least one application for payment has been made by that Collector (E3.105).

Waiting time

9.24   As Magistrates' Courts devote most of their time to criminal offences, tax debts tend to be given low priority. A Collector may therefore face a lengthy wait before being given the opportunity to present his case.

Procedure

Commencement

9.25   The collection office will start summary proceedings by preparing a *complaint* (Form SP25) and a *summons* (Form SP24). The complaint is held by the Court and the summons is normally served on the taxpayer by post. The summons shows full particulars of the debt together with the time, date and place of the Magistrates' Court hearing. It should be served at least ten days before the date set for the hearing (E3.207).

If the taxpayer pays the full sum shown on the summons (including costs) to the Inland Revenue before the date set for the hearing, no further action should be taken and the Collector should notify the Court that the action has been discontinued.

The hearing

9.26   If the debt remains unpaid at the date of the hearing, the Collector will need to present evidence of the unpaid tax to the Court. This is done by presentation of a *certificate(s) of debt*, which should be sufficient evidence of the debt (see paragraph 7.19). Although the taxpayer is able to present his case at the hearing, the Magistrates are likely to make an order for payment in the sum requested by the Collector. The reasons for this are explained in paragraph 7.17 *et seq.*

9.27   If the taxpayer wishes to dispute the liability, or to seek an instalment arrangement, it is best to contact the Collector before the day of the hearing. However, if this has not been done, the taxpayer should arrive at the Court early on the day of the hearing and try to speak to the Collector before going into Court.

- This may provide an opportunity for the parties to agree an instalment arrangement, which the Magistrates may endorse. Magistrates are sometimes unaware that they have power to order that an income tax liability - as a civil debt - be paid by weekly or monthly instalments (Magistrates' Court Act 1980, s58). The taxpayer may request such an order by drawing their attention to this legislation and to Form 106 *Order: Civil Debt*, on which orders for payment by instalments may be set out.[3]

- If the taxpayer has copies of very recent correspondence that he has sent to his tax district disputing the liability, of which the Collector is unaware, the Collector's instructions are to request an adjournment of the hearing (E3.305).

Enforcement

9.28   When an order for payment which has been issued by a Magistrates' Court is not complied with, the debt can be enforced in one of two ways - a distress warrant or a judgment summons.

Distress warrant

9.29   The Court may be asked for an order that distraint be levied on the taxpayer's possessions and this is called a *distress warrant*. However, this is not commonly sought in the case of a tax debt since the Inland Revenue has its own statutory powers of distraint, which may be exercised without any Court order and the Collector should normally have considered the exercise of these powers *before* commencing summary proceedings (see Chapter 8).

9.30   Nevertheless, a Collector may seek the issue of a distress warrant following summary proceedings where information has come to light after an order for payment has been granted, which suggests that such action may be productive.

9.31   In these cases, the Collector issues by post a *copy minute of order for service* (Form SP26B), which sets out the terms of the Magistrates' order and states 'that in default of payment the amounts be levied by distress and sale of the defendant's goods'.

9.32   If there is no response within seven days, the Collector may apply to the Magistrates' Court for the issue of a *distress warrant* (Form SP35) (E3.403).   A private bailiff authorised by the Court will then visit the taxpayer's premises to seize his possessions to the value of the Court debt. Unlike Inland Revenue Collectors[4] and bailiffs used by the County Court, private bailiffs are not bound by self-imposed restraints. Their charges are not regulated, the goods that may be seized are less limited and the process of distraint is very difficult to stop once it has begun.

---

[3] This power to order payment by instalments is not even mentioned in the Inland Revenue leaflet *Collection 2 Magistrates' Court proceedings*.

[4] See paragraph 8.7 and Chapter 8 generally.

Judgment summons

9.33 The *judgment summons* (Form SP27) is normally served on the taxpayer personally (E3.413). It sets out the terms of the Magistrates' order and requires the taxpayer to appear before the Magistrates at a specified date and time

> 'for an inquiry to be made as to the means you have had since the order for payment was made ... and to show cause why you should not be committed to prison in accordance with section 96 of the Magistrates' Court Act 1980, in default of payment'.

9.34 At the hearing, if the Magistrates take the view that the taxpayer has had the means to pay the sum ordered and has refused or neglected to do so, they may order that he be sent to prison for up to six weeks (E3.419). However, in practice the Magistrates may make a suspended order on condition that payment is made over a specified period. In the event that the taxpayer is committed to prison, the tax debt is remitted when he has served his prison sentence.

9.35 If the taxpayer fails to attend Court, he may receive a *witness summons*. This must be served personally on the taxpayer, or be left with a responsible adult at the taxpayer's residence or place of business (E3.416). It must be accompanied by *conduct money*, a sufficient amount to cover the cost of travel to the Court by public transport. If the taxpayer still does not attend Court or does not pay what the Magistrates order, he may be arrested (E3.417).

9.36 In view of the serious consequences that may follow the issue of a judgment summons, the Collector should not take such action without first carefully reconsidering the taxpayer's age, health and financial position. This may involve asking the taxpayer to attend the collection office for an interview, or contacting the tax district or the taxpayer's employer for recent details of income (E3.408). In practice, the issue of a judgment summons is quite rare.

Fees and costs

9.37 The following fees will be added to the tax debt:

Complaint	£3.50
Summons and copy	£3.50
Order and copy	£16.50
Warrant of distress and copy	£6.50
Judgment summons application	£3.50
Order of commitment	£6.50

In addition, for a distress warrant there are private bailiff's charges which may be significant.

9.38   In addition, the following costs may be awarded against the taxpayer at the discretion of the Court:

- to obtain an order for payment   £5.00 maximum

- to obtain a judgment summons   £15.00 maximum

Other implications

9.39   *Interest* stops accruing on the tax debt from the date of issue of a Magistrates' Court summons (E1.207). However, this makes little difference in practice since:

- the majority of taxpayers settle their debts before their first hearing date, and

- the liability involved generally will be low, because of the monetary limits governing such proceedings.

9.40   There is no *credit blacklisting* as there is when judgment is entered in the County Court or when a taxpayer is made bankrupt (see paragraph 7.38 *et seq)*.

Key points to consider

9.41   The Collector should not start summary proceedings unless all the necessary conditions are met. In particular:

- There are strict time limits (see paragraph 9.11 *et seq*).

- There is a £1,000 monetary limit (see paragraph 9.9).

- The health, age and other circumstances of the taxpayer should be reviewed (see paragraph 9.18).

The Collector may not have all the necessary information to consider these factors and so, upon receipt of a summons (or threat of one), the taxpayer should check whether he may claim the benefit of any of the restrictions.

9.42   Where the liability is undisputed, the taxpayer should consider carefully whether there are *any* ways of obtaining the necessary funds to pay off the debt, in which case the action will be discontinued (see paragraph 9.25). Given the disproportionate powers of the Magistrates compared with the relatively small tax debts with which they have to deal, settlement of the debt should not be delayed.[5]

9.43   The taxpayer should consider whether the liability claimed on the summons may be disputed in any way, or an instalment arrangement

---

[5]   It is worth noting that County Court proceedings are relatively benign, despite the fact that the tax at stake may be twenty times as great (see Chapter 10).

reached and, if so, he should contact the Collector before the date of the hearing. If no prior contact is made, it may be possible to speak to the Collector before going into Court. It is not advisable to try to argue about the accuracy of the debt before the Magistrates (see paragraph 9.26 *et seq).*

9.44 If the travelling distance to the court is unreasonable, the taxpayer may ask for proceedings to be moved to a local Court (see paragraph 9.23).

9.45 If the Magistrates make an order which is not paid and the Inland Revenue obtains a judgment summons or a witness summons, this should be taken very seriously (see paragraph 9.28 *et seq).*

Chapter 10

County Court proceedings

County Court proceedings are the most common form of Court action used to recover tax debts. Although they may have serious consequences, there are advantages which may be of use in certain situations. This chapter covers the following:

From paragraph

- Background   *10.1*
- The basic conditions   *10.7*
- Procedure leading up to judgment   *10.11*
- The effect of a judgment   *10.50*
- Striking out and setting aside   *10.63*
- Variation and administration orders   *10.68*
- After the judgment   *10.86*
- Enforcement powers   *10.95*
- Adjustments to the tax liability after proceedings
  commence   *10.123*
- Discrepancies in County Court procedures   *10.132*
- Key points to consider   *10.136*

Background

10.1   Court proceedings to recover tax debts are most commonly taken through the County Courts. 38,920 new actions were commenced in 1995/96.[1]

10.2   A County Court judgment is a serious matter. If the taxpayer does not make payment in accordance with its terms, the Collector may ask the Court for payment to be enforced in a number of different ways. The judgment is also listed by credit reference agencies, which may prevent the taxpayer from obtaining credit in the future.

---

[1]   Source: Inland Revenue

10.3 On the other hand, County Court proceedings are not wholly disadvantageous. In particular, interest stops running on the debt and there are clear procedures to establish instalment arrangements, set by reference to what the taxpayer can afford.

10.4 Most County Court actions are conducted purely by way of paperwork, without any need for a hearing. This gives rise to a plethora of forms to be used for different purposes and the necessary references are given in this chapter.

10.5 The power to institute County Court proceedings is given to the Collector under TMA 1970, ss66 and 69, and cases are handled by local collection offices. The process is more time-consuming than distraint or summary proceedings, and so Collectors are instructed not to initiate County Court action until those other methods of recovery have been ruled out.

10.6 In all cases the Inland Revenue must comply with the law governing County Court proceedings. Furthermore, Collectors should also follow normal Inland Revenue practice, which tends to offer the taxpayer further protection (see paragraph 7.7). Most of the relevant guidelines are to be found in the *Inland Revenue Enforcement Manual* and, in this chapter, the relevant paragraph numbers are shown in brackets, prefixed by the letter 'E'.

The basic conditions

10.7 County Court proceedings may be taken in respect of any kind of tax debt, and action may be taken against an individual, partnership or limited company. There are no time limits for commencing action, beyond those discussed in paragraph 2.98 *et seq.* However there are certain restrictions, which are discussed below.

Monetary limits (E1.305)

10.8 The sum recoverable must not exceed:

- £10,000 in the case of sums due from an employer under Income Tax (Employments) Regulations 1993 SI 1993/744 or from a contractor under Income Tax (Sub-contractors in the construction industry) Regulations 1993 SI 1993/743.

- £20,000 in any other case.

In the event that the liability exceeds these limits and the debt cannot be recovered by distraint - for which there is no monetary limit - the normal Inland Revenue practice is to refer the matter to the Enforcement Office for consideration of bankruptcy proceedings (see Chapter 11).

10.9   The above limits refer to the tax only. Any interest chargeable may be added, even if it takes the total over the relevant monetary limit given above.

Other factors

10.10 A Collector should *not* commence County Court proceedings if:

- The taxpayer owes the Inland Revenue less than £100 in total (E1.303).

- The taxpayer is not an undischarged bankrupt.

- Application has been made for an interim order in respect of an individual voluntary arrangement (E1.303).

- The sum is due under a contractrual settlement following a tax district investigation or PAYE audit, *and* the amount outstanding (excluding interest) is more than £5,000 (E1.105).

Procedure leading up to judgment

Commencement

10.11   The process commences with the Collector *entering a plaint*. This involves preparing a County Court *summons* (Form N1 - see Appendix 3) and delivering or posting it to the County Court together with the necessary Court fee.

10.12   The summons includes details of the tax debt, referred to as the *particulars of claim*. The plaint is normally entered at the local collection office's home Court - invariably the County Court which is nearest to the collection office.

10.13   Upon receipt of the summons, the Court office issues a *plaint note* to the Collector, which provides a receipt for the payment and specifies the case number allocated to the summons, which is also entered on the front of the summons.

10.14   The summons is then *served* on the taxpayer. The Court will normally send it to him by first class post, although in cases of urgency the Inland Revenue may arrange to serve it on the taxpayer in person (E4.211 and E4.212).

10.15   The date of service is deemed to be the seventh day after posting (CCR 1981, Order 7, rule 10)· A summons must be served within four months of its issue, although application may be made for an extension, normally for a further four months and exceptionally up to a further 12 months (CCR 1981, Order 7, rule 20).

Responding to the summons

10.16 The taxpayer has 14 days from the date of service (see paragraphs 10.14 and 10.15) to respond to the summons.

10.17 If the taxpayer takes no action within that period, the Collector will ask the Court to enter judgment immediately, referred to as a *default judgment* (E4.303). The taxpayer will then be sent a *Judgment for Plaintiff* (Form N30) which orders payment 'forthwith'. If the taxpayer fails to pay, the Collector may take enforcement action of the kinds described in paragraph 10.95 *et seq*. If the Collector fails to apply for a default judgment within 12 months of service of the summons, the Court will strike out the action (E4.218) (CCR 1981, Order 9, rule 10).

10.18 If the taxpayer does not dispute the liability shown on the summons and has the means to settle the debt and Court fee immediately, he should make the payment to the Collector before judgment is entered. The Collector should then take no further action in respect of the summons which will lapse automatically after 12 months (E4.302).

10.19 Even if the taxpayer does not have the means to settle the debt immediately, he may be able to persuade the Collector - without returning the Admission form described below - to suspend recovery proceedings by making an offer of payment by instalments which will settle the debt over a relatively short period. If the debt is then settled, the Collector should take no further action in respect of the summons and no judgment is entered.

10.20 In other cases, the taxpayer may use the machinery of the County Court to:

- request time to pay (see paragraph 10.22 *et seq*), and/or

- dispute the amount claimed (see paragraph 10.41 *et seq*).

10.21 In either event he should follow specified procedures, using either or both of the two forms that should accompany the summons.

Requesting time to pay

10.22 Under the terms of a County Court judgment, the taxpayer may be ordered to pay the tax debt either

- forthwith (i.e. immediately), or

- in one sum on a specified future date, or

- by monthly instalments (CCA 1984, s71 and CCR 1981, Order 22).

10.23 In practice, most requests for time to pay involve settlement by instalments and the following paragraphs refer to such arrangements, although they may apply equally to orders for payment on a specified future date.

10.24 Requests for time to pay are made on an *Admission* (Form N9A - see Appendix 4), a blank copy of which is normally sent with the summons.

Full admissions

10.25 Where the taxpayer admits the claim in full[2], but cannot afford to pay the whole sum immediately, he should complete the *Admission* form and send it to the Collector who is identified as the plaintiff on the front of the summons. The form asks for details of the taxpayer's financial circumstances and has space for him to make an offer to pay the debt by specified monthly instalments.

10.26 Upon receipt of the Admission, the Collector should

- Consider whether the offer of instalments is reasonable in relation to the information on the form.

- Consider contacting the taxpayer directly to see if he can obtain a better offer.

- Review the accuracy of the information provided on the Admission against other details already held, for example income reflected in tax returns or knowledge of the taxpayer's lifestyle (which may have been obtained in the course of earlier negotiations about time to pay, see Chapter 6). The existence of inconsistencies may offer him grounds for challenging an order for instalments by the Court, see paragraph 10.37 below (E4.305).

10.27 If he considers that the taxpayer's offer (or increased offer - see paragraph 10.26) is reasonable, the Collector should advise the Court office accordingly, and judgment will be entered for payment to be made by the proposed (or agreed) instalments. The taxpayer will be sent a *Judgment for Plaintiff (Acceptance of Offer)* (Form N30(1)) which states the amount of each monthly instalment and the date that the first payment should be made to the Collector.

10.28 If the Collector does not accept the taxpayer's offer, he will notify the Court accordingly and give reasons for his objection. This will usually be because he considers that the offer of instalments is insufficient in relation to the information provided on the Admission and the Collector will propose a higher instalment figure.

10.29 The Court's administrative staff then review the Admission and calculate an appropriate instalment order, solely on the basis of its contents.

---

2 Part admissions are discussed in paragraph 10.48 *et seq*.

In reviewing the form, the Court's staff are instructed not to question whether the level of expenditure is too high, unless it contains *frivolous or non-essential items*, which should be disallowed.[3] Non-essential items are defined to include pocket money, cigarettes, holidays and (except for work purposes) newspapers and magazines.

10.30 They then calculate an instalment order by using a standard formula, as set out on their *Determination of Means Calculator* (Form Ex120 - see Appendix 5). Broadly this involves:

- adding the taxpayer's declared income to 1/12th of his savings, and

- deducting the total of his living expenses plus regular outgoings in respect of repayment of priority debts, Court orders and credit debts.

10.31 The net figure so reached is his *total disposable income.*

10.32 Provided this is a positive figure (i.e. broadly, that income exceeds outgoings), an order for payment by instalments will be set at the *lower* of:

- total disposable income, and

- the rate of instalments requested by the Collector.

10.33 However, should the taxpayer's offer on the Admission be higher than the figure so calculated, then the instalments are set at the level offered by the taxpayer.

10.34 If the calculation on Form Ex120 reflects a negative figure for total disposable income (i.e. broadly, outgoings exceed income), the matter is referred to a District Judge who may make an order for instalments without a hearing. District Judges are not bound by *Determination of Means Notes for Guidance* and can make whatever order they think fit, including an order that no payments be made at all.

10.35 In either event, the Court then issues a *Judgment for Plaintiff (determination without hearing)* (Form N30(2)) which states that the Court has considered the offer of the taxpayer and objections from the Collector and sets out the amount of each monthly instalment as determined by the Court and the date the first payment should be made to the Collector. The form goes on to state that either party may object to the payment rate fixed by the Court, by providing their reasons in writing to the Court within 16 days of the date shown on the postmark and that the matter will then be determined at a hearing.

---

3 *Determination of Means Notes for Guidance* Lord Chancellor's Department, May 1991

Disposal hearings

10.36 A *disposal hearing* will be held if either party objects to the level of instalments determined by the Court, or if the Court considers that the information provided on the Admission is not sufficient to enable instalments to be set.

10.37 In practice, the Collector should not object to the instalments set by the Court, unless he has evidence to suggest that the taxpayer's means, as reflected on the Admission, are not stated accurately. He should then take recent evidence of the taxpayer's means to the hearing, in support of his objection (E4.407) (see paragraph 10.26).

10.38 The District Judge will hear both parties and then decide upon the level of instalments to be paid (CCR 1981, Order 9, rule 3). Details are then recorded on a *Judgment for Plaintiff after hearing or reconsideration* (Form N30(3)), which is issued by the Court.

10.39 In practice, such disposal hearings are rare. Collectors are instructed that they will gain little by forcing a disposal hearing, unless the Court has overlooked important evidence or fresh evidence has come to light (E4.305).

10.40 However, in the event of such a hearing, it may assist the taxpayer to speak to the Collector in advance. This may provide the opportunity for a revised instalment offer to be agreed between the parties, which the District Judge may agree to endorse at the hearing.

Objecting to the debt shown on the summons

10.41 The summons should also be accompanied by a blank *Defence and Counterclaim* (Form N9B - see Appendix 6), on which the taxpayer may dispute that he owes part or all of the amount claimed. This form should be completed and returned to the Court office.[4]

10.42 For defences received in respect of claims over £3,000, the Court arranges a *pre-trial review* hearing. For claims under £3,000, known as *small claims*, the matter is referred automatically to an *arbitration* hearing (CCR 1981, Order 19, rule 3). Both types of hearing are held before a District Judge informally in his chambers.

The hearing

10.43 Both parties have the right to be heard. Whatever arguments the taxpayer raises, the Collector will present evidence of the unpaid tax in the form of *certificate(s) of debt*, which should normally be sufficient to

---

[4] Although the form has space for making a counterclaim, counterclaims are prohibited in actions by the Crown for the recovery of taxes and so this part of the form should be disregarded (CCR 1981, Order 42, rule 9(1)).

determine the matter in his favour, for the reasons explained in paragraph 7.17 *et seq.*

10.44 Accordingly, such a hearing is rarely a suitable forum for a taxpayer to dispute the sum claimed by the Collector. It is generally preferable to try to resolve such disputes by urgent negotiation with the Collector (and Inspector, if appropriate), relying upon the safeguards discussed in Chapter 3 if agreement is not possible.

10.45 Should the taxpayer's objections be unresolved by the date set for a hearing, the taxpayer should ask the District Judge to adjourn the matter to allow time for the dispute to be settled following the normal procedures provided under tax law and practice. If this fails and judgment is given in the amount claimed by the Collector, the amount outstanding under the judgment debt may subsequently be reduced by any tax discharged following resolution of the dispute between the taxpayer and the Inland Revenue (see paragraph 10.130 *et seq*).

10.46 A separate difficulty with pre-trial reviews and arbitration hearings is that they generally lead to a judgment for payment 'forthwith', even if the taxpayer lacks the means to settle the amount ordered. Indeed, if the taxpayer was disputing the full amount claimed by the Collector, it will not have been appropriate to submit an Admission asking for payment by instalments.

10.47 One solution is for the taxpayer to bring a completed Admission to the hearing. Should the District Judge indicate that he intends to give judgment for the Collector, the taxpayer may then present the Admission and ask for an order to pay by instalments. Alternatively, after an order to pay 'forthwith' has already been given, the taxpayer may apply for a variation order (see paragraph 10.69 *et seq)*.

Part admissions

10.48 If the taxpayer admits part of the Inland Revenue's claim *and* he requires time to settle that amount, this is known as a *part admission*. In such cases both the *Admission* and *Defence and Counterclaim* should be completed, and *both* sent to the Court office.

10.49 The dispute over the liability is then dealt with in the way described in the previous section and the submission of the Admission should ensure that, when the Court makes an order, this is for payment by instalments and not for payment forthwith.

The effect of a judgment

Advantages for the taxpayer

10.50 There are two significant advantages to the taxpayer in having judgment entered against him.

Freezing of interest

10.51 Interest stops accruing from the date of 'entry of plaint' (see paragraph 10.11) and this is a rare situation where interest on a tax debt may be frozen. The Inland Revenue has advised TaxAid:

> 'Although the Inland Revenue are entitled to charge interest beyond the date of entry of plaint either under the provisions of the Taxes Acts or under the County Court Order (in relevant cases), we do not at present do so, basically because it is not generally cost-efficient for the usually small amounts involved.

> 'The practice is however kept under review and a change is likely with the introduction of self-assessment.'

10.52 Indeed, a canny taxpayer unconcerned about the drawbacks of a County Court judgment might even go so far as to ask a Collector to obtain a judgment against him for the sole purpose of freezing interest. However, Collectors are instructed that they 'should *not* start County Court proceedings solely for the purpose of minimising the interest payable by the defaulter' (E1.207).

Manageable instalments

10.53 The level of instalments payable under a County Court order is determined purely by reference to the taxpayer's ability to pay, without regard to the size of outstanding debt or the period that it will take to clear the sum owed. In some cases, the Court will order nominal instalments or no payment at all, which may have the result that the debt is never cleared. It should be noted that the Collector may always return to the Court at a later date to ask for an increase in the instalments payable, if it comes to his attention that the taxpayer's means have changed (see paragraph 10.76). However, in practice Collectors do not devote significant resources to observing the continuing circumstances of those who are complying with Court orders.

10.54 The Court's approach contrasts sharply with that adopted by Collectors in negotiations, whose primary concern will be to clear the tax debt over an appropriate period (see paragraph 6.124 *et seq*).

10.55 Accordingly, if the taxpayer is contacted by the Collector after submitting an Admission form and asked to consider increasing the instalments he has offered (see paragraph 10.26), he should bear in mind that his original offer might well be acceptable to the Court and that there may be no advantage in acceding to the Collector's request.

10.56 So while such approaches may be turned down by the taxpayer, an alternative response might be to offer increased instalments on an informal basis, in return for an undertaking from the Collector not to seek a judgment. In the unlikely event that such a proposal is accepted, it would enable the taxpayer to avoid 'credit blacklisting' (see below), although it entails the disadvantage that interest will continue to accrue.

Disadvantages for the taxpayer

10.57 The main drawbacks of a judgment being entered are:

- credit blacklisting,

- enforcement, and

- costs and fees.

Credit blacklisting

10.58 When judgment is entered in the County Court, details are included on a Register of County Court judgments which is maintained by Registry Trust Ltd, 173-175 Cleveland Street, London W1P 5PE.[5] This register is open for inspection to credit reference agencies, and the implications of this are described in paragraph 7.38 *et seq*.

10.59 It should be noted that if the amount claimed by the Inland Revenue is settled within one month, the judgment is deleted from the Register (see paragraph 10.87).

Enforcement

10.60 Once judgment has been entered, the Collector will have several different methods available to enforce payment (see paragraph 10.95 *et seq*). The taxpayer needs to be aware of these enforcement procedures if he fails to comply with the terms of the judgment.

Costs and fees

10.61 The Court's fees are added to the amounts due from the taxpayer and the current levels are as follows:

Claim not exceeding	£100	£200	£300	£400	£500	£600	£1000	£5000	Over £5000
Fee	£10	£20	£30	£40	£50	£60	£65	£70	£80

10.62 There are additional charges ranging between £10 and £50 for the enforcement of judgments, appeals or setting aside judgments and certain other court proceedings. The fees are listed in the leaflet *County Court Fees*, available from County Courts.

---

5 The Register of County Court Judgments Regulations 1985 (SI No 1807) (as amended).

Striking out and setting aside

10.63 These are two separate processes whereby County Court proceedings brought by a Collector may be effectively expunged, before and after judgment respectively.

Striking out

10.64 Prior to a judgment, the taxpayer may ask the Court to dismiss the proceedings by striking them out (CCR 1981, Orders 13 and 21). The taxpayer makes his application on the Court's Form N244 or by making a verbal request at a hearing.

10.65 Striking out may occur in three different situations:

- Where the whole or part of any pleading

    - discloses no reasonable cause of action or defence,
    - is scandalous, frivolous or vexatious,
    - may prejudice, embarrass or delay the fair trial, or
    - is otherwise an abuse of the process of the Court.

- If the Collector does not appear at a hearing, the Court may strike out the proceedings, although these may later be restored on application from the Collector (CCR 1981, Order 21, rule 1).

- If the Collector fails to take steps to deliver any pleading or particulars which are necessary for the Court to make a decision (CCR 1981, Order 13, rule 2).

In practice, it is extremely unusual for these grounds to exist in the case of an action by the Inland Revenue.

Setting aside judgment

10.66 The taxpayer may ask for a judgment to be set aside. Application should be made on the Court's Form N244, stating the grounds for the application, ideally within 14 days of any hearing that has been held. The application does not operate as a stay of execution, but the Court may order a stay depending upon the facts of the case.

10.67 A judgment may be set aside on the following grounds:

- the taxpayer did not receive the summons, e.g. because it was sent to the wrong address (CCR 1981, Order 37, rule 3), or

- it was obtained at a hearing in the taxpayer's absence (CCR 1981, Order 37, rule 2), or

- proceedings did not comply with the County Court rules (CCR 1981, Order 37, rule 5).

A judgment will be set aside only if the District Judge considers that the taxpayer also has a defence which has some prospects of success. Since such defences are rare in tax cases (see paragraph 10.43), it is very unusual for a judgment obtained by a Collector to be set aside.

Variation and administration orders

10.68 Where a judgment has been given and the taxpayer does not have the means to settle the payment(s) ordered by the court, or has other unsecured debts, he may apply for:

- a variation order changing the payments required under the terms of a judgment, or

- an administration order which consolidates the payments due on his tax and other debts, subject to certain conditions.

Variation orders

10.69 A taxpayer may apply to the Court for a *variation order* at any time after a judgment has been made, provided bankruptcy proceedings have not commenced (CCR 1981, Order 22, rule 10 and see paragraph 11.51 *et seq*).

10.70 This may be appropriate, for example:

- Where for any reason, including neglect of his affairs by the taxpayer, a judgment has been given for payment 'forthwith' and he does not have the means to settle the full sum due immediately.

- Where the taxpayer's financial circumstances have deteriorated and he can no longer afford instalments currently due under a judgment.

10.71 The taxpayer's application is made to the Court on Form N245, setting out the proposed terms of payment and grounds on which application is made. This form is very similar to the Admission form, discussed in paragraph 10.24 *et seq*. It is treated in exactly the same way, in that Court staff will use the *Determination of Means Calculator* (Form Ex120 - see Appendix 5) to arrive at a monthly instalment order.

10.72 The Court sends a copy of a variation application to the Collector and, if he does not object to the proposed variation within 14 days, the Court staff use the determination of means guidelines to determine the new level of payments, which is contained in the variation order.

10.73 Both parties then have 14 days to ask the Court for a *reconsideration* if they do not agree with the terms of the variation order and this application should normally be made by letter. If so, a hearing is arranged at the taxpayer's home Court (usually close to where he lives) and the case is automatically transferred there. At the hearing, the District Judge may make whatever order he thinks fit.

10.74   If the taxpayer is unable to afford a payment, he may apply to pay nothing. The Court has the power to make a variation order in these terms, so long as it is satisfied that he is unable to pay. Such an application should be made on a Form N244 enclosing a financial statement, since the Form N245 does not contain a space to request such an order.

10.75   As applies in the case of an Admission, the Collector is unlikely to object to the making of a variation order, unless he has evidence that the taxpayer's circumstances are not properly disclosed on the forms submitted to the Court.

10.76   Should the Collector ever have grounds for believing that the taxpayer is able to clear the debt more quickly, he may apply to the Court for a variation order requiring an increase in instalments or that the remaining debt be settled in one lump sum.

Administration orders

10.77   *Administration orders* are designed to enable an individual with more than one debt to:

- avoid bankruptcy, and

- discharge his debts under an affordable arrangement with the assistance of the Court.[6]

10.78   To qualify for an administration order, the taxpayer must have:

- at least one unsatisfied County Court (or High Court) judgment against him, and

- total debts of no more than £5,000 (CCA 1984, s112(1)).

10.79   An administration order is sometimes called a *small debtor's bankruptcy* and has the following consequences:

- The taxpayer makes monthly payments to the Court, which it distributes among his creditors quarterly in proportion to the debts that they are owed. The Court charges a 10% 'handling fee' for this service (CCR 1981, Order 39, rule 18).

- Interest is frozen on all judgment debts within the administration order (County Court (Interest on Judgment Debts) Order 1991, article 4(3)).

- Once an administration order is granted, it is unlawful for any creditor to approach the taxpayer for individual payment or to sue him for a debt included in the order, without permission of the Court.

---

6   It may be noted that the Insolvent Partnerships Order 1994 introduced an analogous provision for partnerships (see paragraph 11.139).

- If the taxpayer fails to make any payment due under the order, the Court may revoke it and direct that the taxpayer may not apply for credit of £250 or more without disclosing the revocation of the administration order, and disqualify him from acting as a company director for up to two years.[7]

- The presentation of a bankruptcy petition by any creditor will normally be stayed, unless the debt exceeds £1,500 and the petition is presented within 28 days of the creditor receiving notice of the administration order (CCA 1984, s112(4)).

- A *composition order* may be applied for, so that part of the taxpayer's debts are ultimately written off (see paragraph 10.83).

Procedure to apply for an administration order

10.80 Application is normally made on Form N92, on which the taxpayer lists:

- all his debts and any arrears of rent, mortgage, maintenance, community charge/council tax, hire purchase, and consumer credit agreements,

- his personal details, and

- his income and outgoings.

10.81 Upon receiving the completed form, the Court staff fix a proposed provisional level of monthly payment by the taxpayer and notification is sent to the taxpayer and to all creditors. If there are objections to the proposals, the Court will arrange a date for hearing where a District Judge will decide whether and on what terms, an order is to be granted. There is at present no statutory limit on the duration of an administration order, although the Lord Chancellor's guidance to court staff indicates that it should not normally extend beyond three years.

10.82 It should be noted that the Court has power to make an administration order without any application, for example where it appears that the taxpayer owes considerable sums to other creditors, which he is paying off (CCR 1981, Order 39 rules 1 and 2(2)).

Compositions

10.83 Where the taxpayer does not have sufficient net income to clear his debts in full during the period of an administration order, there is discretion to order that the payments will be 'to such extent as appears

---

[7] IA 1986, s429. These consequences are similar to restrictions on bankrupts (see paragraphs 11.12 and 11.14).

practical to the court under the circumstances of the case' (CCA 1984, s112(6)). Effectively this gives the court power to make an administration order whereby just part of the taxpayer's indebtedness will be cleared over the duration of the administration order and any sum unpaid at the end of that period is written off. Such orders are often called *compositions* or *composition orders* and may be applied for on Form N244 or at a hearing, as there is no space on Form N92 to enter the details.

The Court will look very carefully at a taxpayer's circumstances before granting a composition order, which may assist an individual on a low income whose circumstances are unlikely to improve, such as those who are long-term unemployed or disabled.

Inland Revenue instructions

10.84 In relation to administration orders and composition orders, the Inland Revenue is not given any preferential rights amongst creditors. Its internal instructions to Collectors simply state: ' You must never in any circumstances advise a taxpayer to apply (or not to apply) for an administration order.' (E4.803)

10.85 The instructions express no general views on the acceptability of administration orders, but the tenor suggests that the Inland Revenue will review any applications by tax debtors very carefully to ensure that they are accurate, while applications for composition orders may attract particularly careful scrutiny since they involve the prospective write-off of tax.

After the judgment

Satisfaction of judgment

10.86 When the debt due under a County Court judgment has been paid by the taxpayer, he may apply to the Court for a *certificate of satisfaction*. Before issuing this certificate, the Court will check with the Collector that the debt has been settled.

10.87 If the debt is paid within one month of judgment, the Court should ask the Registry Trust Limited to delete the entry from the Register of County Court Judgments. If it is settled later, the word *satisfied* should be entered against the judgment on the Register.

Non-compliance with the judgment

10.88 If the taxpayer does not comply with the terms of the judgment, then the Collector can apply to the Court for enforcement of the judgment. The enforcement methods available are discussed in the next section (CCR 1981, Order 25, rule 1).

10.89 However, unless the taxpayer ignores all communications, enforcement can usually be avoided for the following reasons:

- Upon receiving the summons, the taxpayer will have had the opportunity to apply for an order to pay the debt by instalments and the Court should normally set these at an affordable level (see paragraph 10.25 *et seq)*.

- If the taxpayer failed to apply for instalments and an order was given for payment forthwith, he may subsequently apply for a variation order under which the judgment debt becomes payable by instalments (see paragraph 10.69 *et seq)*.

- Collectors will often agree informally for instalments to be paid, which are less than the amount actually due under the order, reserving the power to take enforcement action if the taxpayer does not comply with the agreement. In practice, such agreements may be helpful to a taxpayer with a short-term inability to meet the terms of an instalment order. However, if the problem may be long-term, it is generally preferable to seek a variation order from the Court since this prevents the Collector from unilaterally raising his demands later on.

- In some cases, a judgment will be in an excessive amount because the sums claimed by the Collector are open to challenge, perhaps by one of the methods discussed in Chapter 4 (e.g. making a late appeal, submitting a claim, error or mistake relief, or equitable liability). In such cases, the taxpayer may negotiate appropriate reductions with the Inspector and Collector, even after judgment, and any tax discharged will reduce the remaining liability under the judgment to the amount properly due (see paragraph 10.130).

Action by the Collector

10.90 Before making an application for enforcement, the Collector should ensure that he has sufficient information regarding the taxpayer's income or assets, so as to select the most appropriate method to recover the tax. If more details are needed, he may:

- interview the taxpayer, or
- obtain details from the tax district or the taxpayer's employer, or
- apply for *oral examination* of the taxpayer (E4.602).

Oral examination

10.91 An *oral examination* brings the taxpayer before the Court, to be questioned under oath about his ability to pay the judgment debt (CCR 1981, Order 25, rule 3). Following such examination, the Collector should be better placed to decide which method of enforcement is most likely to succeed.

10.92 The Collector's instructions state that he should consider applying for oral examination only after all other lines of enquiry have been exhausted and where it is believed that the taxpayer has sufficient goods or assets. An application should not be made where the Collector believes the issue of a judgment summons is likely to be the only method of enforcement available (E4.615).

10.93 The *Order for Oral Examination* (Form N37) instructs the taxpayer to attend the Court on a specified date to be examined under oath, normally by the Chief Clerk or a District Judge. If the taxpayer fails to attend, a Form N39 warning of imprisonment for contempt of Court, is served on the taxpayer personally by a Court bailiff and *conduct money* handed to him. This must be a sufficient amount to cover the cost of travel to and from the Court by public transport.

10.94 If the taxpayer still does not attend Court or does not pay the judgment debt, the collection office will ask the Court to issue a *Warrant of Committal* (Form N40) and the taxpayer may be arrested. The taxpayer may only be discharged from custody by purging his contempt, i.e. making a written apology to the Court and asking for release from custody on the grounds that he has made amends for his failure to comply with the order of the Court. He will also need to supply evidence of means. Unlike committal following summary proceedings, the tax debt is *not* remitted.

Enforcement powers

10.95 There are six methods of enforcement available and the Inland Revenue's official order of preference (at E4.630) is:

- warrants of execution

- garnishee proceedings

- charging orders

- attachment of earnings orders

- bankruptcy proceedings

- judgment summonses

Warrants of execution

10.96 A warrant of execution instructs a Court bailiff to:

- call at the taxpayer's house, business premises or wherever the taxpayer's goods may be found, and

- remove and sell sufficient of those goods to satisfy the judgment and the costs of sale. If there are insufficient goods, the warrant is returned unsatisfied.

This process is similar to distraint, discussed in Chapter 8, although in this case it is carried out by a Court official and not a Collector. If the debt is below £5,000, the work is done by County Court bailiffs who tend to be helpful and are subject to guidelines laid down by the Lord Chancellor's Department detailing goods exempt from distraint (see paragraph 8.38 and E4.701). Debts of £5,000 or more are handled by High Court bailiffs (High Court and County Courts Jurisdiction Order 1991).

10.97 The Collector applies to the Court for a warrant of execution to be issued for the whole or part of a debt (CCR 1981, Order 26, rule 1). The minimum sum outstanding under the judgment must be at least £50 or one month's instalment, whichever is the greater. A warrant may be issued for the full sum remaining unsatisfied under the judgment, even if only one instalment has been missed (CCR 1981, Order 26, rule 1(2)).

10.98 The Court first issues a *Notice of Issue of Warrant of Execution* (Form N326) which gives the taxpayer at least seven days notice of the warrant's existence and the bailiff's intention to call. If payment is not made and provided there are sufficient effects, the bailiff will 'levy' on the taxpayer's goods.

10.99 The remaining process is quite similar to distraint described in Chapter 8. In particular, there is usually a *walking possession agreement*, and sale can take place after the goods have been held for five days, provided that payment has not been made (CCA 1984, s93).

10.100 The legal restrictions on goods which may be taken by bailiffs are contained in CCA 1984, s89(1). Exempt goods are:

- such tools, books, vehicles, and other items of equipment as are necessary for use personally in employment, business or vocation, and

- such clothing, bedding, furniture, household equipment and provisions as are necessary for satisfying the basic domestic needs of that person and family (see paragraph 8.37 *et seq)*.

10.101 A warrant remains in force for one year from the date of issue and cannot be issued more than six years after the date of judgment or order, except by leave of the Court (CCR 1981, Order 26, rules 5, 16(5) and 17(6)).

Suspension of a warrant of execution

10.102 When a taxpayer receives notice of issue of a warrant of execution, he may apply for issue of the proposed warrant to be suspended (CCR

1981, Order 25, rule 8). This is done by completing Form N245 (i.e. the same form as for a variation order) and it may assist to attach a covering letter explaining, for example that:

- A warrant will not work because the taxpayer has insufficient goods of value.

- The only valuable asset that may appear available for seizure is exempt, because it is necessary for use in the taxpayer's work.

Garnishee orders

10.103 A garnishee order instructs a third party who owes money to the taxpayer (the 'garnishee') to pay it to the plaintiff instead, or pay over sufficient to satisfy the judgment debt (CCR 1981, Order 30). This is known as *attaching the debt*. Many debts can be attached in this way, but in practice it is used mainly to obtain money held in the taxpayer's bank or building society account.

10.104 The Collector makes an application to the Court, which is considered by a District Judge who may make a *garnishee order nisi* (interim order), which orders the garnishee to attach sufficient debt to satisfy the judgment or order, i.e. effectively freezing the money if held in an account, pending a hearing.

10.105 At the hearing, the taxpayer or garnishee may show good reason why the order should not be made absolute, for example if the account is overdrawn or the taxpayer is holding the money for a third party. Otherwise the Court will make a *garnishee order absolute*, under which the garnishee is required to pay the sum to the Collector. It is difficult for a taxpayer to prevent a garnishee order from being made if funds are available.

Charging orders

10.106 A charging order secures the judgment debt against equity in the taxpayer's real property or other capital asset (e.g. government stocks or shares) and effectively converts an unsecured debt into a secured one (CCR 1981, Order 31 and Charging Orders Act 1979).

10.107 The Inland Revenue has advised TaxAid that at present:

> 'the Revenue only applies for charging orders in a very small number of cases, usually against real property. The use of charging orders to secure debt is under review.'

10.108 Collectors are instructed that charging orders should normally be restricted to cases where the property is up for sale, and also that in such cases normally they should seek a solicitor's undertaking in preference to a charging order (E4.720 and E4.721). As with garnishee orders, an interim *charging order nisi* is made prior to a hearing, at which the order may become *absolute*. The Court is not obliged to make a charging order, although it will generally grant the application. An order may be refused, for example, where it would prejudice the rights of other creditors or where the taxpayer is insolvent.

Attachment of earnings orders

10.109 This is a process by which the Court orders the taxpayer's employer or occupational pension administrator to deduct a specified sum from his earnings or occupational pension, until the judgment debt is satisfied (Attachment of Earnings Act 1971 and CCR 1981, Order 27).

10.110 An attachment of earnings order can be made on any unpaid judgment debt over £50 and fixes:

- the amount of the weekly or monthly deductions to be made by the employer[8], called the *normal deduction rate*, and

- the amount below which the Court considers that the taxpayer's pay or pension - after deduction of tax, national insurance and pension contributions - should not be reduced. This is called the *protected earnings rate* and is set by reference to current income support and family credit levels. The scales appropriate to different family situations are published in the *Inland Revenue Enforcement Manual*, Volume IV, Appendix 4.

10.111 The Collector applies for an attachment by submitting to the Court a *Notice of Application for Attachment of Earnings Order* (Form N55). The Court sends this to the taxpayer, together with a questionnaire (Form N56) requesting details of his employment, income, liabilities and proposal for payment. This form should be returned within 8 days and failure to do so, or provision of false information, can lead to imprisonment (Attachment of Earnings Act 1971, s23(1)).

A Court officer will use the information supplied on the Form N56 together with the Determination of Means Calculator (Form Ex120). The same procedure is used as detailed in paragraphs 10.30 *et seq.*

10.112 There is space on Form N56 to request that only a *suspended attachment order* is made, under which the taxpayer agrees to make regular payments directly. An attachment of earnings order will then not be made unless he fails to keep up with the agreed payments. This is particularly helpful if the taxpayer does not want his employer to know of the judgment debt.

10.113 A taxpayer may apply for a *consolidated attachment of earnings order* where he has two or more judgment debts, of which at least one is

---

[8] The employer may withold £1.00 each time a deduction is made, to cover administrative costs.

subject to an attachment of earnings order (Attachment of Earnings Act 1971, s17 and CCR 1981, Order 27, rules 18-22). The sums due under all the judgments are then included within the same order. Application is made on Form N244 supported by a financial statement and proposals for payment under the consolidated order.

10.114 The official Inland Revenue view is that this method of enforcement is slow and fairly expensive (E4.630). It is of no assistance to the Collector where the taxpayer is self-employed, nor where he has a large family and a modest income falling below the protected earnings rate.

Bankruptcy proceedings

10.115 Although only fifth in the 'pecking order' of enforcement measures to be considered by a Collector (see paragraph 10.95 above), this method is used quite frequently by the Inland Revenue and 3,866 bankruptcy petitions were issued in 1995/96, with 2,217 bankruptcy orders in the same period.

10.116 Bankruptcy is considered in detail in Chapter 11 (since it is not a County Court remedy as such) and in every case the local collection office will pass the file to the Inland Revenue's Enforcement Office in Worthing for proceedings to be taken. Once the file has been transferred, it becomes more difficult to dissuade the Inland Revenue from taking the matter to bankruptcy, because the Enforcement Office operates a shorter timescale when considering requests for time to pay:

- At the local level, Collectors are instructed: 'Where the debtor is able to bring his/her tax position up to date within three or four years, the Collection Manager should give favourable consideration to making an instalment arrangement in preference to recommending bankruptcy or winding-up proceedings.' (E4.752)

- Once the matter is being handled by the Enforcement Office, different considerations apply. The Inland Revenue has advised TaxAid:

    'The Enforcement Office only becomes involved when it has proved impossible to negotiate a settlement locally. In certain circumstances, the Enforcement Office may agree that payment can be made by instalments... The Enforcement Office will expect settlement under an instalment arrangement to be made in the shortest time possible and usually within 12 months... In cases of genuine hardship, consideration will be given to instalment arrangements over a longer period although it would be unusual for these to extend for longer than 24 months.'

10.117 Accordingly, the taxpayer's best chance of avoiding bankruptcy may be by ensuring that the case never reaches the Enforcement Office, either:

- by negotiating an instalment arrangement at local collection level, or

- by using the provisions for payment by instalments under County Court judgments (including variation orders) discussed earlier in this chapter.

10.118 It should be noted that in determining whether a taxpayer has a debt of at least £750, the minimum necessary to commence bankruptcy proceedings, a judgment debt under a County Court order cannot be included if the taxpayer has complied with the terms of the order (IR 1986, rule 6).

Judgment summonses

10.119 A judgment summons is served on the taxpayer requiring him to attend Court to explain why the money due under the judgment has not been paid (CCR 1981, Order 28). The taxpayer will be examined under oath in open Court before a Judge to establish his financial position. The extent to which judgment summonses are used varies widely between collection offices.

10.120 A taxpayer who fails to attend Court as ordered, or ignores an order of the Judge at the hearing, can be imprisoned. Therefore, it is important for the Collector to decide whether committal proceedings are desirable. If the taxpayer is elderly or infirm or if it is a partnership debt, a judgment summons should not be issued (E4.756).

10.121 The *Judgment Summons* (Form N67) is served personally by the Court bailiff and orders the taxpayer to attend Court on a specific date. If the taxpayer fails to attend Court, an order to attend at an adjourned hearing (Form N69) may be served personally on the taxpayer and *conduct money* handed to him (see paragraph 10.93). If the taxpayer still does not attend Court or pay the judgment debt, he may be arrested and can be imprisoned for up to six weeks.

10.122 The issue of judgment summonses frequently leads to the Court ordering a lengthy instalment arrangement and can prove to be a slow process as there are often difficulties serving the forms on the taxpayer.[9] When granting an instalment arrangement, the Judge may also grant a *suspended committal order*, which gives the Collector a powerful weapon to ensure that the taxpayer complies with the payment order.

---

[9] If the original judgment summons has not been served within four months of its issue, the Collector must apply to the Court to extend the time limit.

Adjustments to the tax liability after proceedings commence

10.123 It is very common for County Court summonses to be issued, or judgments to be given, in amounts which include excessive tax liabilities, perhaps because:

- The debt includes a liability on an unappealed estimated assessment.
- There is a claim for equitable liability.
- There is scope for a claim to be made.
- Further relief is due for a tax credit or set-off, or an unrecorded payment.

10.124 It has already been explained in paragraph 7.19 *et seq* that many such issues may not be raised in the course of enforcement proceedings and that, even where they do constitute admissible defences, the Court may be persuaded by an over-zealous Collector to enter judgment in an excessive amount.

10.125 Accordingly, it becomes important to understand the procedures that apply where a dispute as to the amount of the tax due is resolved, between the taxpayer and the Inspector or Collector, with the result that all or part of a liability is discharged after a summons has been prepared.

If the summons has not yet been served

10.126 If the debt is discharged fully, the Collector should ask the Court to suspend service of the summons and no further action should be taken.

10.127 If the debt is reduced in part, amended particulars of claim should be prepared by the Collector and sent to the Court for service on the taxpayer (E4.210 and E4.902).

After service of the summons but before entry of judgment

10.128 If the liability is discharged in full, the same provisions apply as for full payment after service of a summons, i.e. no further action is taken (see paragraph 10.126).

10.129 If part of the liability is discharged, the Collector should obtain a judgment based upon the remaining debt.

After judgment

10.130 If the liability is discharged in part or in full, the amount remaining unsatisfied under the judgment is reduced accordingly (and repayment made if appropriate) (CCR 1981, Order 42, rule 10). If the debt is fully discharged within one month of judgment, the entry should be deleted from the Register of County Court debts (see paragraph 10.87).

10.131 However, the amount of the reduction is not regarded as a payment under the judgment, i.e. if an order for instalments has been made, these must continue until the reduced amount due under the judgment has been paid (CCR 1981, Order 42, rule 10 and see footnote to paragraph 4.82). The Collector should advise the taxpayer and Court in writing of the amount of the discharge (E4.902).

Discrepancies in County Court procedures

10.132 It will be noted from this chapter that there are a range of procedures in the County Courts designed to give protection to debtors, ranging from the opportunity to dispute the amount claimed on a summons or apply for payment by instalments, to variation of the terms for paying judgment debts, to provisions for hearings before a District Judge before enforcement proceedings are taken.

10.133 Much of the responsibility for the administration of these safeguards, and the determination of instalments to be paid, is devolved to Court staff. As there are 270 County Courts in England and Wales, it is not surprising that complaints arise of errors and inconsistencies in the administration of justice.

10.134 Problem areas include the following:

- Court staff failing to use the Determination of Means Calculator in calculating instalments.

- Cases not being transferred to the debtor's local court, when a hearing is required.

- Court staff accepting plaintiff's objections out of time, or failing to act appropriately in response to an application by a debtor.

- Errors by the Courts in carrying out their functions.

10.135 If it is considered that the Court has not carried out its functions in the correct manner, expert advice should be sought. Fortunately there are now many advisers across the country who are experts in County Court procedures (see Chapter 13).

Key points to consider

10.136 A County Court order should not always be resisted, given that it offers the taxpayer an opportunity to settle the debt by manageable instalments and the freezing of interest. However, these advantages must be viewed in the light of the main drawbacks being 'credit blacklisting' and the range of enforcement methods open to the Collector (see paragraph 10.95 *et seq)*.

10.137 An order to make payment forthwith, or to pay by instalments that have become unaffordable, can always be amended by applying for a variation order (see paragraph 10.69 *et seq*). Action should be taken quickly, or the Collector might seek enforcement of the outstanding sums due.

10.138 If a taxpayer is in a desperate financial position and his total debts are less than £5,000, an administration order may be obtained, possibly combined with a composition order. This will enable the taxpayer to pay what he can afford, normally over three years, and the balance outstanding after this period to be written off (see paragraph 10.77 *et seq*).

10.139 The County Court is rarely the appropriate forum to dispute the sum claimed by a Collector. If the taxpayer has grounds for obtaining a reduction in the sum due and payable, the best approach is to seek a delay in proceedings, usually by asking the Collector to defer entry of judgment or asking the Court to adjourn a hearing, according to the state the proceedings have reached (see paragraph 10.44 *et seq*).

10.140 If tax is discharged after proceedings have commenced or an order has been given, appropriate adjustments should be made (see paragraph 10.123 *et seq*).

10.141 Although several procedures in the County Courts are conducted by paperwork, there are many circumstances where a hearing may be held. Such hearings should not be ignored, as they may lead to an adverse judgment or, in some extreme cases, imprisonment.

10.142 If it is considered that Court officials or a District Judge has failed to follow County Court procedures, seek expert advice (see paragraph 10.132 *et seq*).

Chapter 11

Bankruptcy proceedings

The circumstances in which the Inland Revenue will petition for bankruptcy, and the procedures and remedies are complex. This chapter considers the following main areas:

From paragraph

- Introduction   *11.1*
- Effects of bankruptcy on the individual   *11.6*
- Inland Revenue considerations   *11.24*
- Procedures leading up to a bankruptcy hearing   *11.29*
- The bankruptcy hearing   *11.60*
- A debtor's petition   *11.77*
- Events following bankruptcy   *11.84*
- Meeting the claims of creditors   *11.92*
- The bankrupt's estate   *11.100*
- The bankrupt's home   *11.115*
- Insolvent partnerships   *11.139*
- The tax implications of bankruptcy   *11.147*
- Costs and fees   *11.159*
- Ending the bankruptcy   *11.163*
- Voluntary arrangements   *11.181*
- Key points to consider   *11.209*

Introduction

11.1 The Inland Revenue's ultimate sanction is to petition for bankruptcy, and in 1995/96 it served 3,866 bankruptcy petitions and obtained 2,217 bankruptcy orders.[1] All Inland Revenue petitions are presented in the High Court in London.

11.2 Although the monetary threshold for a bankruptcy petition is £750, it is relatively unusual for the Inland Revenue to commence bankruptcy proceedings in respect of tax debts of below £5,000 (see paragraph 6.67).

---

[1] Source: Inland Revenue

11.3 In certain circumstances, it may be appropriate for a taxpayer to petition for his own bankruptcy and this is known as a *debtor's petition*. In such cases, both the High Court in London and certain County Courts have jurisdiction.

11.4 Much of the administration in relation to bankrupts' affairs is carried out by the Official Receiver, who works within the Insolvency Service of the Department of Trade and Industry and is an officer of the Court for the area covered by his office.[2]

11.5 The main legislation governing bankruptcy is contained in the Insolvency Act 1986 and the Insolvency Rules 1986. In this chapter, unless otherwise stated, section references and rule numbers (e.g. r6.3) refer to the 1986 Act and Rules respectively.

Effects of bankruptcy on the individual

The main financial implications

11.6 This section outlines the main financial implications. More detailed explanation is given in subsequent sections of this chapter.

Loss of assets

11.7 Shortly after a bankruptcy order is made, the *bankrupt's estate* (see paragraph 11.100 *et seq*) vests in his *trustee in bankruptcy* (see paragraph 11.88), who will seek to dispose of it for the benefit of creditors (see paragraph 11.92 *et seq*). With limited exclusions, this comprises all property belonging to the bankrupt at the date of the bankruptcy order. The trustee also administers and controls the bankrupt's financial affairs until he is discharged from bankruptcy, which is normally after three years (see paragraph 11.176 *et seq*).

11.8 Banks and building societies must freeze any accounts in the bankrupt's name, or in joint names with any third parties, upon receipt of a notice of the bankruptcy order. If the bankrupt requires an account to receive future earnings, he will need to open a new one. The policy adopted by each bank or building society towards bankrupts varies, but several will permit the operation of an account which cannot be overdrawn.

After-acquired property and income

11.9 The bankrupt must notify the trustee of property acquired, or of any increases in income, during bankruptcy. The trustee may claim after-acquired property, or obtain an income payments order, for the benefit of the bankrupt's estate (see paragraph 11.107 *et seq*).

---

[2] At 31 March 1995, there were 29 Official Receivers managing 33 offices in England and Wales; Insolvency Service staff numbered 1,757.

The taxpayer's business

11.10 If the taxpayer has been proprietor of a business with valuable premises, equipment or stock, normally this will be closed down. Trading may be allowed to continue where closure would be impractical, or where the business might be marketed as a going concern, for example:

- a farm, or
- a newsagent's shop with a delivery round.

11.11 If the taxpayer runs a business with no valuable assets, there is no prohibition against his continuing to trade, although he may have difficulties because of credit or professional restrictions discussed in this section. The bankrupt is entitled to retain necessary equipment and the obligation to inform the trustee of after-acquired property does not apply to property acquired in the ordinary course of the business, although the bankrupt may be required to supply the trustee with periodic accounts (r6.200(5)).

Obtaining credit

11.12 It is an offence for a bankrupt to obtain credit of £250 or more, without declaring his status (s360(1)(a) and see paragraph 11.91). Bankruptcies are recorded by credit reference agencies and are normally retained on their records for about eight years following the order. The implications of this are described in paragraph 7.38 *et seq.*

Fees and costs

11.13 The bankruptcy process is extremely expensive (see paragraph 11.159 *et seq*) and it has been estimated that on average 60% of a bankrupt's assets will be swallowed up in the fees and costs of administration.[3] Accordingly, bankruptcy should always be avoided if the taxpayer is actually solvent.

Other implications

11.14 An undischarged bankrupt is disqualified from holding various positions including:

- a Member of Parliament (s427)

- a local councillor (Local Government Act 1972, ss80 and 81)

- a Justice of the Peace (Justice of the Peace Act 1979, s63A)

- a director of a limited company (Company Directors Disqualification Act 1986, s11)

---

[3] *Law Society Gazette* 12 April 1989

- an estate agent (Estate Agents Act 1979, s23(1))

- a receiver or manager of a limited company (s31)

- an insolvency practitioner (s390)

11.15 Beyond that, many professional bodies automatically expel any member becoming bankrupt and those working in other regulated businesses may encounter difficulty. For example, a chartered accountant will find that his Institute membership is terminated and licensed taxi drivers in London may not be permitted to operate as 'owner drivers' while they are undischarged bankrupts; there are also restrictions on the work of financial advisers.

11.16 The 'stigma' of bankruptcy will trouble some individuals more than others. Although every bankruptcy order is published in the *London Gazette* and a local paper, many bankrupts manage to keep their status secret even from close friends and relatives.

11.17 More materially, the bankrupt's status may affect his current employment status or future prospects of obtaining employment. He may be obliged under an employment contract to reveal his status, or his employer may learn of it through media publicity or a third party. The Official Receiver will not normally inform an employer of an employee's bankruptcy.

11.18 A bankrupt may lose his right to occupy a rented domestic property. Contracts for domestic lettings sometimes include a clause providing for termination upon the tenant's bankruptcy (see paragraph 11.138). The Official Receiver will usually need to advise a landlord of his tenant's bankruptcy.[4]

11.19 The bankrupt must also:

> '(a)   give to the trustee such information as to his affairs,
>
> (b)   attend on the trustee at such times, and
>
> (c)   do all such other things,
>
> as the trustee may for the purposes of carrying out his functions ... reasonably require' (s333(1)).

'Advantages' for the taxpayer

11.20 All the above drawbacks must be viewed in terms of the benefits that bankruptcy offers.

---

[4] Official Receiver's leaflet *What will happen to my home? Information on your home when bankruptcy occurs*

Removal of pressure from creditors

11.21 Bankruptcy can remove the uncertainty and anxiety caused by repeated contact from creditors threatening recovery action. Once a bankruptcy order is made, creditors having debts provable in the bankruptcy cease to have any remedy against the taxpayer personally and must claim against the bankrupt's estate (s285(3)) (see paragraph 11.92 *et seq)*.

A chance to clear debts and make a fresh start

11.22 Although the bankrupt may lose valuable assets owned at the time of the order and may have to contribute to creditors from income received or assets acquired during bankruptcy, he will usually be discharged after three years and is then released from virtually all claims for pre-bankruptcy debts (see paragraph 11.180 for exceptions to this rule). This is a shorter period than it would take many individuals to clear their tax debts by way of instalments under County Court judgments and in most bankruptcies the creditors receive no more than a fraction of the claims lodged by them.

11.23 If the taxpayer has minimal assets and little or negative equity in his home, there may be no change in his financial circumstances and he may well be permitted to continue his job uninterrupted.

Inland Revenue considerations

11.24 All bankruptcy action is initiated by the Inland Revenue's Enforcement Office, at Durrington Bridge House, Barrington Road, Worthing, West Sussex BN12 4SE. The legal formalities are carried out by the Inland Revenue's Solicitor's Office.

11.25 If the Enforcement Office is unable to reach an acceptable agreement with the taxpayer and it is not an acceptable case for remission, bankruptcy will be considered:[5]

> 'The factors we take into account when deciding whether or not to go ahead (with bankruptcy) include:
>
> - the size of the debt and the rate at which it is likely to increase
> - whether any tax previously over-paid can be set-off against this debt in the near future
> - offers of payment, including the success of any earlier arrangements to pay
> - your income and outgoings, assets and other liabilities

---

[5] For further discussion of remission and instalment arrangements with the Enforcement Office, see paragraphs 6.105 *et seq,* 6.145 *et seq* and 10.116.

- how we have been treated compared with other creditors

- your past tax compliance record

- your age, health and domestic circumstances

- whether there have been transactions, such as sales at below true value to people outside the jurisdiction of the British Courts, which may have been made so you could avoid paying tax...

'In some cases we may decide, in light of the above, that we need to start bankruptcy ... proceedings even though there may appear to be little prospect of recovering the debt owed at the time' *(Code of Practice 6 Collection of Tax pp7-8).*

Internal guidance

11.26 There is not much guidance in the published Inland Revenue guidance manuals on how the above rather general statement is applied, although the following reference is of note:

'A case may be considered suitable for bankruptcy ... proceedings where other methods of enforcement are unavailable or unsatisfactory **and** either

- there is evidence of assets (for example, a house) which give a reasonable prospect of recovering a worthwhile sum, or

- the debtor has no (or negligible) means or assets **and** the overall tax position is worsening because further liability has arisen/will arise, or

- the debtor has already been imprisoned for failing to pay part of a judgment debt' *(Inland Revenue Enforcement Manual* paragraph E4.752).

11.27 *Inter alia,* this statement reinforces the final sentence in the quote from the Code of Practice, that bankruptcy proceedings may be taken without any expectation of a financial yield for the Inland Revenue.

11.28 A further consideration by the Enforcement Office will be the extent of the Inland Revenue's expected preferential rights following bankruptcy, since this will determine the likely 'dividend' (see paragraph 11.94 *et seq).*

Procedures leading up to a bankruptcy hearing

11.29 The following paragraphs consider the procedures where a bankruptcy petition is presented by the Inland Revenue. The position where a taxpayer files a debtor's petition is discussed in paragraph 11.77 *et seq.*

Statutory demand

11.30 A necessary pre-requisite for any bankruptcy petition is that the debtor appears unable to pay, or has no reasonable prospect of paying, the debt (s267(2)(c)). Under the Insolvency Act, this may be satisfied in one of two ways:

- The creditor has served a *statutory demand* on the debtor, and

    - a period of at least three weeks has elapsed since service, and

    - the demand has been neither complied with nor set aside, and

    - there is no outstanding application for it to be set aside.

- Execution or other process issued in respect of the debt on a judgment or court order has been returned unsatisfied (s268(1) and r6.8(2)).

11.31 In practice the Inland Revenue always commences bankruptcy proceedings by the former process, i.e. the service of a statutory demand *(Collection 4 Bankruptcy and winding up)*.

11.32 A statutory demand is a formal document stating the amount claimed by the Inland Revenue and requiring the taxpayer to pay the debt or to secure or compound for it to the creditor's satisfaction.[6] The Inland Revenue uses a modified version of the prescribed Court Form 6.1 (see Appendix 7).

Service

11.33 The Inland Revenue's practice is to serve the statutory demand on the taxpayer in person if at all possible *(Collection 4 Bankruptcy and winding up)*.

11.34 If this is not possible, the Inland Revenue is required 'to do all that is reasonable for the purpose of bringing the statutory demand to the debtor's attention' (r6.3(2)):

- This may include service by post, in which event service is deemed to be effected on the seventh day after posting.

- In extreme cases, if the taxpayer may be keeping out of the way to avoid service in relation to a debt which is payable under a judgment or court order, service may be by advertisement (r6.3(3)).

11.35 Once service has been effected, the demand is not invalidated by an error, for example the use of the wrong form or an overstatement of the

---

6 The word *compound*, in this context, means to pay by instalments and/or full settlement by less than 100p in the £.

amount due, unless the error actually misled the taxpayer (*Re a Debtor* (No 1 of 1987) [1989] 2 All ER 46).

Responding to the statutory demand

11.36 While some commercial creditors issue statutory demands as a threat to encourage settlement of debts, with no intention to petition for bankruptcy, the Inland Revenue invariably proceeds to bankruptcy unless the taxpayer either:

- complies with the demand to the Inland Revenue's satisfaction, which in practice requires immediate payment or an offer to settle the debt over a very short period, or

- successfully applies to have it set aside.

Application to set aside a statutory demand

11.37 The application to set aside a statutory demand must be made to the High Court within 18 days after the date of service, using court Form 6.4 accompanied by a copy of the demand and a supporting affidavit (on Form 6.5) stating the grounds for the application. Four copies of the application and affidavit must be lodged.

11.38 The Court has a general power to grant an extension of the 18 day period under s376, although it is understood that only very limited extensions are granted. There is a fee of £20.

11.39 The Court may dismiss an application without a hearing if the application does not show sufficient cause. Otherwise a hearing date will be fixed and the parties should be given at least seven days' notice (r6.5).

11.40 The Court may set aside the statutory demand on any of the following three grounds:

- The debt is disputed on substantial grounds.

- The creditor has security which equals or exceeds the debt.

- The Court is satisfied that the demand should be set aside on other grounds (r6.5(4)).[7]

Disputes on substantial grounds

11.41 It is necessary to dispute the entire debt; a demand will not be set aside if it is overstated or only part of the debt is disputed.[8]

---

[7] The Insolvency Rules include a fourth possible ground - where the debtor has a counterclaim, set-off or cross-claim against the creditor - but this ground does not apply to debts due to the Crown.

[8] *Re a Debtor* (No 1 of 1987) [1989] 2 All ER 46. If the undisputed sum is less than £750, this may be grounds for opposing a bankruptcy petition at a later date, see paragraph 11.71.

11.42   If the demand is based on a judgment, the Court cannot go behind the judgment or enquire into the validity of the debt, nor should it generally adjourn the application to await the outcome of an application to set aside a judgment or order (*Practice Note (Bankruptcy: Statutory Demand: Setting Aside)* [1987] 1 WLR 119).

11.43   In *Re a Debtor (No 657/SD/91), ex p. CIR v The Debtor* (Ch D [1992] STC 751), the Inland Revenue had served a statutory demand on an uncertificated sub-contractor in the construction industry to recover £39,736, including £14,811 in respect of an unsatisfied judgment debt. The Inland Revenue admitted that it held some £24,000 in respect of deductions by contractors creditable against the taxpayer's liabilities, although the set-off had not been finalised. The Registrar's order to set the demand aside was overturned by the High Court on the grounds that it could not enquire into the validity of the debt and that even if the debt was overstated, this was not sufficient grounds for the demand to be set aside.

11.44   Similarly, a demand should not be set aside on the grounds that the taxpayer has unagreed losses available for carry back, or that the Inland Revenue's claim is based upon excessive assessments confirmed by the Commissioners (*Re a Debtor (No 383/SD/92), Neely v CIR* [1992] TL 3342 and *Re a Debtor (No 960/SD/92), ex p. The Debtor v CIR* Ch D [1993] STC 218).

The Inland Revenue has security which equals or exceeds the debt.

11.45   This argument was advanced by the taxpayer in *Re a Debtor (No 960/SD/92), ex p. The Debtor v CIR.* He had written to the Inland Revenue in general terms offering his house as security, without providing details of its value or other charges against it, although it appeared subsequently, from evidence given in Court, that there was sufficient equity to cover the Inland Revenue's claim. Nevertheless, the Judge refused the application to set aside, saying: 'The Revenue does not hold security in respect of the debt which it claims by the demand. The most there has been has been a general offer without any specific details of the value of the property or the other encumbrances on the property.' (Ch D [1993] STC 218 at p220).

11.46   In practice, this ground is unlikely to be of assistance in tax debt cases. If the Inland Revenue has agreed to accept security, then it should not issue a statutory demand except in cases of gross maladministration.

Other grounds satisfactory to the Court

11.47   This is a 'mopping up' provision. Grounds that might be considered satisfactory may be inferred from the suggested reasons, provided by way of example, on the court Form 6.5 on which the taxpayer makes his affidavit:

●   The taxpayer admits the debt, but it is not payable now.

- Part of the debt is admitted and the taxpayer will pay it now, but denies the balance of the debt.

- The taxpayer admits the debt and is prepared to secure or compound for it to the creditor's satisfaction by ...9

- Execution of the judgment has been stayed.

- The demand does not comply with the Insolvency Rules in that ...

11.48 A demand may be set aside under the last point where the Inland Revenue has not complied with statutory requirements necessary for tax to become due and payable, for example in relation to the service of documents.

11.49 In *Re a Debtor (No 1240/50/91), ex p. The debtor v CIR* (Ch D [1992] STC 771) the taxpayer had been heavily engaged in fighting extradition to the USA and had not attended a Commissioners' hearing of a tax appeal. Notification of determination under TMA 1970, s55(9) was sent to his previous place of business, but this did not comply with the requirement of delivery to the 'usual or last known place of residence, or his place of business or employment' (TMA 1970, s115(2) and paragraph 2.18). As the notice was not properly served, the tax was not yet due and payable and the statutory demand was set aside.

11.50 In *Re a Debtor (No 415/SD/1993)* (Ch D [1994] 1 WLR 917) a debtor applied for a statuory demand to be set aside on the grounds that he had made an offer of security and settlement by instalments, which had been unreasonably refused by the creditor. The Court declined to set the demand aside, noting that these might subsequently be grounds for dismissing the bankruptcy petition itself (see paragraph 11.66 *et seq*).

Obtaining a variation order

11.51 Statutory demands by the Inland Revenue are normally founded upon County Court judgments. Where the Court has ordered payment by instalments, there is no 'debt' for the purposes of a statutory demand, unless and until the taxpayer fails to comply with the order. Accordingly a taxpayer is safe from bankruptcy proceedings in respect of such a judgment debt for as long as he complies with the terms of the order.

11.52 Frequently, however, statutory demands issued by the Inland Revenue are based upon County Court orders requiring payment 'forthwith', because the taxpayer did not realise that he could apply for an instalment order. The position is not irremediable after the judgment, because the taxpayer can subsequently apply for a variation order requiring payment by instalments (see paragraph 10.69 *et seq)*.

---

9   Unless the taxpayer is able to provide proof of the Inland Revenue's acceptance, an application on this ground will not succeed.

11.53   However, it is understood that a Court may refuse a variation order where bankruptcy proceedings have already commenced by way of the issue of a statutory demand, and so it is essential that any variation order is applied for beforehand.[10]

Creditor's petition

Grounds

11.54   The Inland Revenue may present a bankruptcy petition if the following five conditions are met:

- The debt owed to the Inland Revenue by the taxpayer is equal to or exceeds the 'bankruptcy level', currently £750 (s267).

- The debt is a liquidated sum payable immediately or at some certain future time and is unsecured (s267).

- The taxpayer appears unable to pay the debt or has no reasonable prospect of being able to pay (s267 and see next paragraph).

- There is no outstanding application for a statutory demand to be set aside (s267 and see paragraph 11.37 *et seq*).

- The taxpayer is domiciled or personally present in England and Wales on the day on which the petition is presented, or at any time in the previous three years has been resident or carried on a business in England and Wales (s265).

11.55   The third condition is satisfied in respect of any tax debt included in a statutory demand which has been served at least three weeks prior to the petition and has not been complied with nor set aside.   An expedited bankruptcy petition may be presented before that period has elapsed if there is the possibility that the taxpayer's property will be diminished significantly, although a bankruptcy order cannot be given until three weeks after the service of the statutory demand (ss268(1), 270 and 271(2)).   If the statutory demand was served more than four months previously, the Inland Revenue must provide an affidavit stating reasons for the delay.   If an adequate explanation is not given, the Court may dismiss the application (s266(3) and r6.12(7)).

Procedure

11.56   All Inland Revenue petitions are filed in the High Court in London together with an affidavit verifying that the statements in the petition are true, or are true to the best of the petitioner's knowledge, information and belief (r6.12(1)), and an affidavit verifying service of the statutory demand. The Inland Revenue uses a modified version of the prescribed Court Form 6.7 (see Appendix 8).

---

[10] *The County Court Green Book* (Note to CCR 1981, Order 22, rule 10)

11.57 The petition should be served personally on the taxpayer, by an officer of the Court or the Inland Revenue (r6.14(1)) and in practice this is normally done by a local collection office. If personal service cannot be effected, for example because the taxpayer is keeping out of the way to avoid service of the petition, the Court may order substituted service in such manner as it thinks fit (r6.14(2)).

11.58 The petition cannot be heard for 14 days after service, unless the taxpayer has absconded, the taxpayer consents, or the Court is satisfied that there is some other good reason for an expedited hearing (r6.18).

11.59 The taxpayer may oppose the petition using Form 6.19 which must be filed at the Court not less than seven days before the hearing and a copy sent to the Inland Revenue (r6.21). This must specify the grounds on which he objects to the making of a bankruptcy order against him. The grounds which might be acceptable to the court are discussed in paragraph 11.66 *et seq.*

The bankruptcy hearing

11.60 Inland Revenue petitions are heard in private before a Bankruptcy Registrar in the High Court in London. There is a Citizens Advice Bureau in the main hall which is able to provide advice on bankruptcy, but will not offer representation.[11]

11.61 If the taxpayer is opposing the petition, or wishes to obtain an adjournment, he should attend the Court on the date and time shown on the petition and advise the Registrar's clerk that he is present.

11.62 It may also be appropriate to seek out the representative of the Inland Revenue before the hearing to advise him of the action intended, to ascertain whether he will oppose it. Usually he will be a staff member of Inland Revenue Solicitor's Office with little detailed knowledge of the case and will usually be at the Bankruptcy Court to represent the Inland Revenue in respect of several petitions, most of which will be unopposed. If the taxpayer has contacted the Enforcement Office about a proposed adjournment prior to the hearing, the Inland Revenue representative should be able to indicate whether he will be opposing an adjournment.

The Court's jurisdiction

11.63 The Court has a wide jurisdiction but should not make a bankruptcy order unless it is satisfied that the tax debt which is due at the date of the petition has not been paid, nor secured or compounded for (s271(1)).[12]

---

[11] It is open Monday-Thursday, between 10.00 am and 12.30 pm, although on Tuesdays and Thursdays clients are seen by appointment only. Telephone: 0171 936 7120

[12] Under the Insolvency Act, petitions may also be presented in respect of future debts, for which different provisions apply, but these are not discussed as the Inland Revenue's practice is to petition only for debts payable immediately.

11.64 It may dismiss a petition if it is satisfied that the taxpayer is able to pay all his debts (s271(3)). To succeed on this ground, the taxpayer needs to provide detailed evidence of his assets and liabilities. If the court dismisses the petition, it would then be up to the Inland Revenue to secure payment through an alternative enforcement procedure. Dismissal on this ground would be rare, since the case would not ordinarily get as far as a bankruptcy hearing in such circumstances.

11.65 Alternatively, the Court may dismiss the petition if it is satisfied that:

- the taxpayer has made an offer to secure or compound for a debt in respect of which the petition is presented, and

- the acceptance of that offer would have required the dismissal of the petition, and

- the offer has been unreasonably refused (s271(3)).

Opposing the petition

Offers to secure or compound the liability

11.66 A taxpayer may argue that an offer to secure or compound the liability has been unreasonably refused. In principle, such an offer might comprise any arrangement to settle the debt in part or in full, immediately or over a period of time, with or without the granting of security over an asset.

11.67 In *Re a Debtor (2389 of 1989)* ([1990] 3 All ER 984) a creditor holding approximately 50% of unsecured debts had used his vote to veto an individual voluntary arrangement (IVA), which was acceptable to all the other creditors.[13] The debtor argued that this constituted an unreasonable refusal under s271(3) but the Court held that a proposed IVA could not be regarded as an offer to each creditor capable of being accepted or refused by the petitioning creditor within the meaning of that section.

11.68 In *Re A Debtor (No 32 of 1993)* ([1994] TLR 1 March) a major insurance company had refused an offer of 50% of the debt, to be settled by a third party on behalf of the debtor. Holding that a creditor's refusal is 'unreasonable' only if it is beyond the bounds of any reasonable action by a creditor in the circumstances of the case, and taking the view that a large commercial creditor was unlikely to adopt an unreasonable attitude in light of its experience of debt recovery, the Court concluded that the refusal was not unreasonable.

---

[13] An IVA requires more than 75% approval (see paragraph 11.182).

11.69   In practice, taxpayers frequently consider that they have made very reasonable offers of part payment in full settlement, i.e. to compound the debt, particularly in cases where it is clear that a bankruptcy order will realise little or no proceeds for the creditors.   However, as a matter of policy the Inland Revenue does not agree to compound debts and may proceed to bankruptcy even if there appear to be no assets (see paragraph 11.27).   Given the broader public policy role of the Inland Revenue in administering taxes, it may be difficult in practice to obtain the agreement of the Registrar that such a refusal is 'unreasonable'.

11.70   Where the taxpayer has offered to realise an asset sufficient to cover the whole of the tax debt, the Registrar will in practice consider whether it is 'bankable' in the sense that it may be realised within about three months.   The Registrar is obliged not to keep a bankruptcy action hanging over a taxpayer's head indefinitely and would normally accept that a charge on a taxpayer's home, or a solicitor's undertaking, falls within s271(3) only if contracts have already been exchanged or there is evidence that exchange is imminent.

Reducing the debt below £750

11.71   If the debt is reduced below the bankruptcy level of £750 by the date of the hearing, an order for bankruptcy should not be made (*Re Patel* [1986] 1 WLR 221).

'Technical' objections

11.72   It is sometimes possible to object to the making of an order on the grounds that a 'technical' requirement has not been met, which may provide the basis for a dismissal or an adjournment of proceedings.   For example:

- Sometimes the statutory demand will not have been properly served, or insufficient time may have elapsed since service (see paragraphs 11.33 *et seq* and 11.55).

- Occasionally, notice of the bankruptcy hearing is served less than 14 days before the hearing, which will normally entitle the taxpayer to be granted an adjournment.

- Where execution on a County Court judgment debt is involved, a taxpayer may apply for a stay or suspension of proceedings (r6.25(2) and CCA 1984, s71(2)).   The making of such an order will not prevent a creditor's petition being presented, although the Registrar will not normally make a bankruptcy order while a stay is in force and will adjourn the petition so long as the stay persists.

Other practical points

11.73 Quite often the amount claimed by the Inland Revenue will be wholly or partly based upon sums which are capable of being reduced by way of a late appeal, a claim for relief or any of the other 'challenges' described in Chapter 4.

11.74 In law, this is of no assistance to the taxpayer, since the correctness of an assessment cannot be raised in proceedings to enforce a tax debt (see paragraph 7.19 *et seq*). In *Calvert v Walker* (QB [1899] 4 TC 79), the Inland Revenue lodged proof in bankruptcy in respect of unpaid tax charged by an unappealed assessment and the Court held that this could not be expunged even upon evidence that the taxpayer did not make the profits assessed.

11.75 Nevertheless, the Registrar should be amenable to granting a short adjournment of proceedings, for a matter of weeks, to allow the taxpayer to settle any outstanding matters with the Inland Revenue, if there is clear evidence that this may lead to the discharge of the debt. This may be provided by way of an accountant's letter explaining the basis on which the liability should be reduced. Provided such action leads to a reduction of the debt below the bankruptcy level of £750, a bankruptcy order will not be made (see paragraph 11.54).

Appeals

11.76 Appeals against decisions of the Registrar lie to the High Court; the appellant must show that there has been an error of principle or law in the way that the Registrar exercised his powers (s375(2)).[14] Beyond that appeals may be made, with leave, to the Court of Appeal and the House of Lords.

A debtor's petition

11.77 A taxpayer may present his own bankruptcy petition if:

- he is unable to pay his debts, which may be in *any amount* (s272(1)), and

- he is domiciled or personally present in England and Wales on the day on which the petition is presented, or has been resident or carried on a business in England and Wales at any time in the previous three years (s265).

11.78 The petition should be presented to the High Court in London for taxpayers who:

---

[14] As this is relatively rare in tax debt cases, it is beyond the scope of this handbook.

- have been resident in the London insolvency district for the greater part of the six months preceding presentation, or

- are not resident in England and Wales.

In other cases it may be presented to the taxpayer's local County Court with bankruptcy jurisdiction, or if it is desired to expedite matters, to his nearest bankruptcy Court listed in Schedule 2 of the Insolvency Act.

11.79   The taxpayer must complete a Debtor's Bankruptcy Petition (Form 6.27), which should be accompanied by a statement of affairs (Form 6.28). The statement of affairs is verified by an affidavit which can be sworn at the Court office. The taxpayer will also be required to pay a £250 deposit and a £25 fee, in cash.

11.80   The matter comes before a Registrar or District Judge who may:

- Make a bankruptcy order.

- Make a bankruptcy order and issue a certificate for the *summary administration* of the bankrupt's estate. This is a simplified procedure where total debts are less than £20,000[15] and the taxpayer has not been adjudicated bankrupt in the last five years. The main implication for the taxpayer is that he may be discharged after two, rather than three years.

- Appoint an insolvency practitioner to prepare a report under s273 (see paragraph 11.184).

11.81   At the High Court in London, the taxpayer may obtain assistance from the Court staff in preparing all the necessary forms, which are then passed to a Registrar for consideration. In simpler cases, the Registrar may make the bankruptcy order without a hearing. The order is normally made on the day that the petition is presented.

Reasons for a debtor's petition

11.82   Some 'advantages' of bankruptcy have been discussed in paragraphs 11.20 *et seq*. In particular, it can terminate the immediate pressure of claims from creditors and give the taxpayer a chance to clear his debts and make a fresh start.

11.83   While the Inland Revenue will often 'assist' by presenting a creditor's petition, there are some circumstances in which a debtor's petition may nevertheless be considered. For example:

- If the taxpayer wishes to expedite the process. Unless the debt is very large, it may take the Enforcement Office a year or two to

---

[15] This is known as the 'small bankruptcies level' and is set by the Insolvency Proceedings (Monetary Limits) Order 1986 (SI 1986/1996).

present a petition, even where the taxpayer offers no opposition. This delays the ultimate date of discharge. A debtor's petition will bring forward the date from which he will be able to make a fresh start.

- If the taxpayer's total unsecured debts are less than £20,000, he may be discharged after a two-year summary administration, instead of the normal three-year period following a creditor's petition (see paragraph 11.177).

- An individual's tax debts may be too small to be transferred to Enforcement Office (i.e. normally below £5,000), in which case the Inland Revenue will not present a petition. The Inland Revenue may also decide against presenting a petition for other reasons (see paragraph 11.25 *et seq*).

- The taxpayer may be subject to a County Court judgment and be making instalments which are onerous and will not clear the debt for many years. He may be able to clear his debts more quickly by missing a payment and presenting a debtor's petition.

Events following bankruptcy

11.84 The bankruptcy order is prepared by the Court and copies are sent to the Official Receiver (see paragraph 11.4). The Official Receiver will send one copy to the bankrupt and advertise the making of the order in a local newspaper and in the *London Gazette*. The Official Receiver must also inform the Chief Land Registrar so that an entry is made in the Land Register (r6.34(2)).

11.85 Normally a bankrupt will receive a letter from the Official Receiver enclosing a copy of the bankruptcy order stating a time and date to attend his office for an interview. In some cases the Official Receiver may wish to interview the bankrupt on the same day as the bankruptcy order, or the following day, if his office is near to the bankruptcy Court. The interview is with the bankrupt, although an adviser may be present.

11.86 The bankrupt will be given an 'Examination Booklet' (Form B40.01) to complete before the interview. This booklet is 40 pages in length and requires details of the bankrupt's Inland Revenue tax district reference number, VAT registration number, national insurance number, details of insurance and pension policies, shares, premium bonds, property, debts owed to the bankrupt, a list of creditors, outstanding judgments, assets on hire purchase, etc.

11.87 The initial interview may last anything from less than an hour to several hours. The Official Receiver will review the information given in the Examination booklet and attempt to determine what property is exempt, and what will require reasonable replacement (see paragraph 11.103). He will also be interested in ascertaining the likelihood of obtaining an income payments order (see paragraph 11.108 *et seq*). He may retain the bankrupt's business records, credit cards, keys to business premises and vehicles, and documents and certificates in relation to investments and insurances.

Vesting of assets

11.88 Immediately following the bankruptcy order, ownership of the bankrupt's assets vests in the Official Receiver as *receiver and manager* of the bankrupt estate (s287). Within the following months, a *trustee* must be appointed, to control and administer the affairs of the bankrupt's estate and to realise and distribute its assets. The assets automatically vest in the trusteee when he takes office.

Appointment of a trustee

11.89 The Official Receiver must decide within 12 weeks whether it is appropriate to summon a general meeting of the bankrupt's creditors for the purpose of appointing an insolvency practitioner as trustee of the bankrupt's estate (s293(1)). If so, the meeting must be held not more than four months from the date of the bankruptcy order (r6.79(1)).

11.90 It is Government policy for an insolvency practitioner to be appointed whenever possible, provided there are sufficient assets to justify this. Broadly this will be the case where there are at least £5,000 gross assets, although in some cases insolvency practitioners are appointed for much smaller estates and there are variations throughout England and Wales.

In the majority of cases there are negligible or no assets available. The Official Receiver will then not summon a creditors' meeting and must notify the Court accordingly. He then becomes the trustee of the bankrupt's estate himself (s293(3)).[16] In summary administration cases, the Official Receiver invariably acts as trustee; an outside trustee is not appointed unless the Court directs under s297(2).

Bankruptcy offences

11.91 At his first meeting with the Official Receiver, the bankrupt's attention should be drawn to offences for which a bankrupt may be prosecuted, in relation to conduct before or after the bankruptcy order:

- Non-disclosure of information (s353).

- Concealment of property (s354).

- Concealment or falsification of books and papers (s355).

---

[16] In the year to 31 March 1995 there were 23,828 new bankruptcy cases and insolvency practitioners were appointed trustee in 7,196 cases.

- False statements or material omissions (s356).

- Fraudulent disposal of property (s357).

- Absconding from the country (s358).

- Fraudulent disposal of property obtained on credit (s359).

- Obtaining credit in excess of £250 without disclosing bankrupt status (s360).

- Failure to keep proper accounts of a business (s361).

- Engaging in rash and hazardous speculations (s362).

Meeting the claims of creditors

11.92 After payment of costs and fees of bankruptcy (see paragraph 11.159 *et seq),* the trustee must distribute the bankrupt's remaining estate (if any) among creditors who had claims against the bankrupt at the date of the bankruptcy order. Creditors must lodge a claim to the Official Receiver or trustee, which is known as *proving* for the debt. A debt which is capable of being proved for is called a *provable debt* (r6.96).

11.93 Provable debts include claims by creditors 'whether they are present or future, certain or contingent, ascertained or sounding only in damages' (r12.3). The only important exceptions are sums due in respect of fines, and under matrimonial proceedings, which are not provable and continue to be enforceable against the bankrupt personally, even after discharge (see paragraph 11.180).[17]

11.94 Provable debts are settled in the following order: preferential debts rank first, then unsecured debts, and finally deferred debts.

11.95 The full list of *preferential debts* is:

- Arrears payable under the PAYE Regulations 1993 and the Income tax (Sub-contractors in the construction industry) Regulations 1993, for the 12 months prior to bankruptcy.

- One year's class 2 and class 4 national insurance contributions.

- Arrears of VAT for the six months prior to bankruptcy.

- All arrears of contributions to occupational and state pension schemes.

---

[17] After the making of a bankruptcy order, creditors with provable debts cease to have any right of action against the bankrupt personally (s285(3)). There are two limited exceptions to this rule: allowing a landlord to distrain for up to six months unpaid rent (s347) and a creditor to retain the benefit of an execution completed before the making of the bankruptcy order (s346).

- Arrears of remuneration due to employees for up to four months prior to bankruptcy, subject to a limit of £800 per claimant.

- 12 months' arrears of car tax.

- 12 months' gaming duties (IA 1986, 6 Sch).

11.96 *Unsecured debts* are those which are neither preferential nor deferred; *deferred debts* are defined by the Insolvency Act as those due to a spouse (s329).

11.97 The Inland Revenue has advised TaxAid that

'partnership tax debts rank as deferred in a sole bankruptcy unless all partners are bankrupt or the Inland Revenue is the petitioning creditor, when they rank as non-preferential (i.e. unsecured).'

Accordingly, where a former partner in a business is bankrupt or insolvent, the Revenue may tend to concentrate its work to collect partnership tax arrears on the remaining partner(s), which does sometimes give rise to complaints of unfairness (see paragraph 5.71 *et seq)*.

11.98 Creditors with *secured debts*, such as a home mortgage or other debt charged on the bankrupt's property, may prove for their debt in the bankruptcy only if either:

- they are willing to give up their security for the benefit of all the bankrupt's creditors, or

- their proof is expressed to be made only in respect of the unsecured part of the debt (i.e. to the extent that the debt is greater than the estimated value of the asset against which it is charged).

11.99 In either event, the debt proved then ranks with unsecured debts (ss269 and 383, and r6.109). In the latter case (or if they do not prove), they retain their pre-existing rights to enforce their security to the extent of the value of the asset at the time of bankruptcy.

The bankrupt's estate

11.100 The bankrupt's estate comprises 'all property belonging to or vested in the bankrupt at the commencement of the bankruptcy' and any property which by virtue of the Insolvency Act is to be treated as falling within the bankrupt's estate (s283(1)), apart from any items which are expressly excluded (see paragraph 11.102 *et seq)*.

11.101 In practice, the main items may be the bankrupt's home (see paragraph 11.115 *et seq)*, car, insurance policies and savings. It is currently unclear whether rights under personal pension contracts vest in the trustee; occupational pension entitlements do not.

Property which is excluded

11.102 The bankrupt's estate does not include:

- Property held in trust for any other person (s283(3)).

- Tools, books, vehicles and other items of equipment necessary for personal use by the bankrupt in his employment, business or vocation (s283(2)(a)).

- Clothing, bedding, furniture, household equipment and provisions necessary to satisfy the basic domestic needs of the bankrupt and his family (s283(2)(b)).

11.103 However, if the trustee considers that the realisable value of an excluded item within the second and third categories above exceeds the cost of a reasonable replacement, he may claim that item for the estate and must apply part of the disposal proceeds towards providing the bankrupt with a replacement (s308). This is most likely to occur in the case of a motor vehicle. As a rule of thumb, the Official Receiver in London will consider making such a claim if the expected net proceeds of sale exceed £500.

11.104 Beyond the statutory exclusions, trustees will not seek possession of low value household and personal chattels, since these are unlikely to yield any benefit to the bankrupt estate after accounting for disposal costs.

Disclaimers

11.105 The trustee may disclaim any *onerous property* of the bankrupt, being:

- any unprofitable contract

- any other property which is not readily saleable or which may give rise to a liability to pay money or perform any other onerous act (s315)

Typical examples are leasing or hire purchase agreements. Any person who suffers in consequence of such a disclaimer may prove for the loss or damage as a bankruptcy debt.

Adjustment of prior transactions

11.106 The trustee may apply to the Court for an order to overturn certain transactions, i.e. to restore the position to what it would have been had the taxpayer had not entered into the transaction:

- *Transactions at an undervalue* at any time within five years before the presentation of the bankruptcy petition (s339). This provision is designed to prevent a bankrupt from avoiding the claims of his creditors by giving away assets, or selling them at undervalue, before bankruptcy.

- *Voidable preferences* given within six months prior to the bankruptcy petition, this period being extended to two years where the recipient is an associate of the bankrupt (s340). Such a preference is given if the bankrupt has done anything, or allowed anything to be done, for one of his creditors or the guarantor of a debt which puts that person in a better position than he would otherwise have been in, where the bankrupt was influenced by a desire to prefer that person over his other creditors.

- *Extortionate credit* transactions entered within three years prior to the presentation of the bankruptcy petition (s343). This applies where the bankrupt has obtained credit on grossly extortionate terms and allows the Court to set the arrangement aside.

The conduct underlying such transactions may also constitute bankruptcy offences (see paragraph 11.91).

After-acquired property

11.107 Property acquired by the bankrupt, before discharge from bankruptcy, may be claimed by the trustee for the bankrupt's estate (s307) and the bankrupt is required to notify the trustee of any such property (s333(2)). To exercise this right, the trustee must give the bankrupt notice within 42 days from the date on which he first became aware that the property had been acquired by, or devolved upon, the bankrupt. Such property may include, for example, a large redundancy payment or an inheritance.

Income payments orders

11.108 The trustee may apply to the Court for an order that part of the bankrupt's income be paid to the bankrupt's estate, provided that he is left with sufficient income to meet the domestic needs of himself and his family. The order may direct that payment be made either by the bankrupt, or by a third party such as his employer (s310).

11.109 Income payments orders can be made at any time before discharge from bankruptcy (see paragraph 11.176 *et seq*) and cease to operate after discharge, except in the following circumstances:

- In the case of automatic discharge (after two or three years), the order may specify that payments will continue thereafter, although the order itself cannot continue for a period of more than three years (s310(6)).

- Where discharge is by order of the Court (after at least five years), it may be conditional upon income payments continuing (ss310(6) and 280).

11.110 Most income payments orders are obtained by the Official Receiver, who is becoming more active in this respect. In 1994/95 the Official Receiver obtained 1,063 orders, compared with 742 in 1993/94 and 181 in 1992/93.

11.111 Many orders are obtained by the Official Receiver before the appointment of an insolvency practitioner as trustee. In assessing whether an order should be obtained and the appropriate level of payment, he will consider actual figures of income and expenditure, and attempt to agree a level of contribution with the bankrupt. Where expenditure figures are unavailable or disputed, the Official Receiver uses the Family Expenditure Survey compiled annually by the Central Statistical Office.

11.112 In practice, income payments orders are rare where the bankrupt's income is well below average earnings or where he has significant family responsibilities. Also, the Official Receiver does not in practice seek an order where the monthly income available, after expenditure, does not exceed £75.

11.113 In cases where the bankrupt disputes the making of an income payments order or does not agree with the amount sought by the Official Receiver, a Court hearing is held at which the bankrupt will be given an opportunity to show cause why the order should not be made in the amount applied for by the trustee (r6.189). A common area of dispute is expenditure associated with the bankrupt's home, where it is subject to high mortgage outgoings. In such cases, the Official Receiver may want the bankrupt to move to the rented sector to release money for an income payments order. For further discussion of the home, see paragraph 11.115 *et seq.*

11.114 Once an income payments order is in operation, the onus is on the bankrupt to inform the trustee of any change in circumstances, in particular if his income increases (s333(2)). Only in exceptional cases will the Official Receiver contact a bankrupt's employer, for example if there has been a failure to comply with an order or there is good reason to believe the bankrupt has underdeclared his stated income.

The bankrupt's home

11.115 If the bankrupt is an owner-occupier, his beneficial interest in his home may be his only asset of significant value. This interest vests in the trustee, who will wish to realise it for the benefit of the creditors.

11.116 However, an immediate disposal of the property may be prevented by:

- Rights of occupation of a spouse, minor child or other third party (see paragraph 11.123 *et seq)*.

- Financial considerations, in cases of 'negative equity' or where the value of the property is not significantly greater than the value of loans secured against it (see paragraph 11.134 *et seq).*

Due to the complex issues of property and matrimonial law involved, it is recommended that anyone facing the possible loss of his home should seek expert advice.

The bankrupt's beneficial interest

11.117 The *bankrupt's beneficial interest* in the property may be defined as his interest in the proceeds of sale of the property, after settling the claims of secured creditors.[18] It is loosely referred to as the bankrupt's share of the equity and the term *negative equity* is used where the value of secured loans exceeds the market value of the property.

Sole and joint owners

11.118 If the bankrupt is the sole owner of the property, then his beneficial interest usually will be equivalent to the equity in the property.

11.119 Where the property is jointly owned, because the legal title is in joint names or where another person has an equitable interest in the property, then it is a fraction of the equity. For example, where the property is co-owned with a spouse, then the bankrupt's beneficial interest is usually equivalent to half of the equity.

Protecting the beneficial interest

11.120 The Inland Revenue, and subsequently the Official Receiver and the trustee, will wish to ensure that the beneficial interest is preserved for the benefit of the bankrupt's estate.

11.121 Accordingly, where the property is registered land, the Inland Revenue will lodge *a creditor's notice* against the property at the Land Registry when petitioning for bankruptcy. This puts potential purchasers on notice that the title-holder, or one of the title-holders, faces a bankruptcy petition. In practice, the existence of such a notice makes it difficult for a tax debtor, who has been served with a petition, to obtain a secured loan from a third party to meet the Inland Revenue's claims and avoid bankruptcy.

11.122 Upon the making of the bankruptcy order, a *bankruptcy inhibition* is registered, which effectively prevents a disposal of the property except for the benefit of an existing secured lender and the bankrupt's estate until the property vests in the trustee.

---

[18] The rights of a mortgagee as a secured creditor are discussed in paragraphs 11.98-11.99.

Rights of occupation

11.123 Where the bankrupt has no spouse or minor children living with him, he has no rights of occupation as against the trustee and cannot prevent a sale at any time after the trustee is appointed.

The spouse

11.124 Where the bankrupt is married, the trustee cannot dispose of the property without an order of the Court having jurisdiction over the bankruptcy:

- Where the property is jointly owned, the trustee will require an order under the Law of Property Act 1925, s30.

- Where the property is owned solely by the bankrupt, the spouse will have rights of occupation under the Matrimonial Homes Act 1983, which can only be terminated by an order of the Court (s336).

11.125 Whether the matrimonial home is solely or jointly owned, the Court may not make the relevant order during the first 12 months following the date of the trustee's appointment, without considering the needs of the spouse, children and all the circumstances of the case. In practice, this gives the spouse (and the bankrupt) a period of 12 months to organise their affairs, which may involve seeking an alternative home or trying to 'buy out' the bankrupt's beneficial interest (s336) (see paragraph 11.135 *et seq*).

11.126 After the end of the year, the trustee can apply for the relevant order and, *unless the circumstances of the case are exceptional*, the interests of the creditors will outweigh all other considerations (s336(5)). No statutory guidance is given on the italicised words, but there is some case law which tends to favour creditors:

- The fact that the wife and children of the bankrupt will lose their home and may be unable to buy or rent a comparable home in the same area is not ordinarily regarded as an exceptional circumstance (*Re Lowrie* [1981] 3 All ER 353 and *Re Citro* [1990] 3 All ER 952).

- On the other hand, an order for sale *may* be postponed where a disposal of the property will cause very serious problems in relation to the children's educational or housing needs (*Re Holliday* [1981] Ch 405).

In most cases, a Court will not consider the circumstances 'exceptional'.

Children

11.127 If there is no spouse but the bankrupt has been living in the property with children under 18 years old, he gains rights of occupation analogous to those of a spouse discussed above (s337).

The bankrupt's separated or former spouse

11.128 Where a property is occupied by a separated or former spouse, protection is available under the same provisions as apply to a spouse (see paragraphs 11.124-11.126). Occupation will be secure for 12 months and thereafter the interests of creditors become paramount. However, there will be a greater chance of persuading the Court that the circumstances are 'exceptional' where the marriage breakdown occurred some time prior to the insolvency and the disposal of the property will cause hardship to an 'innocent' former spouse or children who are still in education (*Harman v Glencross* [1986] 1 All ER 545 and *Austin-Fell v Austin-Fell* [1990] 2 All ER 455).

11.129 A property adjustment order under the Matrimonial Causes Act 1973, s24, which transfers a bankrupt's interest in the matrimonial home, if consented to after presentation of a bankruptcy petition, may be overturned by the trustee as a 'voluntary conveyance' (*Re Flint* [1992] TLR 1617).

Third parties

11.130 If another person, such as a relative or cohabitee, is a legal co-owner of the property, he may be able to obtain a postponement of sale in an exceptional situation (s336). In *Re Mott* [1987] 6 CL 29 the sale of a property co-owned with the bankrupt's sick mother was postponed until after her death.

11.131 Any person apart from the bankrupt may have acquired a beneficial interest in a property by making a financial contribution, perhaps towards a deposit or mortgage instalments. In *Re Sharpe* ([1979] 1 WLR 219) the Court held that the bankrupt's aunt had acquired an equitable interest entitling her to rights of occupation where she had made financial contributions to the property on the understanding that she could live there. The trustee was refused an order for sale.

Realising the bankrupt's beneficial interest

Significant equity cases

11.132 If there is significant equity, the trustee will wish to realise the bankrupt's beneficial interest by disposing of the property as soon as any rights of occupation, discussed above, have terminated. The net proceeds of disposal, after satisfying the claims of secured creditors, are apportioned between the bankrupt's estate and any co-owner(s) in accordance with their entitlements, and the normal presumption is that each co-owner is entitled to an equal share of the equity.

11.133 In such cases, a non-bankrupt co-owner or other third party (e.g. a friend or relative) may be able to prevent a sale to a third party by 'buying out' the bankrupt's beneficial interest, i.e. by offering a contribution to the trustee which is equivalent to the amount the bankrupt's estate might expect to realise on a disposal to a third party. The arrangement would have to be negotiated with the trustee who, in cases where there is significant equity, would invariably be an insolvency practitioner (see paragraph 11.90).

Insignificant or negative equity

11.134 Where there is little or no equity, there will be no point in the trustee seeking to sell the property. A disposal may then be deferred indefinitely and the bankrupt's beneficial interest may remain vested in the Official Receiver as trustee long after discharge from bankruptcy. Alternatively, where the trustee is an insolvency practitioner, he must apply to the Court for a charge on the property sufficient to clear outstanding bankruptcy debts plus interest at the judgment rate or contractual rate, whichever is the higher. In either event, the bankrupt may continue to live in the property (possibly for many years) but, when it is sold, the bankrupt's share of any equity is first applied to meet outstanding debts of the bankruptcy. The Official Receiver will monitor the value of the property and may at any time require a sale so as to realise the beneficial interest or charge.

Alternative options

11.135 If an *insolvency practitioner* is acting as trustee, a co-owner or third party may approach him with a view to 'buying out' the bankrupt's beneficial interest. The trustee may agree to do so for a modest sum if he considers that there is little prospect of realising a greater amount in any other way, and this has the advantage of avoiding the long-term consequences outlined in the previous paragraph.

11.136 Where the *Official Receiver* is acting as trustee and the home is jointly-owned registered land, a co-owner may take advantage of a special scheme to acquire the bankrupt's beneficial interest. It is outlined in the Official Receiver's leaflet *What will happen to my home? Information on your home when bankruptcy occurs*, and is operated in conjunction with a firm of solicitors in Bristol. The co-owner will have to pay:

- For a solicitor or licensed conveyancer to act for him.

- £211 to cover the Official Receiver's costs, although part of this may be refunded if costs amount to less.

- The cost of an independent valuation, unless there has recently been one.

- An agreed purchase price for the beneficial interest acquired. In cases of negative equity, this is set at £1.

Once this transfer of the beneficial interest has been effected, the Official Receiver will have no further entitlement in respect of the property. Under this scheme, the bankrupt's legal title is also transferred and secured lenders have not in practice raised any objection to this aspect of the arrangement.

11.137 In cases which do not qualify for the above scheme - because the property is solely owned or unregistered - a spouse, relative or friend of the bankrupt may nevertheless approach the Official Receiver with a view to 'buying out' the bankrupt's beneficial interest. Should he agree to such a transfer, the Official Receiver would expect to receive at least the current value of the bankrupt's beneficial interest, without making any allowance for estate agents' or solicitors' costs that would have to be borne on a sale.

Domestic tenancies

11.138 If the bankrupt is a tenant, normally his lease will vest in the trustee unless it is a protected or secure tenancy, or he is a statutory tenant under the Rent Acts. On vesting, the trustee becomes liable for rent and covenants unless he disclaims the property as *onerous* (see paragraph 11.105), which will determine all the bankrupt's rights in the property. The trustee may also apply to the Court for the property to be vested in an appropriate person, normally the landlord, although any person in occupation of the property, or entitled to occupy it, may apply to the Court for the property to be vested in them. Certain leases contain a *forfeiture clause* which entitles the landlord to seek repossession before the term has expired, in the event of the tenant's bankruptcy, and he will usually be advised of such a bankruptcy by the Official Receiver (see paragraph 11.18).

Insolvent partnerships

11.139 The Insolvent Partnerships Order 1994 (SI 1994/2421) specifies the provisions of the Insolvency Act 1986 that apply to partnerships and modifies certain of the provisions. There are four alternative procedures (discussed below) and, in addition, the Order introduced:

- partnership voluntary arrangements, and

- partnership administration orders.

These achieve some of the same objectives, in the partnership context, as individual voluntary arrangements and administration orders discussed elsewhere (see paragraphs 11.182 *et seq* and 10.77 *et seq*), but in view of their complexity specialist advice should be sought and they are beyond the scope of this handbook.

Winding up the partnership as an unregistered company

11.140 This is the most common way of dealing with a partnership insolvency and does not involve the bankruptcy of individual partners, although they may face disqualification under the Company Directors Disqualification Act 1986.

11.141 A petition may be presented to wind up a partnership under Part V of the Act by:

- A creditor or creditors, on the grounds that the firm is unable to pay its debts, has ceased trading, or where for other reasons the Court considers it is just and equitable (s221(5)).

- The firm itself, provided it has at least eight partners and it is insolvent. The same grounds apply as for a creditor's petition.

- An individual partner,

    - provided the firm has at least eight partners, or

    - upon leave from the Court having satisfied the Court that he is owed at least £750 by the firm under a judgment, has taken all reasonable steps to enforce it and has served a statutory demand.

Winding up the partnership and making individual partners bankrupt

11.142 This involves a petition on the firm itself, together with petitions on at least two individual partners. This may be appropriate where the objective is to dissolve the partnership and, at the same time, ensure that there are personal assets available to meet the firm's debts.

11.143 There must be an outstanding partnership debt of at least £750 and failure by the firm to comply with a statutory demand. While an individual partner may apply to set aside the statutory demand (see paragraph 11.37 *et seq),* the partnership itself cannot do so.

Petition against one or more individual partners

11.144 As partners are jointly liable for partnership debts, a creditor may demand payment of a debt owed by the partnership from one or more of the partners individually. If payment is not forthcoming, a bankruptcy petition can be presented against that partner without involving the other partners, or the partnership itself, in the proceedings. If this action is taken the normal bankruptcy procedures, discussed in this chapter, apply.

Partners' own petition

11.145 The partners may jointly petition for their individual bankruptcy and this is the partnership equivalent of an individual debtor's petition (see paragraph 11.77 *et seq).* All the partners must be willing to become bankrupt and no certificate of summary administration can be issued.

11.146 This may be appropriate where they wish to avoid a winding up order against the firm. In consequence, the partners are not liable to be disqualified from being directors under the Company Directors Disqualification Act 1986, although they may not be directors while they are undischarged bankrupts.

The tax implications of bankruptcy

'Standing'

11.147 A bankrupt has no legal 'standing' to challenge tax debts which are provable in the bankruptcy. Any application for relief, for example by making a late appeal or under the principle of equitable liability, must be submitted by the trustee. If the trustee declines to challenge the Inland Revenue's proof (see 11.92), perhaps because he considers that the costs would outweigh the likely benefit, the bankrupt cannot compel him to do so (*Soul v CIR* CA [1966] 43 TC 662). In practice, however, the trustee and the Inland Revenue may not object to the bankrupt handling the necessary negotiations directly, although there may be practical difficulties where the trustee holds all the business papers required by the taxpayer to prepare outstanding accounts or returns.

Assessment of post-bankruptcy profits

Income tax

11.148 Subject to the 'tax holiday' described in paragraph 11.151 *et seq,* income received by the bankrupt after bankruptcy is assessable directly on him (*Hibbert v Fysch* CA [1962] 40 TC 305).[19] This rule applies even where the bankrupt is required to make payments under an income payments order and the level of payments should accordingly be set by reference to the net income due.

11.149 If the bankrupt has been self-employed and continues trading, the making of a bankruptcy order does not trigger a 'cessation' of the business. However, if the business is continued on a smaller scale or is conducted in a different way - perhaps because premises are disposed of - then this may constitute a cessation under general tax rules (*Kirk & Randall Ltd v Dunn* KB [1924] 8 TC 663, *Seaman v Tucketts Ltd* Ch D [1963] 41 TC 422 and *J G Ingram & Son Ltd v Callaghan* CA [1968] 45 TC 151).

Capital gains tax

11.150 Capital gains are treated differently. Since the bankrupt's interest in the asset will ordinarily vest in the trustee, any capital gains liability on a disposal by the trustee falls on the bankrupt estate and is treated as a cost of administration (*In re McMeekin* QB (NI) [1973] 48 TC 725).

---

[19] It should be noted that creditors having debts provable in the bankruptcy are forbidden from taking proceedings against the bankrupt in respect of non-provable debts, while he is undischarged, without leave of the Court (s285(3)). Accordingly, if the Revenue has petitioned for or proved in the bankruptcy, it may have difficulty enforcing post-bankruptcy liabilities.

The 'tax holiday'

11.151 A bankrupt may enjoy a 'tax holiday', to the extent that tax on post-bankruptcy income is provable in the bankruptcy and therefore cannot be enforced against him personally (see paragraph 11.93).

Guidance from the Inland Revenue Manuals

11.152 Paragraph 3.112 of the Inland Revenue Insolvency Manual states:

'Where a taxpayer who is an employee under PAYE becomes insolvent ... tax imposed for the year in which (the bankruptcy order is made) is regarded as a debt for which proof is to be lodged. In such cases the District will

- instruct the current employer to stop deducting tax

- repay any tax deducted after the (date of the bankruptcy order)'.

11.153 The implications of that paragraph are as follows:

- The bankrupt should be paid without deduction of income tax under PAYE from the date of bankruptcy to the following 5 April and any tax incorrectly deducted from income earned during this period should be refunded to the bankrupt personally.

- The Inland Revenue may claim the Schedule E liability from the bankrupt's estate, the extent of recovery being dependent upon the sufficiency of its assets.

- The bankrupt will have no personal tax liability, although an indirect contribution may be required if his income is sufficient to render him subject to an income payments order (see paragraph 11.108 *et seq*).

Further guidance

11.154 TaxAid sought advice from the Inland Revenue on the extent to which this provision applies to employees changing jobs, and to self-employed taxpayers, and the following guidance has been received:

'The basic principle

'The tax liability for the whole tax year in which the bankruptcy falls is in principle a provable debt in the bankruptcy. But it can only be provable if it is a liability of the bankrupt, at least contingently, at the time the order is made. All that happens is that the Revenue rights of recovery become limited as a result of the bankruptcy order. The liability of the trustee only extends to distributing the available assets in accordance with the Insolvency Act and we must be content to claim and accept whatever dividend is available.

'The basic position under the current regime is that where tax has already been imposed for the tax year in which the order is made, the full year's tax liability on any contract of employment existing at the date of the bankruptcy order is a provable debt. This was embodied in 'Regulations' agreed with the Board of Trade many years ago and later revised as 'Best Practice' notes agreed with the DTI. We do not include tax already imposed for years subsequent to the year of bankruptcy or tax on a fresh source arising during the year as it was not a contingent liability at the time of the order.

PAYE deductions made before the order

'There is no implication for PAYE deductions made before the date of the bankruptcy order which are simply credited against our total claim. After the bankruptcy order is made, deductions have to stop because we are confined to proving for whatever remains outstanding for the rest of the tax year.

Change of employer

'If there is a change of employer after the bankruptcy order, the 'tax holiday' ends and PAYE deductions can recommence on a Month 1 basis.

Application to self-employment

'The Schedule E rules were extended with modifications to the sub-contractor scheme when it was introduced. The rationale was that, although sub-contractors might have many individual contracts for services, similar principles would apply for the year of bankruptcy provided they were contracts of a similar nature in the same basic trade. (This cannot be taken for granted: a sub-contractor made bankrupt might be forced to switch to labour-only work from a more substantial trade.) Accordingly, where income tax is deducted at source, it is refunded to the trustee in bankruptcy.

'In the case of any other trade or profession, the position is different because no deduction is made at source. If such a source continues with no 'cessation' during the period from the date of the bankruptcy order to the following 5 April (inclusive), then the tax liability of the year of bankruptcy is provable in the bankruptcy. Again, any payments made prior to the order are credited against our claim.

'If there is a 'cessation' between the date of the order and the following 5 April, then the liability in respect of profits arising up to the date of cessation is provable. Tax on any income arising from a trade or profession commenced after the time of the order is not provable in the bankruptcy.'

260

Practial implications of the above guidance

11.155 In the case of employees, it will be significant whether the bankruptcy order falls early or late in the tax year; the earlier it falls, the longer the tax holiday. If bankruptcy is threatened towards the end of a tax year, it may be advantageous to stave off the order until after 5 April.

11.156 It may also be advantageous to ensure, as far as possible, that earnings during the tax holiday are received gross rather than relying upon a subsequent refund of tax deducted under PAYE. If a significant refund is obtained, the bankrupt will be obliged under s333(2) to advise his trustee of the receipt, which may result in a claim for 'after-acquired property' (see paragraph 11.9).

11.157 For uncertificated sub-contractors, there is no tax holiday as there is no provision for payment to be made 'gross' in the absence of a 714 certificate, and so tax must continue to be deducted and the Inland Revenue's practice is to pay the refund to the bankrupt's estate.

11.158 For other self-employed workers, provided there is no 'cessation' of the trade (see paragraph 11.149), any unpaid liability for the tax year of bankruptcy is provable and cannot be recovered from the bankrupt personally. Again, this suggests a benefit where the order falls early in the tax year.

Costs and fees

11.159 Costs and fees can be considerable and for this reason bankruptcy should always be avoided by a taxpayer who is solvent. The charges are governed by The Insolvency Fees Order 1986 as amended and the main items are as follows:

Presentation of petition:

- Debtor's petition   - Deposit of £250 and Court fee of £25

- Creditor's petition   - Deposit of £300 and Court fee of £55

Preliminary acts of Official Receiver prior to appointment of trustee:

- For performance of his general duties   - £320

- For expenses   - £175 plus further charges in relation to the summoning of creditors' meetings

On the recovery of funds for the bankrupt's estate in his capacity as receiver and manager, the Official Receiver may charge a fee according to the following scale:

On the first £5,000 @ 20%
On the next £5,000 @ 15%
On the next £90,000 @ 10%
On all further sums @ 5%

11.160 Where an insolvency practitioner is appointed to act as trustee, his fees are agreed by the creditors' committee and will rarely be less than £5,000 - £10,000, although the ultimate figure will depend upon the extent and complexity of the case.

11.161 In addition, there is a fee charged by the Secretary of State, in relation to his 'general duties' and based upon sums recovered for the bankrupt's estate by the Official Receiver as receiver and manager and by the trustee (sometimes referred to as the DTI's fees):

On the first £50,000 @ 15.00%
On the next £50,000 @ 11.25%
On the next £400,000 @ 9.75%
On the next £500,000 @ 5.625%
On the next £4,000,000 @ 3.00%
On all further sums @ 1.50%

11.162 By way of example, where the assets realised are £120,000 the charges might be as follows:

Charges by Official Receiver

General duties	£320
Expenses	£175
Summoning of meeting	£65

Secretary of State's fees

On the first £50,000 @ 15%	£7,500
On the next £50,000 @ 11.25%	£5,625
On the next £20,000 @ 9.75%	£1,950
Insolvency practitioner's fees, say	£7,000
Total	£22,635

Ending the bankruptcy

11.163 A bankruptcy may be ended in a number of ways:

- annulment under s282

- annulment following the approval of an IVA

- rescission

- discharge from bankruptcy

Annulment under s282

11.164 A bankruptcy order may be annulled if at any time it appears to the Court:

- that on any grounds existing at the time the bankruptcy order was made, the order ought not to have been made (s282(1)(a)), or

- that since the making of the order, the debts and expenses of the bankruptcy have been paid or secured in full (s282(1)(b)).

The bankruptcy order ought not to have been made

11.165 This allows for annulment where, for example, the bankruptcy petition was not properly served, or was based upon a false claim.

11.166 Where the Inland Revenue is the petitioner, if the taxpayer appeared at the bankruptcy hearing and there was any prospect that the debt could quickly be discharged by settling an outstanding tax dispute, the Registrar should normally have granted an appropriate adjournment (see paragraph 11.73 *et seq)*. Accordingly, it is unusual to have grounds for an annulment in the case of an Inland Revenue bankruptcy petition.

11.167 If the taxpayer did not appear at the hearing, the Court will consider whether his appearance at that hearing would have made any difference to the outcome. In one case a sub-contractor in the construction industry, with SC60 tax credits in excess of the debts claimed on the petition, had received a telephone assurance from the Inland Revenue that he need not attend the hearing at which a bankruptcy order was made. An application to annul was successful.

Debts paid or secured in full

11.168 Under this heading it is not sufficient for debts claimed in the Inland Revenue's petition to be settled. The bankrupt must pay or secure *all* debts and costs that have been proved in the bankruptcy, and reasonable time must be given for all creditors to prove their debt. Accordingly, credit card debts and personal loans will have to be cleared, even if the creditors concerned would not, in the absence of bankruptcy action by the Inland Revenue, have pressed for settlement.

Procedure

11.169 An application for an annulment is heard by the Court, although it may stay any proceedings in advance of the hearing. If a debt is disputed or a creditor cannot be traced, the bankrupt may have to provide security either as money paid into Court or by way of a bond.

11.170 If he has already notified the creditors of the bankruptcy, the Official Receiver must notify them of the annulment (r6.212) and the order should provide for removal of the registration of the bankruptcy at the Land Registry (r6.213). The former bankrupt can require the Secretary of State to advertise and gazette the making of the annulment order (at the bankrupt's expense) (r6.213).

11.171 Before an order to annul will be made, the question of costs must be settled. Both the Inland Revenue and the Official Receiver's costs must be satisfied and may be considerable (see paragraph 11.159 *et seq)*. Where an annulment is consequent upon a failure by the Inland Revenue (e.g. see paragraph 11.167), it may agree to waive its costs.

11.172 In appropriate cases where an order is annulled, an order also should be sought to dismiss the bankruptcy petition as well. If no order is sought to dismiss the petition, whilst the bankruptcy order will be annulled, the bankruptcy petition will be re-listed for hearing.

Annulment following the approval of an IVA

11.173 Where a creditors' meeting approves an IVA after bankruptcy (see paragraph 11.184), the Court may annul the order (s261(1)), although this cannot be until at least 28 days after the decision of the meeting was reported to the Court, nor if there is an application pending to challenge the decision of the meeting.

Rescission

11.174 There is a wide discretionary power given to any Court with jurisdiction in bankruptcy to 'review, rescind or vary orders' (s375). The grounds which might justify the Court in rescinding a bankruptcy are analogous to those for annulment under s282 including, for example, that all debts have been paid.

11.175 A bankruptcy order should not be rescinded solely on the grounds that the bankrupt has no assets or other means of clearing his liabilities (*Re Field* [1978] Ch 371).

Discharge from bankruptcy

11.176 Unless the order is annulled or rescinded, a person against whom a bankruptcy order has been made remains a bankrupt until he is discharged.

11.177 In most cases discharge is given automatically:

- after two years where a certificate of summary administration made on a debtor's petition is in force (see paragraph 11.80), or

- after three years in all other cases,

although in either event the Official Receiver may apply for the discharge to be suspended on the grounds that the bankrupt has not complied with his obligations under the Insolvency Act (s279).

11.178 Discharge is not automatic where:

- a person has been an undischarged bankrupt at any time during the last 15 years, or

- in cases of criminal bankruptcy.

In such cases, the bankrupt must apply to the Court for discharge and application cannot be made until at least five years after the order (ss279(1)(a) and 280).

11.179 When a bankrupt has been discharged the Court must, at his request, issue to him a certificate of his discharge stating the date from which it was effective (r6.220). The former bankrupt can require the Secretary of State to advertise and gazette his discharge (at the bankrupt's expense) (r6.220).

11.180 When a bankrupt is discharged, he is released from all pre-bankruptcy debts except the following:

- fines

- maintenance orders and other payments due in respect of family proceedings

- damages in relation to personal injury claims

- obligations incurred by fraud or fraudulent breach of trust

- any other debts not provable in the bankruptcy, for example secured debts (see paragraph 11.93) (s281)

Voluntary arrangements

11.181 If the taxpayer wishes to avoid bankruptcy - and has exhausted the scope for reducing the debt and negotiation with the Collector (see Chapter 6) - he may consider entering an individual voluntary arrangement (IVA). It should be noted that the Insolvent Partnerships Order 1994 (SI 1994/2421) extended voluntary arrangements to partnerships. This provision is beyond the scope of this handbook and specialist advice should be sought.

Individual Voluntary Arrangements (IVAs)

11.182 An IVA is a formal arrangement governed by the Insolvency Act 1986, under which creditors may agree:

- to accept less than 100p in the £ on their debts, and/or

- to some deferment in the time allowed for payment of their debts, in full and final settlement of their claims. An IVA requires assent by over 75% of the taxpayer's creditors by value. If this is obtained, its terms are binding on *all* creditors (see paragraph 11.201).

11.183 An IVA is usually initiated by the taxpayer approaching an insolvency practitioner for advice on the prospects of successfully establishing an IVA as a means of staving off bankruptcy. Most practitioners will agree to a short meeting, without any charge, to discuss a prospective IVA, and the terms on which they might commence acting as *nominee*.

11.184 An IVA may also be established:

- Where a taxpayer has presented a debtor's bankruptcy petition but, on hearing the application, the Court appoints an insolvency practitioner to enquire into his affairs and report on whether a meeting of creditors should be summoned for the purpose of considering an IVA. It is a condition that the taxpayer's unsecured debts are less than the 'small bankruptcies level' (£20,000 - see paragraph 11.80) and the bankrupt's estate would be more than £2,000 (s273).

- After bankruptcy, an application may be made by the bankrupt, his trustee or the Official Receiver and, if the IVA is approved, the Court may annul the bankruptcy (ss253 and 261).

This section focuses on the considerations where a taxpayer is considering entering an IVA to avoid bankruptcy.

Will an IVA be acceptable to creditors?

11.185 This is the first hurdle and, if the insolvency practitioner considers that an IVA is unlikely to be acceptable to more than 75% by value of creditors voting on the resolution, he should advise against proceeding with an IVA (r5.18(1)).

Making a successful proposal

11.186 An IVA is unlikely to be successful unless there are sufficient funds to pay the insolvency practitioner who will act as supervisor and to provide a reasonable dividend for creditors, and as a broad rule of thumb it requires that the taxpayer has:

- at least £10,000 of gross assets, or

- sufficient funds to make an initial payment of £1,500-£3,000 to the insolvency practitioner to set up the arrangement (see paragraph 11.206) plus an expectation of substantial income or capital receipts in the future.

11.187 There may be a greater chance of success where:

- A third party (e.g. a spouse, partner or relative) offers to assist by putting up money, a guarantee, or their beneficial interest in a jointly-owned property.

- Friends or relatives who are owed money agree to defer their claims in favour of commercial creditors.

- The taxpayer can demonstrate that by carrying on his business, he will be able to sell it as a 'going concern' or trade out of trouble.

Satisfying the Inland Revenue

11.188 In practice, the Inland Revenue will frequently hold sufficient 'votes' to veto any IVA proposal and so it is essential to consider the Inland Revenue's likely response. Its published policy, in relation to taxpayers who wish to enter an IVA so as to remain in business, is set out in *Code of Practice 6 Collection tax* at page 7:

> 'We will treat any proposal for a voluntary arrangement as sympathetically as we can. We will take account of your past tax history and the likelihood of sending future payments and tax returns on time. Whether or not we can accept an arrangement will depend on the particular facts, but our main concerns will be:
>
> - whether we think the proposal will work, including the likely future trading position and the business's ability to pay future tax debts
>
> - that we are not disadvantaged compared with other creditors in a similar position
>
> - that you are not entering into the arrangement just to avoid paying tax
>
> - how the arrangement compares with what we would be paid in bankruptcy ...'

11.189 Although this general statement appears unobjectionable, the tax authorities are nevertheless perceived as being predisposed against IVAs, and as having unpublished criteria as to the minimum dividend that an IVA should yield. Some criticism has appeared in the professional press, together with an official response.

'High' rejection rate

11.190 In answer to one query, the Inland Revenue observed that it voted against only 1,445 IVA proposals out of 9,977 in the two years to 31 March 1993.[20] Although this may superficially be taken to imply that

---

[20] *Taxation Practitioner* November 1993 p3

any taxpayer has an 85% chance of Inland Revenue approval, it is possible that the 9,977 cases were the cream of the crop and that many other prospective IVAs were abandoned because the insolvency practitioner warned that any proposal was unlikely to satisfy the Inland Revenue.

Schemes to make payments out of income

11.191 In response to criticism that it is predisposed against IVAs which rely on payments out of future income, rather than existing assets or lump sums from third parties, the Inland Revenue has stated: 'Most schemes supported by the Revenue are funded almost entirely on future earnings spread over some two to five years. Indeed, the Revenue rejects only a minority of schemes.'[21]

Minimum yields

11.192 The Inland Revenue has also denied the suggestion that it expects a minimum yield of 100p in the £ for preferential debts and 30p in the £ for non-preferential.[22]

Casting votes in excess of the 'true' debt

11.193 A further criticism concerned the Inland Revenue seeking to cast votes by reference to tax liabilities based upon excessive estimates, when the ultimate liability proved to be much lower. The Inland Revenue replied: 'The chairman of the relevant creditors' meeting has the power to admit or reject a creditor's claim in whole or in part (r5.17(4)). Where the Revenue's claim includes an estimated liability which is under negotiation with the Inspector (who accepts that it will be reduced), the Revenue will be content for the chairman to exercise his statutory power by anticipating the reduction and reducing the claim appropriately; on some occasions the Revenue will file a reduced claim prior to the date of the meeting.'[23]

Comprehensive policy statement

11.194 In view of continuing concerns in this area, TaxAid has sought a comprehensive statement and has been advised by the Inland Revenue:

> **'Outline of Revenue criteria**
>
> The Revenue has not adopted a policy of opposing a proposed Voluntary Arrangement where it would yield less than 30p in the £. Each case is considered on its merit, taking into account a number of factors. For example, the Revenue need to look at proposals in the light of the past history of the taxpayer and consider

---

[21] *Taxation Practitioner* February 1994 p29
[22] *Taxation Practitioner* February 1994 p29
[23] *Taxation Practitioner* February 1994 p29

the prospects for payment of future liabilities as well as the provision of outstanding Accounts and Returns. The viability of the scheme also needs to be considered as well as the basis of the funding. And there has to be some certainty about the assets and liabilities so that the financial position of the debtor can be quantified with some precision. Similarly, income only proposals should be based on a firm foundation, not simply optimistic estimates of future earnings, with proposals for improved dividends if earnings continue.

Statutory duty to collect tax that is due

The Revenue perspective is normally wider than that of the insolvency practitioner proposing the Arrangement. The Department is concerned with preserving integrity of the Collection system and not merely whether the balance is favourable in a particular case between the Arrangement and other possible outcomes of Insolvency (such as bankruptcy); although some comparison of the expected yield from the Arrangement with that which could otherwise be expected in bankruptcy is necessary.

Duty to the public

The Revenue in its deliberations also needs to protect the interests of the vast majority of taxpayers who pay their tax in full and on time. It is important that these taxpayers are not disadvantaged by the Voluntary Arrangement procedures where returns to the Public purse are likely to be appreciably less from those who put forward proposals for a Voluntary Arrangement than those who settle their liabilities on time.'

Procedures

Preliminary stages

11.195 The taxpayer must prepare a *proposal* and this is normally done with the help of an insolvency practitioner. This *must* explain briefly why, in the taxpayer's opinion, an IVA is desirable and why his creditors are likely to concur with it. It should also provide, *inter alia*, details of:

- His assets, with estimates of their values, and the extent to which they are charged.

- The extent to which any of his assets are to be excluded from the arrangement, and to which any assets are to be made available by third parties (e.g. a spouse or friend).

- His liabilities and how they are proposed to be met. In particular, how preferential creditors and associates of the taxpayer are to be treated.

- The proposed duration of the IVA, and proposed dates and amounts of distributions to creditors.

- Arrangements for remuneration and expenses payments to be made to the nominee and the supervisor.

- The name and address of the person proposed as supervisor and confirmation that he is qualified to act (r5.3).

The proposal is a crucial document which sets out the terms of the arrangement. It may not affect the rights of secured or preferential creditors without their consent.

11.196 The taxpayer usually then applies to the County Court or High Court for an *interim order*, to give him protection from his creditors while the matter is taken further (s253) and the Court has wide discretion to grant such an order (s255 and r5.1(1)). The interim order has the effect that no bankruptcy petition may be presented or proceeded with, and that no other proceedings, execution or legal process may be commenced without leave of the Court. The order is initially for 14 days.

11.197 The insolvency practitioner, in his capacity as *nominee*, then considers the proposal and must deliver to the Court a *report* in which he gives his opinion as to whether a meeting of creditors should be called to consider the taxpayer's proposal, and a proposed date and venue. If the Court is satisfied that such a meeting should be called, it will extend the interim order to allow the further time necessary (s256).[24]

Approval by creditors

11.198 Notification of the creditors' meeting is sent to every creditor with a copy of the taxpayer's proposal, his statement of affairs and the nominee's comments on the proposal (r5.13 and r5.14). It is essential to identify all creditors, as any who are not notified will not be bound by the IVA.

11.199 The creditor's meeting is then held for the purpose of considering the proposed IVA, which requires the approval of over 75% by value of the creditors present in person or by proxy and voting on the resolution (r5.18(1)). The meeting is normally chaired by the nominee. The creditors may propose modifications to the taxpayer's proposal, for example a supervisor of their own choice rather than the nominee being appointed as supervisor. The Inland Revenue used to have a standard form for setting out its proposed modifications, which was manually completed to reflect the circumstances of the case. Nowadays it uses a word-processed document.

---

[24] In practice, the nominee may use a *Concertina Order* which is an abbreviated procedure adopted by the Courts, allowing the interim order and the nominee's report to be considered at the same hearing.

11.200 After the conclusion of the meeting, the chairman must report the decision of the meeting to the Court (s259). If the meeting has declined the taxpayer's proposal, the Court will discharge the interim order and the taxpayer is thereafter at the mercy of his creditors.

Implementation

11.201 If the IVA is approved by the creditor's meeting, the arrangement takes effect as if made by the taxpayer at the meeting and binds all creditors who had notice of, and were entitled to attend and vote at the meeting, whether or not present or represented there (s260).[25] The nominee, or possibly an alternative choice of the creditors (see above), becomes the *supervisor* of the IVA (s263(2)), and the taxpayer must immediately put him in possession of all assets included in the IVA.

11.202 The supervisor's responsibilities include the realisation of those assets included in the IVA and the payment of creditors in accordance with the proposals. He must keep accounts of all receipts and payments, and supply annual accounts to the Court, the taxpayer and the creditors (r5.26). The only fees chargeable are those sanctioned under the terms of the IVA (r5.28).

11.203 The taxpayer commits an offence if he makes any false representation or commits any other fraud for the purpose of obtaining the approval of his creditors to an IVA. The maximum penalty is seven years' imprisonment (r5.30).

11.204 A significant number of IVAs fail because, for example;

- The taxpayer fails to meet his obligations under the proposal.

- Information contained in the proposal was false in a material particular.

- The taxpayer fails to comply with a reasonable request of the supervisor.

The only remedy in such situations is for the supervisor, or a creditor, to petition for the taxpayer's bankruptcy (ss264(1)(c) and 276). Indeed it is usually a standard term of an IVA that the supervisor *must* petition for bankruptcy in such circumstances.

Other practical considerations regarding IVAs

11.205 An IVA may be preferable to bankruptcy because:

- It enables the taxpayer to avoid the stigma and financial implications of bankruptcy (see paragraph 11.7 *et seq)*, and can,

---

[25] The decision of the creditors' meeting may be challenged on the grounds of unfair prejudice or material irregularity (s262).

for example, enable the owner of a viable business to 'trade out' of trouble.

- It offers the taxpayer greater power to determine how his assets are dealt with and how creditors are satisfied. For example, he may persuade creditors to allow him to retain certain assets, such as his car or his home.

- It allows greater flexibility, in that *any* workable proposal can be put forward. This may include postponing the sale of a property or other asset for a specified period.

- The overall costs and fees are likely to be lower under an IVA than in a bankruptcy (see paragraph 11.59 *et seq*).

11.206 However, there are also limitations, for example:

- An IVA can be vetoed by any creditor(s) holding at least 25% of the votes at the creditors' meeting.

- Although less costly than a bankruptcy, an IVA may nevertheless be expensive and is frequently ruled out because the taxpayer cannot afford the fees. An insolvency practitioner will generally require an initial payment of £1,500-£3,000 to progress matters up to the creditor's meeting, and there will be further (usually significant) charges for acting as supervisor.

- A supervisor's power to enforce an IVA is limited to the sanction of applying for a bankruptcy order, which ends the IVA.

- IVAs are registered with the Department of Trade and the details are recorded by credit reference agencies. The taxpayer's credit rating may be adversely affected for a number of years (see paragraph 7.38 *et seq*).

Deeds of arrangement

11.207 An older scheme, which preceded IVAs, is for the taxpayer to enter a *deed of arrangement* under the Deeds of Arrangement Act 1914, under which he contracts to make payments to all or a majority of his creditors, without necessarily clearing the debts in full. He is then released from the claims of the assenting creditors and protected from enforcement proceedings by them.

11.208 The limitation of a deed of arrangement is that it is binding only on the creditors who execute the deed or expressly assent to its terms. Creditors who do not assent are *not* bound and may pursue other enforcement remedies available to them. In view of this weakness, deeds of arrangement have largely been superseded by IVAs.

Key points to consider

11.209 Is the debt correctly stated? Even though the accuracy of an asssessment cannot be challenged in enforcement proceedings, the Bankruptcy Court will usually permit an adjournment to allow a liability based upon estimates, or otherwise considered excessive, to be revised to the 'correct' figure (see paragraph 11.73 *et seq).*

11.210 In practice, it is best to act as early as possible. Where a demand is based upon a County Court judgment requiring payment forthwith, an application for a variation order made prior to the issue of the statutory demand may avoid bankruptcy (see paragraph 11.51 *et seq).*

11.211 In any event, consider whether the tax payable immediately can be reduced below the bankruptcy level of £750 (see paragraph 11.71*).*

11.212 In situations of insolvency, consider whether bankruptcy might, on balance, actually be a solution by removing the pressure from creditors and enabling the taxpayer to make a fresh start (see paragraph 11.20 *et seq).* If it is, consider expediting matters by submitting a debtor's petition (see paragraph 11.77 *et seq).*

11.213 Where a taxpayer is insolvent but may be able to avoid bankruptcy, perhaps by obtaining help from a friend or relative, consider the overall implications of bankruptcy and their likely impact. In particular, have regard to:

- The possible loss of his home, whether owner-occupied or rented, and whether it might be protected by third party rights of occupation or a 'buy out' (see paragraphs 11.123 *et seq* and 11.132 *et seq).*

- Restrictions and difficulties in obtaining credit, which may inhibit the establishment of a new business for several years (see paragraph 11.12).

- Restrictions on positions he may hold, or on his profession or employment (see paragraph 11.14 *et seq).*

- Whether his business will be sold (see paragraph 11.10 *et seq).*

11.214 Bankruptcy is never a solution where the taxpayer is solvent, since costs and charges on the bankrupt's estate can mount up even where the bankruptcy is annulled shortly after the initial order (see paragraph 11.159 *et seq).*

11.215 If the taxpayer wishes to oppose bankruptcy he should be aware that the Inland Revenue may be supported by the Court in refusing to accept what seems like a reasonable 'offer' (see paragraph 11.69). In such cases, he may have more success with an IVA, but should be aware of Inland Revenue strictures on such arrangements (see paragraph 11.188 *et seq).*

11.216 If the taxpayer considers that the Inland Revenue has not followed published guidance on bankruptcy or acceptance of an IVA, consider a complaint under one of the procedures mentioned in Chapter 3, especially a complaint to the Adjudicator (see paragraph 3.110 *et seq*).

11.217 Timing can be important:

- An application to set aside a statutory demand must be made within 18 days of service, while notice of intention to oppose a bankruptcy petition must be filed at least 7 days before the hearing (which may be only 7 days after receipt of the petition) (see paragraph 11.37 and 11.59).

- If the taxpayer is entitled to a 'tax holiday', a bankruptcy order early in the tax year is particularly favourable (see paragraph 11.151 *et seq)*.

11.218 If the taxpayer has a reasonable income, he should be prepared for an income payments order to be made against him, as the Official Receiver is becoming more pro-active in this respect (see paragraph 11.108 *et seq)*.

Chapter 12

Self-assessment

This chapter introduces the main changes that will affect tax debts following the introduction of self-assessment from 1996/97. The following issues are considered:

		From paragraph
■	The background to self-assessment	*12.1*
■	How a tax debt will arise	*12.6*
■	Tax returns and payments	*12.9*
■	Assessments and determinations	*12.35*
■	Enquiries into tax returns	*12.44*
■	Interest, surcharges and penalties	*12.51*
■	Partnerships	*12.69*
■	Transitional provisions for 1996/97	*12.73*
■	Tax debts under self-assessment	*12.80*

The background to self-assessment

12.1   Self-assessment is the biggest change in tax administration since the introduction of PAYE in 1944/45. Under the new system, responsibility for assessment and payment of tax is transferred largely from the Inland Revenue to the taxpayer, thus bringing the UK system of taxation closer to that of the United States of America and Australia.

12.2   An unprecedented publicity campaign has been embarked upon by the Inland Revenue, to promote self-assessment as a positive reform, while at the same time warning taxpayers of the requirements and obligations that will be placed upon them. Comprehensive training, lectures, conferences and seminar programmes have been arranged, both by the Inland Revenue and the professions, and numerous books and articles have been published on the subject. Among the best known of these is the Inland Revenue's *SAT 2 (1995) Self-assessment: The legal framework*, which has been distributed free to tax practitioners.

12.3   A key aspect of the new regime is the move to the current year basis of assessment (CYB). CYB took effect from 1994/95 for businesses which commenced trading after 5 April 1994 while, for those already trading at that date, CYB takes full effect from 1997/98, with transitional rules for 1996/97. The detailed provisions of CYB are beyond the scope of this text, but a good summary is given in the Inland Revenue's *SAT 1 (1995) The new current year basis of assessment.*

12.4   Aspects of the CYB have proved controversial, particularly the Inland Revenue's initial suggestion that accounts should be prepared in line with the tax year - known as *fiscal accounting*. This was resisted successfully by the professions, but has resulted in some very complex legislation; in particular the concepts of 'overlap relief' and certain anti-avoidance provisions regarding the transitional year 1996/97.

12.5   The changes introduced by self-assessment are considerable and far beyond the scope of a single chapter. The following paragraphs cover the main amendments affecting payments to the Inland Revenue. References in this chapter to Taxes Management Act 1970 and the Income and Corporation Taxes Act 1988 are to those sections applicable for 1996/97 and subsequent years.

How a tax debt will arise

12.6   Chapter 2 examined the main ways in which a tax debt could be created under the old system, namely:

- By the Inspector making an *assessment.*

- Under the terms of a *contractual settlement* between the taxpayer and the Inland Revenue following a tax investigation.

- Where the taxpayer makes a payment to a third party of a kind which is required to be paid under *deduction of tax at source*, for example a salary payment to an employee.

12.7   The main impact of self-assessment is to change the first of these provisions. The vast majority of tax liabilities, which previously would have originated from the making of an assessment by an Inspector, will now be created by the taxpayer's own self-assessment on a tax return (TMA 1970, s59B).

12.8   There will be several circumstances where tax liabilities may still be triggered by an action by the Inspector. The most important situations will be:

- Where a tax return does not contain a computation of the tax due - either because the taxpayer has opted for the Inland Revenue to do the calculation or for any other reason - the Inland Revenue should complete the self-assessment. In this event, the self-assessment is still treated for all purposes as 'made' by the taxpayer (TMA 1970, ss9(2) and 9(3)) (see paragraph 12.14). In such cases, the legal charge to tax is created by the Inland Revenue's issue of the notice of tax payable.

- Where a self-assessment contains an obvious error or mistake, the Inspector may amend the self-assessment to correct it. The Inland Revenue refers to this as a *repair* (TMA 1970, s9(4)) (see paragraph 12.33).

- Where the taxpayer has failed to submit a tax return and the Inspector makes a *determination* (TMA 1970, s28C) (see paragraph 12.40 *et seq*).

- Where a self-assessment is, upon an enquiry, considered inadequate by the Inspector, he may make an *amendment*:

  - to avoid a loss of tax to the Crown, or

  - to effect amendments which the taxpayer declines to make upon the conclusion of the enquiry (TMA 1970, s28A) (see paragraph 12.47 *et seq*).

- Where an Inspector *discovers* that profits assessed have been inadequate, that any assessment is insufficient, or that relief given is excessive, he may make an *assessment* (TMA 1970, s29) (see paragraph 12.36 *et seq*).

Tax returns and payments

12.9 The new system depends upon the Inland Revenue being aware that an individual is chargeable to tax, so that a tax return may be issued to him, together with sanctions for failure to self-assess.

Notification of chargeability

12.10 Anyone who has profits chargeable to income tax or capital gains tax, and who has not received a tax return form, must notify the Inland Revenue within six months of the end of the tax year (i.e by 5 October). This requirement generally does not apply in respect of income where the full tax liability is satisfied by deductions made at source (TMA 1970, s7).[1]

12.11 Failure to notify chargeability may give rise to a penalty not exceeding the tax unpaid at 31 January following the end of the tax year. It should therefore be noted that no penalty will arise if a liability outstanding at 5 October is settled on or before 31 January.

---

[1] For the Inland Revenue's proposed practice in relation to penalties for failing to notify income assessable under Schedule E, see *Statement of Practice 1/96*.

12.12   The purpose of notification is to trigger the issue of a tax return by the Inspector. If no return is then issued, due to a failure by the Inland Revenue, no liability can arise. It is possible that some disputes over tax debts may centre around questions over whether tax returns were issued and/or received.

Tax returns

12.13   In the vast majority of relevant cases, tax returns will in fact be issued. A tax return must be completed and returned to the Inland Revenue by the later of:

- 31 January following the tax year end, and

- three months after the date on which the return is issued.

The latter provision will apply where a return is issued after 31 October. For example, if the return covering 1996/97 is issued on 1 January 1998, it must be submitted by 1 April 1998 (TMA 1970, s8A).

12.14   If the taxpayer does not wish to do the self-assessment calculation, he may ask the Inland Revenue to do it for him. In such cases the remainder of the tax return should be completed and returned to the Inland Revenue by the later of:

- 30 September following the tax year end, and

- two months after the date on which the return is issued.

12.15   The Inland Revenue should then take the necessary action to ensure that the taxpayer is given details of the self-assessment (including the tax payable) in time for the payment date discussed below. It should be emphasised that this is still considered a self-assessment and in computing the tax the Inland Revenue is deemed to be the agent of the taxpayer (TMA 1970, s9(3)). This means that, if an error on the return leads to the Inland Revenue's computation understating the tax due, the fault is regarded as the taxpayer's and he cannot blame the Inland Revenue for failing to identify the error on the return.

12.16   The Inland Revenue has made it clear that it will carry out the self-assessment calculation even where the deadline in paragraph 12.14 is not met, but it cannot then guarantee to complete the exercise in time for the due date for payment, in which case interest and surcharges may arise.

12.17   For a taxpayer who does not wish to compute his own tax, the most significant change is the obligation to ensure that his tax return is complete in all other respects. It will not be sufficient to enter 'as per accounts to follow' or 'as returned by my employer'. The return itself must contain all the information necessary for the Inspector to complete the self-assessment calculation.

Payment dates

12.18   The present system, whereby tax under different parts of the taxes legislation is payable on a range of different dates, is replaced by a single set of payment dates (see paragraph 2.29).

12.19   In general terms, a taxpayer will be required to make two *payments on account* towards his total income tax and class 4 national insurance contributions liability for any year of assessment.   A third *balancing payment* to meet any income tax and class 4 national insurance contributions still outstanding, together with the capital gains tax liability for the year, will then be due on the filing date for the return, as set out in paragraph 12.13.   If tax has been overpaid, then a refund is due on the tax return filing date.

12.20   The Inland Revenue will issue a *taxpayer statement* in advance of each payment date, setting out details of all outstanding liabilities still to be settled.   This statement will reflect sums due for each year separately (so that interest charges and surcharges may be properly made) and it represents an innovation in setting out in one document the total indebtedness of the taxpayer to the Inland Revenue. The taxpayer statement will not include liabilities of 1995/96 and earlier years, except where assessments are issued after 5 April 1998.   For consideration of the implications of these changes, see paragraph 12.81 *et seq.*

Payments on account

12.21   If a taxpayer has been liable to make a self-assessment for any year, or has otherwise been assessed to tax for that year, he may be required to make payments on account for the following year.   These will be due on:

- 31 January within the year of assessment, and

- 31 July immediately following the year of assessment (TMA 1970, ss59(2) and 59A(1)).   For the special provisions for 1996/97, see paragraph 12.76 *et seq.*

12.22   Payments on account will be calculated by reference to the *relevant amount*, which is broadly the total income tax and class 4 national insurance contributions liability for the previous year, less tax credited or deducted at source.

12.23   This may be illustrated by reference to an example in *SAT 2 (1995) Self-assessment: The legal framework*:

A taxpayer's self-assessment for 1997/98 shows:

Gross income tax assessed	£8,500
Gross capital gains tax assessed	£2,360
Gross class 4 national insurance contributions	£650
SC60 tax deducted at source	£1,750
Tax credits on dividends received	£345

The relevant amount is income tax assessed for 1997/98 less tax credits for 1997/98.

The relevant amount of income tax for 1997/98 is therefore:

$$£8,500 - (£1,750 + £345) = £6,405$$

The relevant amount of class 4 national insurance contributions for 1997/98 is simply

$$£650 - £0 = £650$$

The total relevant amount is £6,405 + £650 = £7,055

Therefore the payments on account required for 1998/99 are

31 January 1999:   £3,202.50 + £325 = £3,527.50

31 July 1999:   £3,202.50 + £325 = £3,527.50

12.24 If the *relevant amount* of income tax or class 4 national insurance contributions is less than a *de minimis* figure, or a *de minimis* fraction of the previous year's total liability (*before* deduction at source or tax credits), then no payment on account will be required (TMA 1970, s59A(1)). The *de minimis* thresholds are to be set by Statutory Instrument and had not been announced at the time of writing. However, they are expected to be £500 and 20% respectively.[2] This will relieve the vast majority of taxpayers, apart from the self-employed, from the obligation to make payments on account.

12.25 Tax on capital gains is excluded from the computation of payments on account. Therefore, any capital gains tax liability will be payable only as part of the balancing payment.

Balancing payments

12.26 The self-assessment will reflect the taxpayer's remaining liability to tax (or repayment due), net of tax credited or deducted at source and payments on account. If the Inland Revenue does the self-assessment calculation, the figure will be notified to the taxpayer.

12.27 A balancing payment, or refund, is due on 31 January following the tax year end, or three months after the issue of the tax return if later (TMA 1970, ss59B(3) and 59B(4)). It should be noted that usually this will be the same due date as for the first payment on account for the following tax year, which may in practice give rise to some confusion.

12.28 Where a taxpayer pays tax through PAYE, he may opt for a balancing liability of up to £1,000 to be 'coded in' and collected by

---

[2] These figures were subsequently confirmed by an Inland Revenue Press Release on 26 June 1996.

deduction at source, and not to pay it directly, provided he submits his return by no later than 30 September following the tax year end (*SA/BK1 Self Assessment - A general guide*).

Reduced payments on account

12.29 Where a taxpayer's liability tends to be fairly constant from one year to the next, it will be met broadly by the payments on account and any balancing payment or refund will be small. If his liability increases from one year to the next, there is a cash flow advantage in that the extra tax does not become payable until 10 months after the tax year end and no interest begins to run until then.

12.30 However, where his liability is expected to fall, the standard provisions for payments on account described above will give rise to an overpayment. In these circumstances, the taxpayer may make a claim that each payment on account should be reduced to 50% of what he calculates will be the balance of his tax liability for the current year, after taking account of deductions at source and tax credits. This may involve reducing the payments on account to nil. The reduced amounts must be specified in a claim and, if the claim is made after one or both instalments have been paid, a refund will follow. A form to make the claim will be included with the taxpayer statement.

12.31 If a claim to reduce payments on account is made negligently or fraudulently, a penalty may be charged (TMA 1970, ss59A(3) to 59A(6)). Penalties are discussed in paragraph 12.62 *et seq*. Also, should the payments made on account prove insufficient to meet the liability for the year, interest is chargeable from the due date of each payment to the extent that the claim was excessive. The payments that would have been due had the claim been accurate are compared with the payments actually made; each shortfall attracts interest from the due date for the payment on account (TMA 1970, s86(4)).

Correction of errors

12.32 A taxpayer may amend his tax return by notifying the Inland Revenue, normally within 12 months of the filing date. This includes the right to make belated claims for any allowance or relief (TMA 1970, ss9(4) to 9(6)). If an error is discovered after the deadline, it may be remedied by an error or mistake claim (see paragraph 4.55 *et seq*).

12.33 The Inland Revenue may correct any 'obvious errors or mistakes', for example errors of principle or arithmetic, and notify the taxpayer of the adjustment to his liability accordingly. This is known as a *repair* and must be carried out within nine months of the date on which the return is submitted (TMA 1970, ss9(4) to 9(6)). If the Revenue discovers an error after the deadline, it may exercise its powers to make a discovery assessment or start an enquiry (see paragraphs 12.36 *et seq* and 12.44 *et seq*).

12.34 In either event, any additional tax will be payable on the later of:

- the due date for filing the tax return, and

- 30 days after the notification of the amendment to the self-assessment,

although interest will usually run from the filing date (TMA 1970, s59B(5)).

Assessments and determinations

12.35 There are two important powers given to the Inland Revenue to create a tax debt where it appears that there would otherwise be an underpayment, or excessive relief granted.

Discovery assessments

12.36 An Inspector may make an assessment, known as a *discovery assessment*, if he finds that inadequate profits have been assessed, that any assessment is insufficient, or that relief given is excessive. This should be in the amount which he believes is necessary to make good to the Crown the loss of tax.

12.37 Such an assessment cannot be made unless either of the following situations applies:

- The loss of tax is due to fraudulent or negligent conduct on the part of the taxpayer, in which case the assessment may be made at any time within 20 years following 31 January after the tax year end (TMA 1970, ss29 and 36(1)).

- It is too late to commence an enquiry and the Inspector could not reasonably have been expected, on the basis of the information made available to him before that time, to be aware of the situation giving rise to the loss of tax. In such cases the assessment may be made at any time within five years following 31 January after the tax year end (TMA 1970, ss29 and 34(1)).

12.38 Problems over what an Inspector might be 'reasonably' expected to be 'aware of' have already been discussed in the context of discovery assessments under the old system (see paragraph 2.25 *et seq*). Considerable concerns were expressed by professional bodies that the Inland Revenue's views of its powers to raise discovery assessments would give rise to great uncertainty under self-assessment, particularly where returns are electronically filed. The Inland Revenue relented by modifying its views as to when a discovery may be made and the new policy is set out in *Tax Bulletin* June 1996 pp313-315.

12.39   The tax charged by a discovery assessment is normally due and payable 30 days after the assessment is issued. An appeal may be made and tax postponed pending settlement of the appeal, in the same way as applied under the old system, except that interest is charged under TMA 1970, s86 with effect from the filing date for the tax return, i.e. normally 31 January following the tax year end (TMA 1970, s59B(6)).

Determinations

12.40   Where a taxpayer fails to file his self-assessment tax return by the due date, the Inspector may make a *determination*, 'to the best of his information and belief', of the amount of tax to which the taxpayer is liable. Notice of a determination should be issued to the taxpayer and should state its date of issue (TMA 1970, s28C).

12.41   The determination is treated as if it were the taxpayer's self-assessment and has the following consequences:

- Since the normal date for making the balancing payment will have passed, the tax shown is payable and enforceable immediately. There is no 30 day delay before enforcement can commence.

- There is no right of appeal or, consequently, postponement. The only way that the determination can be displaced is by the taxpayer submitting his own self-assessment, by way of a tax return. If the tax return does not include a computation of the tax due, then the determination is not displaced until the Inland Revenue has done the computation. In practice, Collectors may agree to suspend enforcement proceedings pending completion of the Inland Revenue's calculation.

- If recovery proceedings have already commenced on the basis of a determination and the taxpayer's self-assessment is then made, the proceedings may be continued, but the sum due must be amended to reflect the liability shown on the self-assessment.

12.42   These provisions end the scope for abuse, which existed under the old system, whereby a taxpayer could appeal against an assessment and apply to postpone all the tax charged, as a way of delaying recovery proceedings.

12.43   However, the new provisions do permit the Inland Revenue to place extreme pressure on a taxpayer to sort out his affairs - by taking enforcement proceedings for tax due on a determination which may include a very high estimate of income - in cases where the taxpayer has failed to submit his tax return through no fault of his own.

Enquiries into tax returns

12.44 Self-assessment places great reliance on the taxpayer getting his return right and so the Inland Revenue is given significant powers to check compliance by way of conducting *enquiries*. These will replace the investigations that have been conducted under the old system, but there are a number of important differences.[3]

12.45 Whereas investigations have been conducted on a non-statutory basis, there is a legislative code governing enquiries (TMA 1970, ss9A, 19A and 28A). In particular:

- An enquiry must commence within 12 months of the filing date for the tax return. If the return or an amendment is filed after the correct filing date (see paragraph 12.13), then the enquiry may commence within 12 months of the end of the quarter in which the return or amendment is filed (quarters end on 31 January, 30 April, 31 July and 31 October). After the deadline for commencing an enquiry has passed, the liability for the year is final and may not be altered, except by way of a discovery assessment (see paragraph 12.36 *et seq*).

- An Inspector must notify the taxpayer upon commencement of an enquiry and upon its completion. The taxpayer has the right to ask the Commissioners to order the conclusion of an enquiry, for example if he considers that there are no grounds for its continuation, or if it is being prolonged unduly.

- There is no longer a requirement for the Inspector to state, or even to have, 'grounds' for commencing an enquiry - indeed it is the Inland Revenue's intention to select some cases randomly as a way of 'encouraging' compliance with the new regime.

- There are powers for the Inspector to require documents to assist him in course of the enquiry.

12.46 The broad purpose of an enquiry is to identify any errors on, or omissions from, a tax return which result in an understatement of the tax due. Such matters may be remedied, upon the conclusion of the enquiry, by the Inspector inviting the taxpayer to amend his self-assessment to correct the errors or omissions. Any additional tax is payable 30 days after the date of the amendment.

12.47 The Inspector also has powers to make amendments to the self-assessment himself in the event that:

- the taxpayer declines to amend his self-assessment at the conclusion of an enquiry, or

---

[3] For a discussion of such investigations, see paragraph 2.30 *et seq.*

- underdeclarations come to light in the course of the enquiry which may lead to a loss of tax if not remedied immediately.

In either event, the taxpayer has the right to appeal to the Commissioners and to apply for tax to be postponed. However, in the latter situation, such an appeal will not be heard or determined until the enquiry is completed (TMA 1970, ss28A, 31(1)(a) and 31(1A)).

12.48 In the Inland Revenue's view, the formal procedures ensure that both parties' rights are protected, but it expects that

> 'in the vast majority of cases, settlement will be by agreement and by an amendment to the self-assessment to reflect any adjustments agreed. The facility to agree a contract settlement for all outstanding items will remain broadly as now.'[4]

Accordingly, it is expected that many enquiries will be concluded by the taxpayer offering a lump sum reflecting tax, interest and penalties in much the same way as described in paragraphs 2.32-2.33, and that in such cases amendments will not be made.

12.49 It should be noted that an enquiry is the only method open to an Inspector to remedy any (apparent) inaccuracy on a tax return, unless it is an 'obvious' error or mistake falling within the *repair* provisions discussed in paragraph 12.33.

12.50 Concerns have been expressed that the introduction of self-assessment, together with the scope for conducting 'random' enquiries, could lead to heavy-handed conduct by Inspectors. To deflect such criticism, the Inland Revenue intends that all taxpayers facing enquiries will be provided with information concerning the conduct of an enquiry and their rights. If it is considered that the enquiry may lead to a significant amendment to their self-assessment, they should be given a copy of the new *Code of Practice 11 Enquiries into tax returns by local Tax Offices.* This explains how enquiries should be conducted and the avenues for complaint in cases of abuse or unfairness.

Interest, surcharges and penalties

Interest on tax paid late and on refunds

12.51 Fundamental changes are being introduced to the regime for charging interest on tax and paying interest on repayments.

12.52 The old provisions have allowed for:

- charges to interest on unpaid tax from a 'reckonable date', and

---

[4] *SAT 2 (1995) Self-assessment: The legal framework*, p52

- repayment supplement on tax overpaid, which cannot accrue until at least 12 months after the end of the tax year to which the refund relates.

Both have been calculated at the same *rate* (see paragraphs 2.65 *et seq* and 4.77 *et seq*).

12.53 Under self-assessment, interest on tax payable and repayable is normally calculated from the same date, but at different rates. The rate charged on tax paid late will be set in line with the average rate of borrowing, while the rate paid on tax refunds will be lower, set in line with the average return on profits.[5]

12.54 Interest charges will arise automatically on all tax paid late. They will be reflected on the taxpayer statement, no matter how small the amount. Such charges may arise in respect of, for example:

- late settlement of a payment on account

- late settlement of a balancing payment

- tax payable following an amendment to an assessment, whether made by the Inland Revenue or the taxpayer

- tax payable on a discovery assessment by the Inland Revenue

- tax payable following a postponement in relation to a discovery assessment or an amendment to a self-assessment as a result of an enquiry

12.55 Where a payment due on account is made late, or an underpayment results from a claim for a reduced payment (see paragraph 12.31), interest runs from the date(s) on which payment fell due. In all other cases listed above, it runs from the filing date for the tax return, normally 31 January following the relevant tax year end (see paragraph 12.13), even though the due date for payment may be later. Similarly, interest on refunds normally runs from that date.

Surcharges

12.56 The Inland Revenue takes the view that interest charges simply reflect commercial restitution for late payment of tax. In order to deter taxpayers from using the Inland Revenue as a 'bank' offering relatively cheap credit, a scheme of surcharges is introduced to encourage prompt payment (TMA 1970, s59C).

12.57 A surcharge may be imposed whenever tax remains unpaid more than 28 days after the filing date for the tax return (see paragraph 12.13). This can apply to tax due, for example:

---

[5] *SAT 2 (1995) Self-assessment: The legal framework*, p40

- By way of a balancing payment (including cases where a determination is made).

- On an amendment to a self-assessment.

- On a discovery assessment.

12.58 The initial surcharge is 5% of the tax underpaid, with a further 5% imposed on any sums still unpaid within 6 months from the due date. Interest is charged on the surcharge if not settled within 30 days from the date on which the formal notice of surcharge is issued to the taxpayer (TMA 1970, s59).

12.59 A taxpayer may appeal against the imposition of a surcharge on the grounds of 'reasonable excuse'. It is not yet known how the Commissioners and the Courts will interpret this phrase, but cash flow difficulties are expressly ruled out as grounds for mitigation (TMA 1970, s59C). The Inland Revenue has undertaken to publish guidelines on what it considers to be a reasonable excuse, before the surcharge regime comes into effect.

12.60 Quite separately, the Inland Revenue has powers to mitigate surcharges and the Government has stated that no charge should be made on a taxpayer who discovers a bona fide mistake on a self-assessment, which he volunteers and corrects promptly ((1994) STI 239), although interest will still be due. The Inland Revenue has stated that it could use the power of mitigation:

- In a case where an instalment agreement is reached to allow the taxpayer to settle a tax debt over time. The Inland Revenue could waive or reduce the surcharge provided the instalment agreement was kept to.

- In cases of hardship.[6]

12.61 A surcharge will not be levied if a penalty is sought under TMA 1970, ss7, 93, 95 or 95A in respect of the same tax (TMA 1970, s59C(4)). In such cases, the Inland Revenue would normally seek a penalty of at least the same amount as the surcharge waived.

Penalties

12.62 There is a battery of penalty provisions available to the Inland Revenue to ensure compliance with the new regime. It should be emphasised that many of the more serious statutory provisions described below usually will be invoked by an Inspector in the course of an enquiry and the amount charged may therefore be included as part of a contractual settlement (see comments in paragraphs 2.85 and 12.48).

---

[6] *SAT 2 (1995) Self-assessment: The legal framework*, p39

12.63 For returns not filed by the due date, there may be:

- An initial fixed penalty of £100.

- A further fixed penalty of £100 if the return is still outstanding after 6 months.

- A penalty not exceeding the liability to tax if the return is still outstanding after 12 months.

The second penalty listed above is waived if the Inspector has already applied to the Commissioners for a daily 'non-filing' penalty of up to £60 per day, although this power will only be used in serious cases, where 'the tax risk is believed to be high'. The total penalty charged in any case cannot exceed the balancing payment of tax shown to be due by the return (TMA 1970, s93).

12.64 The flat rate penalties are subject to mitigation on the grounds of 'reasonable excuse', with rights of appeal to the Commissioners. In the case of a penalty determination for a tax-geared penalty, the grounds of appeal are not specified and so they are wider and will take account of the normal factors that might justify mitigation, whether in the course of negotiating a contractual settlement or on an appeal against a penalty determination (see paragraph 2.87).

12.65 Existing tax geared penalties for filing of incorrect returns continue to apply (TMA 1970, s95) (see paragraph 2.83).

12.66 Members of a partnership may each individually be liable for the non-filing penalties where a partnership return is filed late (TMA 1970, s93A).

12.67 Some other important penalty provisions are as follows:

- Failure to notify chargeability - a penalty of up to 100% of the tax unpaid by 31 January following the tax year end (see paragraph 12.10).

- Failure to keep records - a penalty of up to £3,000 although this maximum charge is expected to be extremely rare (TMA 1970, s12B(5)).

- Failure to comply with a notice requiring documents, accounts or particulars - an initial penalty of £50 followed by daily penalties (TMA 1970, s97AA).

- A tax penalty where profits are moved to take advantage of the transitional provisions for moving to the CYB (see paragraph 12.75).

12.68 Interest is charged on penalties outstanding after the due payment date, which is normally 30 days after the imposition of the penalty (TMA 1970, s69).

Partnerships

12.69 Fundamental changes to partnership taxation are introduced by self-assessment. Under the old system, the profits of a trade or profession carried on by a partnership have been taxed by an assessment on the firm itself, which is then primarily liable to pay the tax charged and to take any other appropriate action concerning the assessement. The partners have been jointly liable for the income tax and class 4 national insurance contributions due (see paragraph 5.70 *et seq*).

12.70 Under self-assessment, there are to be no partnership assessments. Each partner is to be assessed on his share of the partnership profit and each partner will be liable individually for the tax due on his share. Accordingly, individual partners are required to include their shares of partnership profits on their own tax returns and self-assessments. Joint liability ceases (ICTA 1988, s111).

12.71 The rules for determining the precise date from which partners are liable for tax only on their own profits, in relation to any particular partnership, are explained in paragraph 5.77 *et seq*. Broadly, for firms set up after 5 April 1994 this new provision will apply from the outset, while in other cases joint liability will not apply in respect of profits assessed from 1997/98, or from the date of a deemed cessation if earlier.

12.72 There has been some concern expressed in the professional press that the new wording of TMA 1970, s36(2) gives the Inland Revenue a residual power to claim joint liability where an assessment is made following 'fraudulent or negligent conduct'. The Inland Revenue has given assurances that it does not intend to interpret the legislation in this way, i.e. there will be no joint liability.

Transitional provisions for 1996/97

12.73 Self-assessment is designed to be more 'user-friendly' in that:

- Computation of liabilities should be simpler. In particular, the preceding year basis of assessment (PYB) is to replaced by the current year basis of assessment (CYB). This should ease the calculation of liabilities arising from sources of income assessable under Schedule D Cases I to V.

- The process by which tax liabilies are determined is less bureaucratic. The old system, involving estimated assessments (with attendant appeals and postponements) and a number of different payment dates for different kinds of liabilities, is replaced by a single set of payment dates with liabilities based upon the taxpayer's own figures. Payments on account are determined by reference to the previous year's self-assessment.

However, both of these innovations require transitional measures in 1996/97 and there are also special rules for partnerships.

Moving from PYB to CYB

12.74   Very broadly, sources of income previously assessable on the PYB will be taxed on that basis for all years up to 1995/96 and on the CYB with effect from 1997/98, with transitional provisions in 1996/97. The extensive provisions covering this change are beyond the scope of this handbook[7], apart from the following remark.

12.75   The normal way in which the taxpayer will move from PYB to CYB, is by paying tax for 1996/97 on a 12 month average figure, based upon the profits for the period:

- *from* immediately after the end of the period which formed the basis of his assessment for 1995/96,

- *to* the accounting period end falling in 1996/97.

To prevent taxpayers from exploiting the transitional provisions by the diversion of profits, there are penalties which may be triggered by a change or modification of an accounting policy, a change of business practice, self-cancelling transactions or transactions with connected persons. However, a change of accounting date ending in 1996/97 which moves it closer to 5 April 1997 will not attract the anti-avoidance provisions (FA 1995, 22 Sch). Details are given in *SAT 1 (1995) The new current year basis of assessment*, Chapter 10.

Payments on account for 1996/97

12.76   The first payments on account under self-assessment will fall due on 31 January and 31 July 1997. As taxpayers will not previously have self-assessed, it is necessary for the Inland Revenue to notify them of the amounts due on each date and taxpayer statements will be sent out November and December 1996.

12.77   In contrast with the normal rules explained in paragraph 12.21 *et seq*, the liability for 1995/96 will be split between 31 January 1997 and 31 July 1997 as follows:

- The payment due on 31 January 1997 will be equal to the aggregate of:

---

[7] A comprehensive and useful explanation is given by the Inland Revenue in its *SAT 1 (1995) The new current year basis of assessment* which has been distributed free to practitioners.

- One half of the 1995/96 liability under Schedule D Case I or II (including class 4 national insurance contributions).

- All of the 1995/96 liability under Schedule D Cases III to VI.

- All of the 1995/96 liability under Schedule A.

- The payment due on 31 July 1997 will be:

    - One half of the 1995/96 liability under Schedule D Case I or II (including class 4 national insurance contributions).[8]

If the assessment for 1995/96 has been issued on or after 1 June 1996, then the apportionment is different. Each payment on account for 1996/97 is one-half of the aggregate liability for 1995/96 under Schedule A and Schedule D Cases I to VI (including class 4 national insurance contributions).[9]

If an assessment for 1995/96 is still under appeal at the time that the taxpayer statement is issued, the payments on account will be based upon the tax charged by that assessment which has not been postponed. Once the appeal is determined, the Inspector will recalculate the payments on account by reference to the final liability for 1995/96. If, in consequence, the taxpayer is found to have paid an insufficient sum on account on 31 January or 31 July 1997, interest will be charged on any underpayment. It is therefore important to finalise liabilities for 1995/96 before 31 January 1997 wherever possible.

It should be noted that whatever liabilities would fall due under the above provisions, claims may be made to reduce the payments on account by reference to the anticipated liability for 1996/97, under the rules outlined in paragraphs 12.30-12.31.

12.78 The payments on account for 1996/97 will disregard any liability to higher rate tax on investment income received net of tax, which previously would have been due for payment on 1 December following the tax year end. The liability for 1996/97, in respect of this income, will be settled simply as part of the balancing payment for 1996/97.

Partnership assessments for 1996/97

12.79 For firms that were trading prior to 6 April 1994 and have not had a 'deemed cessation' prior to 6 April 1997, a composite partnership assessment will be made for 1996/97, as in previous years. In most cases this will be made on an estimated basis, with the traditional rights of appeal

---

[8] *SAT 2 (1995) Self-assessment: The legal framework*, p40

[9] This reflects the fact that the income tax charged under Schedule D Cases I and II will have been payable in a single instalment, which makes the normal apportionment (outlined on page 40 of *SAT 2*) more difficult to apply.

and postponement, and instalments falling due on 1 January and 1 July 1997. The reckonable date for interest charged under TMA 1970, s86 will be 1 July 1997, or 30 days after the issue of the assessment if later. When each partner comes to make his self-assessment for 1996/97, his share of the tax borne by the partnership will be available as a credit against his personal liability.[10]

Tax debts under self-assessment

12.80 The new tax regime changes substantially the processes whereby tax, which is not deductible at source, becomes due and payable to the Inland Revenue. However, once the liability is established, the Inland Revenue's collection practices should remain much the same as before. Many of the techniques and approaches discussed in this handbook will remain relevant, as will negotiation and enforcement procedures explained in Chapters 6 to 11.

Taxpayer statements

12.81 An important innovation under self-assessment is the *taxpayer statement*, which will provide a running total of each taxpayer's indebtedness including any interest, surcharges and penalties that have accrued to date (see paragraph 12.20). This will provide the taxpayer with a clearer picture of his overall liability than under the old system, where computerised demands tend to relate to individual assessments (and do not mention payments due on other assessments) and letters from local collection offices do not always provide a comprehensive list of tax liabilities, let alone the interest that has accrued.

12.82 However, the taxpayer statement will also provide the Collector with a permanent continuing record of liabilities, which should assist Collectors in enforcing tax debts. It is understood that the Inland Revenue is still to decide whether remitted liabilities should be deleted from the taxpayer statement and, if so, at what stage.

12.83 From 6 April 1998, the taxpayer statement will incorporate unsettled debts for the years up to 1995/96 which are assessed after 5 April 1998. Pre-self-assessment liabilities assessed before 6 April 1998 will never be included in the taxpayer statement. Nevertheless local Collectors and the Enforcement Office will be instructed to pursue all liabilities due from any individual (whether or not reflected on the taxpayer statement) as a single exercise.

---

[10] The Inland Revenue procedures are explained in *Tax Bulletin* April 1996 pp293-298.

Partnerships

12.84 One welcome departure will be the end of joint liability for members of partnerships, although it should be noted that this does not apply until 1997/98 for those receiving composite assessments for 1996/ 97 (see paragraphs 12.71 and 12.79).

New compliance measures

12.85 In many cases, the new scheme of penalties, interest and surcharges could add significantly to the tax arrears at stake. To some extent, this depends upon the extent to which the Inland Revenue agrees to mitigate the charges. If it proves inflexible, the Commissioners may be swamped with appeals on the grounds of 'reasonable excuse', in much the same way as happened with the enforcement of VAT some years ago.

Reduced Commissioners' powers

12.86 Under the old system, the Commissioners have offered unrepresented taxpayers a practical safeguard against excessive estimated assessments, in those cases in which tax returns and accounts have not been submitted on time, or have been challenged by the Inspector. Provided an appeal was made, the assessment could not become final before the matter was determined, either by an agreement between the taxpayer and the Inspector, or by a Commissioners' determination. Tax could be postponed pending settlement of the appeal.

12.87 The listing of a Commissioners' hearing has therefore offered the taxpayer a chance to explain his level of profits to an independent tribunal and in many cases Commissioners have adjusted assessments on a rough and ready basis without the need for much additional evidence. Although resort to the Commissioners is not usually the best course of action in tax debt cases (see paragraph 3.33 *et seq)*, their existence can be a vital protection where relations break down and the taxpayer considers that estimates have been pitched at an unreasonably high level.

12.88 Under self-assessment, a taxpayer who fails to submit his tax return will receive a *determination*, which can only be displaced by the submission of a self-assessment (i.e. tax return) and there is no right of appeal (see paragraph 12.40 *et seq)*. Should the taxpayer not be able to make his return immediately (perhaps because he cannot gain access to certain essential records or because of illness), recovery proceedings may commence and there is no legal defence against the claim for tax shown on the determination, even if the Inspector's underlying estimate of income is unduly high. The procedures for *complaint* discussed at Chapter 3 are unlikely to be of much help in such cases.

12.89 Further problems may arise where the Inland Revenue has also levied a penalty for non-submission of the return, against which the taxpayer *does* have the right of appeal. When the appeal reaches a hearing, an unrepresented individual may believe that he has to address the Commissioners on the level of the determination itself, only to be told that this matter is outside their jurisdiction. This will inevitably be a cause of confusion and grievance.[11]

Estimated liabilities and equitable liability

12.90 Self-assessment also marks the end of tax debts based upon estimated assessments which have become final. As discussed in paragraph 4.61 *et seq*, these have arisen under the old system where a taxpayer has failed to submit a tax return and/or accounts, and an estimated assessment has been made, in circumstances where:

•   it is too late for an appeal to be admitted, or

•   the Commissioners have determined an appeal by confirming the Inspector's estimate.

12.91 Under self-assessment such problems will not arise for some time, for reasons best explained by the Inland Revenue itself, in the remaining part of the statement reproduced in paragraph 4.63:

> 'Self-assessment will change the way in which liability is established and will remove the Inland Revenue's reliance on estimated assessments. The liability that taxpayers declare on their returns should normally reflect their proper liability and there should be no need for the Inland Revenue to review those cases in the way described above (i.e. at paragraph 4.63).

> 'However, where a taxpayer has not submitted his or her return, the Inland Revenue can determine the taxpayer's likely tax liability so that the tax can be pursued. There is no right of appeal against such determinations and the tax determined is legally enforceable. Taxpayers can displace the determination with their own self-assessment at any time up to the fifth anniversary of the filing date for the year of assessment in question (or one year after the determination was issued, if later).

> 'It is unlikely therefore, that the point will often be reached where a determination can no longer be displaced. Where exceptionally that point does occur and the conditions of the practice described are fulfilled, then the Inland Revenue will be prepared to consider extending their practice to meet this situation.'[12]

---

[11] See article on this subject in *Taxation* 9 May 1996 pp140-141.
[12] *Tax Bulletin* August 1995 p246. See also the footnote to paragraph 4.63.

Providing for tax where the liability is uncertain

12.92 Under the old system, where there was a dispute about a tax liability, the taxpayer could protect himself against interest charges by appealing against an assessment and postponing tax, while purchasing a certificate of tax deposit (see paragraph 4.97).

12.93 It is understood that such certificates are likely to be abolished in the course of the next few years, following the withdrawal of the facility to apply them in settlement of corporation tax liabilities. When this occurs, the only safeguard will be for a taxpayer to make a deliberate overpayment and ask the Collector to hold this in a suspense account.

Increased use of summary proceedings

12.94 There is likely to be greater use of summary proceedings as a method of enforcing tax debts, since two of the practical limitations on the Collector's use of this power have been eased:

- The monetary limit has been doubled to £2,000 (see footnote to paragraph 9.9).

- The more efficient way of establishing tax liabilities and underpayments should make it less difficult for Collectors to meet the normal six-month deadline for commencing summary proceedings.

12.95 Given the serious potential implications of such enforcement action and the lack of protections for the taxpayer in contrast with those which are offered by County Court proceedings, this will result in a tougher regime for tax debtors.

Interest on County Court judgment debts

12.96 It was noted in paragraph 10.51 that the Inland Revenue does not charge interest beyond the date of entry of plaint, but that this practice is 'likely' to change with the introduction to self-assessment. Such a change would make it more difficult for tax debtors to clear their liabilities.

Assessing tolerances

12.97 The old assessing tolerances will no longer apply to taxpayers who are required to complete self-assessment tax returns (see paragraphs 3.83-3.84). All tax and interest will have to be paid. The position regarding taxpayers outside the scope of self-assessment - in particular the vast majority of those taxed under PAYE - is currently subject to an internal Revenue review.

Chapter 13

Advice and advisers

This chapter discusses the sources of advice available to taxpayers facing tax debts, and the roles played by different professionals. In particular, it considers:

From paragraph

- The role of the professional tax adviser *13.1*
- Free tax advice and assistance *13.31*
- Agencies offering money advice *13.38*
- Representation at hearings *13.48*
- Legal aid *13.55*

The role of the professional tax adviser

13.1   Quite commonly, tax debts demanded by Collectors are excessive in that they include sums charged on estimated profits, disregard allowances or reliefs available to the taxpayer, or contain errors. It is therefore essential that any tax debt is reviewed by a competent tax adviser, to check whether it is capable of being reduced by way, for example, of one of the 'challenges' discussed in Chapter 4 of this handbook.

13.2   It is unwise to rely upon help from the Inland Revenue or a non-specialist adviser in checking the liability:

- While the Inland Revenue is bound by the Taxpayer's Charter 'To help you to get your tax affairs right', it is unrealistic to expect an Inspector to be completely independent when reviewing the work of colleagues.

- Most voluntary agencies acknowledge their own limitations in advising on tax matters, particularly in relation to small businesses and the self-employed (see paragraph 13.35).

13.3   If the taxpayer has already been employing a tax adviser and is satisfied with his services, then that person will normally be well placed to check the accuracy of the Inland Revenue's demands.

13.4   If no tax adviser is acting, or the taxpayer is unhappy with the service being provided by his present adviser, then it may be necessary to appoint a new adviser.

Choosing a tax adviser

13.5 A taxpayer may appoint virtually anyone to act for him in his tax affairs. While tax advisers are frequently referred to as 'accountants' or 'tax accountants' (see TMA 1970, s20A), there is no requirement to be a qualified accountant or indeed to hold any qualifications at all.[1]

13.6 The Inland Revenue will deal with any adviser appointed by the taxpayer, regardless of his qualifications or apparent competence, and will usually refer to him as the taxpayer's 'agent'.

13.7 In principle, a taxpayer should appoint an adviser who has knowledge and experience of taxation appropriate to his affairs, and who will provide the service required for an acceptable fee. In practice, this is easier said than done, since few taxpayers have a sufficiently detailed understanding of taxation to make the necessary judgments. In such cases it may assist to consider the following points.

Does the prospective adviser belong to a appropriate professional body?

13.8 There are a number of organisations whose members are required to pass professional examinations and to keep up to date by way of continuing professional development. They are also regulated by codes of conduct and disciplinary rules, and are subject to a requirement (or recommendation) to hold professional indemnity insurance.

13.9 For taxpayers in England and Wales, the main professional bodies are:

Professional body	Designation	Contact address and telephone number
The Chartered Institute of Taxation (CIoT)	FTII or ATII	12 Upper Belgrave Street, London SW1X 8BB. Telephone: 0171 235 9381
The Institute of Chartered Accountants in England and Wales (ICAEW)	FCA or ACA	Chartered Accountants' Hall, Moorgate Place, London EC2P 2BJ. Telephone: 0171 920 8100
The Law Society	Solicitor	113 Chancery Lane, London WC2A 1PL. Telephone: 0171 242 1222
Chartered Association of Certified Accountants	FCCA or ACCA	29 Lincoln's Inn Fields, London WC2. Telephone: 0171 396 5700

13.10 These organisations can assist the public by referring them to individual members or firms which are available to assist with tax matters. For example, a caller to the CIoT and ICAEW may receive a list of local

---

[1] See TaxAid Research Report *Regulation of Taxation Advisers in the UK* by Sue Green, December 1995

members who are available for consultation. Professional bodies will also provide confirmation as to whether a particular individual claiming to belong to their organisation is in fact a member.

Does the prospective adviser have requisite knowledge and experience?

13.11 Whether or not the prospective adviser is a member of a professional body, confirmation should be obtained that he is skilled and experienced in the relevant areas of taxation. Ideally this is done by seeking a 'reference' from a third party whose opinion may be trusted, perhaps a friend or relative of the taxpayer who is an existing client.

13.12 There are many advisers who are not members of any professional bodies who provide an excellent service. Quite often they will have a strong background, for example previously having been an Inspector of Taxes.

Is the proposed fee level reasonable?

13.13 The fees to be charged should be ascertained before appointing a tax adviser. The Members Handbook of the ICAEW advises:

> 'A member should inform a client in writing prior to commencement of any engagement of the basis upon which any fee he proposes to charge that client for his services will be calculated and, on request and where practicable, the level of fees likely to be charged for any assignment.'[2]

13.14 A fee dispute is less likely if a written quotation or estimate is given at the outset, which clearly indicates the total expected (annual) charge. A statement of hourly rates is not very helpful, unless there is a commitment as to the number of hours expected to be involved.

13.15 It is unwise to appoint a tax adviser on the basis of the lowest quote obtained. Greater weight should be attached to adviser's professional qualifications, skill and experience.

Making the choice

13.16 It may be sensible to interview two or three tax advisers before making a choice. Most will agree to an initial meeting without any charge, to discuss the services that they can offer and their fee arrangements.

13.17 At such meetings, the taxpayer will have the opportunity to question each adviser on the points discussed in paragraphs 13.7- 3.15 above, and to form an opinion as to whether it will be easy to work with him. Great care should be taken over the appointment, since the taxpayer is legally

---

[2] ICAEW *Members Handbook*, section 1.210 paragraph 2.0

responsible for the work carried out by the tax adviser (see paragraph 13.19 *et seq)*.

13.18 Once appointed, the adviser will need to provide the Inland Revenue with written authorisation from the taxpayer, confirming his appointment. This is normally done on an Inland Revenue Form 64-8. Should the professional relationship break down, the taxpayer may cancel the authorisation by notifying the Inland Revenue directly.

The tax adviser's remit

General appointments

13.19 Tax advisers are usually appointed to assist with *all* matters in relation to a client's tax affairs and the use of the term *agent* (see paragraph 13.6) is entirely appropriate since the acts or omissions of the tax adviser are generally deemed to be those of the taxpayer. For example:

- When an Inspector reaches an agreement to settle an appeal with an agent, this is binding in the same way as if the agreement was made with the taxpayer (TMA 1970, s54(5) and *CIR v West* CA [1991] STC 357).

- Accounts submitted by an agent are deemed to have been submitted by the taxpayer, 'unless he proves that they were submitted without his consent or connivance' (TMA 1970, s97(2)).

- The taxpayer can be guilty of fraud or neglect, even where the relevant act or omission was that of his agent. In *Clixby v Pountney* (Ch D [1967] 44 TC 515) the taxpayer had signed incorrect returns prepared by his agent, without checking them, and it was held that assessments could be made under provisions for 'fraud or wilful default'. In *Mankowitz v Special Commissioners* (Ch D [1971] 46 TC 707) the taxpayer was liable for penalties for failure to comply with a tax notice, where this was due to negligence on the part of his accountant.

13.20 Accordingly, it is rarely a defence to an action by the Inland Revenue to argue that a tax adviser should bear responsibility for a negligent act or omission, although Inspectors will sometimes suggest that the taxpayer considers an action for negligence against his adviser. The problem in tax debt cases is that the taxpayer will rarely have the funds available to risk on such a venture, given the difficulties of proving professional negligence and of demonstrating the extent of the loss attributable to it.

Correspondence

13.21 Most correspondence passes directly between the adviser and the Inland Revenue, although certain documents are invariably sent to the taxpayer, for example tax return forms and copies of all assessments.[3]

13.22 Demands for unpaid tax, and related correspondence from Collectors, are generally sent to the taxpayer although *Code of Practice 6 - Collection of Tax* states:

> 'If you have an accountant or other agent to handle your tax affairs we will normally deal with him or her if you want us to. However, you will always be personally responsible for paying your tax, and if we cannot make progress with your agent we will have to contact you direct.'

Limited appointments

13.23 An alternative arrangement that is sometimes appropriate in cases of tax debt is to appoint a tax adviser for a limited purpose, perhaps to examine the history of the debt and to advise on action that might be taken to mitigate the situation.

13.24 In such cases the taxpayer may remain responsible for his ongoing tax affairs, and the Inspector need only be authorised to correspond with the adviser in relation to the years to which the tax debt relates.

Special arrangements for settling fees

13.25 An adviser may be appointed on the basis that he will be paid at a later date, when the taxpayer's financial circumstances are expected to have improved. It may assist negotiations with the Inland Revenue to advise the Inspector or Collector of such special arrangements, because it emphasises the taxpayer's limited resources and may assist in negotiations.

13.26 Sometimes the taxpayer's ability to pay will depend upon a successful outcome of the matter in dispute. Historically, professional bodies have frowned upon conditional or contingent fee agreements. Nowadays, they are not completely barred but are still discouraged:

- Chartered accountants are advised that these arrangements are permitted for most non-audit work, but 'such methods of charging may be perceived as a threat to objectivity and should, therefore, only be adopted after careful consideration.'[4]

---

[3] Under self-assessment, agents will receive details of relevant information contained in *taxpayer statements*; *Inland Revenue Press Release* 29 July 1996.

[4] ICAEW *Members Handbook*, section 1.210 paragraph 4.0

- Solicitors are now permitted to enter conditional fee arrangements for certain kinds of work, but this does *not* include disputes between taxpayers and the tax authorities.[5]

13.27 It should be noted that a fee payment to an adviser prior to the presentation of a bankruptcy petition may constitute a voidable preference under Insolvency Act 1986, s340, if the bankrupt's 'desire', or one of his desires, in making the payment is to put the payee in a better position than he would otherwise be in. However, a payment to a tax adviser for current work, which is motivated by the desire to stay in business or avoid bankruptcy, should normally avoid this pitfall (see *Re M C Bacon Ltd* [1990] 3 WLR 646 and *Re Ledingham-Smith* (1992) Vol 5 *Insolvency Intelligence* p65).

Mandates for tax refunds to be paid to advisers

13.28 The Inland Revenue provides a form R38, on which a taxpayer may mandate the payment of a tax refund directly to his agent. Completion of this form may be helpful to the adviser, as it gives greater assurance that he will be paid for his work. However, both parties should recognise the limitations of such mandates.

13.29 The taxpayer needs to be certain that, in the event that the refund obtained exceeds the fees properly due to the adviser, the excess will be passed on to him. Once the repayment has been made under the terms of the mandate, the Inland Revenue will not intercede in a fee dispute between client and adviser.

13.30 The adviser should be aware that the taxpayer may unilaterally cancel the mandate, or that the Inland Revenue may inadvertently breach the mandate and make a refund directly to the client. A recent complaint by a firm of accountants, following an erroneous repayment directly to a client company which went into liquidation before paying its fees, was rejected by the Parliamentary Ombudsman who held that the accountants' loss arose from the client's insolvency and not from Inland Revenue maladministration.[6]

Free tax advice and assistance

13.31 The UK has a long tradition of voluntary sector organisations offering free advice on a wide range of subjects. While many such agencies offer help with tax queries, an individual requiring a review of a tax debt should seek advice only from those having advisers who are qualified or experienced tax professionals.

---

[5] The Conditional Fee Agreements Order 1995 SI 1995/1674
[6] *Accountancy Age* 15 February 1996 p3

TaxAid

13.32 TaxAid is a registered charity offering free advice and assistance on tax and tax debt to individuals who cannot afford to pay professional fees. Advice is given by qualified tax professionals or former tax inspectors, most of whom work as volunteers. The emphasis of the work is self-help; the adviser examines the problem and explains the courses of action open to the client. In complex cases, TaxAid may agree to engage in correspondence, negotiation or representation on a client's behalf. Advice is given at interviews at TaxAid's office near Central London and by telephone to those who are unable to reach its offices. Client advice and appointment line: 0171 624 3768 (9.00-11.00 am weekdays). Address: TaxAid, Linburn House, 342 Kilburn High Road, London NW6 2QJ.

Mary Ward Legal Centre

13.33 The Mary Ward Legal Centre offers free self-help advice on tax and financial matters, using the services of volunteer professionals. Advisers sometimes work in conjunction with solicitors and money advisers based at the Centre. For an appointment, telephone: 0171 831 7079. Address: Mary Ward Legal Centre, 42 Queen Square, London WC1N 3AQ.

The Green Form advice scheme

13.34 Many solicitors offer advice through this scheme which is funded by the Legal Aid Board and is discussed further in paragraph 13.57 *et seq*. While in principle the scheme may be used to provide free tax advice to individuals with limited means, only a small minority of solicitors offering Green Form advice have expertise in tax matters.

Citizens Advice Bureaux (CABx)

13.35 The CAB network is more fully described in paragraph 13.42 *et seq*. CABx offer help with most tax queries from the public and can provide assistance on a broad range of personal tax debt-related subjects, for example entitlement to allowances and making tax appeals. However, they acknowledge that the problems of small business (Schedule D) tax debt can be complex, and many place limits on the assistance that they offer.[7]

13.36 At one end of the spectrum, some bureaux have 'honorary financial advisers' - typically local accountants who volunteer their time - who will engage in most aspects of tax debt advice and assistance. At the other

---

[7] *Responding to small business debt enquiries - Guidance on good practice* Admin Circular DEV 10.G, November 1993

extreme, all CABx will give basic advice and may then refer the client on to an appropriate third party.

Birmingham Settlement Business Debtline

13.37 The service offered by the Business Debtline is described in paragraph 13.44 *et seq.* One of its advisers is a former tax professional, which enables the organisation to offer specialist advice.

Agencies offering money advice

13.38 Beyond the assistance required to ensure that a tax demand is correct, a taxpayer may require further help in:

- negotiating with the Collector (see Chapter 6),

- responding to enforcement action by the Inland Revenue (see Chapters 7 to 11), and

- coping with a situation of multiple debt, i.e. debts to other parties as well as to the Inland Revenue.

13.39 Quite often this will be available from the same adviser or organisation that has assisted in checking the accuracy of the debt, but they may not always be willing or able to provide the further help required.

13.40 In such cases, a large number of voluntary agencies can offer assistance. Many of their advisers will have some training in debt advice, and several employ specialist *money advisers* who have experience of negotiations with creditors, and a working knowledge of the enforcement procedures used by the Inland Revenue (especially the County Courts).

13.41 When using a voluntary agency, a tax debtor should ensure that the adviser understands the ways in which the Inland Revenue differs from other creditors, as discussed in this handbook. If there are particularly complex tax issues which may be relevant to the negotiation or enforcement process, it may be appropriate for a tax adviser and money adviser to work together.

Citizens Advice Bureaux (CABx)

13.42 There is a chain of CABx across the UK, offering free and independent advice and assistance to any member of the public on a wide range of issues. There is no means test. In recent years CABx have developed extensive experience in all areas of debt advice, and in complex cases they can call upon specialist help from Money Advice Support Units. As part of its function, a CAB will be seeking to maximise a client's net income and will be alert to the particular tax opportunities and pitfalls facing vulnerable groups such as unemployed people, pensioners and single parents.

13.43 A number of bureaux are situated within court buildings. For example, there is a CAB at the Royal Courts of Justice in London which can assist taxpayers facing bankruptcy proceedings, although it will not represent them in Court (see paragraph 11.60). The telephone numbers and addresses of CABx may be found in local telephone directories.

The Birmingham Settlement

13.44 The Birmingham Settlement pioneered money advice in the UK and now offers a number of services including:

- *National Debtline* - free telephone advice and a free self-help information pack. Telephone: 0121 359 8501.

- *Business Debtline* - money advice for self-employed and micro-businesses facing debt problems. This service is restricted to clients based in the Birmingham area, although callers from other parts of the UK may be sent a self-help information pack priced at £10. Telephone: 0121 359 7333. Address: Business Debtline, Birmingham Settlement, 318 Summer Lane, Birmingham B19 3RL.

Law centres

13.45 A number of law centres across the country offer free legal advice and assistance, and many have expertise in debt. Their addresses and telephone numbers may be found in telephone directories or through local libraries.

Other advice agencies

13.46 There are a large number of other advice agencies which offer debt advice. Some are funded by local authorities to serve clients living or working in their area. Others are established to serve special groups, such as individuals with disabilities. Details may be obtained through local libraries.

Insolvency practitioners

13.47 A tax debtor may wish to consult a professional insolvency practitioner to ascertain whether bankruptcy may be avoided through an *individual voluntary arrangement*, and most practitioners will offer a free initial interview (see paragraph 11.183). Insolvency Practitioners are regulated by the Department of Trade and Industry (DTI) or through one of seven *recognised professional bodies* including the Institute of Chartered Accountants in England and Wales and The Law Society (in the case of practitioners who are also chartered accountants or solicitors, respectively). A complete list is given in *The Directory of Authorised Insolvency Practitioners* produced by the DTI, published by HMSO and available from many local libraries (ISBN 0 11 515383 7).

Representation at hearings

13.48 In all tax disputes which reach a hearing, the taxpayer may appear in person or be represented. Rules and practices on representation vary according to the tribunal or Court involved.

Representation at tax appeals

13.49 At a Commissioners' hearing, the taxpayer has the right to be represented by a person who is legally qualified or a member of an incorporated society of accountants. The Commissioners may also agree to hear any other person at their discretion (see paragraph 3.25).

13.50 On an appeal to the Courts, the taxpayer may be represented by a barrister, or a solicitor who has the right of audience in the Court concerned, and the taxpayer may qualify for Civil Legal Aid (see paragraph 13.59 *et seq*). Reported cases reveal that unrepresented taxpayers rarely succeed, although this may have as much to do with the merits of appeals taken in person as the mechanics of representation.

Representation in enforcement proceedings

13.51 In the Magistrates Courts, County Courts and Bankruptcy Court the taxpayer may be represented by a solicitor or barrister, or any other person at the Court's discretion. In the unusual event of an appeal proceeding to the High Court or beyond, the rights of audience are the same as for appeals against Commissioners' determinations (see paragraph 13.50).

13.52 In the Magistrates Courts and County Courts, the practice has developed of allowing defendants to be represented by 'MacKenzie friends', unqualified individuals with some knowledge of the law or of the defendant's case. Quite commonly this role is filled by money advisers.

13.53 Registrars in the Bankruptcy Court welcome representation by tax advisers, if this may assist in clarifying the issues. For example, if the adviser provides evidence that a late appeal is being made, and explains that this may lead to the discharge of the assessment underlying the debt which is the subject of the petition, the Registrar may agree to an adjournment to allow time for the appeal to be settled (see paragraph 11.75).

13.54 While legal representation may be perceived to offer a taxpayer greater protection, it is of limited benefit in most proceedings to enforce tax debts, where there are few legal defences available (see paragraph 7.19 *et seq*). In the exceptional case where the taxpayer does have legal grounds for opposing the Inland Revenue's claim or petition, legal representation should be considered.

Legal aid

13.55 Legal aid is commonly used to describe the provision of support by way of:

- *Green Form advice* on matters of law, and

- *Civil Legal Aid* in legal proceedings.

13.56 Legal aid is administered by the Legal Aid Board, which makes payments directly to solicitors for services and disbursements under the scheme. The service is means-tested.

Green Form advice

13.57 Up to two hours of free advice may be obtained from a solicitor on most matters of UK law, including tax law. If more time is required, the solicitor may apply to the Legal Aid Board for an extension.

13.58 The client must meet specified conditions of financial eligibility, set by reference to disposable income and capital. These are set out in a leaflet *Legal Aid - financial limits*, available from the Legal Aid Board. Broadly:

- Anyone in receipt of income support, family credit or disability working allowance will qualify provided that his savings are within certain limits - for example £1,000 in the case of a person with no dependants. The value of the client's home, household effects and tools of trade are disregarded, although from 1 June 1996 a property is taken into account if its market value exceeds £100,000.

- Clients not in receipt of the above benefits can receive advice if their 'disposable income' - i.e. after deductions for tax and national insurance contributions and specified allowances for dependants - is no more than £75 per week.

Civil Legal Aid

13.59 This is available to provide *representation* for litigants in cases in the County Courts, High Court, Court of Appeal and House of Lords. It does not apply to proceedings before most tribunals, and so is not available for Commissioners' hearings, although *advice* concerning such proceedings may be obtained under the Green Form scheme.

13.60 Civil Legal Aid will be granted provided the following conditions are satisfied:

- The client is *financially eligible*.

- The case has *legal merit*.

- It is *reasonable* to take the case.

13.61 Anyone in receipt of income support is automatically financially eligible for Civil Legal Aid. In other cases, the means tests are less stringent than for Green Form advice: for example, the capital limit for a person with no dependants is £3,000.

13.62 While Civil Legal Aid is therefore available free to those on the very lowest incomes:

- in other cases it may be subject to a monthly contribution from the client for the duration of the case, and

- in cases where money is recovered or preserved, a successful litigant's legal costs will be deducted from his award (although he may seek a costs order against the other side).

13.63 The legal merits test involves a consideration of whether it is reasonable to take or defend the case, which must always rely on a point of law. A taxpayer *defending* an appeal by the Inland Revenue against a ruling of the Commissioners or a lower court is likely to pass this test, while a taxpayer *appealing* against an adverse decision may have more difficulty.

13.64 The reasonableness test involves a consideration of whether it is appropriate for Civil Legal Aid to be granted in the client's particular case. This should be satisfied if a person in similar circumstances - but with sufficient means to exclude him from legal aid - would be advised ordinarily to proceed with the action. The test exists primarily to exclude unreasonable cases, for example where the amount at stake is small, or the costs are likely to exceed the value of any benefit gained.

13.65 Applications for Civil Legal Aid are usually made by a solicitor on the client's behalf. It is considered by the local area office of the Legal Aid Board, which may decide to grant a limited certificate, for example, for the purpose of obtaining Counsel's opinion. It may also refuse legal aid, in which case there is usually a right of appeal to the Area Committee.

Practical issues

13.66 Firms of solicitors are not obliged to offer services under the legal aid scheme and many, if not most, firms with tax expertise do not work within either of the two schemes discussed above.

13.67 This makes it difficult to obtain tax advice within the constraints of the Green Form scheme, since this depends upon identifying a solicitor with sufficient specialist knowledge and experience. Civil Legal Aid may be less problematic; provided there is a clear point of law in issue, a competent solicitor with general experience may conduct such a case with the aid of good research or reference to expert advice on technical points.

13.68 The Law Society has a database of firms offering their services under legal aid, and the areas in which they offer help. Telephone: 0171 242 1222. Alternatively, a local CAB may have a list of legal aid practices able to help.

Distraint Notice and Inventory

**Inland Revenue
Collector of Taxes**

Distraint Notice and Inventory

To _____

of _____

Note that I have today seen and distrained the goods in the inventory below at *the above address

_____

for the sum of _____

being _____

due and described below and that these goods will be sold unless that sum together with the costs of the distress, is paid to

me within **five days** from this date. I have obtained verbal confirmation from _____

that these goods belong absolutely to the above named.

Collector of Taxes _____ *Date* _____

	£	p
Amount deductible from payments to sub-contractors due for the month(s)/*year(s) ending 5 19		
Income Tax PAYE due for the month(s)/*year(s) ending 5 19		
Class 1 NI contributions due for the month(s)/*year(s) ending 5 19		
Income Tax Schedule(s) due for the year(s) ending 5 April 19		
Class 4 NI contributions due for the year(s) ending 5 19		
Capital Gains Tax due for the year(s) ending 5 19		
Corporation Tax due for the accounting period(s) ending 19		
Interest accrued/*due under Section Taxes Management Act 1970 *see computation attached		
Total *excluding costs*		
Costs *see scale over the page* • levy		
• possession *for one day only*		
Total amount if paid today ... . † ..		
Add _____ per day until distress is fully paid *Maximum £* _____		
Total *including additional days possession fees, if any*... ... ... † ..		

Delete as appropriate † *exclude from totals fractions of a penny*

How to pay You must pay the total amount plus the costs of this distress to the Collector of Taxes _____ Collection

Inventory

Continue over the page if necessary

C204A(New)

Printed in the United Kingdom for Her Majesty's Stationery Office
7872/1181L Dd 8174865 9/89 C1600 Gp636 19232

Inventory *continued from previous page*

Scale of distraint costs

When working out any of the percentages shown below a fraction of £1 will be rounded up to £1. VAT may be added to the amounts shown below.

Levying distress   Where the total sum *excluding costs*

- is up to £100
- is more than £100

£12.50
12½ per cent on the first £100 of the amount to be recovered
4 per cent on the next £400
2½ per cent on the next £1500
1 per cent on the next £8000
¼ per cent on any additional sum.

Possession   Where

- close possession is taken, £4.50 *for the day of levy only*
- walking possession is taken, 45p per day. The walking possession fee is payable for the day of the levy and up to 14 days thereafter.

Appraisement

The costs to be charged are the reasonable fees, charges and expenses of the appraiser(s).

Removal and storage of goods

Reasonable costs and charges of removal and storage.

Sale   Where

- the sale is held on the **auctioneer's premises** the auctioneer's commission, which includes all out-of-pocket expenses other than charges for removal and storage is
                         15   per cent on the sum realised
plus the reasonable cost of advertising, removal and storage

- the sale is held on the **debtor's premises** the auctioneer's commission is
                         7½ per cent on the sum realised
plus out-of-pocket expenses actually and reasonably incurred.

Walking Possession Agreement

Walking-Possession Agreement

To the Collector of Taxes _____

_____

For my convenience and in consideration of your not taking into close possession the goods and chattels distrained by you (as listed in the inventory dated _____)

I hereby acknowledge and agree that

1. by not taking the said goods and chattels into close possession you have not abandoned the distress;

2. I will pay the fees for walking possession;

3. while the distress is in force you and your man will be given access to the goods and chattels distrained at any time for the purpose of inspection or completion of the distress;

4. I will not allow any goods or chattels so distrained to come into the possession of any other person; and

5. I will inform any person who may seek to levy any other distress or execution that you are already in possession of the goods so distrained and that I will inform you of any such visit.

Dated this _____ day of _____ 19

Signed _____

C204B

Printed in the United Kingdom for Her Majesty's Stationery Office
A2509/2340L Dd FAL 0200759 2/92 C750 Gp636 19232

County Court Summons

County Court Summons

Case Number	*Always quote this*

In the

County Court

The court office is open from 10am to 4pm Monday to Friday

(1)

Plaintiff's
full name
address

(2)

Address for
service (and)
payment
(if not as above)
Ref/Tel no.

Telephone:

Seal

(3)

Defendant's
name
address

This summons is only valid if sealed by the court
If it is not sealed it should be sent to the court.

What the plaintiff claims from you

Brief
description
of type of
claim

Particulars of the plaintiff's claim against you

Amount claimed

Court fee

Solicitor's costs

Total amount

Summons issued on

What to do about this summons

You can

- **dispute the claim**
- **make a claim against the plaintiff**
- **admit the claim in full and offer to pay**
- **pay the total amount shown above**
- **admit only part of the claim**

**For information on what to do or if you
need further advice, please turn over.**

Signed
Plaintiff('s solicitor)
(or see enclosed particulars of claim)

N1 Default summons (fixed amount) (Order 3. rule 3(2)(b))

Keep this summons, you may need to refer to it

You have 21 days from the date of the postmark to reply to this summons

(A limited company served at its registered office has 16 days to reply.)

If you do nothing	Judgment may be entered against you without further notice.
If you dispute the claim	Complete the white defence form (N9B) and return it to the court office. The notes on the form explain what you should do.
If you want to make a claim against the plaintiff (counterclaim)	Complete boxes 5 and 6 on the white defence form (N9B) and return the form to the court office. The notes at box 5 explain what you should do.
If you admit all of the claim and you are asking for time to pay	Fill in the blue admission form (N9A). The notes on the form explain what you should do and where you should send the completed form.
If you admit all of the claim and you wish to pay now	Take or send the money to the person named at box (2) on the front of the summons. If there is no address in box (2), send the money to the address in box (1). Read How to Pay below.
If you admit only part of the claim	Fill in the white defence form (N9B) saying how much you admit, then **either:** Pay the amount admitted as explained in the box above; **or** Fill in the blue admission form (N9A) if you need time to pay

Interest on Judgments

If judgment is entered against you and is for more than £5000, the plaintiff may be entitled to interest on the total amount.

Registration of Judgments

If the summons results in a judgment against you, your name and address may be entered in the Register of County Court Judgments. **This may make it difficult for you to get credit.** A leaflet giving further information can be obtained from the court.

Further Advice

You can get help to complete the reply forms and information about court procedures at any county court office or citizens' advice bureau. The address and telephone number of your local court is listed under "Courts" in the phone book. When corresponding with the court, please address forms or letters to the Chief Clerk. Always quote the whole of the case number which appears at the top right corner on the front of this form; the court is unable to trace your case without it.

How to pay	To be completed on the court copy only
● PAYMENT(S) MUST BE MADE to the person named at the address for payment quoting their reference and the court case number.	Served on
● DO NOT bring or send payments to the court. THEY WILL NOT BE ACCEPTED.	By posting on
● You should allow **at least 4** days for your payments to reach the plaintiff or his representative.	
● Make sure that you keep records and can account for all payments made. Proof may be required if there is any disagreement. It is not safe to send cash unless you use registered post.	Officer
● A leaflet giving further advice about payment can be obtained from the court.	Marked "gone away" on
● If you need more information you should contact the plaintiff or his representative.	

Printed in the UK for HMSO 07/94 D.8424532 C15000. 36625

Admission

Admission

When to fill in this form
- Only fill in this form if you are admitting all or some of the claim **and** you are asking for time to pay
- If you are disputing the claim or you wish to pay the amount claimed, read the back of the summons

How to fill in this form
- Tick the correct boxes and give as much information as you can. **Then sign and date the form.**
- Make your offer of payment in box 11 on the back of this form. **If you make no offer the plaintiff will decide how you should pay.**
- You can get help to complete this form at **any** county court office or citizens' advice bureau.

Where to send this form
- **If you admit the claim in full**
  Send the completed form to the address shown at box (2) on the front of the summons. If there is no address in box (2) send the form to the address in box (1).
- **If you admit only part of the claim**
  Send the form **to the court** at the address given on the summons, together with the white defence form (N9B).

What happens next
- **If you admit the claim in full and offer to pay**
  If the plaintiff accepts your offer, judgment will be entered and you will be sent an order telling you how and when to pay. If the plaintiff does **not** accept your offer, the court will fix a rate of payment based on the details you have given in this form and the plaintiff's comments. Judgment will be entered and you will be sent an order telling you how and when to pay.
- **If you admit only part of the claim**
  The court will tell you what to do next.

How much of the claim do you admit?
- ☐ I admit the full amount claimed as shown on the summons **or**
- ☐ I admit the amount of £ [   ]

---

1 Personal details

Surname [   ]

Forename [   ]

☐ Mr ☐ Mrs ☐ Miss ☐ Ms

☐ Married ☐ Single ☐ Other *(specify)* [   ]

Age [   ]

Address [   ]

Postcode [   ]

In the [   ] **County Court**

Case Number	*Always quote this*	

Plaintiff *(including ref.)*

Defendant

---

2 Dependants *(people you look after financially)*

Number of children in each age group

under 11 [   ]   11-15 [   ]   16-17 [   ]   18 & over [   ]

Other dependants *(give details)* [   ]

---

3 Employment

☐ **I am employed as a** [   ]

My employer is [   ]

Jobs other than main job *(give details)* [   ]

☐ **I am self employed as a** [   ]

Annual turnover is..................... £ [   ]

☐ **I am not** in arrears with my national insurance contributions, income tax and VAT

☐ **I am** in arrears and I owe.......... £ [   ]

Give details of:
(a) contracts and other work in hand [   ]
(b) any sums due for work done [   ]

☐ **I have been unemployed for** [   ] years [   ] months

☐ **I am a pensioner**

---

4 Bank account and savings

☐ **I have a bank account**

☐ The account is in credit by .... £ [   ]

☐ The account is overdrawn by.... £ [   ]

☐ **I have a savings or building society account**

The amount in the account is .... £ [   ]

---

5 Property

I live in ☐ my own property   ☐ lodgings

☐ jointly owned property   ☐ council property

☐ rented property

N9A Form of admission and statement of means to accompany Form N1 (order 9, rule2) (1.95)   *Printed by Satellite Press Limited*

6 Income

My usual take home pay *(including overtime, commission, bonuses etc)*	£	per
Income support	£	per
Child benefit(s)	£	per
Other state benefit(s)	£	per
My pension(s)	£	per
Others living in my home give me	£	per
Other income *(give details below)*		
	£	per
	£	per
	£	per
Total income	**£**	**per**

7 Expenses

(Do not include any payments made by other members of the household out of their own income)

I have regular expenses as follows:

Mortgage *(including second mortgage)*	£	per
Rent	£	per
Council Tax	£	per
Gas	£	per
Electricity	£	per
Water charges	£	per
TV rental and licence	£	per
HP repayments	£	per
Mail order	£	per
Housekeeping, food, school meals	£	per
Travelling expenses	£	per
Children's clothing	£	per
Maintenance payments	£	per
Others *(not court orders or credit debts listed in boxes 9 and 10)*		
	£	per
	£	per
	£	per
Total expenses	**£**	**per**

8 Priority debts

(This section is for arrears only. Do not include regular expenses listed in box 7.)

Rent arrears	£	per
Mortgage arrears	£	per
Council Tax/Community Charge arrears	£	per
Water charges arrears	£	per
Fuel debts: Gas	£	per
Electricity	£	per
Other	£	per
Maintenance arrears	£	per
Others *(give details below)*		
	£	per
	£	per
Total priority debts	**£**	**per**

9 Court orders

Court	Case No.	£	per

Total court order instalments	**£**	**per**

Of the payments above, I am behind with payments to *(please list)*

10 Credit debts

Loans and credit card debts *(please list)*

	£	per
	£	per
	£	per

Of the payments above, I am behind with payments to *(please list)*

11 Do you wish to make an offer of payment?

- *If you take away the totals of boxes, 7, 8 and 9 and the payments you are making in box 10 from the total in box 6 you will get some idea of the sort of sum you should offer. The offer you make should be one you can afford.*

☐ I can pay the amount admitted on _____
or

☐ I can pay by monthly instalments of £ _____

12 Declaration

I declare that the details I have given above are true to the best of my knowledge

Signed _____   **Dated** _____

Position *(firm or company)* _____

Determination of Means Calculator

Determination of Means Calculator

Defendant [_____] **Case Number** [_____]

- Check addition of boxes 6, 7, 8, 9, and 10 on Form N9A/N245 is correct.
- All figures used must be **either** monthly **or** weekly but not a combination of both.
- If you disallow any of the defendant's expenses, you must complete D below.

Part A

Sums shown in boxes 4 and 11 must be divided by 12 (50 for weekly figures) before being entered in the calculator

* Bank account credit (**Box 4**) ÷ 12   £

* Amount in savings/building society account (**Box 4**) ÷ 12   £

Any expenses not allowed *(complete box below with reasons for disallowing items)*   £

Total income (**Box 6**)   £

Sub total (part A)   £   A

All sums shown on this form are

☐ per month
☐ per week

Part B

Total expenses (**Box 7**)   £

Priority debts (**Box 8**)   £

Court debts (**Box 9**)   £

Sums shown in box 10 must be converted to monthly/weekly figures where defendant has shown total owed

* Regular credit debt payments (**Box 10**)   £

Sub total (part B)   £   B

Deduct B from A to give disposable income, C

$$A - B = C$$

Part C

Total disposable income   £   C

Defendant's offer   £

Plaintiff's figure   £

Court order   £   per   [____]

Part D   **Reasons for disallowing expenses**
(set out here any other factors you have taken into account in making the order eg. defendant's savings)

Signed _____   Dated _____

Ex120   Determination of means calculator   Printed in the UK by HMSO 801216 Dd 8252142 C5000 5/91 PP CRC Supplied.

Defence and Counterclaim

Defence and Counterclaim

When to fill in this form

- Only fill in this form if you wish to dispute all or part of the claim **and/or** make a claim against the plaintiff (counterclaim).

How to fill in this form

- Please check that the correct case details are shown on this form. You must ensure that all the boxes at the top right of this form are completed. You can obtain the correct names and numbers from the summons. The court cannot trace your case without this information.

- Follow the instructions given in each section. Tick the correct boxes and give the other details asked for.

- If you wish only to make a claim against the plaintiff (counterclaim) go to section 5.

- Complete and sign section 6 before returning this form.

Where to send this form

- Send or take this form immediately to the court office at the address shown above.

- If you admit part of the claim and you are asking for time to pay, you will also need to fill in the blue admission form (N9A) and send **both** reply forms to the court.

- Keep the summons and a copy of this defence; you may need them.

Legal Aid

- You may be entitled to legal aid. Ask about the legal aid scheme at any county court office, citizen's advice bureau, legal advice centre or firm of solicitors displaying the legal aid sign.

What happens next

- If you complete box 3 on this form, the court will ask the plaintiff to confirm that he has received payment. If he tells the court that you have not paid, the court will tell you what you should do.

- If you complete box 4 or 5, the court will tell you what you should do.

- If the summons is not from your local county court, it will automatically be transferred to your local court.

1 How much of the claim do you dispute ?

☐ I dispute the full amount claimed *(go to section 2)*

or

☐ I admit the amount of £ [_____]

If you dispute only part of the claim you must **either**:

- pay the amount admitted to the person named at the address for payment in box (2) on the front of the summons or if there is no address in box (2), send the money to the address in box (1) (see How to Pay on the back of the summons). Then send this defence to the court.

or

- complete the blue admission form and send it to the court with this defence.

Tick whichever applies

☐ I paid the amount admitted on [_____]

or

☐ I enclose the completed form of admission

(go to section 2)

In the [_____] **County Court**

Case Number *Always quote this* [____]

Plaintiff *(including ref.)*

Defendant

The court office is open from 10am to 4pm Monday to Friday

2 Arbitration under the small claims procedure

How the claim will be dealt with if defended

If the claim is for **£1,000 or less** it will be dealt with by arbitration (small claims procedure) unless the court decides the case is too difficult to be dealt with in this informal way. Costs and the grounds for setting aside an arbitration award are strictly limited. If the claim is for £1,000 or less and is not dealt with by arbitration, costs, including the costs of a legal representative, may be allowed.

If the claim is for **over £1,000** it can still be dealt with by arbitration if either you or the plaintiff asks for it and the court approves. If the claim is dealt with by arbitration in these circumstances, costs may be allowed.

Please tick this box if the claim is worth over £1,000 and you would like it dealt with by arbitration. ☐

(go on to section 3)

3 Do you dispute this claim because you have already paid it ? *Tick whichever applies*

☐ No *(go to section 4)*

☐ Yes I paid £ [_____] to the plaintiff

on [_____] *(before the summons was issued)*

Give details of where and how you paid it in the box below *(then go to section 6)*

[_____]

N9B Form of defence and counterclaim to accompany Form N1 (Order 9, rule 2)

Case No. [   ]

4 If you dispute the claim for reasons other than payment, what are your reasons ?

Use the box below to give full details. *(If you need to continue on a separate sheet, put the case number in the top right hand corner.)*

[   ]

5 If you wish to make a claim against the plaintiff (counterclaim)

If your claim is for a specific sum of money, how much are you claiming? £ [   ]

- If your claim against the plaintiff is for more than the plaintiff's claim against you, you may have to pay a fee. Ask at your local court office whether a fee is payable.

- You may not be able to make a counterclaim where the plaintiff is the Crown (e.g. a Government Department). Ask at your local county court office for further information.

What are your reasons for making the counterclaim?

- Use the box opposite to give full details. *(If you need to continue on a separate sheet, put the case number in the top right hand corner.)*

(go on to section 6)

6 Signed
(To be signed by you or by your solicitor)

Position
(firm or company)

Give an address to which notices about this case can be sent to you

Dated

Post code

Printed in the U.K. for H.M.S.O. 10/92 Dd.8365392 C15000 38806 G4891

Statutory Demand

Form 6.1

Statutory Demand
under section 268(1)(a)
of the Insolvency
Act 1986.
Debt for Liquidated
Sum Payable
Immediately.
(Rule 6.1)

WARNING

- This is an **important** document. You should refer to the notes entitled "How to comply with a Statutory Demand or have it set aside".
- If you wish to have this Demand set aside you must make application to do so **within 18 days** from its service on you.
- If you do not apply to set aside **within 18 days** or otherwise deal with this Demand as set out in the notes **within 21 days** after its service on you, you could be made bankrupt and your property and goods taken away from you.
- Please read the Demand and notes carefully. If you are in any doubt about your position you should seek advice **immediately** from a solicitor or your nearest Citizens Advice Bureau.

NOTES FOR CREDITOR
- If the Creditor is entitled to the debt by way of assignment, details of the original Creditor and any intermediary assignees should be given in part C on page 3.
- If the amount of debt includes interest not previously notified to the Debtor as included in the Debtor's liability, details should be given, including the grounds upon which interest is charged. The amount of interest must be shown separately.
- Any other charge accruing due from time to time may be claimed. The amount **or** rate of the charge must be identified and the grounds on which it is claimed must be stated.
- In either case the amount claimed must be limited to that which has accrued due at the date of the Demand.
- If the Creditor holds any security the amount of debt should be the sum the Creditor is prepared to regard as unsecured for the purposes of this Demand. Brief details of the total debt should be included and the nature of the security and the value put upon it by the Creditor, as at the date of the Demand, must be specified.
- If signatory of the Demand is a solicitor or other agent of the Creditor, the name of his/her firm should be given.

* Delete if signed by the Creditor himself.

DEMAND

To

Address

This Demand is served on you by the Creditor:

Name

Address

The Creditor claims that you owe the sum of £ ,
full particulars of which are set out on page 2, and that it is payable immediately and, to the extent of the sum demanded, is unsecured.

The Creditor demands that you pay the above debt or secure or compound for it to the Creditor's satisfaction.

[The Creditor making this Demand is a Minister of the Crown or a Government Department, and it is intended to present a Bankruptcy Petition in the High Court in London.] [Delete if inappropriate].

Signature of individual

Name
(BLOCK LETTERS)

Date   day of   19   .

*Position with or relationship to Creditor:
*I am authorised to make this Demand on the Creditor's behalf.

Address

Tel. No.   Ref. No.

N.B. The person making this Demand must complete the whole of pages 1, 2 and parts A, B and C (as applicable) on page 3.

[P.T.O.

1

Particulars of Debt
(These particulars must include (a) when the debt was incurred (b) the consideration for the debt (or if there is no consideration the way in which it arose) and (c) the amount due as at the date of this demand).

NOTES FOR CREDITOR

- If the Creditor is entitled to the debt by way of assignment, details of the original Creditor and any intermediary assignees should be given in part C on page 3.
- If the amount of debt includes interest not previously notified to the Debtor as included in the Debtor's liability, details should be given, including the grounds upon which interest is charged. The amount of interest must be shown separately.
- Any other charge accruing due from time to time may be claimed. The amount or rate of the charge must be identified and the grounds on which it is claimed must be stated.
- In either case the amount claimed must be limited to that which has accrued due at the date of the Demand.
- If the Creditor holds any security the amount of debt should be the sum the Creditor is prepared to regard as unsecured for the purposes of this Demand. Brief details of the total debt should be included and the nature of the security and the value put upon it by the Creditor, as at the date of the Demand, must be specified.
- If signatory is a solicitor or other agent of the Creditor, the name of his/her firm should be given.

Note:
If space is insufficient continue on page 4 and clearly indicate on this page that you are doing so.

2

320

Part A
Appropriate Court for Setting Aside Demand

Rule 6.4(2) of the Insolvency Rules 1986 states that the appropriate Court is the Court to which you would have to present your own Bankruptcy Petition in accordance with Rule 6.40(1) and 6.40(2). In accordance with those rules on present information the appropriate Court is [the High Court of Justice] [County Court] (address)

Any application by you to set aside this Demand should be made to that Court.

Part B
The individual or individuals to whom any communication regarding this Demand may be addressed is/are:
Name...
(BLOCK LETTERS)

Address...

....

....

Telephone Number...

Reference..

Part C
For completion if the Creditor is entitled to the debt by way of assignment.

	Name	Date(s) of Assignment
Original Creditor		
Assignees		

How to comply with a Statutory Demand or have it set aside (ACT WITHIN 18 DAYS)

If you wish to avoid a Bankruptcy Petition being presented against you, you must pay the debt shown on page 1, particulars of which are set out on page 2 of this notice, within the period of **21 days** after its service upon you. Alternatively, you can attempt to come to a settlement with the Creditor. To do this you should:

• inform the individual (or one of the individuals) named in Part B above immediately that you are willing and able to offer security for the debt to the Creditor's satisfaction; *or*

• inform the individual (or one of the individuals) named in Part B above immediately that you are willing and able to compound for the debt to the Creditor's satisfaction.

If you dispute the Demand in whole or in part you should:
• contact the individual (or one of the individuals) named in Part B immediately.

If you consider that you have grounds to have this Demand set aside or if you do not quickly receive a satisfactory written reply from the individual named in Part B whom you have contacted you should **apply within 18 days** from the date of service of this Demand on you to the appropriate Court shown in Part A above to have the Demand set aside.

Any application to set aside the Demand (Form 6.4 in Schedule 4 of the Insolvency Rules 1986) should be made within 18 days from the date of service upon you and be supported by an Affidavit (Form 6.5 in Schedule 4 to those Rules) stating the grounds on which the Demand should be set aside. The forms may be obtained from the appropriate Court when you attend to make the application.

Remember: From the date of service on you of this document:
(a) you have only **18 days** to apply to the Court to have the Demand set aside, and
(b) you have only **21 days** before the Creditor may present a Bankruptcy Petition.

3

321

Appendix 8

Creditor's Bankruptcy Petition

Form 6.7
Creditor's
Bankruptcy
Petition on
Failure to Comply
with a Statutory
Demand for a
Liquidated Sum
Payable Immediately
(Rule 6.6)

No.   **of 19** .

IN THE†

In Bankruptcy

†Enter "High Court of
Justice" *or* "———
County Court" as
the case may be.

. *Re‡*

‡Insert full name of
Debtor (if known)

(1) Insert full name(s)
and address(es) of
Petitioner(s).

I/We (^{1})

(2) Insert full name,
place of residence and
occupation (if any) of
Debtor.

Petition the Court that a Bankruptcy Order may be made against
(^{2})

(3) Insert in full any
other name(s) by
which the Debtor is or
has been known.

[also known as (^{3})

         ]

(4) Insert trading name
(adding "with another
or others", if this is
so), business address
and nature of business.

[and carrying on business as (^{4})

at

as

         ]

(5) Insert any other
address or addresses
at which the Debtor
has resided at or after
the time the Petition
debt was incurred.

[and lately residing at (^{5})

         ]   *i*

(6) Give the same
details as specified in
note (4) above for any
other businesses
which have been
carried on at or after
the time the Petition
debt was incurred.

[and lately carrying on business as (^{6})

at

as

         ]

and say as follows:—

1. The Debtor has for the greater part of six months immediately preceding the presentation of this Petition (^{7}) [resided at] [carried on business at] (^{8})

(7) Delete as
applicable.

(8) Insert address.

(9) Or as the case may
be following the terms
of Rule 6.9.

within the District of this Court (^{9})

(10) Please give the
amount of debt(s),
what they relate to
and when they were
incurred. Please show
separately the amount
or rate of any interest
or other charge not
previously notified to
the Debtor **and the
reasons why you are
claiming it.**

2. The Debtor is justly and truly indebted to me[us] in the aggregate sum of
£ (^{10})

(11) Insert date and time (before/after 1600 hours Monday – Friday, before/after 1200 hours Saturday) of (personal) service of a Statutory Demand (or date alleged on affidavit of subservice).

3. The above-mentioned debt is for a liquidated sum payable immediately and the Debtor appears to be unable to pay it.

4. On (^{11}) the   day of   19   , a Statutory Demand was served upon the Debtor by (^{12}) [personal service before [after]   hours [post] [advertisement] [insertion through letter box] in respect of the above-mentioned debt. To the best of my knowledge and belief, the Demand has neither been complied with nor set aside in accordance with the Rules and no application to set it aside is outstanding.

(12) State manner of service of Demand [delete as appropriate or as the case may be].

(13) If 3 weeks have not elapsed since service of Statutory Demand, give reasons for earlier presentation of Petition, (see section 270).

(^{13})

5. I/We do not, nor does any person on my/our behalf, hold any security on the Debtor's estate, or any part thereof, for the payment of the above-mentioned sum.

OR

(14) Delete as applicable.

I/We hold security for the payment of (^{14}) [part of] the above-mentioned sum. I/We will give up such security for the benefit of all the creditors in the event of a Bankruptcy Order being made.

OR

I/We hold security for the payment of part of the above-mentioned sum and I/we estimate the value of such security to be £   . This Petition is not made in respect of the secured part of my/our debt.

Presented and Filed the   day of   19   , at   hours   and allotted to

(14) Delete as applicable.

(^{14}) [Mr. Registrar] [District Judge]

See Endorsement

ENDORSEMENT

This Petition having been presented to the Court on
IT IS ORDERED that the Petition shall be heard as follows:—

Date: day of   19   .

Time: .   hours

Place:

⁽¹⁵⁾ Insert name of Debtor.

and you, the above-named (¹⁵)   , are
to take notice that if you intend to oppose the Petition you must not later than 7 days before the day fixed for the hearing:—

(i) file in Court a notice (in Form 6.19) specifying the grounds on which you object to the making of a Bankruptcy Order; and

(ii) send a copy of the Notice to the Petitioner or his Solicitor.

(16) Only to be completed where the Petitioning Creditor is represented by a solicitor.

The Solicitor to the Petitioning Creditor is:—(¹⁶)

Name

Address

Telephone Number

Reference

We certify that there are no prior Petitions against the within-named Debtor within the last three years *or*

Delete if not required by the court where petition is filed.

We certify that all prior Petitions against the within-named Debtor have been dismissed.
The last Petition was dismissed on the   day of   19   .
We certify that we are unable to certify the full christian names of the debtor.

Solicitors for the Petitioning Creditor.

This is the Petition marked "A" referred to in the Affidavit

of

SWORN before me this

day of   19   .

Solicitor/A Commissioner for Oaths

Index

Accountants *see* Advisers
Accounts *see* Business accounts
Accounts Offices *see also* Inland Revenue, structure
- demands 1.9, 7.2
- handling of cases 6.48-6.52
- time to pay 6.140-6.144
Actors 5.55
Adjudicator *see* Taxpayer's Charter, Adjudicator
Admission 10.24-10.26, Appendix 4
Administration order 10.77-10.85
Advisers Chapter 13
- choosing an adviser 13.5-13.18
- difficulties faced by advisers 1.4-1.6
- fees 3.133, 5.93, 13.25-13.30
- free tax advice 13.31-13.37
- Legal Aid *see* Legal Aid
- lien over business records 4.24
- money advice 13.38-13.47
- remit of the adviser 13.19-13.24
- representation at hearings 13.48-13.54
Age of taxpayer *see* Taxpayer, age
Agency workers 5.34, 5.55
Appeals 3.1-3.36, 3.144-3.148, 4.4-4.7
- agreement, resiling from 4.31-4.32
- agreement, settlement by 3.13-3.20, 3.33-3.36, 4.14, 4.31-4.32, 4.58
- costs 3.27, 3.35-3.36
- Courts' evolving approach 3.56-3.76
- Courts, to the 3.30-3.32, 3.54-3.55, 4.44
- determination by Commissioners 3.21-3.29, 4.58, 4.62
- determination, review of 4.40-4.44
- difficult situations 4.4-4.44
- directions, against 5.59, 5.62
- equitable liability *see* Equitable liability
- grounds 3.9-3.12
- hearing 3.5, 3.15-3.17, 3.26-3.27
- hearing, drawbacks 3.35-3.36
- hearing, postponement of 3.18, 4.34-4.37, 4.39
- hearing, taxpayer's absence 4.38-4.39, 4.41
- judicial review 3.69
- late 4.62, 7.30, 4.8-4.16
- notice 3.3-3.4, 3.7-3.12
- postponement *see* Postponement
- representation 3.25, 13.49-13.50
- self-assessment 12.39, 12.41, 12.47, 12.59, 12.64, 12.85-12.89
- time limit 3.7
- withdrawal 3.13

Assessing tolerances 3.83-3.84, 12.97
Assessments 2.14-2.29
- alternative 2.27
- amended 2.28, 3.13, 3.20
- appeals, *see* Appeals
- capital allowances 4.54
- contents 2.20-2.22
- death, after 5.12-5.14
- discovery 2.23-2.26, 12.8, 12.33, 12.36-12.39
- error 2.22
- estimated 2.14-2.15, 12.73
- finality *see* Enforcement, 'finality principles'
- further 2.23-2.27
- incapacity 5.17-5.19
- issue 2.17
- making 2.14-2.16
- MIRAS clawback 5.142
- non-resident taxpayer 5.160
- not received 2.19, 4.11
- service 2.18, 6.100
- time limits 2.56-2.57, 2.59
- vacation 2.28
- withdrawal 2.28, 3.13
Attachment of earnings 10.109-10.114
Bailiff
- private 8.14-8.16, 9.32
- County Court 8.38, 10.96
Bank interest, tax on 6.103
Bankrupt, undischarged 8.9, 9.18, 10.10
Bankruptcy proceedings Chapter 11
- adjournment 11.75
- 'advantages' 11.20-11.23
- after-acquired property 11.107
- annulment 11.164-11.173
- appeals 11.76
- assets, excluded 11.87, 11.102-11.104
- assets, vesting 11.88
- bankrupt's estate 11.100-11.114
- bankruptcy level 10.118, 11.2, 11.54, 11.71
- business closure 11.10-11.11
- complaints 3.130, 3.134-3.135, 11.216
- costs and fees 11.13, 11.159-11.162
- County Court judgments, enforcement of 10.115-10.118
- 'credit blacklisting' 11.12
- credit, extortionate 11.106
- credit, obtaining 11.12, 11.91
- creditors, claims of 11.92-11.99, 11.180
- criminal 11.178

- debts, deferred   11.96-11.97
- debts, preferential   11.28, 11.95
- debts, proving for   11.92-11.93
- debts, secured   11.98-11.99, 11.117
- debts, unsecured   11.96
- deed of arrangement   11.207-11.208
- discharge   11.176-11.180
- disclaimers   11.105
- disqualifications   11.14-11.15
- domicile   11.54, 11.77
- employment, impact on   11.17
- ending   11.163-11.180
- estate, bankrupt's *see* bankrupt's estate
- events following bankruptcy   11.84-11.91
- fees *see* costs and fees
- financial implications   11.6-11.13
- hearing   11.58, 11.60-11.75
- home   11.115-11.138
- home, domestic tenancy   11.18, 11.138
- home, realising beneficial interest
    11.132-11.137
- home, rights of occupation   11.123-11.131
- income payments order   11.87, 11.108-
    11.114, 11.148
- individual voluntary arrangements
    see Individual voluntary arrangements
- Inland Revenue policy   6.25, 10.115-
    10.117, 11.25-11.28, 11.36, 11.69
- Insolvency Service   11.4
- investigations   5.91
- jurisdiction of Court   11.63-11.65
- monetary threshold *see* bankruptcy level
- negotiating with Collector   6.11
- offences   11.91
- Official Receiver   11.4, 11.84-11.91
- order   11.55
- partnerships *see* Partnerships, insolvent
- petition, creditor's   11.54-11.59,
    Appendix 8
- petition, debtor's   11.77-11.83
- petition, opposing   11.59, 11.66-11.72
- publicity   11.16, 11.84, 11.170, 11.179
- reasonable replacement   11.87
- receiver and manager   11.88
- representation   13.51, 13.53
- rescission   11.174-11.175
- residence   11.54, 11.77
- small bankruptcies level   11.80
- statutory demand   11.30-11.53,
    Appendix 7
- statutory demand, setting aside
    11.37-11.50, 11.54-11.55
- stigma   11.16
- summary administration   11.80
- 'tax holiday'   11.151-11.158
- tax implications   11.147-11.158
- tenancy, domestic *see* home, domestic
    tenancy
- timescale   6.80, 6.147
- transactions at undervalue   11.106
- transactions, prior   11.106

- trustee   11.19, 11.88-11.90
- vesting of assets *see* assets, vesting
- voidable preferences   11.106, 13.27
**Birmingham Settlement Business
    Debtline**   13.37, 13.44
Business accounts
- alternative approaches   4.28-4.30
- capital allowances   4.54
- cessation   5.93, 5.98-5.100
- error or mistake   4.55-4.59
- estimates, use of   4.30, 5.99-5.100
- records unavailable   4.23-4.30
- submission before Commissioners'
    hearing   4.41
Business closure   6.26
- bankruptcy   11.10-11.11
- cessation   11.149, 5.93-5.100
- distraint   8.10, 8.30
Business records
- bankruptcy   11.87, 11.91
- lien   4.24
- self-assessment   12.67
- unavailable   4.23-4.30, 5.98
Capital allowances
- claim for   4.54
Capital gains tax   5.187, 6.102, 12.25
Certificate of debt   7.19, 9.26, 10.43
Certificate of disclosure   2.47, 2.102
Certificate of satisfaction   10.86
Certificate of tax deposit   4.97,
    12.92-12.93
Cessation *see* Business closure, cessation
Charging order   10.106-10.108
**Chartered Association of Certified
    Accountants**   13.9
Chartered Institute of Taxation
    page ix, 13.9
Citizens Advice Bureaux   3.110, 11.60,
    13.35-13.36, 13.42-13.43
Claims   4.45-4.54
- after enforcement started   1.19, 7.30
- form of   4.46
- late   3.86, 4.48, 4.73, 7.30
- repayment, for   4.72
- self-assessment   12.32
- supplementary   4.49
- time limits   4.47-4.48
Codes of Practice   3.85-3.89, 6.4-6.5
- Collection   6.14-6.21, 6.25
Collection *see* Enforcement
Collection offices *see also* Accounts
Offices, Collectors, Enforcement Office
    and Local collection offices
- enforcement methods   7.3-7.5
- structure   2.7-2.11
Collectors *see also* Collection offices *and*
    Negotiating with the Collector
- authority of   6.156, 6.159
- computation of liabilities   1.10, 4.1, 6.75
- liaison with Inspectors   1.18, 2.10, 4.3,
    6.72-6.74, 7.14-7.16, 7.26-7.28

- powers   6.77-6.80
Commissioners   3.21-3.25; *see also* Appeals
- General   3.22
- self-assessment, role under   12.85-12.89
- Special   3.23
Company directors   5.57-5.65
- directions under PAYE Regulations
  5.58-5.62
Company officers *see* Company directors
Complaint   9.25
Complaints
- Adjudicator *see* Taxpayer's Charter,
  Adjudicator
- appropriate course of action   3.144-3.148
- bankruptcy   11.216
- case studies   3.128-3.135, 4.107, 5.146
- distraint   8.69
- equitable liability   4.70
- investigations   2.49-2.51
- mishandling of   4.114
- negotiating with the Collector   6.17-6.18,
  6.58, 6.64, 6.70
- Parliamentary Ombudsman, to   3.136-
  3.143
- self-assessment   12.48, 12.88
- Taxpayer's Charter, under   3.110-3.135
Composition order   10.83-10.84
Construction industry, sub-contractors
  5.101-5.130
- bankruptcy annulment   11.167
- deduction at source   5.104-5.108
- future changes   5.129-5.130
- Inland Revenue assistance   5.113-5.114
- negotiating with the Collector   6.94
- problems   5.115-5.118
- SC60s missing   5.109-5.112
- set-off   11.43
- status issues   5.125-5.128
- tax certificates   5.119-5.124
- 'tax holiday'   11.154, 11.157
Contractual settlements   2.30-2.51; *see
  also* Enquiries *and* Investigations
- company directors   5.65
- self-assessment   12.48
- tax due under   2.33, 8.9, 10.10
- taxpayers with limited means *see*
  Investigations, taxpayers with limited
  means
- time allowed for payment   2.45
- time limits   2.60, 2.99
Corporation tax
- directors' liability   5.65
County Court proceedings   Chapter 10
- adjournment   10.45
- adjustment of tax liability   10.123-10.131
- administration order   10.77-10.85
- Admission form   10.24-10.26,
  Appendix 4
- arbitration hearing   10.42-10.47
- attachment of earnings   10.109-10.114
- bailiff   8.38

- bankruptcy, consideration of   10.115-
  10.118
- certificate of debt   10.43
- charging order   10.106-10.108
- complaints   3.131
- composition order   10.83, 10.84
- costs and fees   10.61-10.62
- Court, home   10.12
- 'credit blacklisting'   10.58-10.59
- Defence and Counterclaim   10.41,
  Appendix 6
- Determination of Means Calculator
  10.30, 10.71, 10.111, Appendix 5
- discharge of tax   10.45, 10.123-0.131
- discrepancies in procedure   10.132-
  10.135
- disposal hearing   10.36-10.40
- disputing the claim   10.41-10.47
- enforcement, prevention of   10.89
- fees *see* costs and fees
- garnishee order   10.103-10.105
- hearing   10.4
- instalments, payment by   10.22-10.40,
  10.48-10.49, 10.53-10.56, 10.70, 10.131
- interest, 'freezing'   10.51-10.52, 10.79,
  12.96
- judgment, default   10.17
- judgment, forms of   10.22
- judgment for plaintiff   10.27, 10.35, 10.38
- judgment summons   10.119-10.122
- monetary limits   10.8-10.10
- negotiating with the Collector   6.11,
  10.19, 10.26, 10.55-10.56
- oral examination   10.91-10.94
- particulars of claim   10.12
- partnership dispute   5.76
- payment by instalments *see* instalments,
  payment by
- payment of tax   10.18, 10.123
- plaint, entering   10.11-10.12
- plaint note   10.13
- pre-trial review hearing   10.42-10.47
- Register of County Court Judgments
  10.58-10.59
- representation   13.51-13.52
- satisfaction   10.86-10.87, 10.130-10.131
- scope   10.7
- set-off   4.82
- setting aside   10.66-10.67
- striking out   10.64-10.65
- summons   10.11-10.15, Appendix 3
- summons, responding to   10.16-10.21
- variation order   10.69-10.76, 11.51-11.53
- warrant of execution   8.37, 10.96-10.102
County Court Summons   10.11-10.15,
  Appendix 3
'Credit blacklisting'
- bankruptcy   11.12
- County Court proceedings   10.58-10.59
- Credit reference agencies   7.38-7.42
- distraint   8.68

- individual voluntary arrangement 11.206
- spouse, effect on 5.3
- summary proceedings 9.40
Creditor's Bankruptcy Petition 11.54-
 11.59, Appendix 8
Creditors, other 1.21, 6.89-6.90, 6.130,
 11.106, 13.38-13.41
Credit reference agencies *see* 'Credit
 blacklisting'
Criminal proceedings 2.100-2.104; *see
 also* Bankruptcy proceedings, offences
 and Imprisonment
- complaints 3.122
Death 5.12-5.16
- assets passing by survivorship 5.12, 5.92
- investigations 5.92
- 'widow's clemency cases' 6.86-6.87
Debt
- tax debt *see* Tax debt
- to third parties *see* Creditors, other
Deduction of tax at source 2.52-2.55;
 see also Construction industry, sub-
 contractors *and* Tenants of non-resident
 landlords
Defence and Counterclaim 10.41,
 Appendix 6
Determination of Means Calculator
 10.30, 10.71, 10.111, Appendix 5
Determinations
- appeals 3.1
- time limits 2.58
- interest 2.80
- Regulation 49 5.38-5.47
- self-assessment 12.8, 12.40-12.43, 12.88
Directions under PAYE Regulations
- appeals 5.59, 5.62
- directors 5.58-5.62
- employees 5.42-5.44
- judicial review 5.60-5.61
Directors see Company directors
Distraint Chapter 8
- appraisal 8.53
- assets, exempt 8.21, 8.26, 8.34-8.41
- assets, jointly owned 8.35, 8.41
- auction 8.55
- bailiff 8.14-8.16, 8.38, 8.50
- business closure 8.30
- close possession 8.50
- complaints 3.131, 8.69
- costs and fees 8.47, 8.59-8.61
- Distraint Notice and Inventory 8.42-
 8.46, Appendix 1
- entry 8.17-8.21,
- entry, forced 8.18, 8.23
- fees *see* costs and fees
- hardship 8.48
- levy 8.30
- media publicity 8.10, 8.30
- negotiating with the Collector 6.11
- pre-distraint call 8.11
- prior distraint 8.32-8.33

- remission 8.48
- removal, immediate 8.49
- sale 8.51-8.58
- seizure 8.3, 8.26-8.31
- time to pay 8.48
- visit 8.12-8.31, 8.60
- walking possession agreement 8.47-
 8.48, Appendix 2
Distraint Notice and Inventory 8.42-
 8.46, Appendix 1
Distress warrant 9.29-9.32
Employed or self-employed? *see* Status
 disputes, employed or self-employed?
Employee
- bankruptcy, impact on employment 11.17
- complaints 3.132
- directions under Regulations 42(3) and
 49(5) 5.42-5.44
- employer's failure to deduct tax 5.46,
 6.100
- error or mistake 4.60
- national insurance contributions 5.52-
 5.56
- negotiating with the Collector 6.94,
 6.100, 6.103
- overpayment 4.88
- PAYE coding error 4.107
- Schedule D assessment 5.48-5.51
- Schedule E assessment 5.45-5.47
- self-assessment 12.28
- status disputes 5.20-5.56
- 'tax holiday' 11.152-11.155
- tax payments under self-assessment 12.28
Employer
- 'good faith' 5.39
- PAYE audits 5.41
- recovery of tax from employee 5.40
- Regulation 49 determinations 5.38-
 5.41, 5.46
Enforcement
- Accounts Offices 6.48-6.52, 6.78
- checks, internal 7.14-7.16
- Code of Practice 3.88
- Enforcement Office 6.69, 6.80
- evidence 7.17-7.28
- fairness 3.98-3.100
- 'finality principles' 4.15, 7.25, 11.44
- law and practice 7.6-7.7
- local collection offices 6.60-6.64, 6.79
- methods 7.1-7.2
- negotiated arrangements 6.149-6.159
- representation 13.51-13.54
- spouse, effect on 5.3, 6.85-6.87
- stopping or suspending 7.29-7.35
- taxpayer's circumstances *see* Taxpayer
- warning 7.10-7.13
Enforcement Office *see also* Inland
 Revenue, organisation
- address 11.24
- discretion 6.70
- handling of cases 6.68

- other functions   7.5
- referral to   6.65-6.67, 6.148
- remission   6.71
- time to pay   6.145-6.148, 10.116
- 'widow's clemency cases'   6.86-6.87
Enquiries   12.8, 12.44-12.50
Equitable liability   4.61-4.70
- appeal determined by Commissioners
   4.44
- complaints   4.70
- Inland Revenue statement   4.63
- late appeal not allowed   4.13, 4.16
- practical points   4.65-4.70
- procedures   4.64
- self-assessment   12.90-12.91
Error or mistake, relief for   4.32,
   4.55-4.60
- capital allowances   4.54
- self-assessment   12.32
Errors *see* Error or Mistake *and* Inland
   Revenue, mistakes
Estoppel   6.158-6.159
Evidence *see* Enforcement, evidence
Extra-statutory Concessions   3.78-3.80
- Inland Revenue delay   4.99
- late claims   4.73
Fairness *see* Complaints *and* Taxpayer's
   Charter
'Finality principles' *see* Enforcement,
   'finality principles'
Financial circumstances of taxpayer *see*
   Statements of financial affairs
Fraud   2.100-2.104; *see also* Interest on
   tax paid late *and* Penalties
- construction industry, sub-contractors
   5.116
- self-assessment   12.37
Garnishee order   10.103-10.105
Hardship   7.35, 8.48, 8.61, 12.60
- capital gains tax   5.187
- premium due under a lease   5.184-5.186
- rental income not received   5.180-5.183
- statutory reliefs   5.179-5.187
Health *see* Taxpayer, health
Honesty, presumption of   3.108
Imprisonment *see also* Criminal
   proceedings
- summary proceedings   9.3, 9.34
- County Court proceedings   10.94,
   10.122, 11.26
Incapacity   5.17-5.19
Individual voluntary arrangements (IVAs)
- 'advantages'   11.205
- approval   11.198-11.200
- bankruptcy annulment   11.173
- concertina order   11.197
- 'credit blacklisting'   11.206
- failure   11.204
- implementation   11.201-11.204
- Inland Revenue policy   11.188-11.194
- insolvency practitioner   11.183

- interim order   8.9, 9.18, 10.10, 11.196
- limitations   11.206
- offences   11.203
- procedures   11.195-11.202
- proposal   11.186-11.187, 11.195
- report   11.197
Inland Revenue
- collection policy and practice   6.14-6.41
- compensation payments   4.108-4.112
- confidentiality   3.104-3.105
- consolatory payments   4.113
- Controllers   3.112-3.113
- correspondence with agents   13.21-13.24
- delay   3.103, 3.135, 4.99-4.108
- discretion   3.68, 3.77-3.95, 4.107
- duty to collect tax   2.1-2.3
- error *see* mistakes
- maladministration, *see* Complaints *and*
   Taxpayer's Charter
- manuals, internal guidance   3.90-3.92, 6.6
- mistakes   3.86, 3.101-3.102, 6.100
- organisation   2.4-2.11
- publications   1.5, 3.78-3.95, 5.132, 12.2
Insolvency practitioners   11.183, 13.47
Insolvency Service   11.4
Inspectors
- attitude towards tax debt   1.18, 3.34, 4.26
- liaison with Collectors   1.18, 2.10, 4.3,
   7.14-7.16, 7.26-7.28
- office structure   2.5-2.6, 2.9-2.11
Instalment arrangements *see* Time to pay
**Institute of Chartered Accountants in
   England and Wales**   13.9
Interest 'freezing'
- County Court proceedings   10.51-10.52,
   10.79
- County Court proceedings, self-
   assessment   12.96
- negotiating with the Collector   6.38-6.39
- summary proceedings   9.39
Interest on tax paid late   2.61, 2.65-2.80
- certificate of tax deposit   4.97
- death, following   5.13, 5.15
- enforcement   2.70
- 'freezing' *see* Interest 'freezing'
- national insurance contributions   2.66
- payment of tax on account   4.95-4.96
- period for which charged   2.71-2.80
- postponement, after   3.49-3.53
- rate   2.65
- reckonable date   2.78, 3.50
- Schedule E   3.53
- tax liability reduced   2.67
- self-assessment   12.53-12.55
- time to pay arrangements *see* Time to pay,
   interest
- TMA 1970, s86   2.73-2.74
- TMA 1970, s88   2.75-2.80
- waiver   2.68, 2.74, 4.108
Interest on tax repaid *see* Repayment
   supplement *and* Self-assessment, interest
   on tax repaid

International issues
- assessment of non-residents   5.160
- negotiating with the Collector   6.95-6.96
- tenants of non-resident landlords *see*
  Tenants of non-resident landlords
- territorial limitations   5.157-5.161
- unremittable income and gains   5.164-
  5.165
Investigations *see also* Contractual
  settlements *and* Enquiries
- assessments during   2.48, 6.102
- certificate of disclosure   2.47, 2.102
- Code of Practice   3.87
- companies   5.64
- complaints   2.49-2.51, 3.133, 4.68
- conduct   2.34-2.51
- cooperation   2.43, 2.51
- equitable liability   4.68
- interest   2.43
- meetings   2.36
- non-residents   5.161
- penalty mitigation   2.43
- purpose   2.32
- selection   2.30
- statement of assets and liabilities   2.47,
  2.102
- taxpayers with limited means   4.27,
  5.83-5.92
- years covered   2.38
Judgment summons
- County court proceedings   10.119-10.122
- summary proceedings   9.33-9.36
Judicial review   3.61-3.70, 3.144-3.148,
  4.16, 4.44, 5.61
Justices of the Peace   8.23, 9.1
Land Registry   11.121-11.122, 11.84,
  11.170
Law Society   13.9
Legal Aid   13.55-13.68
- Civil Legal Aid   13.59-13.65
- Green Form   13.34, 13.57-13.58
Levy   8.3
Local collection offices *see also* Inland
  Revenue, organisation
- complaints   6.58, 6.64
- discretion   6.64
- enforcement, consideration of   6.62
- function   6.53-6.54
- handling of cases   6.60-6.64
- negotiating with the Collector   6.53-6.64
- priorities   6.56-6.59
- referral to   6.55
London Telephone Unit   6.50
Losses
- claims for   4.48, 4.52
- offset   11.44
Lump sum payments *see* Time to pay,
  lump sums
Magistrates' Court *see* Summary
  proceedings

Maladministration *see* Complaints, Inland
  Revenue *and* Taxpayer's Charter
Married woman   5.1-5.11
- disclaimer by husband   5.10
Mary Ward Legal Centre   13.33
Media publicity   6.10, 6.27, 8.10, 8.30,
  11.17, 12.2
MIRAS   5.131-5.155
- capitalisation of arrears   5.150-5.155
- ceasing to qualify   5.135
- clawback assessments   5.142, 5.147
- difficulties   5.137
- errors by lender   5.144-5.147, 5.155
- failure by borrower   5.142-5.144
- mixed loans   5.138, 5.143, 5.148,
  5.150-5.155
- negotiating with the Collector   6.103
- non-MIRAS loans   5.138-5.140
- notes for lenders   3.94, 5.132, 5.151-
  5.155
- retrospective relief   5.148-5.149
Mistakes *see* Error or mistake, relief for
  and Inland Revenue, mistakes
Money advisers   10.135, 13.38-13.47
Mortgage interest relief at source
  see MIRAS
National insurance contributions
- time limits   2.99
- interest   2.66
Neglect *see* Interest on tax paid late *and*
  Penalties
Negotiated arrangements, enforceability
  of   6.149-6.159
Negotiating with the Collector   Chapter 6;
  see also Accounts Offices, Enforcement
  Office *and* Local collection offices
- after enforcement has commenced   1.18
- collection offices' roles   6.47-6.80
- complaints   6.16-6.18, 6.58
- debt, history of   6.100-6.101
- debt, nature of   6.102-6.103
- debt, size of   6.97-6.99
- Inland Revenue policy and practice
  6.14-6.41
- interest 'freezing' *see* Interest 'freezing'
- part payment in full settlement   6.36-6.37
- preliminary considerations   6.9-6.13,
  6.42-6.45
- publications   6.1-6.6
- purpose   6.8
- taxpayer's circumstances   6.81-6.96
- time to pay *see* Time to pay
- waiver *see* Waiver of tax
Non-residents *see* Bankruptcy proceedings,
  residence, International issues
  and Tenants of non-resident landlords
Notification of chargeability   2.62
- self-assessment   12.10-12.12, 12.67
Official Receiver   11.4, 11.84-11.91
Ombudsman *see* Parliamentary
  Ombudsman

Overseas matters *see* International issues
Parliamentary Ombudsman
- Adjudicator, interaction with   3.123
- complaints to   3.136-3.143
Partnerships   5.66-5.82
- appeals   5.69
- assessments   5.66-5.69
- continuation elections   5.78, 5.81-5.82
- indemnification   5.79-5.80
- insolvent   11.97, 11.139-11.146
- joint liability   5.70-5.80
- negotiating with the Collector   6.103
- self-assessment   5.77-5.78, 12.66,
    12.69-12.72, 12.79, 12.84
- status disputes   5.72-5.76
Part payment in full settlement
    6.36- 6.37
PAYE *see* Employees *and* Employers
Payment of tax   2.88-2.94
- appeal, affect of   3.42-3.43
- determination of appeal   3.46-3.49
- error or mistake claim   4.60
- non-postponed tax   3.44-3.45
- normal due date   2.29, 3.37
- on account   4.95-4.96
- on time   3.109
- post-dated cheques   6.137
- receipt   2.93
- remission *see* Remission
- Schedule E   3.53
- self-assessment   12.18-12.31, 12.34,
    12.39, 12.41, 12.46, 12.56-12.61,
    12.76-12.78
- set-off   7.23, 11.43
- waiver *see* Waiver of tax
Penalties   2.81-2.87
- death, following   5.13
- determination   2.85
- investigation   2.43
- mitigation   2.86-2.87
- self-assessment 12.31, 12.61-12.68, 12.75
- time limits   2.99
Pension contributions, personal   4.53
Pensioner *see* Taxpayer, age *and*
    Taxpayer, limited income pensioner
Permanent local action cases   6.55
Personal circumstances *see* Taxpayer,
    personal circumstances
Personal reliefs   4.51, 5.3
Personal representatives   5.12
Postponement   3.2, 3.37-3.41
- changed circumstances   4.22
- Commissioners' determination   3.40
- difficulties   4.17-4.22
- late applications   3.41, 4.21, 7.30
- time limit   3.37, 4.17
Prison *see* Imprisonment
Remission   6.40-6.41, 6.105-6.108
- Accounts Offices   6.78
- distraint   8.48
- Enforcement Office   6.71

- excessive repayment   6.100
- local collection offices   6.64
- self-assessment   12.82
- summary proceedings   9.34
- unemployed or genuine hardship   7.35
- writing off, distinction   6.40-6.41
Repayment of tax   4.71-4.97
- claim for   4.72-4.76
- construction industry, sub-contractors
    5.107
- equitable liability   4.66
- excessive   4.107, 6.100
- national insurance contributions   4.76
- repayment supplement *see* Repayment
    supplement
- set-off   4.80-4.88
- set-off, Inland Revenue practice   4.81
Repayment supplement   4.71, 4.77-4.79
- relevant date   4.78
- residence of claimant   4.79
- set-off, on   4.89-4.96
Representation   3.25, 7.37, 13.48-13.54
Seafarers   8.9, 9.18
Seize   8.3, 8.26-8.31
Self-assessment   Chapter 12
- appeals   12.39, 12.41, 12.47, 12.59,
    12.64, 12.85-12.89
- assessing tolerances   12.97
- assessment, discovery   12.8, 12.33,
    12.36-12.39
- business records   12.67
- capital gains tax   12.25
- certificate of tax deposit   12.92-12.93
- claims   12.32
- claims, error or mistake   12.32
- Commissioners' role   12.85-12.89
- complaints   12.48, 12.88
- contractual settlements   12.48
- current year basis   12.3-12.4, 12.73
- determinations   12.8, 12.40-12.43, 12.88
- employees   12.28
- enquiries   12.8, 12.44-12.50
- equitable liability   12.90-12.91
- Inland Revenue calculation   12.8,
    12.14-12.17
- Inland Revenue guidance   12.2
- interest, 'freezing'   12.96
- interest on surcharges and penalties paid
    late   12.58, 12.68
- interest on tax paid late   12.53-12.55
- interest on tax repaid   12.53-12.55
- making of   12.7-12.8
- notification of chargeability   12.10-12.12,
    12.67
- partnerships   12.66, 12.69-12.72, 12.79,
    12.84
- payment, balancing   12.19, 12.26-12.28,
    12.78
- payment of tax 12.18-12.31, 12.34, 12.39,
    12.41, 12.46, 12.56-12.61, 12.76-12.78

- payments on account   12.19, 12.21-
12.25, 12.76-12.78, 12.93
- payments on account, reduced   12.29-
12.31
- penalties   12.31, 12.61-12.68, 12.75
- relevant amount   12.22-12.24
- remission   12.82
- repair   12.33
- summary proceedings   12.94-12.95
- surcharges   12.56-12.61
- tax debt   12.80-12.97
- tax debt, creation of   12.6-12.8
- tax return, amendment   12.8, 12.47
- tax return, electronic filing   12.38
- tax return, error or mistake   12.8, 12.15,
12.32-12.34, 12.46, 12.49, 12.65
- tax return, issue of   12.12
- tax return, submission dates   12.13-12.14,
12.63, 12.89
- tax return, submitted late   12.8
- taxpayer statement   12.20, 12.81-12.83
- transitional provisions 1996/97   12.67,
12.73-12.79
Self-employed *see also* Status disputes,
employed or self-employed?
- negotiating with the Collector   6.102
Service of documents
- appeal hearing   3.26, 4.43
- assessment   2.18
- bankruptcy petition   11.57
- Commissioners' determination   11.49
- County Court proceedings   10.11-10.15
- defence in proceedings   7.23
- statutory demand   11.33-11.36
- summary proceedings   9.25
Set-off *see* 'set-off' under Construction
Industry, sub-contractors, County Court
Proceedings, Payment of tax, Repayment
of tax *and* Repayment supplement
Solicitor's undertaking   10.108, 11.70
Spouse *see* Death, Enforcement, spouse,
effect on *and* Wife's profits, tax on
Statements of financial affairs
- investigations   2.47, 2.102
- taxpayers with limited means   5.85
- time to pay applications   6.124-6.134
Statements of Practice   3.81-3.84
Statistics
- Adjudicator   3.117, 3.126-3.127
- appointment of trustee   11.90
- bankruptcy   1.1, 11.1
- complaints about Collectors   6.17
- County Court proceedings   10.1
- criminal prosecutions   2.101
- distraint   1.1, 8.5
- income payments orders   11.110
- Parliamentary Ombudsman   3.137
- summary proceedings   9.4
- tax written off   1.1
**Status disputes, employed or self-
employed?**   5.20-5.56

- construction industry   5.125-5.128
- distinction   5.20-5.22
- Inland Revenue approach   5.27-5.29
- national insurance contributions   5.52-5.56
- proper approach   5.30-5.34
- statutory fiction   5.23-5.29
- tax debts   5.35-5.37
Status disputes, partnership   5.72-5.76
Statutory demand   11.30-11.53,
Appendix 7
Statutory interpretation   3.54-3.60
**Sub-contractors in the construction
industry** *see* Construction industry,
sub-contractors
Summary proceedings   Chapter 9
- adjournment   9.27
- certificate of debt   9.26
- complaint   9.25
- costs *see* fees and costs
- Court, home   9.21-9.23
- 'credit blacklisting'   9.40
- distress warrant   9.29-9.32
- fees and costs   9.32, 9.37-9.38
- hearing   9.20, 9.26-9.27
- instalments *see* order, instalments
- interest, 'freezing'   9.39
- judgment summons   9.33-9.36
- Magistrates' Court   9.1
- monetary limits   9.9-9.10
- order, enforcement of   9.28-9.36
- order for payment   9.26
- order, instalments   9.27
- personal factors   9.18, 9.36
- prison   9.34
- procedural difficulties   9.19-9.24
- remission   9.34
- representation   13.51-13.52
- self-assessment   12.94-12.95
- summons   9.25
- tax, types of   9.16-9.17
- time limits   9.11-9.15
- witness summons   9.35
TaxAid   page x, 1.12, 13.32
Tax Bulletin   3.93
Tax compliance history *see* Taxpayer,
compliance history
Tax Debt *see also* Enforcement *and*
Negotiating with the Collector
- creation   2.12-2.13, 12.6-12.8
- definition   1.23
- history of   6.100-6.101
- Inland Revenue priorities   6.56-6.59
- Inspectors' attitude   1.18, 3.34, 4.26
- investigations of taxpayers with limited
means   4.27
- larger   6.55, 6.58, 6.71, 6.98
- nature of   6.102-6.103
- proceedings to recover   2.95-2.104
- self-assessment   12.80-12.97
- smaller   6.10, 6.59, 6.99
- structured approach   1.12-1.21

- time limits for creation   2.56-2.60
- time limits for recovery   2.98-2.99
Taxpayer
- age   6.82-6.83, 7.16, 8.29, 8.62, 9.18, 9.36, 11.25
- compliance history   6.91-6.92, 11.25
- financial circumstances *see* Statements of financial affairs
- health   1.19, 4.11, 4.43, 6.84, 8.62, 9.18, 9.36, 11.25
- limited income pensioner   6.83
- personal circumstances   4.11, 4.69, 6.10, 6.28-6.33, 6.74, 6.84, 6.106-6.107
- unemployment   6.88, 6.94, 7.35
Taxpayer's Charter   3.96-3.135; *see also* Complaints
- Adjudicator   3.110, 3.113-3.135, 3.148
- appropriate course of action   3.144-3.148
- collection of tax   6.16-6.18
- compensation   3.86, 4.109-4.112
- consolatory payments   4.113
- interpretation   3.98-3.109
- tax debtors, application to   3.109, 6.120
- text   3.96
Tax repayments *see* Repayment of tax
Tax return   2.63-2.64
- capital allowances claim   4.54
- error or mistake   4.55-4.60
- late submission   3.82
- self-assessment *see* Self-assessment, tax return
Tenants of non-resident landlords   5.166-5.178
- negotiating with the Collector   6.103
- new rules   5.172-5.178
- old rules   5.167-5.171
- recovery of tax from future rent   5.171, 5.176
Time limits
- appeals   3.7, 4.8-4.16
- contractual settlements   2.60, 2.99
- creation of tax debts   2.56-2.60
- determinations   2.58
- making assessments   2.56-2.57, 2.59
- national insurance contributions   2.99
- postponement applications   3.37
- recovery of tax debts   2.98-2.99
- summary proceedings   9.11-9.15
Time to pay   6.34-6.35, 6.109-6.148, 7.34; *see also* Negotiating with the Collector
- Accounts Offices   6.140-6.144

- complaints   3.134
- contractual settlement   2.45
- County Court judgments *see* County Court proceedings, instalments, payment by
- distraint   8.48
- enforceability of agreement   6.149-6.159
- Enforcement Office policy   10.116
- financial circumstances *see* Statements of financial affairs
- guiding principles   6.118-6.123
- Inland Revenue error or delay   6.100
- Inland Revenue policy statement   6.109
- instalments, generally   6.109, 6.116-6.117
- interest   6.121
- letter of agreement   6.138
- local collection offices   6.111
- lump sum payments   6.37, 6.117
- part of debt disputed   6.76
- period to clear debt   6.124-6.125, 6.136, 6.146
- post-dated cheques   6.137
- promptness of request   6.101
- refusal   6.139
- review of taxpayer's offer   6.133-6.137
- short-term difficulties   6.112-6.115, 7.12
- solicitor's undertaking   6.137
- summary proceedings   9.27, 9.43
- taxpayers with limited means   5.87-5.90
- tenants of non-resident landlords   5.171
- unilateral arrangements   6.110
Unemployment *see* Taxpayer, unemployment
Unfairness *see also* Complaints *and* Taxpayer's Charter
- judicial review   3.61-3.76
Variation order   10.69-10.76, 11.51-11.53
Waiver of interest on tax paid late   2.68, 2.74, 4.108
Waiver of tax   6.104
- Extra-statutory concession A19   4.99-4.107
- taxpayer with limited means, investigation of   5.88, 5.90
Walking possession agreement   8.47-8.48, 10.99, Appendix 2
Warrant of execution   10.96-10.102
'Widow's clemency cases' *see* Death, 'widow's clemency cases'
Wife's profits, tax on   5.4-5.11
Writing off tax *see* Remission *and* Waiver of tax